The Guardian Postgraduate Guide

The Guardian
Postgraduate Guide

Edited by
Alice Wignall

Published by Guardian Books 2009

2 4 6 8 10 9 7 5 3 1

First published in Great Britain in 2009 by
Guardian Books
Kings Place, 90 York Way
London N1 9GU

www.guardianbooks.co.uk

A CIP catalogue record for this book is available from the British Library

ISBN 978-0-85265-104-9

Text design by Bryony Newhouse
Cover design by Two Associates
Maps by Tony Mills
Map of London boroughs by Ghost

Printed in the UK by Clays Ltd, St Ives plc

Acknowledgments

Thanks to

The universities who responded to requests for information and also to Campus Pi at University, Jonathan Baker, Helen Brooks, Lisa Darnell, Judith Davies, Nick Downing, Hughes, Donald Macleod and Bryony Newhouse.

Contributors

Alice Wignall is a freelance writer and editor. She writes regularly for the *Guardian* and edited the *Guardian University Guide 2009*.

Nic Paton has been a journalist for the past 18 years, writing on business, employment, education and health. He is due to start an MA in October 2009, at which point he will find out how useful his advice really is.

Pam Tate has been a business journalist for several years and will complete her MBA in 2011.

Wendy Berliner is an education specialist. She is a former education correspondent of the Guardian, former education features editor of the *Independent* and most recently was editor of the *Times Educational Supplement*.

Dr Elizabeth Cripps is a lecturer in political theory in the Politics and International Relations Department at the University of Edinburgh.

Robert Hudson reviews non-fiction for various newspapers. He has a PhD in history from Cambridge University.

Contents

Introduction   9
Using this guide   14

Master's degrees

MA/MSc   17
MBA   40
PGCE   60
Postgraduate tables   81

PhD

PhD   119
RAE tables   140

International students

International students   193

University profiles

Reading the profiles   215
London institutions   218

A
University of Aberdeen   221
University of Abertay Dundee   222
Aberystwyth, University of Wales   223
Anglia Ruskin University   224
Arts Institute at Bournemouth   225
University of the Arts London   226
Aston University, Birmingham   227
Bangor, University of Wales   228
University of Bath   229

B
Bath Spa University   230
University of Bedfordshire   231
Birkbeck College, University of
   London   232
University of Birmingham   233
Birmingham City University   234
Bishop Grosseteste University College
   Lincoln   235
University of Bolton   236
Bournemouth University   237

University of Bradford   238
University of Brighton   239
University of Bristol   240
Brunel University   241
University of Buckingham   242
Buckinghamshire New University   243

C
University of Cambridge   244
Canterbury Christ Church
   University   245
Cardiff University   246
University of Central Lancashire   247
Central School of Speech and
   Drama   248
University of Chester   249
University of Chichester   250
Christie's Education London   251
City University London   252
Conservatoire for Dance and
   Drama   253
Courtauld Institute of Art   254
Coventry University   255
University College for the Creative
   Arts   256
Cranfield University   257
University of Cumbria   258

D
De Montfort University   259
Derby University   260
University of Dundee   261
Durham University   262

E
University of East Anglia   263
University of East London   264
Edge Hill University   265
University of Edinburgh   266
Edinburgh College of Art   267
University of Essex   268
University of Exeter   269

G
Glamorgan University   270
University of Glasgow   271
Glasgow Caledonian University   272

Glasgow School of Art   273
University of Gloucestershire   274
Glyndŵr University (formerly
   NEWI)   275
Goldsmiths, University of London   276
University of Greenwich   277

H
Harper Adams University College   278
Heriot-Watt University   279
University of Hertfordshire   280
Heythrop College   281
University of Huddersfield   282
University of Hull   283

I
Imperial College London   284
Institute of Education, University of
   London   285

K
Keele University   286
University of Kent   287
King's College London   288
Kingston University   289

L
Lampeter, University of Wales   290
Lancaster University   291
University of Leeds   292
Leeds College of Music   293
Leeds Metropolitan University   294
Leeds Trinity and All Saints   295
University of Leicester   296
University of Lincoln   297
University of Liverpool   298
Liverpool Hope University   299
Liverpool John Moores University   300
London Business School   301
London Metropolitan University   302
London School of Economics and
   Political Science   303
London School of Hygiene & Tropical
   Medicine   304
London South Bank University   305
Loughborough University   306

M

The University of Manchester   307

Manchester Metropolitan University   308

Marjon (University College Plymouth St Mark and St John)   309

Middlesex University   310

N

Napier University   311

Newcastle University   312

Newman University College   313

University of Wales, Newport   314

University of Northampton   315

Northumbria University   316

Norwich University College of the Arts   317

University of Nottingham   318

Nottingham Trent University   319

O

Open University   320

University of Oxford   321

Oxford Brookes University   322

P

University of Plymouth   323

University of Portsmouth   324

Q

Queen Margaret University   325

Queen Mary, University of London   326

Queen's University Belfast   327

R

Ravensbourne College of Design and Communication   328

University of Reading   329

Robert Gordon University   330

Roehampton University   331

Rose Bruford College   332

Royal Academy of Music   333

Royal Agricultural College   334

Royal College of Art   335

Royal College of Music   336

Royal Holloway, University of London   337

Royal Northern College of Music   338

Royal Scottish Academy of Music and Drama   339

Royal Veterinary College, University of London   340

Royal Welsh College of Music & Drama   341

S

University of St Andrews   342

St George's, University of London   343

St Mary's University College, Belfast   344

St Mary's University College Twickenham   345

University of Salford   346

School of Oriental and African Studies (SOAS)   347

School of Pharmacy   348

Scottish Agricultural College   349

University of Sheffield   350

Sheffield Hallam University   351

University of Southampton   352

Southampton Solent University   353

Staffordshire University   354

University of Stirling   355

Stranmillis University College   356

University of Strathclyde   357

University of Sunderland   358

University of Surrey   359

University of Sussex   360

Swansea University   361

Swansea Metropolitan University   362

T

University of Teesside   363

Thames Valley University   364

Trinity College Carmarthen   365

Trinity Laban   366

U

UHI Millennium Institute   367

University of Ulster   368

University College Birmingham   369

University College Falmouth
  incorporating Dartington College
  of Arts   370
University College London   371

W
University of Wales Institute,
  Cardiff   372
University of Warwick   373
University of the West of England,
  Bristol (UWE Bristol)   374
University of the West of
  Scotland   375
University of Westminster   376
University of Winchester   377
University of Wolverhampton   378
University of Worcester   379
Writtle College   380

Y
University of York   381
York St John University   382

Glossary of abbreviations   383

Introduction

Alice Wignall

One thing's for sure: some people just can't get enough of studying. And those people are around in ever-increasing numbers. According to figures from Hesa (the Higher Education Statistics Authority) the proportion of graduates from full-time undergraduate courses heading straight into some form of further study has risen from 17 per cent in 2002-03 to 25 per cent in 2006-07.

And that's just the people who hop straight from one qualification to the next. Let's not forget those who take a break and return to study, whether it's someone immersing themselves in that physics PhD after one or two years out in the 'real' world, or someone finally realising an ambition to work towards a part-time master's in Renaissance poetry now they have retired.

But why should so many people be drawn to postgraduate study? After all, by the time we've got an undergraduate degree under our belts, most of us are looking back over 16 or so years in full-time education: more than enough, you might think, to stop you from either considering ploughing on for a bit longer, or returning to the classroom.

For many, it comes down – as it always has done – to good old-fashioned love of subject. Some people just cannot get enough of puzzling out complicated algebra or losing themselves in the poems of Wordsworth or charting the migration patterns of sea birds. Don't overlook the proportion of people who carry on, or return to, studying just because it's fun.

In the case of many of these people, their passion is such that they're already considering making a career out of it. It goes without saying that if you are intent on making your mark in academia then a master's and a PhD will almost certainly need to feature somewhere on your CV. They are not only chances for you to garner enough information about your subject to be able to pass it on to undergraduates as a tutor but are also opportunities for you to begin to learn the skills of an academic: researching and writing up your findings, presenting them to colleagues and conferences and (especially if you take on some teaching responsibilities while you're studying) working within a university department.

Postgraduate study does not only carve a path into the sacred groves of academia, however. Not a bit of it. Increasing numbers of courses aim to sharpen up your professional skills before you enter into the recruitment fray. Not sure that your English degree is enough to land you your dream job? How about another year focusing just on journalism or PR or marketing to really hone your skills? Have you developed a passion for statistical analysis during the third year of your history degree, and can only imagine doing a job that has that at its heart? A year of studying to refine your abilities in that area wouldn't hurt. Further study isn't necessarily just for people who've decided to stay in education forever; it can instead be used to serve as a better springboard into employment than just an undergraduate degree.

And then there are those jobs – not just the ones in academia – that demand a few more letters after your name. Teaching is the most obvious example: a PGCE is de rigueur for any aspiring educator. But others, like commercial scientific research, for example, will often be done by people who've spent a few extra years in the lab. Even those hard-nosed captains of industry and financial whiz-kids can sometimes find it useful to spend some time hitting the books, though in their case they will opt for the ultra-vocational MBA.

Or perhaps you don't just want to set yourself on the right track with your postgraduate study, but get yourself off the wrong one. Sometimes an extra qualification – like a relevant master's or an MBA – will have the power to transform your career, putting you in line for more responsibility and more money.

And sometimes the idea is just to get the hell out of your current career for good. Relevant re-training – whether you've decided to become a teacher, or just want to supplement your first degree and subsequent work experi-ence with something that will send you off in a new direction – could make all the difference.

Or perhaps you just want to stand out a little bit more. There was a time when even an undergraduate degree was a relatively rare commodity. Now there are a lot more of them sloshing around the place. Which is good news, of course, but if one degree is good, perhaps two would be better in the eyes of prospective employers?

Not everyone has such thought-through reasons for doing postgraduate work. Some people opt to carry on at (or return to) university because they can't think of anything better to do. While no one could argue against a period of study as good thinking time you're actually supposed to be thinking about your subject, not what you'd really like to be doing with your life. It's possible, of course, that you may suddenly discover a passion for whatever it is you're using to fill in your time or, at the very least, derive some material benefits from the extra qualification you accrue. But don't bank on it. The odds of you making any kind of success of postgraduate work if you're uncommitted to it to begin with are not that great.

Because, make no mistake, you're opting for some hard work. And, unlike during your undergraduate degree, hard work that in all probability not all of your peers are doing. If you're carrying on studying after your first degree, how will you feel seeing your friends disappear up the job ladder while you're spending an extra year living on beans on toast? Even if you're pretty sure you want to stay in academia, will your resolution be tested when other people you know start earning real money and spending it on clothes that don't come from charity shops and wine that costs more that £2.99 a bottle? If you're returning to study after a period of employment the shock will be all the greater. There's no nine to five anymore; no banter with colleagues during the day with clearly demarcated time off in the evening and at weekends; certainly no monthly pay-packet anymore. Just lots of time spent on your own, a feeling there's always more studying you could be doing and a return to a life of penury. Which is not to say that further study does not come with its own rewards. It does, and they are ample, intellectually, socially, professionally and, in time, even materially. But you'll be in a far stronger position to reap them if you are positive about your reasons for becoming a postgraduate student in the first place and have made your peace with any short-term drawbacks.

So, assuming you're still eager, what kind of study are you going to do? If you're a new undergraduate (or a returning student with only an undergraduate degree to your name) in all likelihood you'll be opting for a master's degree. In most cases, this is an extra year of study in your subject or something related. There's a huge range on offer, from purely academic to strongly vocational and your choice will depend largely on your purposes for studying. You can read more in the MA/MSc chapter on page 17.

Some students embark on their master's knowing, or suspecting, that it will be the first step on the road to their PhD, and that desirable 'Dr' prefix to your name. If you've got an inkling that that might be you it naturally brings some other factors into play, especially in your choice of institution. On the other hand, perhaps you've only just realised you want to do a PhD, or still aren't sure if you do. The PhD chapter on page 119 will have more information for you.

If you want to train to become a teacher, either straight from university or as a career-change, it is almost inevitable that you will study for a PGCE (not all teachers have one, but you will be severely limiting yourself in terms of places you can work if you don't). The course varies, naturally, depending on whether you're converting your degree into something you can teach to secondary-level children, or whether you're going to attempt the whole curriculum with primary-level pupils. The latter is going to involve you brushing up on some subjects you waved goodbye to quite a while ago. But there's more to keeping control of a class than just knowing your subject: find out more on page 60.

For a completely different kind of work-related study, you might consider the MBA. And while you'll never see the shining faces of 30 five-year-olds beaming up at you because they just love the way you teach spellings as a result of doing it, it might have its own rewards. Money, for a start. Lots and lots of it. MBA students generally enjoy a significant boost to their earnings when they graduate, and – since most of them return to study after a period spent in a corporate job – most of them aren't on a pittance to begin with. It still means taking time out from your career, though, so what else will an MBA give you? Read the chapter from page 40 to find out.

Each chapter will also give you guidance on other things to think about. There's where to study, of course. Will you take this chance to chose an entirely different university from where you did your undergraduate degree, where the standards are higher (or lower), the weather warmer (or cooler) or the tuition fees heftier (or not)? Or, if you're coming back to study, perhaps with a home and family already established, are you merely going to be looking for the closest university that can offer you the qualification you want? (The postgraduate tables from page 81, RAE tables from page 140 and institution guides from page 213 provide a lot of information to help you with this decision).

Then there's how to study. Full-time is the traditional method but more and more institutions offer part-time courses now; perfect for combining with work, retirement or anything else you've got on. Though, of course, it will take double the time (if not more). If you're happy to spend more time studying on your own, even than a regular postgraduate would, you can also opt for distance learning, meaning you can get your postgraduate qualification from a tropical beach or a mountain crag. (As long as you've got a broadband connection.)

Each chapter will also fill you in on the practical things you need to know. As with many aspects of postgraduate study – not least the study itself – you're considered grown up enough to handle most of the organisation, from applying to providing references, yourself. That includes finding funding to pay for it. Unlike those lucky undergraduates, there's no 'one scheme fits all' Student Loans Company for postgraduates: you'll have to find your own unique ways of getting into debt to finance your study. We will attempt to point you in the right directions – anything from government funding to bank loans (yes, really) to getting your current employer to stump up the cash.

Last but not least on page 193 we provide some specialised information for students coming from other countries to study for their postgraduate qualifications here. A hefty proportion of the UK's postgraduates are international students, and it's not hard to see why. The UK provides a top-class education for a fairly reasonable rate; its qualifications are recognised worldwide; there's a wide range of courses to choose from; and it's got plenty to keep you amused in your weekends and vacations. Much of the information international students need will be found in the chapter relevant to the qualification they aim to study towards, but their dedicated chapter goes into more detail on sources of funding and how to avoid culture shock.

And so, after digesting all of that, there's really only one question left to answer about your foray into postgraduate study... what are you waiting for?

Using this guide

Once you've read the chapter describing the type of postgraduate study you're interested in, you should have a good idea of what it involves, whether it's right for you and how, among other practical considerations, you're going to fund it. The next stage is to get on with the business of choosing which courses and institutions to apply to.

The *Guardian*'s new postgraduate tables (from page 81) tell you which institutions offer your subject at postgraduate level and give details of eight criteria – including completion rates and the cost of courses – that will help you choose between them. These tables cover master's degrees including MAs and MScs, MBAs and the PGCE. Anyone interested in a PhD should consult the tables from page 140, which are based on the latest Research Assessment Exercise (RAE 2008).

When you've put together a list of possible courses, take a look at the institution profiles from page 213 to get more of a flavour of the universities and higher education institutions themselves. These will give you an idea of what a place is like, what it has to offer postgraduate students, what its strengths (and, sometimes weaknesses) are, anything especially noteworthy about it, and, of course, how expensive it's liable to be. We can only scratch the surface here but the contacts and web links will point you in the right direction and enable you to find more precise information.

And when you've done all of that, you really should be well on your way to knowing which institutions could be right for your postgraduate qualification.

A final note on web addresses: while we've tried to ensure that the web addresses in this book are correct, these things can change quickly. We have also tried to recommend useful and reputable sites but editorial policy can change and quality can lapse so we bear no responsibility if you find material there that is useless, wrong or offensive.

Master's degrees

MA/MSc

Nic Paton

If you are thinking about doing an MA or MSc this year, you won't be alone. According to the most recent figures, more than 144,000 people were enrolled on postgraduate master's degrees in 2006-07, up nearly a fifth on five years ago. Britain is also a hugely popular destination for international students, with around 40 per cent of those enrolled on master's courses having come from overseas.

Whether you are a current undergraduate looking to carry on into post-graduate study or you are aiming to return to study after a period away from education, the decision to do an MA or MSc is not one that should be taken lightly. You need to be sure that a master's is the right qualification for you, work out what course is best, what type of study will suit you and even which is the right university or institution.

So, why do it? Why put yourself through one or two years of expensive, brain-achingly hard graft, particularly if you are holding down a day job alongside it or are already heavily in student debt?

There are, of course, as many individual reasons for doing a master's qualification as there are master's students. But the answer for a lot of master's students is employability. Yes, people go into postgraduate education simply because they want to get their grey cells working again or because they are passionate about a subject and wish to pursue it as far as they can. But for the vast majority of students the decision to do an MA or MSc is as much about what they are going to do with the qualification afterwards – and what they hope the qualification is going to do for them – as it is about gaining that precious bit of paper itself.

For some, pursuing an MA or MSc is the first step towards a PhD and a full-blown career in academia. Or it can be that the profession you want to go into requires a postgraduate qualification, with many technical or scientific professions being good examples. Another good reason for doing an MA or

MSc is because you want to change career direction or accelerate the career you already have. Or it may be – and this is particularly the case for students who go straight on to do an MA or MSc after their undergraduate degree – that a master's is a way of getting that little extra something on your CV to help you stand out before going off into the harsh world of paid employment.

Being able to brandish an MA or MSc can set you apart from the lumpen mass of BAs and BScs and give you something extra to talk about in your job interviews, but will it gain you a better job or more money? There is some evidence that it can. A survey in 2007 by the Higher Education Careers Service Unit (Hecsu) found lower rates of unemployment among postgraduates (4.2 per cent) than undergraduates (6.2 per cent) six months after graduating, and research by the Association of Graduate Recruiters has suggested that, among employers who paid a premium to attract graduates, a significant proportion offered on average around £3,500 extra to graduates with an MA or MSc.

Yet it is also important to consider the possible negatives before you take the plunge. If you're attracted to the idea of postgraduate study because you can't think of anything better to do, or enjoy student life and don't want to engage with the 'real world', you certainly shouldn't rush into anything. However you cut it, a master's is hard work and requires a lot of commitment. It has to be something you actively want to do. It's also not a cheap option. If all you're doing is delaying the inevitable while adding significantly to your student debt, you need to think long and hard about whether it is the right thing to do. At the very least, if you are doing an MA or MSc for these reasons you will need to spend the year actively engaging in what comes next and researching your options carefully.

Similarly, if you're returning to academic study and either juggling work alongside it or taking a year out from the nine to five, you need to think about the effect this is likely to have on your career and family or personal life. Are you prepared to give up evenings and weekends, even holidays, for study? What family or financial commitments do you have and how will studying affect them? Will you need to relocate temporarily in order to study? If you are going to be a full-time student, what impact will being out of the workplace for a year have on your career, and how does that weigh up against the potential benefits of having an MA or MSc under your belt?

Postgraduate study is much more independent than undergraduate study, so, on a practical level, it is important to be aware that you may be working by yourself for much of the time. Are you self-motivated enough to survive or will you end up feeling isolated and adrift? This is most likely to be the case if a large element of the course is studied by distance learning or online. Sure, there will normally be forums and chatrooms where topics and issues can be discussed, but a lot of the time you will be on your own.

So, who should you be talking to, to get the answers to all these questions? Clearly, you should be sounding out your family and friends and, perhaps, your employer, particularly if you are going to need to take an extended sabbatical or are looking for some financial support. It also makes sense to speak to the tutor or programme leader on the course that interests you – and don't be afraid to go back to them if you have further questions. (Though do, of course, watch out for the hard sell: postgraduate study is a lucrative income stream for many universities – especially when it comes to international students. Remember that it's in their interests to encourage, or at the very least not put off, students who are showing an interest in their postgraduate courses!)

If you're an undergraduate and your current tutor is recommending you stay on at your current university to do an MA or MSc, it's still worth having a good look around at what other institutions are offering. Is there a better or more relevant course somewhere else? It may also be a good idea to have a word with the university careers office or even approach individual employers or recruiters to get advice on just how helpful a particular MA or MSc will be to your future career. If it's evident that a master's is a 'must have', your decision is clearly going to be much easier. But if the reaction is a dismissive snort, you need to think carefully about whether this is going to be time and money well spent.

Ask any department or university you're interested in if you can speak to current students or alumni. Most will be happy to come up with a few names (and if they aren't that in itself speaks volumes) and such conversations can provide hugely useful information about what the workload is really like, the level of tutor support, employment prospects post-graduation and so on.

Ultimately, if you have a clear goal in your mind as to why it is you want to do an MA or MSc – and it may be that you've decided you really want to do it – then you're likely to benefit from a 'postgraduate premium' – a boost to your finances, your career or even just your sense of personal fulfilment. But the key thing to remember is that your MA or MSc has to be right for you, not your tutor, not your employer (current or prospective) and definitely not just because your friends or peers are doing it.

● How to do it

So, in principle you've made your mind up to do an MA or MSc. Well done! Assuming you now have a fair idea of what your subject is going to be, the next questions should be 'where?' and 'how?'. The first of those we shall come to in a moment, but the 'how' is not as obvious or clear cut as it may at first seem. This is because master's qualifications are now offered in a wide variety of formats and time frames.

The traditional taught master's is a full-time, one-year course where you are predominantly studying and learning on-site through lectures and seminars and in the library. But, as many people these days can't afford to drop everything for a whole year, a popular way of doing an MA or MSc is to do it part-time, normally over two years (although it can be considerably longer). This can be by studying on-site, remotely, or flexibly, or a combination of all three. In fact, according to Hecsu, in 2007 nearly half of all master's students enrolled were part-time students and 47 per cent of master's degrees awarded to UK-domiciled graduates were to people who had studied part-time.

Both approaches have their pros and cons. One of the biggest advantages of doing an MA or MSc full-time is that, while clearly more intensive, you get on with it, have the opportunity to immerse yourself in your subject completely and then rapidly move on. You may also be more likely to develop stronger relationships with the rest of the student cohort on your course if they are also studying full-time.

The main disadvantages of studying full-time are also fairly obvious. First, you won't be working for a living so you are going to need to have enough money to a) fund the course b) live and c) pay the full whack of the tuition fees in one go. Similarly, whether you are going into it straight from university or coming back to it after time in the workplace, you will be out of the job or employment market for 12 months. More mature students may need to consider the effect that not paying into a pension for a year will have on their future retirement income. International students may have to choose between uprooting their family – with all the hassle and expense that that can involve – or opting for a long-distance relationship that necessitates jetting back and forth across continents.

There are similarly important questions to work through when it comes to studying part-time. The fact that part-time courses normally take two years to complete means that you have a greater chance of maintaining some form of employment or paid income alongside it and are therefore less likely to lose touch with the outside world. The corollary of this is that you may feel yourself pulled in all directions, with work, family, personal and study commitments all demanding your time. Many part-time MA and MSc students report that what quickly happens (unless you have a very enlightened employer or have control over the hours you work) is that evenings, weekends and even holidays all get eaten into. So, while a full-time MA or MSc is clearly a major time commitment, it would be wrong to assume that doing it part-time is necessarily an easier option.

Some universities now offer flexible master's courses aimed specifically at people who wish to continue to work while studying. These allow students to select the start date of their course and even the type of tuition and support they wish to receive. Such courses are normally structured around intensive, short blocks of study, sometimes even run over weekends, which students dip in and out of.

A key element of such flexible and part-time courses now is the internet and virtual learning environments, with students often able to access library resources, course documents and discussion boards online, though the level and sophistication of access will vary from university to university. This use of new learning technologies brings us neatly on to the fourth, and increasingly popular, way of doing an MA or MSc: by distance learning. This can take many forms, from 'pure' distance learning where the study is completely carried out remotely, such as through the Open University (www.open.ac.uk), to, more commonly, courses that are predominantly distance learning based but supported by some residential sessions. There may be opportunities to download podcasts or vodcasts and some universities are even moving to embrace cutting-edge web 2.0 technologies such as virtual reality environments and wikis.

The advantages of this type of study are that it is very flexible and you can by and large work when, where (making it a form of study that can be particularly useful for international students or those who are travelling a lot) and how you want. The downside is whether you truly get the same debate, spark and access in online seminars or discussion forums, something that continues to split many within the academic and teaching community. It's also possible that you may end up feeling isolated, perhaps from the university itself, from your fellow students and even, if you rarely communicate with him or her, from your tutor. Either way, distance learning should not be seen as a soft option as it is a method of learning that requires huge focus and self-motivation to rise above the distractions of the day-to-day.

● Where to do it

Where you choose to study for an MA or MSc clearly comes down to individual choices and considerations – we can't tell you where you should go! No one course, university or department will be the same and all will offer different advantages and disadvantages. But there are nevertheless a number of questions you should try to answer before making your choice.

For most students the decision as to where to study is primarily about weighing up course content versus location. If you are an existing student and simply moving on to postgraduate study, the fact that you perhaps already have accommodation and a job, or even an existing circle of friends who are continuing on, can seem like good reasons for staying at the university where you did your first degree. Similarly, for a mature student returning to study, family or personal issues – a partner's work, your work, the children's schooling and so on – are likely to be equally important considerations.

But these need to be weighed against what a particular department or university is actually offering. Is it really the course you want to do or do you feel, deep down, that you are having to compromise because the location is convenient? Are there other, more highly regarded departments or more specific courses out there that make moving further afield seem worthwhile, or does the more conveniently located course tick enough boxes? The *Financial Times*, for example, regularly ranks business schools, while other newspapers including the *Guardian* rank universities.

A long commute to seminars or residentials can be feasible but will inevitably make studying harder and may mean that you miss out on social events or guest lectures held in the evening. If you are going to have to travel, what are the transport links like? If it's a simple train ride the commute might actually provide useful study or thinking time (assuming you can regularly get a seat). The online and remote support on offer can be an important consideration. If you're going to need to spend a lot of time physically in the library then you'll obviously need to be closer to the department than you would on a course where many of the resources are available virtually or online. And, clearly, if your MA or MSc is predominantly remote or distance learning based, geography will be much less important.

Another question to ask yourself, particularly if you are moving directly on from undergraduate study, is how valuable is it to you to maintain a relationship with an existing tutor or supervisor, perhaps because they have overseen your undergraduate dissertation? Try to think more than one step ahead – 'If I do an MA or MSc in this department and then decide I want to go on and do a PhD, is there someone who has a particular interest in my potential field of research, or will I need to move a second time?' If it's the latter, it might make more sense to try and do the master's at the same institution as the possible PhD.

Successful completion of an undergraduate degree is no guarantee that you will secure a place on a postgraduate course in the same department, but if a department or tutor likes and rates you, then the whole process is likely to be much easier than if you are starting from scratch. If however you have the grades and the references and the desire to study elsewhere, the fact that you have not done an undergraduate degree at an institution should normally not be an obstacle. But in both cases it is worth remembering that it is often in a department's interests to keep a student on board or attract a student to a postgraduate course, particularly if it is a relatively new course that the department is trying to get established. What you need to keep clear in your mind is, 'Is this right for me?'

While many of these considerations will be just as important to international students, there will also be other factors to take into account, such as the level of pastoral support the university offers. Most universities these days have extensive international offices that provide a wealth of information about accommodation, fees, scholarships, visas, getting around and so on. But it can also make sense to see whether there is a community of other international students at the university or even a community of your nationality in the wider town or city.

For all students – from the UK and overseas – it is a good idea to check out the alumni services offered by a university. Is there an active alumni society and do they organise many events, whether social or academic? It is useful to gauge whether, having done a master's at a particular university, you will become part of a wider group that will be both fun and rewarding, but just as importantly, offers the potential for networking, making friends and future contacts that will help you in your career.

Finally, and it should really be a lesser issue but inevitably plays its part in the decision making process, you should assess what the location has to offer. While postgraduates tend to be a more sober bunch than undergraduates (though not always), if you're an avid windsurfer or musician or just can't wind down unless you have access to art galleries or rolling moors, the sort of extra-curricular activities available internally and within the wider community may well need to be a factor.

On a more serious note, if there is, say, an internationally renowned library or study centre covering your area of research within striking distance, or maybe interesting local socio-demographic, historical or geographical issues that might feed into your research, this should definitely form part of your decision. Similarly, will the area be likely to offer better employment prospects when you graduate? It might be that it is a centre for the industry or sector on which you are focusing or maybe there is a local college, school or other employer that has close links to the department.

● How to apply

The first thing to know about applying for an MA or MSc is that, unlike for undergraduate courses, there is no central admissions system, so it is up to you to approach the university or department directly. There is an assumption at this level – given the fact that you are going to be doing independent research – that you are capable of researching the courses on offer, finding the application form and applying yourself. Essentially you are being treated as a grown-up.

You will normally be able to download an application form direct from the university, although you may be able to apply through organisations such as

Prospects (www.prospects.ac.uk). It's a good idea at this point to check exactly when the course starts and what the deadlines are for applications – having to wait a full year simply because you have missed the deadline is not fun and you are unlikely to get much sympathy. Courses tend to start at the end of September or in early October, so most applications are made at the end of the previous year or at the start of the year in which the course begins.

To complicate matters, however, most postgraduate degree courses do not have official closing dates and accept applications on a rolling basis. While this means you may technically be able to apply at any time, it goes without saying that if you're keen to start in a particular intake you need to get your application in sooner rather than later. People do join postgraduate courses at the last minute – and if you find yourself in this position it's always worth making enquiries to the admissions staff – but what more commonly happens is that you will be asked to defer for a year.

The application form itself will normally cover your academic career and achievements to date and, if applicable, your subsequent career. You might well be asked to provide a course transcript – a report from your university or tutor that provides details of subjects and courses you have taken and the grades you have obtained. If you are an international student and your transcript is in a different language, you will need to get it translated into English before it is submitted. It's worth checking with the university exactly what is required here. International students will normally also need to provide evidence of competence in English, for instance that your first degree was taught in English or, if not, that you have an International English Language Testing System (IELTS) or Test of English as a Foreign Language (TOEFL) certificate or a GCSE in English. More detailed information about English language tests and requirements are available from British Council offices around the world and can be found at www.britishcouncil.org

If you are applying for a research-based master's, such as an MRes or an MPhil, where you complete a thesis and there are fewer taught elements, it's likely that you'll be asked to write a research proposal outlining the area you wish to investigate, how you intend to go about it and what sources of information you intend to use. For a taught master's you will normally be asked to complete a supporting statement as part of your application. This is something you need to think about carefully and not just dash off in a few minutes, particularly if you are applying for a very competitive course.

The supporting statement should tell the admissions tutors why they should consider you over and above other applicants with good degrees. So you should try to get across some of your enthusiasm for the subject, your reasons for wanting to pursue it, what you hope to get out of it and why you feel you will make a good MA or MSc student. As with any application, it's not wise to take a cut-and-paste approach to this – make it pertinent to the particular course and university, even if you are applying for other courses too.

One of the most important parts of the application process is the references you'll be asked to supply. These will normally be from two people, often tutors who have supervised your work at undergraduate level, who are known as academic referees. But don't despair if university life was decades ago and you no longer have academic references – there is also the option of supplying professional referees, although these will still need to be as relevant as possible to the course for which you are applying.

Choose your referees with care and ask them in advance if they are happy to provide a reference. You'll probably need to send them a copy of the application form and many universities have a set referee letter or form that has to be completed (these can normally be downloaded from the website). It is also important that your referees know what the deadline is for their references, as without them the application process will slow down and can even come to a standstill.

You will be asked for evidence of your degree qualification – particularly so if you are returning to higher education. You will also be asked questions about how you intend to fund your postgraduate study. While it's not vital that you already have a definite source of funding in place it is a good idea to outline as clearly as possible what your most likely source is going to be.

Once the application is in, some admissions tutors (though by no means all) will call potential candidates in for an interview. This will be a great opportunity for you to get to see the department and possibly meet a few tutors and supervisors. For the tutor it is a chance to get to know you better, and find out more about why you should be coming on their course.

Inevitably, the style and type of interview will vary from institution to institution but you will normally be asked about your reasons for choosing the course or particular department, your motivations for studying at postgraduate level and why you feel you will make a good postgraduate student. You may, too, be asked about your career or work experience to date (if that is relevant), what you hope the qualification will do for you and about your studies at undergraduate level.

Before the interview get clear in your mind exactly why it is you are applying and what you want to get from the course. Take a careful look at the course programme online as well as the research interests of the academic staff – for example, is your reason for applying that one of the tutors is world-renowned in the area you are most interested in? Remember, too, that tutors will be looking for people who can work independently and argue around a subject in a critical way. That's not to say they are looking for people who already know the subject area inside out (that is what the course is there to teach you), but you will be expected to have thought carefully about your subject area and motivations.

The interview is also a good opportunity for you to throw some questions back at the tutors – questions that can, in turn, show them how you think and operate. The sorts of things it may be useful to ask will include how the course is run and the sort of research you will be expected to carry out as well as what sort of tutorial or supervisory arrangements will be in place. Are there any changes to the programme being planned before you start or any new courses that will be introduced?

This can also be a good opportunity to ask if it is possible to meet, or at least be put in contact with, any current or past students who will be able to give you the low down on what the course is really like. Ask too about what alumni have gone on to do and the sorts of career paths graduates from the courses have tended to follow. If you want to take this last line further it might well be a good idea to pop across to the university's careers service to get a clearer idea. Once accepted you are normally only offered a provisional place until you have paid a non-refundable deposit, usually a percentage of the course fees. This has to be paid prior to the start of the course, and no later than eight weeks beforehand.

● Funding

Ah yes, money. It would be fair to say that doing an MA or MSc is not cheap. Having said that, the sort of fee you can expect to pay does vary widely, even for courses within the same department. To give an example, the 2008-09 fee for a full-time MSc in accounting and finance management at Lancaster University Management School (www.lums.lancs.ac.uk) was £10,000, while its MA in human resource development and consulting would have set you back just £5,500. All universities list their fees on their website or give links or email addresses to where you can find them. You will also find links to fees and funding information on many of the institution profiles included in the back of this guide.

Bear in mind that if you're coming from overseas (in this instance we mean from outside the EU) you can expect the fees to be much higher. To use LUMS as an example again, the fee for international students for the MSc and MA mentioned above in 2008-09 was £14,000 and £11,000 respectively.

If you are studying part-time you will normally be able to pay half of the fee one year and half the next, which can help to spread the burden, while for some flexible master's you essentially 'pay as you go'. It's also important, however, to factor in living and maintenance costs. These will very much depend on your personal circumstances, though organisations such as Prospects (www.prospects.ac.uk) argue that, as a minimum, you should be budgeting about £10,000 for a year in London and £7,500 elsewhere. Prospects also has a very comprehensive section on funding on its website, which is worth taking a look at. It makes sense to sit down and draw up a realistic budget of what you will need to live off during your time of study, set against any income you might be expecting to get in during it. This is particularly true if you are planning to study full-time. This may well need to include a contingency budget for when or if you are looking for work following the completion of your course.

While many students, particularly those returning to study and using savings or continuing to work while studying, will self-fund their course there are other options and avenues of financial assistance that you can call on.

Loans

The Student Loans Company doesn't cater for postgraduates but postgraduates are able to apply for one of the Department for Innovation, Universities and Skills' (DIUS) (www.dius.gov.uk) Career Development Loans (CDL), which are administered by three high-street banks: Barclays, Royal Bank of Scotland and the Co-operative. These allow you to borrow anything from £300 to £8,000 to fund your studying for up to two years. You cannot use it if you are already eligible for a local education authority grant or if you have a job where your employer is receiving a grant for your training but you can use it to supplement a grant or bursary that does not meet the full cost of your training. You do not need to start repaying the loan until around two months after graduation, with the interest on the loan paid for by the DIUS until this time. If your course is longer than two years it is possible to use a CDL to fund part of it.

Beyond CDLs, it can be worth checking whether you are eligible for a professional studies loan. These are available through a number of banks, including HSBC, for undergraduate and postgraduate study in a range of 'professional' areas such as accountancy, engineering, law and medicine. Applicants can borrow up to £25,000, with repayments needing to start within six months of the end of the course.

Research Councils

These are government-funded agencies that support research in a range of different disciplines and are one of the most important sources of funding of postgraduate students, funding some 10,000 studentships a year between them. There are seven grant-awarding councils, which can be found at www.rcuk. ac.uk Competition for funding is inevitably fierce, with the councils offering a variety of awards, the most common of which at MA and MSc level is a one-year 'advanced course studentship' that normally covers tuition fees, a maintenance grant and a contribution towards expenses such as travel and books.

To be eligible you need to be an EU national who has been resident in the UK for three years prior to your application (in other words normally an undergraduate student) and with a first class or upper second honours degree from a UK university, although the Natural Environment Research Council only requires a lower second degree. Your university should be able to advise you on whether you are eligible for an award and how to go about applying, though you will need to apply directly to the relevant council yourself.

There are a number of other publicly funded bodies that also fund postgraduate study. The Students Awards Agency for Scotland (www.student-support-saas.gov.uk), for example, has a postgraduate students' allowances scheme available to Scottish-domiciled students planning to study in the UK. Similarly, the Department for Employment and Learning in Northern Ireland (www.delni.gov.uk) offers some funding support at postgraduate level for Northern Ireland-domiciled students and UK and EU students who want to study in Northern Ireland. The European Social Fund (www.esf.gov.uk) also supports a number of vocational postgraduate courses in the UK.

Charities, foundations and trusts

Another option is to approach the many charities, foundations and trusts that award partial funding for postgraduate study. These will range in size from the huge Wellcome Trust (www.wellcome.ac.uk), which awards hundreds of studentships each year to much smaller groups. Prospects, again, under its section on funding, offers a pretty comprehensive list and the sorts of areas they cover. Generally you'll be looking at a range of studentships, scholarships, grants, bursaries, competitions and prizes, some focused on very specific research areas and others more general. The size of the award is likely to vary too, sometimes from as little as a few hundred pounds (though no less welcome for that) right up to covering the full cost of tuition.

The key here is legwork – you'll need to go out and source the right body for you. Being charities, they will also want to be sure you have exhausted all other possible avenues of funding and may have strict eligibility criteria but, hey, it's their money.

Teaching, assistantships, scholarships and bursaries

Don't forget your university itself can be a source of funding, although competition will again tend to be fierce. Most higher education institutions offer a range of bursaries and scholarships at postgraduate level, ranging from full-fee studentships and maintenance grants to a contribution to your study costs. Some are designed to alleviate financial hardship or will be for a specific type of project or research. Again, have a close look at the university's website and speak to your department about what options there might be. There may also be the opportunity to pick up a bit of teaching work, perhaps as a research or teaching assistant, although this is something that more commonly happens at PhD level.

Given that universities want to keep you on board, if money is tight it can often be a good idea to ask whether there is any sort of flexible payment schedule of fees. It might be possible to spread the financial pain by paying in termly instalments although, much like paying your car insurance in instalments, there may be a surcharge for doing it this way. Some universities, too, offer reduced postgraduate fees for undergraduate alumni. Students from disadvantaged backgrounds or experiencing financial hardship may be able to access the government's Access to Learning fund, which you apply for through the student services department at your university. Awards tend to range from £100 to around £3,500, though they cannot be used to pay for tuition fees.

Employers

There are really two sorts of funding here: employers fund a sponsorship or a student award through a course or, more commonly, fund either all or part of an employee's study. The first sort of funding is normally advertised through the department and it is simply worth asking about directly.

The latter – getting your boss to stump up the cash – can seem an ideal solution, but it is not without its pitfalls. If you are doing an MA or MSc because you are sick of your current job and want to change career, it is clearly not going to be the best option. But if you are doing something that has the potential to make you a better employee or manager when you return to work, it may be worth considering.

To have any chance of securing this sort of largesse you'll need to put together a business case for why you should have the money. What your boss will want to know is 'what is in it for me?', and don't forget that in all likelihood they will then need to go away and make the case for you to someone higher up. You may also be grilled by other senior managers or the HR department.

What you need to focus on is how having the MA or MSc will help you do your job more effectively, make you a better manager or give you new skills that can be used in a specific way that is beneficial to your company. Don't be too surprised if they ask you in return to commit to staying with them for a specified period of time after graduation or perhaps only agree to pay for a percentage of the costs.

Perhaps the biggest danger here is that the company offers to fund some alternative sort of training instead, such as a number of day release courses. You'll need to have a good answer prepared for this. It's also important to pin down exactly what each side is agreeing to, such as whether you are expected to stump up, say, for your study materials or can claim it back and whether under the agreement you will get any time off for study, exams and so on, or will simply be expected to use your holiday allowance.

International students

Many of the scholarships and bursaries that are available to EU and UK students will be available to international students and can therefore be searched for in the same way. Many universities also offer specific international scholarships, which will be listed on their own websites. Other useful sources are your own education ministry and the British Council (www.britishcouncil.org), which runs Education UK (www.educationuk.org) specifically for international students. This also has a section on scholarships.

The UK Council for International Student Affairs (www.ukcisa.org.uk) is another useful site, while the Overseas Research Students Awards Scheme (www.orsas.ac.uk) offers grants to allow international students to undertake research degrees. The Association of Commonwealth Universities (www.acu.ac.uk) has information on funding opportunities for postgraduates resident in the Commonwealth.

Disability-related support

While there is no statutory funding for course fees for disabled students at postgraduate level, there are some sources of funding and support that disabled students can look into. You may be able to get Disabled Students' Allowance, which provides grants to help meet any extra course costs incurred as a direct result of a disability. Similarly you may be able to access the Access to Learning fund (see above). Skill, the National Bureau for Students with Disabilities (www.skill.org.uk), publishes a range of free online booklets and has an information service and helpline. Individual charities may also be able to provide support and advice.

There is a wealth of information on this, as well as on Career Development Loans and the Access to Learning Fund, on the government's Direct Gov website, www.direct.gov.uk Other websites that offer useful general information on funding include the National Postgraduate Council (www.npc.org.uk), a charity which promotes postgraduate education in the UK, as well as most individual university careers services' websites.

● What it's like to do an MA/MSc

Ask a roomful of MA or MSc students to describe their experiences of postgraduate study and they'll all have a different story to tell about their course, their tutor, their sense of satisfaction and whether or not it was worthwhile. Nevertheless, when it comes to the structure of a taught MA or MSc what you can expect will normally be pretty standard. Whether you are studying full- or part-time, flexibly or remotely, the common route to achieving a master's is by building up points through a series of core and optional modules and finally, the bit everyone dreads, a dissertation. The best way therefore to get a proper feel for what you are going to be doing during the 12 to 24 months of your course is simply to go on to your relevant department website and follow the links through until you get to the one entitled 'programme structure'.

Let's take as an example King's College London's (www.kcl.ac.uk) MA in public policy. Students on this MA are expected to take three core modules, in the process accruing 75 points. This is followed by a range of optional modules that allow them to specialise in areas such as policy analysis, health policy, urban and environmental policy and so on, adding a further 60 credits to their total. Then finally they are required to complete a 15,000-word dissertation for 60 points which, KCL points out, will need to fall within the remit of the programme of study and be approved by a member of the teaching team. On some courses you might find the dissertation will be longer, perhaps as much as 20,000 words, and the points split slightly differently but most master's will follow this sort of structure.

The timeframe you will be working to is also likely to be fairly standard. For full-time students, this will normally mean an October start with the first and second terms either split between core and optional modules or one term devoted solely to core modules and one solely to optional modules. Then the third term (from about May onwards) and the summer will usually be devoted to the dissertation, which will normally need to be submitted by the end of September. For part-time students it can be a bit more variable but what commonly happens is that the core and optional taught modules are completed during the first year and the dissertation during the second. A variation on this might be an initial term of modules in the second year followed by the dissertation.

So that's the bare bones of it, but what is it actually like to do an MA or MSc and how does it differ from what you will have experienced at undergraduate level? A quote on Kent University's (www.kent.ac.uk) website from a former student nicely encapsulates this: 'It's the difference between studying history and being a historian.' What this means is that, during your three to four years as an undergraduate, your time is heavily scheduled, your hand tightly held and you are guided, normally at quite a gallop, across a wide range of subjects and modules.

As a postgraduate it is very different. First, you will be much more on your own, with much more freedom to prioritise and decide how and when you work. Second, the area you are focusing on will be much narrower and, as such, your relationship with the academic staff is likely to be very different.

At undergraduate level it's still by and large a teacher/pupil relationship, albeit sometimes moving beyond this in the final year if there is a dissertation.

At postgraduate level the relationship is much more equal – you are considered to be more mature, to know your subject and to have already done the reading before you turn up. The tutor or supervisor's role is more about support and guidance than formal stand-up-at-the-front teaching. At a practical level, there is also likely to be much less contact time with the tutor than you had during your undergraduate degree, the study or seminar groups will probably be smaller and the focus may be more on what you can bring to the debate – for instance you may be required to make presentations or lead the discussion within a seminar. Another difference is that you will be taught about research methods and some of the problems and practices around academic research. The dissertation is such an important element of the master's qualification that this training is likely to be crucial.

Of course, you can never truly know whether you are cut out for an MA or MSc until you actually do it. But what you do need to think about is whether you will be happy working in this independent way, whether you have the motivation and are enough of a self-starter not to fall behind or lose momentum. These are attributes that are particularly important when you are on your own during the dissertation period. Good planning and organisation tend to be singled out by postgraduate students as key skills here but stubbornness, focus, stamina, an unwillingness to give in and, of course, a passion for your subject will all help.

While tutors and supervisors will normally make themselves available (to a greater or lesser extent) the fact that you are on your own can sometimes lead you to feel isolated. If it's academic isolation – in that you are feeling adrift in your studies – the key here is simply to speak to your tutor. It is, after all, their job to keep you on track and they should be able to offer support and guide you in the right direction as well as helping to restore your motivation. It can sometimes also be helpful to speak to fellow students, but just be sure you know them well and trust them to be supportive.

Postgraduates also often complain of a sense of physical isolation, both from student life and from the campus itself. It is very easy to feel that you are not properly a part of the university, particularly if you are studying remotely or just visiting the campus for seminars. Other issues that can come into play here include the fact that, as a postgraduate, you will probably be older than the bulk of undergraduates and so may have different priorities and constraints on your time, such as family life or work. Similarly, because an MA or MSc is that much shorter and intense, there can be less time for social activities (and hence more of a sense of dislocation), less time to build up friendships and relationships, and a sense that student life, while fun again, is something you are only revisiting in passing before going back out into the 'real' world.

There are no easy answers to these questions. University clubs and societies, the union — and of course the bars — are as open to postgraduates as they are to undergraduates. But if you start to feel really isolated and depressed it is important to turn to the counselling and support services that all universities now offer because there is nothing worse than suffering in silence.

● Make your MA/MSc work for you

The sense of relief and achievement will be palpable. You've sweated and drafted through a long summer, read and re-read, and finally handed in your dissertation and can now sit back in the knowledge that — yes! — you've done it. So, what now? Well, beyond the pride in a job well done — or possibly deflation that it's all over — there's still a job of work to do if you are going to get the most out of your MA or MSc.

For some, particularly those for whom the master's is the first step to an academic career, the transition is pretty straightforward. In fact what often happens is that students convert or roll their master's research straight into a PhD and continue from there. For the rest of us, maximising the potential of a master's qualification is often a bit more hit and miss.

Perhaps the first thing worth remembering — and this is hugely reassuring given the amount of time and money you have just spent on it — is that an MA or MSc is for life; you may not necessarily see the benefits immediately but they will come. As Hecsu's Dr Charlie Ball explained to this guide: 'The benefits of master's study often come later in the career of graduates — at managerial level, for example.'

For some careers, as we have seen, a master's is almost a prerequisite to entry and so may start to open doors straightaway, meaning it is only a question of getting out into the jobs market. Similarly, where the learning you have gained is relevant to the job you want to go on to do, there will clearly be a direct correlation between your research and the positions you are applying for. Yet even in these scenarios, and even more so if you need to 'sell' your MA or MSc in order to gain employment in an area not directly related to your studies, it is important to sit back and evaluate what you have learned and achieved during the 12 to 24 months of your master's degree.

Ideally, this self-analysis or self-audit should be something you are doing throughout your course but, if not, it should definitely be something you do on completion. It need not take long but it is important to step back and ask yourself what skills as well as academic knowledge you've gained through doing an MA or MSc, and how they make you more valuable to a future employer.

Some examples of this are likely to be evidence of commitment (after all you've completed the damn thing), independent and critical thought, effective time management and planning, data collection, research and analytical skills, the ability to distil complex issues into clearly thought-out arguments, debate and discourse skills, project management, IT skills, self-motivation and drive, oral and written communication skills and, of course, advanced intellectual capability.

These are all highly transferable skills that employers in many areas will value, whether your dissertation was on diseases of ancient Assyria or European credit derivatives. If you want to formalise your thinking draw up an action plan listing the strengths you have gained as well as looking at any weaknesses. Sometimes, too, it can be useful to sit down with a friend or colleague (though they need to be ones you trust) to do a bit of what, in HR parlance, is called 360 degree appraisal – basically getting someone to tell you what they think of you and your abilities. If you are unsure what to do next, these sorts of activities can often help to focus your mind on what it is you actually enjoy doing most and are best at and therefore the sort of area or position in which you might like to work.

At a practical level, it also makes sense to speak to your tutor and supervisor about the sort of options that might be available to you, either within academia or out in the commercial world. Similarly, it may be a good idea to sit down with the university careers service. If you have a particular sector or even a company in mind, research them as closely as you can, identify who to approach and, even if there is not a specific opening advertised, make a speculative approach. It's sensible to think about the negative preconceptions some employers may have about postgraduates and how you will answer these criticisms in an interview if they come up. These could be questions around whether you're too expensive, you're over qualified or why you have spent so long before trying to get a 'proper' job.

Most employers these days also use what are known as 'competency-based' assessment techniques to weed out candidates and will therefore be asking questions both on the application form and in interviews designed to get applicants to show how and when they have used the skills they are arguing they have. The key is to think all the time of examples – how you effectively managed your time on a particular project, an instance where you overcame an obstacle in your research, an example of critical thinking or how you successfully pursued a key goal of your qualification. You get the idea.

In conclusion, by completing an MA or MSc you will have gained a range of hugely valuable skills. Assuming you maintain and enhance them over time, they will give you momentum in your career and future life. What's more, they are skills that are likely to become more important the higher up the career ladder you climb and so it may be that you start to experience a greater 'postgraduate premium' three to five years down the line, with that premium even accelerating as time goes on.

Yes, an MA or Msc is a hard slog but it can also be an immensely fulfilling and worthwhile experience. Nothing of course is guaranteed in this world, but the chances are that you will gain financially, in career terms and, most of all, from the sheer intellectual buzz of diving headlong into the sometimes arcane, sometimes frustrating and sometimes contradictory world of academic thought and rigour. Whatever you choose to study, and however and wherever you choose to do it, you will in all likelihood come out the other end wiser, stronger, clearer-headed and, probably, considerably more argumentative! So, what's to lose?

CASE STUDY 1

The graduate

Debra Hawley completed a one-year MA in TESOL (Teaching English to Speakers of Other Languages) at Bath University in September 2007

For me, doing an MA has been simply about getting off the treadmill of work and doing something I have always wanted to do.

In 1995 I graduated with a first in my undergraduate degree in language studies and professional French at the University College of St Mark and St John in Plymouth. My tutors talked to me at the time about whether I wanted to go on to further study and I would have loved to, but as a single mother with a mortgage to pay, I had to go out and find work.

Then last year I decided it was finally time to go back and do it. In a way I had always felt cheated that I had not had the opportunity before, but now we had money saved up, my husband had a good job, the children were grown up and it just felt like the right time. Even though I was still working, I never even contemplated doing it part-time. If I was going to do it I wanted to do it 100 per cent and so I resigned from my job and went for it.

If I'm being honest, my first choice would have been to do an MA in linguistics because the English language has always been one of the key interests in my life. I did look at a course in Bristol but it wasn't clear whether it was actually going to run and they took weeks to come back to me whereas Bath, which is where I live anyway, came back to me straight away saying I could have a place.

Another reason why I chose the course at Bath is the possible career opportunities it might bring. My career up to now has been in customer service management in the logistics and distribution sector but there is a large immigrant community in Bath and, while I am still in two minds as to exactly what route I will take, this is the sort of qualification that will open doors if I want to go into teaching English to speakers of other languages.

Perhaps the biggest difference I have found between doing an undergraduate and postgraduate degree is that there is much less hand-holding than at undergraduate level and it is much more specialised; you get a chance to go into things in much more depth.

To do a master's effectively you do need to be organised. I sat down and planned it out with military precision. I have deadlines for everything, have a timetable that I make sure I keep to and have it all charted out on a calendar. You also have to be prepared to work hard. Whatever you want to achieve on a master's comes down to you and your own ability. It is not something that you can just cruise through. When I have not been in lectures I have more or less been studying 8am to 5pm, Monday to Friday.

When it came to doing the 15,000-word dissertation, which I started in May, I initially thought it wouldn't be that difficult, essentially just like three 5,000-word assignments, but it is harder than that because, of course, it all needs to be linked together. The research methods you will normally be taught also come in very useful in helping you to prepare for it. A key part of doing the dissertation is remaining motivated. I actually enjoy reading and writing in peace and quiet but, even so, family life can always be a distraction, so at times it can be difficult to keep focused. I particularly found it hard at the beginning when I realised I was spending a lot of time on it but was not being focused enough about what I was doing.

Throughout the MA, the support I have had from my tutor has been excellent. I have constantly submitted drafts to him and gained feedback. I've found it is important when I go into a meeting or seminar with him to have done a lot of preparation and come armed with a list of questions because the time you get with your tutor is very valuable. I've mostly used him simply to make sure that I am going in the right direction.

The best bit for me about doing an MA has been the freedom to be a student again. When you're working you're always restricted because you have to go into the office, sit in meetings and be suited and booted. While I have been quite strict with myself about how hard I work — I don't just want to get an MA, I want a distinction — it has been my choice and it is wonderful to have the freedom to study something at your own pace.

What happens next, of course, is the $10m question. I genuinely don't know what I am going to do next, whether I will go back into a general office manager role or try to move into a teaching role, perhaps at one of the local colleges here. But what I do know is that doing an MA has been a hugely worthwhile experience. I've done something I've always wanted to do and I've proved to myself that I am capable of doing it.

CASE STUDY 2

The tutor

Professor John Lyle, professor in sports coaching at the Carnegie Faculty of Sport & Education at Leeds Metropolitan University and course leader for the MSc in sports coaching practice

Studying for a master's degree is very different to studying for an undergraduate degree. People decide to do master's degrees for many reasons — it can be because they want to gain a professional qualification that extends or deepens some existing knowledge, perhaps from their previous degree or subsequent career, or it may be that they simply want to learn about something completely different.

Either way, probably the biggest change you will find when studying at this level is that it is much more independent. At undergraduate level a lot of time the work is simply presented to you and you have few options to study away from the curriculum. With a master's, there is much less direction and you are expected to be studying by yourself and doing more away from the lectures. Essentially, with a master's it is down to you.

Another big difference when you are doing a master's is that you will be studying at a level of critical understanding and appraisal that is much higher than at undergraduate level. It is not just about acquiring the knowledge but about having a notion of criticality, of applying that knowledge and testing the boundaries of the discipline.

Sometimes students do find both the independence and this type of critical thinking difficult, especially at the beginning and also if they are returning to study after some years away from it. You have to learn to be less accepting; you have to learn to argue a position.

What I look for as a tutor therefore when interviewing or assessing prospective students is, first, that you have a good enough degree. But you also need to demonstrate that you are someone who wants to study the subject at this level and in this depth; that it is not something you are simply looking at as an after-thought or because you are unable to decide on a career. For example, it might be that your undergraduate dissertation was in the area that you now want to study. What I want to see is evidence that this is an area you have thought about deeply and want to engage with.

At a practical level, studying for a master's requires good time management. This is, of course, something that is important for study at any level, but it is particularly important at postgraduate level. When you are doing a master's there can sometimes be the temptation simply to work towards the next assignment. But with a master's, because there is so much less teaching to a curriculum, you will need to be reading around the subject much more widely; you have to be immersing yourself in the subject completely. Tutors at postgraduate level will assume their students are doing this and if they are not, particularly when it comes to assignments, it can sometimes cause problems.

Whether you are studying full-time or part-time — and particularly if you are juggling work and study — the best way to manage your time, I think, is to work out a definite schedule of when you are going to study; to set proper time aside rather than just saying you will get to it at some point. It is also important to make sure that you are keeping on top of the paperwork. You need to be keeping records effectively and making a careful note of what you are reading, what you have done, what you thought about it and what you need to be working on.

If you find yourself getting into difficulties, perhaps with the workload or even the study itself, the best thing is simply to come and talk to your tutor. People do sometimes suggest it is a good idea to speak to another student but I'd really recommend that you speak to a tutor because they will have probably seen a lot of people who have been in similar situations.

What can sometimes happen is that students start to get feedback from their tutors that they are uncomfortable with — it may be that a tutor has said their work is superficial or that they are not doing enough reading — so it is important at that point to sit down and talk to them. Tutors can give guidance and support on what a student needs to be doing to improve; that is what they are there for.

What a master's qualification shows potential employers is that you have acquired knowledge beyond the basic undergraduate level, that you have studied at a higher level either as a way of preparing yourself better for a specific vocation or simply that you have acquired a higher level of intellectual knowledge and critical understanding.

But what you then need to be able to do is to demonstrate how that additional education and training can apply to the job you want. So it might be a case of showing that you have the intellectual capacity to work on your own or to make critical judgements or interpret information. With a master's you are marking yourself out. It can definitely set you apart from the mass of graduates.

CASE STUDY 3

The recruiter

Carl Gilleard, chief executive, The Association of Graduate Recruiters

I'm often asked to speak to students about what employers and recruiters look for from postgraduates and the most important message I try to get across to them is that they shouldn't just think that the qualification will get them a job.

What a lot of employers look for when they are hiring on to their graduate training schemes is simply a graduate with a good first degree, but this certainly does not mean they rule out postgraduate qualifications. Sometimes, in fact, employers will actively be looking for a postgraduate qualification because they are after particularly specialist knowledge. For example, for careers such as research chemist, town planner or, increasingly, HR, a postgraduate qualification is now almost a pre-requisite.

Sometimes, too, an employer may be attracted to someone with an MA or MSc because they are looking for someone with a greater level of maturity. A good example here is management consultancy, where customers want to get advice from people who have a certain level of life experience or industry knowledge under their belts.

Grade inflation can come into it too, though I believe this is often more of an issue for students than it is for employers. Everyone at university now is very conscious of the need to get at least a 2:1 or a first in their undergraduate degree and when 60 per cent are getting them, it's natural to think what else can I do that will give me an edge?

But for the recruiter it needs to be about more than simply proffering the qualification. It is about what you can offer that employer. I have been at recruitment fairs and have been approached by potentially promising candidates with master's qualifications who, when asked why they did this extra study, have said in all seriousness, that it was because they did not know what else to do. Others have admitted that it was because they did not feel ready to go out into the world of work, neither of which tends to go down well.

When you are applying for a job you have to overcome some of the stereotypes and negative preconceptions that some employers can have about postgraduate students.

There can be a suspicion of 'are they simply professional students?' or, even worse, that the person in front of them is now over-qualified to do the job. So it is important to look at these negatives and address them and ask yourself how you will answer these questions.

What employers really want to hear is that you had a real desire to study that particular subject or that you thought it would enhance your job prospects and how. It might be that it has improved your project management skills, or you might want to talk up your prowess at research or working independently or the fact that you have been pushed to a higher level intellectually, or even how what you have learned could be applied to a workplace setting. Employers will be looking at the skills and experience you have acquired, your personal attributes and your motivation. They will want to see that you as an individual are in control of your life and your learning.

Also, if you decide to do an MA or MSc, you have to recognise that you are taking a gamble on the jobs market. Even given the difficult economic climate, graduate recruiters have said they had a very good year in 2008. But that could change and you never know what the situation will be like in one or even two years time.

Ultimately, if you have a real, burning desire to do a particular MA or MSc – however obscure – you have nothing to worry about because that will come through when you speak to employers, and it is not my job as an employer to tell people what they can or can't study. But if it is something you are doing just because you can or because you don't know what else to do that would worry me.

Whatever MA or MSc you choose, what you need to be doing is sitting back and reflecting on the knowledge and skills that you have learned and how that might transfer to a work situation. During the one or two years that you are studying you need to be honing those skills and then using the same passion that you have for your subject to convince an employer that you are the person they should be recruiting.

MBA

Pam Tate

The MBA, that American import, is fast becoming a must-have postgraduate degree in UK business. But besides being a box to tick for those climbing the corporate ladder, what is the MBA and what can it do for your career?

The Master of Business Administration programme is essentially a boot camp for general managers. It's an intense one or two years of business fundamentals, including finance, economics, strategy and organisational behaviour, from which participants emerge with a broad set of knowledge and skills that could not all be acquired through ordinary employment. A good MBA programme teaches you how different business functions fit together and how companies in different industries operate. In recent years, there's also been much more emphasis on teaching 'soft skills': how to manage teams and persuade clients.

The MBA can be a virtual necessity if you want to advance to senior levels in some industries, such as banking and management consulting, whereas some old-line sectors like retail are notoriously wedded to the notion of rising up from the shop floor. But in any sector, the big multinationals will demand MBAs for senior roles in consumer marketing, strategy and even human resources. An MBA won't allow you to parachute into a seat on the board of directors the day after graduation, but it may well mean that five or 10 years down the road when it is your turn for a shot at a top job, you won't be held back by doubts about your all-round business acumen. Finally, an MBA gives you a lasting source of flexibility in your career, because its all-rounder nature certifies you as someone with a firm grounding in principles that apply across the board.

Then there's the prospect of increased pay. The difference between before-and-after MBA salaries remains a key point of comparison on MBA league tables (though it's worth bearing in mind that a programme with a younger student body is going to have an easier time showing big jumps than one peopled by senior managers taking a career break to study). Several programmes in the

UK boast 100 per cent-plus increases in average salaries, albeit with the huge jumps generally arising from students hailing from outside Europe or North America. Still, for students originating from the UK, average salary increases at a good programme are still around 50 per cent – nothing to sniff at.

More difficult to quantify, but just as important, is the extended network of business contacts you'll gain. Naturally, you'll only get out of these relationships what you put in, but if you make an effort to get to know your student cohort and alumni, it will pay off in job leads, industry connections and critical local knowledge of places around the world, quite possibly for the rest of your working life. You'll be working in an intense but often exhilarating environment with these people, many of whom will turn out to be lifelong friends as well.

How do you know if now is the right time to do an MBA? One classic reason for wanting to do an MBA – aside from 'bags more money, please' – is to change careers. Whether in your case it's the well-trodden road between consulting and banking, or a more inspired leap into the corporate world from the public sector, an MBA programme can help you do that. That's because the generalist nature of the MBA makes it a versatile degree and relevant in just about any industry, even non-profit organisations. Moreover – and this is especially true if it's full-time – the programme is set up to flood you with opportunities to explore roles and industries new to you, whether it's through a live consulting project for class, a summer internship or evening drinks with alumni.

Another popular reason for doing an MBA is to advance in your current career, particularly if your job is quite specialised or you want to move from working independently to managing a group. An MBA prepares you for tackling the gamut of business problems and in the process turns you into a manager. Perhaps you're an accomplished widget designer but think you could run the company if only you knew how to read a balance sheet, seek investment capital and negotiate with retailers. The MBA is for you.

Maybe you see yourself as an entrepreneur, with a great idea but with only your mum and dad lining up to invest cash. An MBA will not only teach you how to start and run a business, but should build your credibility with customers or lenders while broadening your network of potential investors.

The main downside to embarking on an MBA is the cost: from £8,000 up to £45,000 a year in tuition, plus the potential expense of relocating yourself and family. If you decide to leave work and commit to a full-time programme, you are looking at sacrificing one or two years of income. Of course, the MBA, once completed, could propel you to a salary higher than what you could have otherwise achieved in the same space of time.

Nearly all business schools have some kind of return-on-investment metrics available on their websites or from the admissions office to help you with this calculation. You can generally find out how quickly graduates find new jobs, what the average post-MBA salary is, how much the average increase is and specifics about tuition and the cost of living.

You'll also need to assess whether now is the right time to undertake such a challenge to your personal and family life. The programme is incredibly intense – you will be crammed full of both theoretical knowledge and practical experience that would otherwise take a whole lifetime to acquire. It would be a mistake to assume that leaving paid work to study will mean life will become easier. You may well be putting in longer hours, with classes from nine to five and study groups and networking taking you well into the evening several times a week.

Speaking of timing, for most people an MBA is not the best choice straight out of undergraduate study. Good MBA programmes want applicants who have a least a few years of work experience under their belts, who have been out in the real world and have had a chance to figure out what they want from the degree. With some practical experience behind you, you're also likely to make a richer contribution to the all-important class discussions and group projects than a shiny new undergraduate whose business dealings have been limited to signing up for a current account. This is reflected in the average age of MBA students: in the UK it is 29/30 and in the US it's a bit younger at 27/28.

What the best MBA candidates have in common is a clear idea of their career goals and a realistic plan to get there. The pace of an MBA programme is gruelling and the stampede for job-placements begins within just a few months of the start of the course. If you are floundering, not knowing which of the hundreds of careers you'd like to pursue, you'll already be at a disadvantage when you start to compete with classmates for the best interviews. That's not to say that if you start off aiming for a specific career you won't change your mind once you get stuck into the coursework – only that if you really don't know what you'd like to do, an MBA is a very expensive way to find out and you are unlikely to get the full benefit of the course.

● How to do it

Over the last decade, there has been a proliferation of MBA programmes in the UK. There's more choice now not only in terms of course content, but also in the type of delivery. Depending on your circumstances, you might choose to study full-time, part-time or by distance learning.

Full-time MBA programmes in the UK and Europe usually last for one year, as opposed to the traditional two-year programme in the US. A typical course has five eight-week terms over the year, during which you take four to six courses per term. The required core classes usually account for 40 to 60 per cent of the programme and are delivered over the first half of the year. The second half of the year will shift to electives.

There are a few two-year full-time programmes in the UK, notably at London Business School and Manchester Business School. These will cover much the same fundamental course material, but you'll have a bit more time to soak it in. You'll also have more time to take electives that could give your career an extra boost, such as languages or a specialisation that opens up a new interest. Unlike most one-year programmes, a two-year programme usually has a lengthy summer internship of eight to 12 weeks built into the curriculum – a serious boon for career changers who will need the hands-on experience and contacts-building more than others on a vertical track in their careers.

One-year programmes generally don't make the internship an integral part of the programme, because you may only have a break of a few days between terms. On the other hand, you'll be finished and back on the job market a whole year earlier. If you're already in senior management with no worries about job prospects post your MBA, the one-year programme is a sensible choice.

The majority of students opt to study part-time in the evenings and weekends, taking from two to eight years to complete their MBA. This has a number of advantages. You'll still have a regular pay cheque coming in, and you're not risking unemployment at the end of the programme. The chances of persuading your employer to foot all or part of the bill are also much greater if you enrol part-time. If you are hoping to advance within your current career, or indeed within the same company – and all you want to do is plug the holes in your CV – then choosing to study a full-time course may be an unnecessary sacrifice of momentum.

But you will have to be realistic about how well work and study can be combined. A typical weekly schedule would have you in class for six hours, with a further six to 10 hours of study. Mastering the coursework and building that all-important network with your classmates will be more difficult if you've got to keep turning up at the office than if you had immersed yourself in a full-time programme. Your performance at work may also suffer as you devote time and energy to school, meaning that you'll probably be unable to add to your responsibilities and increase your salary while you're studying. If you're hoping to use the MBA as a springboard to a new job, remember that part-time students have to be much more self-motivated about using the career services on offer. Most of the recruitment activity, such as fairs and dinners, are set up around the full-time student curriculum, so part-time students generally don't benefit as much.

Distance learning programmes, in which all or part of the coursework is delivered online or through the post, are gaining credibility, but it can be difficult to assess the quality of these courses. On a good course you'll be required to participate in seminars or group project days for at least part of the coursework. Find out whether the course material is the same as that used in the part-time or full-time programmes at the same school and also whether you can switch back and forth between the distance and part-time programmes. Also important is whether the school differentiates between a distance MBA degree and other MBAs to employers or regards them as equivalent. For career changers, it's worth noting that a distance learning programme won't be able to deliver what could be the most critical component of your MBA – the enduring network of contacts in industries and locations you wouldn't otherwise have access to and the exposure to a diversity of ideas and experiences in the form of your fellow classmates.

There is one other MBA format, relatively rare but growing in popularity, worth a brief mention here: the Executive MBA. It's mainly for people in their 30s or 40s, with perhaps 10 or more years experience and a strong track record in management. For these people at a fairly senior level in their career a traditional MBA isn't really suitable. They might meet for just a few days a month over two years and, as such, don't necessarily develop the close relationships that you see in traditional programmes. However a major bonus is that EMBA courses are almost always paid for by the employer.

● Where to do it

By now you should have figured out whether the MBA is the right step at the right stage in your career. You'll have weighed up the impact on your finances and lifestyle of the different options and settled on a route that's either full-time or part-time. But with about 115 MBA programmes to choose from in the UK, your research has really just begun.

This is probably as good a time as any to address the issue of reputation. Perhaps more so than other postgraduate degrees, employers see the MBA as a branded commodity. The institution name attached to your degree will, for better or worse, be treated as shorthand for whether you have been trained as a finance whiz or a general manager, whether your aspirations are international or regional in scope, and where your abilities lie relative to the 26,000 students studying for an MBA in the UK at any given time.

If you've had a look at any of the MBA league tables published by, among others, *Which?*, the *Financial Times*, *BusinessWeek*, the *Wall Street Journal* or *Forbes*, you'll probably have an idea of the broad tiers that schools are sorted into. None of these publications will agree from year to year what the best business school is, but their top 10 or 20 are likely to look pretty similar. Use them as a starting point to assess where your overall profile of work experience, academic record and GMAT score (more on which from page 47) could get you. For more information look online at:

- mba.eiu.com
- www.ft.com/businesseducation/mba
- www.businessweek.com/bschools
- online.wsj.com
- www.forbes.com

Accreditation by an education standards body is another key marker of reputation. In the UK, the Association of MBAs (AMBA) has put its stamp of approval on more than 40 programmes. The European Foundation for Management Development, another quality organisation but with a more international focus, has awarded its EQUIS accreditation to about 15 UK programmes. The main US-based accreditation agency, the Association to Advance Collegiate Schools of Business, has awarded its seal to just a dozen UK programmes. Gaining an accreditation is an expensive and time-consuming process, so the lack of one doesn't necessarily mean the school is cranking out bogus diplomas. On the other hand, if you want to work for a blue-chip multinational or a global investment bank, you would be wise to limit your choice of schools to those with an accreditation. You can find out more about accredited courses online at:

- www.mbaworld.com
- www.efmd.org
- www.aacsb.edu

When it comes to reputation, it's the employer you would most love to work for post-MBA who really has the final say. Which schools does your target company, or the best companies in your target industry, regularly recruit from? Which schools already have a working relationship with these companies in the form of students' consulting projects and management shadowing opportunities? The admissions office of the school should be able to fill you in, or it may even be appropriate to ring up the human resources office at your dream job and ask (politely) which MBA programmes they regard highly.

The curriculum should also factor largely in your choice of school. Even though the MBA is by its nature a generalist degree, every programme is different. The balance between core courses and electives will vary, with some programmes boasting non-business courses such as languages that may or may not be relevant to your career. There are specialisations by function (finance or marketing, for instance) or by sector (health care or military). Do some research into what a school's USP is and decide if it will be of benefit to you, and be aware that the glossy programme brochure may not make it obvious what the school is known for by employers. Talk to people who work in the industry you're aspiring to and look at the kinds of jobs students get when they leave. *Which? MBA* is also a good reference – it covers only a couple of dozen of the top schools in the UK but its programme descriptions include what each one is known for among recruiters and alumni.

Another factor to consider is teaching methods. Only you can assess what kind of environment suits you best for learning. Do you find traditional lectures most effective, or does the case study method suit your outgoing nature better? Do you need to have professors with generous amounts of time available to provide extra help, or would you rather learn from tutors who are immersed in industry now, even if that means they don't have time to see you outside of class?

The biggest clue as to whether an MBA programme is right for you is the participants. Most admissions offices and the programme websites are only too happy to provide statistics about where its students come from, what they did for a living, what they intend to do for a living and whether they are career changers or climbers. Classes are sliced and diced according to salary, gender and family situation. Check that where these people are coming from and where they are going to matches up with what you want the MBA to do for you.

Is location important? Doing a programme close to home means you won't have to worry about the emotional and financial cost of uprooting your life and your family. If you're studying part-time, your choices may be automatically narrowed to just a handful that are within commuting distance. But otherwise, the location of your school should depend on where your aspirations lie after the degree. If you intend to live and work in the same region, then a local university will be rich in the contacts and relevant consulting projects you need. But if you seriously yearn to travel, London, and to a much smaller but growing degree, Manchester, are where the multinational companies in the UK are based. This proximity is reflected not only in the quality of their faculty – tutors are generally working in the industry in one capacity or another while they teach – but also in the strength of their job placement office.

A word on study abroad: as the MBA is an American invention, there are vastly more programmes on offer there – an estimated 1,200 in fact – than in any other country. The cost in terms of tuition is likely to be similar to what you would pay in the UK, but you will of course have to consider the expense and stress of such an extreme relocation. Also, most full-time programmes in the US tend to be two years rather than one, so a longer career break will be necessary.

In the eyes of multinational companies, is there anything in the UK to match the prestige of the top-tier or even second-tier business schools in the US? Yes

– but just a handful. Continental Europe also boasts a number of top-ranked MBA programmes. Check out the league tables mentioned earlier for an idea of the top programmes worldwide. But again, you should only worry about international rankings if you plan to work on the global stage yourself.

A quick note for international applicants about UK work visas: as of 2008 the rules have changed a bit. It used to be the case that MBA graduates of certain UK schools were automatically granted a Highly Skilled Migrant Permit (HSMP), which allowed them to work here. Now the HSMP has been replaced by the Tier 1 visa, which is based on a points system. An MBA, or any postgraduate degree, from the UK will put you well on your way to meeting the necessary points for a work permit, but there are certainly more steps involved than there used to be.

● How to apply

It's often said that the hardest thing about doing an MBA is simply getting on to the best programme you can. Once you're in, the dropout rates are very low. So you should expect to devote a huge amount of effort to your admissions strategy, ideally starting several months before the application process would begin.

In finalising your choice of schools, do try to visit each campus on your shortlist for an information session or a chat with the admissions team. They can often arrange for you to sit in on a class or meet a current student. If a visit really isn't possible, then attending an MBA fair is a must – just be warned that these will be so busy that it can be difficult to have anything more than a superficial chat with the school representatives.

Some schools do rolling admissions, while others have a series of rounds, with the first deadline about 10 months before the programme starts and the final round closing a few months before. Try to apply as early as possible, as your chances are simply greater when there are more places available. Depending on the school, admissions decisions are generally based on all or most of the following: GMAT score, the application essays, undergraduate academic record, professional references and a personal interview.

GMAT stands for General Management Aptitude Test and is another import from the US. For most business schools, you need a GMAT score before you apply and it's up to you to arrange to sit the test. It's a nearly four-hour exam that measures verbal and quantitative skills through a series of multiple-choice questions, plus two short essays. It doesn't test specific business knowledge, so you don't need to be an accountant to do well. However, it would be a huge mistake to go into the exam without having prepared at least a bit. People who are aiming for an extremely good score should set aside six months to prepare for the GMAT, and at a minimum it would be wise to hit the books for eight weeks before the exam.

The GMAT is exclusively owned and regulated by the Graduate Management Admission Council (GMAC), though the actual test giving is outsourced to Pearson testing centres, at least in the UK. To take the exam, you sign up directly with GMAC through the MBA website (www.mba.com); it will also be able to tell you where your nearest test centre is. Schools will want GMAC to send them the transcript and scores of your GMAT. You can choose this option at the time of the exam (for free) or up to five years later (for an additional per-school fee). It costs US$250 (£178) to sit the exam. You can take the GMAT more than once but any school that receives your score report will also know how many times you have sat the exam in the past five years. Your score is valid for five years after you sit the test. After that, it becomes void and you will have to re-sit if you haven't got round to applying to business school in that time and decide you want to.

There are several GMAT preparation guides out there, including one published by the GMAC. The *Princeton Review* and *Kaplan* are also very popular, though if you want a seriously high score, it may be worth using at least a couple of these books as their practice test questions vary. If you need intensive help, there are also test-prep courses both online and in classrooms, but many people find self-study with a couple of good books a cheap and effective option. You can find more information on the following websites:

- www.mba.com
- www.princetonreview.com
- www.kaptest.com

How important is the GMAT score? Think of it as a first hurdle. Most programmes publish an average range of GMAT scores for their student body – often the middle 80 per cent (ie the bottom 10 per cent and the top 10 per cent are excluded from the range). This should give you an idea of what to aim for, although a slightly lower score won't eliminate you if the other parts of your record are strong. While you can re-sit the GMAT, there's little point doing this once you're within range of your target school's cohort. Taking the test again and again to nudge your score up a further 10 points won't give you a proportional edge over another candidate with a similar score. You would be better off spending your time honing your essay and talking to your referees. Some schools offer their own entrance exam as an alternative to the GMAT, or will waive the GMAT requirement if there are other educational or professional qualifications showing you'll be able to hold your own.

Once you've got the GMAT out of the way, focus on the essay part of the application – these are incredibly important in grabbing the attention of the admissions committee. The essay component usually consists of half a dozen questions. There will almost certainly be something along the lines of 'Why do you want to do an MBA, why now, and why at this school?' You should be prepared to describe your short-term and long-term career goals and show how the MBA will be a critical part of that plan. If you've given serious thought to the questions raised in the first part of this chapter, you'll be well on your way.

Remember you've got to differentiate yourself from the swarms of other candidates – especially if you hail from a classic MBA-bound sector like consulting, banking or even engineering and IT. That means flagging up the outstanding or interesting parts of your experience that perhaps wouldn't show up on your CV. Try to be as specific and vivid as possible, with anecdotes rather than generalisations. It will be much better to talk about the time you won a client in Singapore than to state in a vague way that you've had international experience.

Be interesting, but not so quirky that the admissions committee will doubt your ability to handle the tough stuff, like accounting and finance. Tell an interesting story but make sure it's clear that you can roll with the suits as well. It should go without saying that you ought to proofread very carefully, and if possible get someone else to read your essays. Aim to have finished them at least a week or two before the application deadline so that you can leave them for a couple of days and come back to them with fresh eyes.

References should be from two or three people who've worked closely with you and know your strengths and weaknesses well. If you work in a corporation of 10,000 employees, a reference from a CEO you've never met will be of no use to the admissions committee, even if you could convince him or her to write one. It is much better to have a more meaty recommendation from your line manager detailing how you saved a project from desperate ruin.

Some schools will interview candidates who've made the first cut (acceptable GMAT score, good application essays) or offer optional interviews. An admissions officer, a faculty member or an alumnus will conduct these. If it's optional, by all means take it and use the opportunity to sell yourself. Be prepared to verbally answer all of the essay questions about your motivations for doing the MBA, your educational and work experience, and your goals in even greater detail. You should also be able to talk about the top business issues of the day in your chosen industry. And don't forget to dress professionally, just as you would for a job interview.

● Funding

You should start investigating the options for financing your study as soon as you decide to pursue an MBA — the deadline for some scholarships or grants is actually earlier than you would normally be applying for courses. Facing up to how strapped for cash you'll be early on will also force you to assess whether the MBA is right for you, right now and will signal to admissions tutors that you're taking a mature and considered approach to furthering your career.

Course fees run the gamut from about £8,000 for a distance-learning programme at a less competitive school, to around £35,000 to £45,000 for the one- or two-year full-time programme at the UK's top institutions. When you're talking numbers like this, an extra £500 or so for books hardly makes a splash, but sometimes they're not included in the course fees. You might also need to buy a laptop, complete with MBA-ready programmes such as Excel spreadsheets.

Add to these living expenses, which will vary widely depending mainly on the market rate for housing near where you're studying. Obviously it will be much cheaper to house yourself, much less a family, if you're going to Aberdeen rather than London. Some schools provide their own on-campus housing, even for families, and these are often the most affordable option. Check with the admissions office about the cost of living — most MBA brochures at least make a stab at projecting food and housing expenses for single people, couples and families.

How to pay for it all? About two-thirds of MBA students in the UK attend part-time while continuing to work. If you've decided this route is for you, a good place to start looking for funding is with your own employer, especially if you're already in a managerial role and would like to continue your career at the company. Large corporations often have an established sponsorship programme that could pay for some or all of your fees, in exchange for a specified period of work during or afterwards. Indeed, the AMBA says that around half of part-time students have their fees met by their employers.

If you're going to make a pitch to your boss for footing your MBA bill, do it professionally, with a business case showing how the company will benefit. Even if your employer won't help pay for tuition, you should investigate whether it offers salary sacrifice schemes for further education. These are voluntary contracts that would allow you to set aside part of your pay in a tax-beneficial way, much like childcare voucher schemes.

You're unlikely to get any employer sponsorship for a full-time programme unless you're a rising star in one of just a handful of blue-chip companies or elite consultancies. You might be able to wangle an unpaid leave of absence, however, so that your job is still there after you've graduated. In that case, be sure to negotiate your post-MBA increase in salary or responsibilities before you go.

If you do a full-time programme, there may be opportunities for a paid internship during the course. The more elite the school, the more companies will pay its interns: at London Business School, for instance, the median pay for its eight to 12 week summer internship is £1,000 a week. But internships are definitely not a central component of every MBA programme, so research your chosen schools thoroughly if such an internship is important to you.

Many business schools have a range of in-house scholarships, but the application process is usually separate from the admissions one, so get organised early on. They're doled out throughout the admissions cycle and will most likely have dried up for any late applicants. These scholarships can be specific to home country, gender, background industry or any number of other differentiators. Some, but certainly not all, are needs based.

Start by asking the admissions office of your target school to point you in the right direction for scholarships available both within the school and externally. International students should consult the British Council website, which compiles some 270 scholarships for students coming to the UK. Then get over to your local library to consult the *The Grants Register* – a mighty tome published by Palgrave Macmillan, which lists 3,700 scholarships, grants and bursaries available for postgraduate education worldwide. For more information go to www.britishcouncil.org and www.educationuk.org

Once the free (or earned) money options have been exhausted, it's time to think about debt. Remember that with almost any loan scheme you'll be required to stump up some of the funds yourself, often about 20 per cent of course fees.

Career Development Loans are sponsored by the UK government, and you can apply if you live or intend to train in the UK and use that training for work in the UK or Europe. You can borrow up to £8,000 for a course lasting up to two years, or three years if the programme includes a year of work experience. Even if the course is longer, you may be able to use a CDL to pay for part of it. You don't start repaying until a month after the course has finished. These loans are available from Barclays Bank, Co-operative Bank and Royal Bank of Scotland. Go to www.direct.gov.uk for more information.

The AMBA sponsors a business school loan scheme, which is financed by NatWest. Full-time students can borrow up to two-thirds of their previous salary, plus tuition fees and expenses, while part-time students can borrow tuition fees. You won't have to make payments on the loan until after graduation. Distance learning students can borrow up to £10,000 but repayments begin almost immediately.

● What it's like to do a MBA

If you are considering an MBA it's likely to have been a few years since you were in a classroom setting so there'll be an adjustment to make. The MBA experience is also very different from the undergraduate programme.

The workload will be a shock to all but a few people whose jobs already require 16-hour days juggling a multitude of highly varied projects. The first half of the programme is loaded with all the core fundamentals courses including economics, corporate finance, operations, accounting, organisational behaviour, marketing and statistics. Getting through it will be a real test of your stamina, particularly if you're doing the programme full-time. You may well have classes most days from nine to five, with studying, group work and other related activities adding another four or five hours to your day.

The second half of the programme is devoted to electives as well as an internship, final project or dissertation. Many students find this period a bit easier to manage, with much more flexibility in scheduling. However, there's the new stress of securing a post-graduation job to cope with. Some recruitment rounds begin in the first term, within just a couple of months of the students' arrival, but if you don't land your dream job then, there will still be opportunities in the spring. That said, you need to be constantly mindful of your career aspirations and how you make use of everything going on at school to meet them. Even with a full study load, you should devote a few hours a week to your post-MBA career, whether it's through networking with people in your target field, practising mock interviews with career services or researching the companies you'd like to work for.

You will encounter some methods of teaching that are unique to business schools, such as the case study. This involves the class examining a situation, real or hypothetical, at a company and then discussing what the best course of action would be. Often classes using this format will base a large part of the grade on your participation, which can mean an all-out fight for airtime as everyone tries to get his or her twopenn'orth in. That won't suit every personality but it's good practice in thinking on your feet, framing an argument and persuading a sceptical audience.

The tutors, rather than being lifelong academics, will usually come from a mixed academic and commercial background. Often the lecturers are themselves high-level bankers, consultants, or technical experts with a vested interest in ensuring that everything they're teaching will stand up in practical contexts. On one hand that straight-from-the-boardroom energy could ignite your enthusiasm for a subject in a way you never thought possible. On the other hand, your tutor (on his way to that boardroom of course) might not be available for cups of tea and long meandering chats, in the way your English tutor was back at university.

You might want to decide early on what your philosophy about grades is – for example, some students are happy to focus more on the learning experience than aiming for the dean's list. Many MBA programmes operate on a pass/fail basis, so unless you outright fail several classes, you're unlikely to walk away without a degree. But before you relax too much, do find out what your school's policy is about grades disclosure to prospective employers.

One of the biggest differences between MBA programmes and other courses of study is the supreme emphasis on group work. The onslaught of theory during the core phase, with so much new information to absorb about so many relatively dissimilar subjects, forces you to rely on the five or six other members of your appointed study group. Often the school will sort you into groups, in order to achieve maximum diversity (or as it sometimes seems, maximum friction). The workload will need to be meted out among your group in order for everyone to meet it. Trusting people you've only just met to help you succeed can be a real struggle but such lessons are part and parcel of the MBA.

As if the workload wasn't heavy enough, you really won't be able to avoid joining in events outside of class and nor should you. Particularly in the first part of the programme, before people split off into their specialisations, it's important to wade into the many activities organised by pre-professional groups and purely social clubs on campus and get to know the others in your class. You'll be tapping into this network of people in other industries and countries for years to come.

● Making your MBA work for you

Don't put this off until after graduation: making your MBA work for you is a task for the present. It should start even before your degree programme does!

If you are what's known as a career climber – that is, you want to stay in the same company, sector or industry but increase your management potential – then start sounding out your boss about what an MBA is likely to do for you in terms of a promotion or salary increase. Investigate the kind of roles you'd be interested in and make sure your choice of MBA programme can be tailored to give you as much relevant exposure as possible.

Career changers, who are hoping to make the transition from one industry to another, need to do their groundwork to establish a realistic career path early on. Speak to a specialist recruiter about which companies hire MBAs and the level at which they are usually taken on. A good recruitment consultant could also advise you on the best way to progress to your dream job. This is useful to know before starting the MBA programme as you can focus your job placement and internship efforts in a much narrower field.

During the MBA programme, the demands of studying and socialising with your fellow students will leave little time for thinking about the job hunt. However, as we've said before, do keep your toe in the water: keep exploring career options, researching companies and networking as much as possible. If your programme curriculum includes work placements, then you must of course seek out an internship that lets you work in the sector or role you're ultimately aiming for. After all, the best evidence that you can do a particular job is that you have already done it before, even if it was in a school setting.

Networking isn't just a euphemism for a big boozy night out with your study group after exams. It should be about building relationships rather than flitting from handshake to handshake. Take the time to learn about your fellow students, and do try to be helpful should anyone want to pick your brains about your area of expertise.

Finally — and this is something a surprising number of students fail to do — make use of all the career services office has to offer. It's not just about browsing job listings or sipping punch at the annual recruiters' fair. In fact, the older you are (and more advanced in your career) the less likely these channels will be able to deliver for you, as they are frequently aimed at a more junior crowd. But wherever you are in your career, CV workshops and mock interview sessions can teach you how to market yourself. Outstanding career services advisers may even be able to coach you on how to negotiate the position and salary you want. After all, they are in the unique position of knowing exactly what kinds of salaries, bonuses and other perks MBAs just like you are commanding elsewhere.

Even if you decide not to go into business, the MBA can still be incredibly useful throughout your career. Running a charity, setting up a healthcare initiative in a foreign country, or furthering scientific research still involve — at senior levels — the management of people and of money.

CASE STUDY 1

The graduate

Michael Lisboa, Johnson & Johnson Latin America regional supply chain manager, graduated from Cranfield University's full-time MBA in 2007

Before the MBA I was working in Holland for TNT Logistics as a global account manager, which is roughly a sales role. One of my main reasons for doing the MBA was to change function and sector. I wanted to leave the service side and go back into industry. Because I had previous experience in supply chain I thought it would be nice to come back to that but at a different level and using the knowledge acquired in the MBA.

Now I'm a regional manager for Johnson & Johnson Latin America. We are responsible for the overall supply chain — everything to do with planning and distribution — in Latin America which represents 22 countries. As for the salary increase, I consider myself lucky — I managed to get a 60 per cent increase and I was already at a senior level before the programme.

I hope the MBA will eventually lead me to other positions, such as customer development or strategy, not just technical positions within supply chain. I do feel my knowledge is now broader than the traditional engineers, and I can talk the same language as top management and that's something the MBA has provided me with.

I chose to pursue a one-year programme because I was already in senior management. I also had a family — a wife and a five-year-old son — and so really could not afford to stay out of the market for two years.

Cranfield drew me in because of the profile of its students. I didn't want to go for a pure American-style programme where you have mostly younger students. I was 37 when I started the programme and wanted to benefit from the experience of my peers as well as from the coursework.

The family aspect was also very important and I found the university had a strong infrastructure for families, with a huge campus and lots of houses around like a village. Families were integrated quite well, whereas in a big city my wife and son would be alone and isolated all day.

Regarding funding the MBA, I would advise people to apply early in the admissions cycle. You'll have a better chance of getting a scholarship as they have only a fixed amount available. In my case I got a partial scholarship from the university and paid for the rest from savings.

Looking back I can clearly see two stressful phases. The very beginning was a challenge because of the huge change from being a senior manager one day to a full-time student the next. One has to learn how to cope with student life and the family pressure. The other difficult phase was at the end. I went to more than 20 interviews with Johnson & Johnson alone, in different parts of the world, before finding the right role.

Compared with working life, MBA hours were much worse. In a normal day, without tests to prepare for, we worked eight to 10 hours taking into account lectures and group study time. If we had any special projects or exams — and we almost always did — that would go up to 12 to 16 hours work a day. That would be easily 50-60 hours a week and up to 80 during exam time. It's pressure, but a good pressure.

Balancing your work and personal life was tough. You live more with your peers than your family, but you also know that it's for a limited amount of time. My wife and I had talked about it before the programme, about taking the opportunity to immerse myself in the course, but I didn't have a full idea of what was about to hit me. You have to be really careful not to do too much and forget about your family and their needs. It's a daily negotiation, and sometimes I would have to take a day off to regroup.

The structure and sheer workload of the MBA programme means you cannot get through the course without working with and relying on other people. In a study group, everyone has to take their share. For example, when preparing for exams, each person would be responsible for one specific part and then present it to the others.

This is quite different from traditional coursework. It teaches you how to be mature enough to rely on others. It can be difficult, though, as you have some people from other backgrounds and cultures and they may want to do everything themselves.

The university was able to bring a lot of good companies to campus to recruit, and that was how I made the initial contact with Johnson & Johnson. But I don't think the role of the school's careers service is to find you a job — they help you to understand yourself and what you want. They ask the tough questions and make sure you are delivering the right message about yourself when you go for a job.

People have to carefully evaluate the benefit of going for an MBA. You have to know what you want from it — I have friends from the programme still looking for a job because they don't know what they want. It's a huge investment in terms of time and money, and not the magical solution to all your problems. It's something that you have to do consciously knowing it's going to require a lot of work. But it's worth it, not just to increase your salary, but also to increase your network and of course your happiness in work.

CASE STUDY 2

The associate director of MBA admissions

David Simpson, associate director of MBA marketing and admissions, London Business School

You'll only really benefit from doing an MBA if you know what your career goals are in the first place. It's important to have an aspirational but realistic goal when you come into the MBA programme. Expecting to go from being a software engineer with three years' work behind you and no international experience, to becoming a senior manager in an investment bank straight after the MBA, is unrealistic. Taking time out of one's career does have an impact, so it should not be the automatic next step for anybody. Ask yourself if another postgraduate degree or professional qualification would serve you better.

Yes, you can do an MBA immediately after an undergraduate degree. However, unlike most graduate programmes, the MBA really comes into its own by using experience you already have. You'll get core knowledge from any MBA programme, but will you be able to reflect back and apply it to a particular issue or situation? The MBA teaches you to approach any subject and break it down into smaller parts, to really dismantle a problem looking for different outcomes. The way you do that is by putting together all the learning you've had. So really, the best MBAs require you to bring something to the class, whether you're a doctor or a soldier or a consultant.

The time you're spending on the MBA will have an impact on the people around you — your colleagues if you're continuing to work and of course your family if you have one. If you're moving to attend school, that creates further pressure on the family. So when you are deciding whether to do the MBA, you've got to speak to other people around you who will be affected by it. There are going to be certain peaks in study and you've got to figure out how to balance this with your family life. This is truer for the MBA than for other courses.

Once you've decided an MBA is right for you, take a step back and think about which kind of programme is right for you. Look at the calibre of the participants. Is the diversity of students important to you? Is the school known to be strong in any particular areas? Will the programme focus on business internationally or locally? If you're looking to start a local business, for instance, then it makes sense to find a school that will help build a local network. It's very important to look at how well connected the school and its professors are to the types of jobs and industry you're targeting.

In recent years the variety of MBAs in the UK and across the world has grown hugely and so have the ways you can study them — you can study full-time or part-time and choose from programmes of differing lengths. It's important to realise these are set up for different groups, which are defined by ability or career situation or aspiration. Look at the cohort and make sure that profile fits your goals.

You're not just coming in to learn in the classroom — you're there to build a network of people and use that group of alumni. It's more than the 'old boys' network' — this has a very real application in business. You'll meet people from different countries and backgrounds who you'll be calling on for the next 50 years and who will help you succeed. An MBA is as much about the people as the curriculum.

During the admissions process you've got to balance giving a clear, fact-filled description of yourself, with making yourself sound interesting. But don't go over the top — we want to know that you can be solid and successful.

Once you're in the programme, one of the most challenging aspects is managing the sheer diversity of the workload and juggling that alongside the job search. Whether the MBA programme lasts for nine months or two years, you'll be working alongside the careers services office and preparing for internship interviews, or full-time job interviews. If a professor is trying to teach you week 10 of a 12-week accounting course, he's not going to be particularly sympathetic if you've got mock interviews to concentrate on as well. Accept that there will always be more going on than you can do.

There are also the pressures that are brought on by group work, which most MBA programmes insist upon. Working together reflects so much about communication ability. In our programme, if you're a British banker, you're most likely the only Brit in your study group and one of only two bankers. We do that on purpose, because in business you don't get to pick who you work with. It's about challenging the norms of your profession as well as your home nation. If you've worked in accounting for 10 years you're going to think differently from someone with 10 years in marketing. Recognise that you need to learn from these people about their frames of reference and how they solve problems.

In an MBA programme you've got to get really involved beyond reading the books and passing the exams. When you're an undergraduate, student clubs tend to be more about socialising. Here they're about changing careers and creating new opportunities. It's likely that getting a job and getting to know the right people could well be through those clubs. For example, one of the speakers at our India Business Forum is the Indian finance minister. No other setting will provide access to that kind of network.

The MBA really is a tough qualification to do. It's not just the many subjects you'll be studying, it's the fact that you are forced to think in several different ways at the same time. When you approach a business case you've got to look at it from the perspective of an accountant and a marketing person and a senior manager simultaneously. You need to understand what the people around you and underneath you are doing. That's why an MBA still holds its value 30 years after you've done it.

CASE STUDY 3

The recruiter

Helen Bostock, global head of campus recruiting, Credit Suisse

I would encourage prospective candidates to think very hard about their MBA plans. Look carefully at the destination statistics for the students and alumni of your chosen schools. Where are they going to work, in what careers and in what industries? It's no good choosing a school that's close to you if all the people graduating from that programme are going into the public sector and you want to be an investment banker. What is the cohort that you would be part of in terms of their background and destination? Match up the programme with your goals.

Look at the course content. If a programme says it has a bias towards financial theory, can it also leverage relationships within industry? Are you going to have contact with industry practitioners to show there's a real-life commercial application to what you are learning? For example, Credit Suisse delivers certain course modules at a number of business schools and we believe it's a great opportunity for students to have that exposure.

The prestige of the business school and the MBA programme matters more in some industries than others. For example, a senior manager in the NHS would not necessarily need to complete an MBA at Harvard to get them to the next level running a huge complex department. But investment banks tend to focus on the top tier of global business schools because their needs are different.

Investment banks look globally for talent but many of them focus on the top US business schools for historical reasons because the MBA is an American invention. Within the UK there are a number of top league business schools who now compete with the US schools. A good example would be the London Business School or Saïd Business School at Oxford. They all offer different types of programmes, so prospective students really need to reflect on their career aspirations and interests.

It doesn't make much difference to recruiters whether the programme was full-time or part-time. The key is how long it takes to complete and how that fits into your career progression plans. If someone is pursuing an MBA part-time and taking much longer, then the cohort of people they will be competing against when they graduate will be different from when they began. What you don't want is to complete over several years and then try to get a space on an associate programme at an investment bank, as the intake will be at a much earlier point in their careers. As for the distance-learning MBA degrees we see, they tend to be few and far between among those looking to join one of the top banks or consultancies and they tend to be completed at an Executive MBA level while students are still working. However, there may be international students for whom it makes sense to complete some modules online and the rest face-to-face in order to gain accreditation from one of the top business schools.

Part-time students are probably less well served in terms of the recruiting process, so they have to be a bit more proactive. They need to use their careers offices to gain contact with recruiters and use the web to research opportunities. Recruiters may focus on different communication channels that part-time students may not use. Here at Credit Suisse we target high-traffic areas on campus, like the gym, or we try to catch students in the social times, doing sponsorships and the like. Part-time students may not be on campus as frequently as full-time students or they may not have the flexibility to go to evening recruiting events.

The MBA is revered by corporate America and it is considered to be the premier qualification for those who will eventually be senior leaders. But the really good news about the MBA is that it acts as a catalyst for creativity and confidence. You meet so many other people and feed off their ideas. Many people who complete MBA programmes use it as a springboard to change career direction or even to become an entrepreneur and run their own businesses. It acts as a lever to show that the possibilities are endless.

PGCE

Wendy Berliner

There is a big difference between deciding to take a postgraduate teacher training course and most other postgraduate study. Other courses aren't designed to prepare you for a specific job; this one is. If you successfully complete it, you will be qualified to teach.

The financing is very different too. Unlike most postgraduate courses, you can qualify for student loans, means tested grants, even bursaries and, in some parts of the UK, there are tempting golden hellos for teachers of subjects where there is a shortage.

But remember, a Postgraduate Certificate of Education (PGCE) is vocational training as well as education. It is designed to get you ready to be a school teacher so it's not the kind of course you should do to spin out another year at university while you decide what you really want to do. It's meant to be a commitment to a profession and it costs the taxpayer money to train you.

It may be that during your course you realise that it's not for you, but you are more likely to find that out if you do your homework before you sign up and therefore less likely to waste your time and national training resources. A bit of work experience could help you decide whether you can see yourself standing in a teacher's shoes and whether you think you would enjoy it.

So what is a PGCE? In essence it's a crash course in how to be a teacher. Not for you a four-year Bachelor of Education degree course – a PGCE prepares you in one academic year if you opt to do it full-time. In Scotland the PGCE is known as the Professional Graduate Diploma in Education (PGDE).

Successful completion of the course in England and Wales gives you Qualified Teacher Status (QTS), in Northern Ireland you are granted 'eligibility to teach' and in Scotland you get the Teaching Qualification (TQ).

In England, Wales and Northern Ireland you will learn about the national curriculum programmes of study for the subjects you plan to teach, how to plan and prepare lessons and set learning objectives, classroom management

– how to promote good behaviour – and how to use information and communications technology effectively. On top of all of this you will become aware of the professional values expected of teachers in their attitudes towards pupils and colleagues.

Only a small proportion of the year will be spent listening to lectures. A lot of time will be spent in your own classroom – teaching in a real school on supervised teaching practice. If you want to be a primary school teacher, you spend a minimum of 18 weeks on teaching practice. If you are training to be a secondary school teacher, you have to spend at least 24 weeks teaching. By the end of it, regardless of whether you are training to be an early years, primary or secondary teacher, you will have had plenty of exposure to school teaching and should know whether it's the job for you.

The Scottish education system is different from that in the rest of the UK, but broadly speaking the PGDE offers a similar approach providing you with both theory and direct practice of teaching.

Before you go any further you need to ask yourself why you want to do this. Do you have a vocational drive to teach? Perhaps you loved school and always saw yourself as a teacher. Perhaps you have a passion for your favourite academic subject and want to light that same fire in others. Perhaps you are working in another career that isn't fulfilling and are drawn to teaching – a third of new teachers are career changers. Perhaps you have taken time out to bring up children and now feel that teaching is for you. If so, these are good reasons to train as a teacher.

If, however, teaching appeals to you because it is secure, with good pay, a pension and long holidays, or because you can't think of anything else to do or are just fed up with what you are doing, you need to think a lot more carefully before you sign up to teacher training. Whether you are an undergraduate coming to the end of a first degree or someone looking for a change, certain things need to be honestly acknowledged and seriously considered.

Some people are born to teach, some learn to do it very well. But teaching is not for everyone. It can be tough – particularly in those early years when you are still learning – regardless of how good your training was. Even in a school where the kids go home to advantages a child in the inner cities may only dream of, it can be hard if you struggle with maintaining discipline in the classroom or personal time management – children and young people can be very unforgiving and there is a lot of paperwork. That's when vocational drive, character and commitment, combined with the help of supportive colleagues, friends and family, get you through. Do you have that drive? Do you really want to be a teacher?

If you do, this can be the best of jobs, with rewards that are hard to come by anywhere else. People remember good teachers all their lives. Good teachers turn kids round and become role models to those without any. Good teachers ignite interests that last a lifetime. Our children and young people deserve to be taught by people who like them most of the time and really want to prepare the next generation to the best of their ability. If you think you are up for it, read on.

● How to do it

A PGCE is generally based in a university or college of higher education and will specialise in a particular phase of education – primary, middle or secondary. Most people know whether they want to teach in primary or secondary schools before they apply for a place on a training course, but the applications process does allow you to apply for both at the same time. It may also be possible to study for PGCE via flexible distance learning or on a school-centred initial teacher training (SCITT) programme in some parts of the UK.

PGCE courses generally last for one year full-time or up to two years part-time and selection is made on the basis of qualifications and interview.

Qualifications

To qualify you need to have graduate or equivalent status. If you are applying from abroad you can check the equivalence of your qualifications with UK NARIC (www.naric.org.uk), the government agency responsible for providing information and expert opinion on vocational, academic and professional skills and qualifications from over 180 countries worldwide.

In most of the UK you also need:

- A standard equivalent to at least a grade C in GCSE English language and mathematics.

- A standard equivalent to a grade C in a GCSE science subject if you want to teach primary or key stage 2/3 (ages 7-14). If you haven't got that, you may be able to sit a special aptitude test at the university or college you are applying to.

- To have studied the subject/s you are planning to teach, usually up to degree level (for secondary teaching).

The main point of the PGCE course is to develop your teaching skills, not your subject knowledge. In a secondary school you will have to offer a specialist subject to teach and even in a primary school where the class teacher covers all the curriculum there are subject co-ordinators to ensure the subject is being delivered properly by people who may not have studied it since they were 16.

A major exception is given if you have studied chemistry, mathematics, physics, French or German to A-level in England and would like to teach one of them. There is a shortage of teachers in these subjects and, to stimulate supply, people with A-level equivalent qualifications can go on a free pre-PGCE training course to boost their subject knowledge. The science courses take 26 weeks, the modern language courses last for 14. More details can be found at www.tda.gov.uk In Wales there are alternative courses. You can call the Teaching Information Line on 0845 6000 991, or on 0845 6000 992 (for Welsh speakers) to find out more.

The Scottish PGDE entry requirements are based on credits, which are standard across all Scottish universities. If you are applying for a primary PGDE in Scotland you must have at least:

• A degree from a UK university (or an equivalent degree from outside the UK).

• Higher English at grade C or above (or equivalent).

• Standard grade mathematics at credit level (or equivalent).

The universities will also want to see evidence that you have studied at least two of the following: science, social studies, expressive arts, religious and moral education, technology and modern languages.

Experience of working with children in a primary school or in a similar setting such as a youth group or sports club will be welcomed. You'll also need a good understanding of the Scottish primary education system.

For a secondary PGDE, at the very least you'll need:

• A degree from a UK university or an equivalent. The degree should normally contain 80 credit points relevant to the teaching qualification you are studying for. (40 credit points must be at second year undergraduate level or above).

• Higher English or an equivalent qualification.

However, some subjects have very specific demands, so it's best to check with the university where you want to study. For entry requirements to primary and secondary courses in Scotland see www.teachinginscotland.com

Alternative postgraduate routes into teaching

If you are a new graduate with excellent qualifications, attracted to teaching but not sure you want to teach long term, the Teach First programme might suit you. This allows very good graduates to spend two years working in challenging secondary schools in London, Manchester and the Midlands, training to be teachers but with the added bonus of leadership training and work experience with leading employers.

To be considered, you need a minimum of three Bs at A-level, a 2:1 degree and to have demonstrated high levels of leadership and communications skills. The course leads to qualified teacher status but also provides the potential to develop a commercially oriented career. For more information see www. teachfirst.org.uk

There is also on-the-job postgraduate teacher training that is particularly suitable for mature entrants switching careers who need to earn a salary while they train. The Graduate Teacher Programme is available in England and Wales and you can achieve qualified teacher status in a year, or much less with relevant teaching experience. You need the same qualifications as a PGCE course entrant but you are based on the staff of one school and work as an unqualified teacher while training. For more information see www.tda.gov.uk

● Where to do it

This is where you have to think about what works for you. You may be an undergraduate and loving the place you are studying in so the choice seems easy – you switch to the education faculty for a PGCE. But life is rarely that simple. The place you are studying in may work wonderfully now because it is full of friends – but if they are not staying on it may soon feel very different. It's also not automatic that you will get a place on the PGCE course in your current university, particularly if you are offering a subject in which there is no shortage of teachers and lots of applicants.

If you are a mature entrant with close family ties in an area, you will probably want to study locally or you could consider the part-time Open University secondary PGCE course. The subject specialisms on offer are design and technology, geography, mathematics, modern languages (French, German, Spanish), music, science. More information can be found online at www.open.ac.uk

If you are coming to the UK from abroad, you have the whole country to pick from. But would you prefer to study at an institution where there is a large community of international students or surround yourself with students from the UK?

For anyone trying to pick an institution to study at, there are hundreds of courses throughout the country and no two will be exactly the same. Some content will vary, so will the strengths of different courses, the success rates, the entry requirements and the success of students in finding teaching jobs.

Then there is the academic level you wish to study at. In England and Wales the PGCE includes master's level credits, although the number of credits will vary. If you're doing a PGCE a lot of institutions will give you the opportunity to study for the additional master's level credits required to obtain a full master's level qualification after you have completed your PGCE course. It is worth noting that there is also a newer Professional Graduate Certificate in Education qualification, which will provide you with Qualified Teacher Status, but which is the same level, academically, as the final year of an honours degree course.

This point is going to be increasingly important as the government is urging new teachers in England to undertake a master's in teaching and learning (MTL) in their first five years of teaching. In September 2009, the north-west will become the first region in England to offer the MTL to all newly qualified teachers. The idea is to eventually roll out the new qualification to the entire teaching force. Headteachers who in the past would not have bothered about whether a newly qualified teacher had completed master's credits may now start to take it into account because their new recruit will need time to complete the MTL.

Aside from academic differences, there will be significant variation in the student intake on different courses. One third of teaching recruits in England are over 25 and another third over 30. Some PGCE courses will recruit a majority of new graduates, others will recruit a majority of over 25s, others will be more equal. The same goes for gender and ethnic minority mixes. Teaching is an increasingly feminised profession. Four out of five primary teachers are women and more than 60 per cent of secondary teachers are female, with the proportion rising. Teacher training tutors try hard to attract more men, particularly for primary training places, but some are more successful than others. Do you want a course where less than a third of entrants are men or do you want a course where nearly half are? Only you know whether that matters to you. The same goes for ethnic balance. Some big city institutions will have getting on for a third of their intake coming from ethnic minority backgrounds. In other parts of the country, courses will struggle to get intake levels from ethnic minorities above two or three per cent.

The good news is that it is easy to check all these things in England. The Training and Development Agency for Schools (TDA) and its predecessor body the Teacher Training Agency (TTA) has for the last 10 years produced extensive data covering the entry characteristics, Ofsted ratings and trainees' take up of teaching posts of all the teacher training providers. You can look at the profiles online at www.tda.gov.uk You can also find details of full Ofsted inspections of training institutions at www.ofsted.gov.uk/reports

Bear in mind that the TDA data is collected almost two years in arrears so that it can show how many teachers in that year group have got jobs in teaching. (So, for example, the 2008 TDA profiles are based on the 2006-07 academic year.) Remember that a lot can change – for better or worse – in two years.

Professor Alan Smithers and Pamela Robinson of the Centre for Education Employment Research at the University of Buckingham produce an annual Good Teacher Training Guide based on the TDA material. It is an independent report not endorsed by the TDA but it could be helpful in preliminary course research. The 2008 Good Teacher Training Guide ranks institutions in a league table. The top five based on the qualifications expected on entry, Ofsted inspections and employment in schools are: Cambridge, Oxford, Exeter, Warwick and King's College London. Other courses do very well when you look at individual strengths. For example, when the Ofsted grades awarded for management, training and standards are combined by the report's authors, perfect scores are achieved by Canterbury Christ Church University for primary courses and by Cambridge, Oxford, Exeter, Warwick and East Anglia for secondary courses.

Looking at job success – measured by the proportion of trainees in teaching in January after completing their courses the previous year - the top five for primary teacher training are Huddersfield, Birmingham, Reading, Warwick and Anglia Ruskin universities. For secondary it's Birmingham City University, Oxford, Loughborough, Sheffield and King's College, London.

The top five universities asking for the highest entry qualifications in 2006-07 for postgraduate primary courses – at least an upper-second – are Leicester, Cambridge, Exeter, Leeds and Chester. For secondary, the top five are Cambridge, the Central School for Speech and Drama, King's College, London, Oxford and York St John. (See the report at www.buckingham.ac.uk for more details.)

You could also take a look at Unistats – the teaching quality information website created by Ucas which looks at the average Ucas points score for students on entry, student satisfaction with the course and whether they have a job after six months of graduating. See www.unistats.com.

All postgraduate teacher training courses throughout the UK are fully accredited and, as with all other higher education courses, practices are checked by the UK's Quality Assurance Agency. Remember, league tables never tell you the whole story.

For information about teacher training institutions in Wales go to:

• the Higher Education Funding Council for Wales: www.hefcw.ac.uk

• the Teacher Education and Training in Wales: www.teachertrainingwales.org

• Estyn is the office of Her Majesty's Chief Inspector of Education and Training in Wales and the website includes reports on teacher training: www.estyn.gov.uk

For information about teacher training institutions in Scotland go to:

• The General Teaching Council for Scotland: www.gtcs.org.uk

• Teach in Scotland: www.infoscotland.com/teaching

For information on teacher training in Northern Ireland go to:

• Department of Employment and Learning: www.delni.gov.uk

● How to apply

Applications for most PGCE courses and Professional Graduate Diploma in Education (PGDE) courses have to be submitted to the Graduate Teacher Training Registry (www.gttr.ac.uk) which acts as a clearing house for universities and colleges offering initial teacher training courses in England, Wales, and Scotland (apart from the University of the West of Scotland, which handles its own applications) and Northern Ireland, where you contact institutions direct.

For the GTTR system, you can choose up to four courses which can be a mix of primary and secondary, as long as no more than two are primary courses. This is to help people who haven't yet made up their mind which level they want to teach at, but in reality it is rare not to have settled this before you apply. By the time someone applies to be a teacher most will know whether they want to teach their specialist subject — in secondary — or whether they want to teach children the whole range of subjects — primary.

Like Ucas, of which the GTTR is part, the application website has a course search facility where you can find course and vacancy information and a facility to track the progress of your application online.

To apply for any courses through the GTTR, you will need to complete an online application form — in 2008 the fee for this was £15. You cannot submit more than one application in the same cycle. Even if you satisfy academic requirements for entry to the course you want, it is no guarantee of a place. Competition for places can be high, especially for primary courses and popular secondary courses such as physical education.

You can apply through the GTTR for a postgraduate teacher training place up to a year in advance, from early September of the year before you want to start your course — most courses start in September — but there are different rules for primary and secondary courses.

Primary courses

You need to apply by December 1 in the year before you want to start training to guarantee your application goes to your first choice training provider for consideration. Your application is sent to providers one at a time in order of preference. Popular courses fill quickly and it makes sense to get your application in as early as possible to give you maximum choice. Or indeed any choice — training providers do not have to consider any applications for primary teaching courses received at the GTTR after December 1 for courses starting the following year.

Middle years, secondary or further education teaching courses

You can send your application any time between September of the year before you want to start training and June 30, but again promptness is key because

● What are the admissions tutors looking for?

Qualifications

Make sure that your academic qualifications fit what the course is asking for. Some courses only look at students with firsts or 2:1s; others are happy with 2:2s or equivalent qualifications. For nationally set academic qualifications that apply to all courses check the 'How to do it' section earlier in the chapter.

Experience

Tutors will be looking for someone who has had some recent experience of schools. That doesn't mean as a pupil — it means work experience! It can be as little as a fortnight and it can be as informal as sitting in class observing but they need to know that you know what the reality of school life is like. The last thing an admissions tutor needs is someone who decides they don't want to work in a school a few weeks into their course. It's not what you need either.

Even if you have always known you wanted to be a teacher and have gained plenty of relevant work experience in your past, a more recent exposure to school life — say in your last year of university — is a good idea. If you are older and planning to switch careers or train for teaching after raising a family, it's almost more important. Any rose-tinted spectacles have to be removed before you apply.

Personality

You will need to be genuinely enthusiastic about education and working with children or young people and tutors will also be looking for those hugely important interpersonal skills. Education is about communication and you will need to be a good communicator with both your pupils or students and the adults you work with, including the parents.

Most tutors will be looking for a lively personality and strength of character — the kind of person who they can imagine standing up and thriving in front of a class of children or young people. You have to be someone who is happy mixing and mingling with others. A sense of humour helps too — and the ability to demonstrate it.

Knowledge and skills

They will also be looking for people who have done some background research about teaching, education and children's learning. They are not going to be looking for detailed in-depth knowledge but they won't be impressed if you are seemingly unaware of the burning issues affecting teachers, whatever they are at the time.

They will appreciate it if you can bring some extra skill beyond your academic qualifications — perhaps you can play the piano or are keen on fencing, for example, because eventually that will add to the mix of talents in the school staff room.

At interview

Institutions will differ in how they interview you. Some rely on group interviews and exercises; others do individual interviews as well. Your interview day may also include time spent in a school that is partnered with the institution so that you can be observed interacting with pupils.

At interview tutors may well ask you the obvious — 'Why do you want to be a teacher?' — but not always. They are using the interview to assess whether you have what it takes to become a teacher both in personality and habits. They want to recruit people who are resilient and who have some sense of the education system. They will be interested in your study habits and organisational skills — teaching involves a large amount of bureaucracy and you will need to be good at planning, preparing and recording. The idea of the interview will be to get a good dialogue going with you.

As selection days differ it is important to understand what will be happening so you can prepare properly for it. For example, many institutions will also administer a maths and English test on the day so it's good to know what form that will take and what it is testing.

Finding information

You must ask the questions you need answered by the tutors at your interview. Remember also that you can check online and find thousands of students talking about their courses and experiences. Just Google PGCE blog and you'll find lots of material.

Some institutions run their own Facebook groups and encourage prospective teaching candidates to use forums and blogs when they are deciding where to apply.

the application will only be sent to training providers that have vacancies. Some courses fill up early.

Late applications

From mid-March to the end of June, late applications (or additional applications from students who have failed to secure a place on one of their preferred courses) can be submitted via the GTTR Extra scheme, to providers that still have spaces on their courses. Applications received after June 30 are put into the GTTR Clearing system for any remaining teacher training vacancies. GTTR will have details of courses with spaces to fill and you contact institutions direct to find out whether or not they can consider you.

● Funding

The funding of PGCE and PGDE courses varies throughout the UK and, to some extent, between institutions. There are different rules applying to part-time students, EU nationals and international students. There is a wealth of information available online and on institutional sites which can help you work out what you are likely to have to pay and what loans, grants or bursaries may be available in your particular circumstances. What follows will give you a general introduction to what the costs are and what support is available.

England

Postgraduate teaching trainees, including part-time trainees, qualify for the same student loans and grants available to students doing their first higher education course. They also have access to excellent tax-free bursaries.

TUITION FEES The maximum tuition fee for home/EU students for PGCE courses in 2008-09 is £3,145. In 2007-08 all PGCE students who met residency requirements were entitled to a £1,230 non-means tested tuition grant from their local authority and up to £1,535 was also available through a means tested grant. For the least well-off students, institutions will top up the difference, effectively making the course tuition free. Students need to contact their local authority for application details and up-to-date financial information. The tuition fee does not have to be paid up front. More information is available on the government website at www.direct.gov.uk

LOANS AND GRANTS If you are a resident of the UK, you'll be able to get a student loan for tuition fees to cover your fees in full and to help with accommodation and living costs. Loans do not have to be repaid until you are earning more than £15,000 per annum. For more information see www.studentfinancedirect.co.uk and www.ucas.ac.uk

For 2008-09, full-time PGCE students were able to get a maintenance grant or special support grant of up to £2,835. Only part of this is means tested, and qualifying students got £1,260 no matter what their household income.

Individual universities or colleges also give bursaries. Details are available direct from the institutions.

You may be entitled to loans and grants if you're doing a part-time course - as long as it doesn't take more than twice as long to complete than the equivalent full-time course, or it's classed as a flexible postgraduate initial teacher training course

BURSARIES Secondary PGCE students receive a tax free £6,000 training bursary and primary students receive £4,000. Students who plan to teach in subjects in which there is a shortage of teachers get even more − £9,000. The qualifying subjects are mathematics, science, ICT (information and communication technology), religious education, modern foreign languages, design and technology, and music.

These shortage subjects also qualify for a taxable 'golden hello' of up to £2,500 after successfully completing the induction period, or £5,000 in the case of mathematics and science.

For more information see www.tda.gov.uk

Scotland

TUITION FEES If you are a Scottish student your tuition fees are paid for you. If you normally live elsewhere in the UK but want to do your postgraduate teacher training in Scotland, you would have to pay tuition fees of £1,735 a year.

GRANTS Scotland has a system of loans, bursaries and special support grants for certain categories of student. If you want to do a PGDE in a priority subject, fees and bursaries are paid for you no matter what your previous qualification is. The priority subjects for 2008-09 are biology, business education, English, Gaelic, geography, history, home economics, maths, modern languages (French, German, Italian, Spanish and Chinese), physical education, physics, religious education, technological education and primary (all courses including Gaelic medium). For more information see www.gttr.ac.uk/students/studentfinance/costoftraining/traininginscotland

Wales

TUITION FEES The maximum tuition fee for home/EU students for PGCE courses in 2008-09 will be £3,145 − the same as England. If you normally live in Wales and are also studying there, you may be entitled to a tuition fee grant of £1,890 which does not have to be repaid. As in England, you can get loans for your tuition fees and pay them back once you are earning more than £15,000 per annum. For more information see www.studentfinancewales.co.uk and www.cyllidmyfyrwyrcymru.co.uk

GRANTS For PGCE courses starting in September 2008, trainees in maths and science received a training grant of £7,200 and a taxable teaching grant – also known as the 'golden hello' – of £5,000 at the end of the induction year. Trainees in modern foreign languages, design and technology, information and communications technology, Welsh, music and religious education received a training grant of £7,200 and a teaching grant of £2,500. Trainees in art, geography, history, physical education and English (including drama) received a training grant of £4,200 but no teaching grant. Primary trainees received a training grant of £2,200.

For detailed financial information see www.studentfinancewales.co.uk

Northern Ireland

TUITION FEES From September 2008, institutions in Northern Ireland have also been able to charge variable tuition fees of up to £3,145 to graduates starting PGCE courses. All eligible students can choose to take out a fee loan that they repay when they leave higher education and earn more than £15,000. Details may be obtained from the Education and Library Board which serves the area in which you normally live. You can find the contact details for the ELBs at www.studentfinanceni.co.uk For more information see www.deni.gov.uk

EU nationals

If you are an EU national or the family member of an EU national, you can get information about the financial support arrangements while you are studying at college in England from www.direct.gov.uk/studentfinance-eu

International students

International students have to pay a fee set by the institution, which is at the discretion of each place and therefore varies. (As a guide, fees tend to be around £8,000 to £10,000 for the year.) Contact institutions direct to find out about their fees and remember that it is a competitive market and you should compare prices from a range of courses you like the look of.

● What it's like to do a PGCE

A PGCE is no soft option. The pace is fast because there is a lot to pack in. Mature entrants often cope better than new graduates because they are used to juggling many things in the work place or whilst bringing up a family. New graduates who have had to concentrate academically on just their chosen subject are faced with learning many new skills while tackling what for most is the biggest challenge of all – teaching children and young people for the first time.

The taught part of the course comes in the form of compulsory lectures and seminars combined with teaching placements. Good time-management is crucial. If you get behind by a couple of weeks you may not catch up and you won't qualify.

Many elements on the courses are standard because they have to meet national requirements for a qualified teacher. The big differences between the courses centre on whether you are training to teach in a primary or a secondary school.

If you are on a primary course, you have to spend 18 weeks on teaching practice in schools – half the course. If you are training to be a teacher of secondary aged children, you spend 24 weeks on teaching practice in schools – two thirds of the course. But even the taught element of the course differs substantially between the two types of trainee teacher.

Primary content

Trainee primary teachers need more time in college because they have to learn how to teach all the subjects of the national curriculum. Unlike their secondary colleagues who concentrate on teaching their specialist subject to differing age groups, primary teachers are usually in charge of a whole class of one age group, or mixed ages that are close together, and teach them everything.

Typically the PGCE course will start with two weeks spent observing in a primary school followed by a densely packed timetable of seminars, lectures and workshops at university or college – not unlike a school timetable in the way it is organised. Each subject on the national curriculum will be on the timetable and the trainees will be taught how to teach it to primary-aged children.

An audit of individual student skills will almost certainly have been done in the core curriculum subjects – literacy, numeracy and science – before the start of the course so the tutors will know subject knowledge strengths and weaknesses of both individual trainees and groups. Aspects of subject knowledge, like phonics (a method for teaching children to read), which may be unfamiliar to most students are likely to be dealt with at group level. The content will be taught directly and the students will undertake tasks to embed the learning. For example, they may have to look at samples of children's spelling, and identify and classify the problems they spot so that they can see what role phonics plays in learning how to spell.

Students may be asked to prepare an explanation on a topic for their fellow students – a good way of ensuring they really understand the material – but they may also need to take their own subject-specific weaknesses into account. For example, a history graduate who is hazy on the laws of friction in science will have to catch up through independent study. But even science graduates with an understanding of the laws of friction will be tested to update their subject knowledge.

To break up the intensity of this part of the course, many colleges will punctuate it with a week in which the timetable is suspended and students concentrate on an integrated subject group – the humanities or arts, for example.

On top of the subject content seminars, students will typically have lectures followed by workshops on generic teaching topics – how children learn, assessment, ethnic diversity, cultural diversity, teaching English as an additional language, behaviour management and child protection. Threaded through lectures will be the psychology and sociology of education.

The pattern of work placements do vary from course to course but you can expect a short teaching placement during the autumn term, followed by a longer block of four to five weeks in the same school in the spring term and the whole of the summer term in a different school.

Expect to do mostly observation and small bursts of teaching in your early teaching practice and to be teaching pretty much full-time by the end of the summer placement. You may go back to college for individual seminar days to reflect on your professional experience and to receive additional teaching input, perhaps three times during your teaching practice.

Secondary content

Trainee secondary teachers spend less time being taught in college because they are subject specialists and don't need to be brought up to speed with the content of the rest of the national curriculum. What they need to learn is how to teach different age ranges in their subject - in England, Wales and Northern Ireland this means key stage 3 (11-14 year-olds), key stage 4, which is GCSE and equivalents (14-16), and A-level and equivalents (16-18). (The Scottish education system is different from that in the rest of the UK and the PGDE reflects that.)

It's not uncommon for trainee secondary students to try out on each other activities they will use in the classroom once they are qualified teachers. These classes can give them real insight into how these methods work and the merits and disadvantages that teachers might need to consider. These teaching sessions also support understanding of behaviour management because even postgraduate students can display typical 'teenage' behaviour. For example, they may talk over the tutor or, when put into groups, someone will dominate while others sit back and contribute little.

In common with primary students they will typically have lectures followed by workshops on generic teaching topics such as how children learn, assessment, ethnic and cultural diversity, behavior management and child protection.

One of the big differences between a secondary level course and a primary level course is the time spent on teaching practice. For secondary level trainees, a common pattern would involve spending two weeks in a school before beginning their college-based sessions. This could be in a primary and secondary school so that students will know something of how, and crucially what, their pupils have been taught before they arrive at secondary school.

In the middle of the autumn term they will do a placement in a secondary school and spend the spring term on teaching practice at the same school. In the summer term they will be on teaching practice at another secondary school. They will come back to college during their teaching practice for perhaps five or six seminar days, which provide time to reflect and consolidate, and for more taught input.

Trainees will start off small, doing short spells of teaching, but should be capable of teaching full lessons by the end of the course. Most knowledge of behaviour management will be learned through observing colleagues managing real live classrooms. For something as practical and personal as the way you deal with the people you are teaching, theoretical work can only go so far.

Sometimes a secondary trainee will shadow a pupil for the day and see at first hand how the atmosphere in the classes the pupil attends differs. The pupil might behave well in some classes and not in others. Whole classes under some teachers may be better behaved. Trainee teachers need to learn early on that they have to earn the respect of their pupils and students. Sadly, it doesn't just come with the job title as it perhaps once did!

Assessment and support

Whether you are training to teach primary aged children or secondary, you will be assessed both as a teacher and on the work you do for your own tutors.

Again the pattern will differ from place to place but a good course will give you a lot of support in your teaching placements. You will be attached to your principal tutor (at primary level that will be the teacher of the class you are working with, and a subject teacher if you are a secondary student). Many courses have a subject tutor who works with the individual student, and a professional tutor who works with all the teaching students in a school.

You may also have extra support through a mentor in school – a more senior member of staff.

A good system may provide weekly meetings with your principal tutor in which targets set for the week are evaluated and the nitty gritty of learning how to teach is discussed. A monthly meeting with your mentor will look at the bigger picture – for example, how you are developing your assessment of students to aid their learning, or how to use your voice assertively, or to plan a class plenary session. The university tutor would talk to all three – trainee, principal tutor and mentor to see how they are meshing together.

During the year you can expect five reports evaluating your progress to date. If there is any cause for concern, you will get a letter from your university detailing the problem and the action plan to tackle it.

● Making your PGCE work for you

We are always going to need teachers. There will be peaks and troughs in demand caused by a rising or falling child population but until the day technology comes up with something better than an empathetic and passionate human being in front of a class who can inspire children and young people – teaching at its best – you will have a job (or, even better, a vocation) for life if you want it.

You can easily spot the demographic shifts that affect job opportunities because they move slowly in waves – a fall in population takes years to pass through the system – and you can make your decisions accordingly. Numbers are currently falling in secondary schools but rising in primaries, for example. Some years there will be proportionately more jobs in primary than secondary or vice versa but new teachers will still be needed because of retirement and people moving into other careers. And the pattern of falling numbers won't be even. In some areas of the country, such as the new city of Milton Keynes, extra schools are being built to cope with expanding population while other areas see downward drifts in school populations.

Economic shifts affecting job opportunities can move much more rapidly and increase the supply of teacher trainees – and competition for posts. Teaching is seen as a safe career option with good pension prospects. At times of economic uncertainty when there are fewer job opportunities elsewhere, teaching traditionally attracts more recruits than it does in booming economic times. For example, in February 2007 applications for secondary PGCEs in physics, chemistry and maths were all down on the previous year – a real worry because, as a nation, we are already short of people who want to teach these subjects. By August the numbers were recovering as the credit crunch bit into other potential career routes, particularly in the finance industries where international banks were cutting jobs. (Though numbers applying were still down overall, with the biggest falls showing in Scotland and Wales.)

That's not to say you can always get a job in your local school. Both the PGCE and the PGDE are recognised by schools nationwide and throughout the world and when there is a lot of competition for jobs you may have to consider moving to find one. That may be much easier for a young graduate than for a mature entrant with children or other family commitments that tie them to a particular area.

In 2007 some new recruits were having a much tougher time finding jobs in Scotland and the north of England because of bigger populations falls. But if a candidate was prepared and able to move to London, with its huge teaching force and turnover, or could teach one of the subjects where there is a perennial shortage of teachers, there were jobs to be had. Even in Scotland a candidate who was prepared to be placed anywhere for their first year qualified for a £6,000 golden hello.

However, if you are one of the minority who can't find a job where you need to be or you just decide teaching is not for you, a successfully completed PGCE course is a fine indication that you are someone who has been able to tackle one of the toughest postgraduate courses there is and learned time management, behaviour management, and team- and people-skills along the way. The kinds of attributes that will always be valued by good employers.

CASE STUDY 1

The newly qualified teacher

Stephen Ryan, newly qualified physics teacher at St Cuthberts RC Comprehensive, Rochdale. First degree: anatomical sciences, Manchester University. Completed a science PGCE at Manchester University in 2008

I had a very good biology teacher at school. You could have a laugh with him but he knew where to draw the line and he put the onus on us to study. I might not have gone to university if it wasn't for him. When I was coming to the end of my degree I was at a bit of a loss as to what to do. There were a lot of things I could have done with a science degree but I thought 'I had such a good experience at school. Why not give teaching a go and put something back?'

At the start of the course they gave us a lecture where they said, 'This course is going to change your lives.' We were all saying, 'How can a course change your life?' But it does. I didn't find a lot of the work difficult, certainly not as challenging as my degree, but it is a different kind of challenge to learn a new skill — to learn how to teach. To go into a class for the first time is the scariest thing.

My first work placement was in the Isle of Man in a nice comprehensive. We did a bit of observation in the first week and then we had to start teaching in the second, although there was always another teacher there. I was most scared to begin with that the kids wouldn't listen to me because I was a student teacher.

But it was a Year 7 class and the kids were new to the school and I was just another teacher to them so they did.

I had good lessons all that first week but the last one I did was dreadful. I was doing a Year 7 lesson on materials and I was going to burn magnesium but the gas didn't work and 15 minutes of my lesson plan went in a moment and I just flapped. At the end of it I thought, 'Can I really do this? Can I really be a teacher?' I am a confident kind of person and I think it hit me harder because of that. I wondered if I had bitten off more than I could chew. I was staying in a B&B on the island and I went back to it and, as the weekend went on, I got more and more stressed about it. Eventually I rang my mentor – a teacher at the school – at home and told her how I was feeling. She said, 'Everyone feels like this at some point. You can't control every lesson. Even I can't.' It was really sound advice.

Although teaching is hard – and almost everyone will meet someone when they say they're going to be a teacher who says, 'Oh my God, teaching! I could never do THAT!' – you need to know that the support is in place to help you through it. The emphasis is on getting you good enough to teach with the skills you have, because no two people teach the same way, not setting a benchmark and failing everyone who doesn't reach it.

Behaviour management was easier for me than for some. I have a decent sense of humour and it helps so much. My second placement was at a tough school in Gorton, Manchester, and when I came into my first lesson with a Year 11 class this one kid told me he was going to stab me in the leg, steal my phone and sell it to buy a Happy Meal. I told him my phone wasn't worth that much and he might just have to settle for a double cheeseburger. All his friends laughed and I never had any more trouble.

You have to think on your feet. You have to know when to use humour and when to rein it in. Reputation can be really helpful in a school. If you teach an older brother or sister and they think you're all right, you will be OK with the younger ones.

One of the best things I learned during the seminars was about the importance of planning lessons. Teachers have a saying: 'Fail to plan and plan to fail.' There was only one time I didn't do enough planning. I'd planned half the lesson and thought I had free periods when I could plan the other half. But I'd got the time wrong for the lesson and I had to go and blag half of it. It was horrible.

The best advice I could give to someone who decides to take a PGCE course is to remember not to let it take over your life. Teaching is more involved than some jobs and you do have to work in the evenings but you have to have a life outside it too.

You have to remember, too, that teaching is a public speaking role and you have to do it every day of school. It doesn't suit everybody – about 10 per cent of our course dropped out. If you are in your shell a bit, it does draw you out – but there has to be something in the shell to be drawn out.

There are great moments when you are able to explain something in your own words and the pupil gets it and you see their eyes light up because they understand what you've said when they didn't understand what was in the text book. And it's great when they are working on something and you are wandering around the desks looking at what they are doing and you hear someone say, 'This is really interesting.' I wouldn't change what I do for the world now.

The teacher trainer

Professor Debra Myhill, head of the School of Education and Life Long Learning, Exeter University School of Education

I am looking for students who have a good command of their subject knowledge but are able to recognise when learners are finding it hard and think of ways of adapting their teaching to help them. You need to be someone who is independent and responsible for your own learning too. There are a lot of influences set by other peoples' agendas − course tutors, schools, the government − it is easy to be swayed every which way. The good student is able to synthesise all of this and make their own decisions and grow. I know how good the teacher education course has been by how quickly the student leaves it behind. The weakest students are still doing the same thing 10 years later − the ideas are fossilised.

You have to consider the emotional and the personal too. A student teacher needs resilience. They get a lot of knocks in their PGCE year. It's the first time they are facing hard judgments on what they do. They are all academically successful but now they are on the line. Things go wrong and some students are dragged down by this, others aren't. You can't get through your PGCE years without 'failing' in some way. Your future success depends upon how quickly you can pick yourself up. Some people are too cautious − but this is the year to make mistakes because you have the support. You need to be able to take criticism too and that can be very hard − it can challenge your identity. A lot of people can take it, some learn to take it during the course but some take it too much to heart. Very few of our students fail but the kind of person who can fail a PGCE course is the kind that can't hear criticism and doesn't listen to advice.

I have had students who are doing well who don't finish the course because there is a gap between their ideal of what a teacher is and the realities of school life. It's a shock for some to find out that not all kids want to learn but there is also the bit to do with education policy. They see being a teacher as being about creativity and the discussion of ideas and then they find that school is framed by targets and testing and they realise it's not for them.

The PGCE course is very different from undergraduate study. Those who come straight from a degree course can find it a bit of a surprise. In my subject, English, you have very few lectures at undergraduate level and you have a lot of time for reading and writing. On a PGCE course most of the day is occupied and attendance is compulsory. You also have to juggle several things − you could be updating your subject knowledge, writing up an assignment, preparing for school, all at a similar time − rather than being immersed in just one course module. People who have already spent time in the workplace or have been primary carers of young children have learned to multi-task and find it less of a problem.

The academic level is high. Most PGCEs are at master's level − ours is − and it isn't in your degree subject and you usually do it in a year. You have to learn a lot of new things whether it's psychology or quantitative analysis or learning to teach children. You are pulled in a lot of directions and it's challenging.

It also gives you the chance to be taught by research leaders in the subject. Ofsted have reported back to us that our students appreciate being taught by people at the cutting edge of the subject. The research also gives you a perspective. I have seen endless numbers of classrooms and schools and English teachers. So if a student is struggling I can tell them there are other schools that might suit them better because I've seen them.

There are pitfalls to watch out for. Time management is one thing students sometimes fall down on. It's a very full course. From the moment they start in September until they finish in July it is pretty much helter skelter. As a tutor I would love to be able to build in time for reflection but I can't. So you can't afford to fall behind in your work otherwise you can get on a downwards spiral with no time to catch up.

You are also very dependent on people – your course tutor and your school tutor. If it doesn't work, it can be very hard. We tell them to work at the relationship with their school tutor and make clear that it is a professional one. They don't have to like them – they need to be adult about it and not get trapped in confrontation. If they are really having a problem in a school placement we will move them on to another but only when the situation cannot be reconciled. It is very rare to do that. We have 620 PGCE students and out of that number we would probably only move two.

How well a student does at PGCE is no prediction of how well they will do as a teacher. I have seen teachers who only just passed their course who have gone to teach in schools where they have been given freedom, encouragement and nurturing and who have turned into brilliant heads of departments. I've also seen the reverse. The message is an encouraging one to take – that the future isn't set.

But they need that magic spark. You can cope with problems the student might have in time management, classroom management, even subject knowledge – you can teach them all of that. But the seed of inspiration has to be there. They need to be driven by a vision of education in which they can alter the outcomes of the children they teach – particularly those who are disaffected and disadvantaged and come from different backgrounds from their own. Teaching is not just a job. It's the teachers who make the difference.

CASE STUDY 3

The teacher

Caroline Williams, foundation year teacher at Hardwick Primary School, Cambridge. Completed her PGCE at Homerton College, University of Cambridge

The PGCE prepared me for work because it gave me a good knowledge of all the expectations and national requirements for the children I was teaching. I had a good idea of what to expect from the NQT [newly qualified teacher] year although every school is very different, often despite geographical proximity. The course prepares you with strategies for effective behaviour management, assessing pupils, planning formats and so on, which you are then able, as I have done, to mould to the particular school in which you are working.

Homerton was really, really good at preparing you to teach and instilling confidence in you. But it's always going to be quite nerve-wracking when you teach your first class alone – no training college can prepare you completely for that. You have to just deal with it yourself.

When you are a student teacher the class knows that you are a trainee and that the real teacher is sitting at the back observing. It's like taking driving lessons — you feel safe when the instructor is there with you. When you take your first class alone you have ultimate authority. But you begin by teaching just one lesson a day and by the end of the course you are teaching pretty much all of the time so you feel built up and fully able to take a class on your own.

The course developed my self-esteem and self-confidence and the practical experience in the classroom — particularly seeing the good practice of teachers — was the most useful part of it. I have carried that away with me and can use it in my own teaching.

As a primary trainee you have more lectures and less teaching practice than the secondary trainees. Some of the paper work from the course I haven't used. For example, I didn't need the notes on teaching a science class because my school did topic teaching. I haven't made much reference to lecture notes from the course although I still have many of them and books that I was advised to buy for the course, so I have these to fall back on should I need them. I would advise against concentrating on making lengthy notes in lectures as they are often well organised with handouts which refer to key points.

The best part of the course is definitely the teaching practice and the opportunity to interact with teachers and grasp how education works and what makes for successful teaching. I was very keen to get into the classroom because I've known I wanted to teach since I was at high school. Homerton was famous for teaching training and I did my undergraduate degree — religious studies with education — there too.

As a primary teacher you have to teach every subject and we had lectures that gave us a taster of all the curriculum subjects and what they looked like to children, which was useful. It was also helpful to see what successful lessons looked like.

My advice to a trainee teacher would be that you have to be very reflective about what you do. Not every lesson goes well and you need to share that and reflect on it with mentors. I got a great deal of good advice from teachers and my mentors — both in the school and back at college — which was very helpful. Homerton was very good at encouraging you to pay attention to the most important parts of the course and I would stress the importance of asking questions and seeking advice as and when you need it. It is better to ask when you are uncertain about something rather than leaving it, particularly on placements. It enables you to learn more from these experiences in schools.

I felt supported by both school colleagues and the college tutors who came in several times while I was training to see how things were going. In the first year of teaching I felt that, if I had needed to, I could have rung them if I'd hit a problem and they would have been able to help.

I made very good friends while I was training and was able to share experiences with them, not only over the job application process but in my NQT year and beyond. Many of these friends I see and speak to regularly and will hopefully continue to do so.

I enjoy the job. You can keep learning in teaching. I find it very rewarding because you build such good relationships with other teachers and you support one another. And it's exciting when the children you are educating grasp something new.

Postgraduate tables

The number of people wanting to study for postgraduate degrees has been rising steadily for years. The costs may be substantial – in contrast to undergraduate study which is heavily subsidised or free (in Scotland). But this has not deterred the growing army of master's and doctors who see an added qualification as a good investment.

Unfortunately the advice and information available for potential students putting their precious money and time on the line has not kept pace with the need.

The university tables published by the *Guardian* and other newspapers are based on the experience of undergraduates and what you can expect if you do a first degree at particular institutions. The *Guardian*'s online tables attract around 17m hits a year from around the world and among those hundreds of thousands of prospective students must, we suspect, be many who are looking to study at postgraduate level.

Our new tables are for them. In our first effort at producing postgraduate tables we are not attempting to rank universities and colleges for different subjects – although visitors to our website (www.educationguardian.co.uk) can do their own rankings on various criteria from completion rates to the cost of courses.

Postgraduate study covers a range of very different courses and we have felt it most useful to limit our tables to master's degrees including MBAs, and qualifications such as the PGCE for teachers.

Doctoral research degrees (PhDs) are very different and for anyone interested the key criterion will be the research rating of the department. Tables based on the latest Research Assessment Exercise (RAE 2008) can be found on our website and on page 140.

The tables are compiled in association with EducationGuardian.co.uk by Campus Pi, an applied research department at Brunel University, which also compiles our undergraduate university guide.

They use the most recent figures available – official 2006-07 returns from universities and higher education colleges to the Higher Education Statistics Agency (Hesa).

For financial information we are grateful to Mike Reddin who compiles an annual breakdown of fees at UK universities (www.publicgoods.co.uk).

We give eight measures for each university in each subject:
- Number of postgraduate students, full-time and part-time
- Percentage of students from outside the UK
- Expenditure per student
- Student:staff ratio
- Completion rate for full-time postgraduate students
- Completion rate for part-time postgraduate students
- Tuition fees for UK/European Union students
- Tuition fees for international students

Number of postgraduate students

Full-time and part-time study are often very different experiences and the balance of provision can vary widely between departments with similar overall numbers.

Percentage of postgraduate students from outside the UK

Depending on the subject this may indicate the international standing of a university. The figures given here are for all students from outside the UK, including those from within the EU. Students from other countries may be reassured by the presence of fellow visitors to the UK, but they may also want a British experience of higher education and that means being able to learn with Brits.

Expenditure per student

We don't publish the actual figures for spending per student. This score is marked out of 10 in bands to allow for comparisons. Spending on medical students is always going to be higher than on historians, for instance.

Spending per student is based on combined figures for undergraduate and postgraduate teaching in each subject, including central academic services. It does not include the costs of academic staff as these are already counted in the staff:student ratio. The amount of money is divided by the number of students given as full-time equivalents (FTEs) ie numbers of part-time students are converted to full-time equivalents.

Student:staff ratio

This is based on combined figures for undergraduate and postgraduate teaching in each subject. The figure given in our tables represents the number of students (FTEs) to each member of staff.

Completion rates

For full-time postgraduate students and part-time postgraduate students. Fields have been left blank where insufficient data was available.

Tuition fees

For UK/European Union students and international students. These figures are compiled by Mike Reddin, who publishes an annual survey on his website (www.publicgoods.co.uk). However, fee data is not provided at subject level so the figures are general guidelines only and students should check the price of particular courses with the institutions concerned.

With regard to data provided by Hesa, please note that Hesa does not accept responsibility for any inferences or conclusions derived from the data by third parties.

Locating tables

To help you locate the tables you are looking for more easily, related subjects have been grouped together over the following pages:

Art and design	84
Engineering	88
Humanities	91
Medical sciences	94
Modern langauges	99
Physical sciences	100
Social sciences	105

● Art and design

	Full-time/ part-time	% students from outside the UK	Expenditure per student (FTE)	Student:staff ratio	Full-time completion rate	Part-time completion rate	Tuition fees: home/EU students	Tuition fees: international students
Architecture								
Bath	17 / 48	28%	7	19.9	100%	94%	£4,000	£13,150
Birmingham City	58 / 129	10%	4	23.2	100%	100%	£4,700	£9,400
Brighton	81 / 62	41%	5	20.6	90%	88%	£3,630	£11,000
Cardiff	15 / 25	55%	7	15.2	62%		£3,300–£11,130	£11,700
East London	24 / 18	50%	5	27.1	64%	100%	£4,560–£9,600	£14,220
Edinburgh	50 / 6	64%	7	20.3	90%		£4,600	£14,000
Edinburgh College of Art	86 / 13	45%	4	19.8	96%		£3,315–£4,975	£9,630
Glasgow School of Art	112 / 19	29%	4	24.4	88%	91%	£3,315	£10,440
Greenwich	53 / 95	27%	7	23.3	74%	75%	£3,600–£7,410	£10,600
Huddersfield	69 / 59	22%	4	34.6	96%	87%	£3,900	£9,500
Kingston	10 / 136	22%	4	27.6		11%	£3,400	£11,000
Leeds Met	58 / 140	8%	3	25.8	96%	99%	£3,400	£8,300
Lincoln	90 / 72	26%	4	23.0	89%	89%	£3,338	£9,243
Liverpool John Moores	48 / 13	7%	3	32.1	100%		£3,145	£8,950
London South Bank	54 / 163	16%	4	34.1	0%	77%	£3,890	£9,355
Newcastle	9 / 42	29%	5	19.2		100%	£4,070	£12,970
Nottingham	44 / 53	57%	7	17.8	93%	83%	£3,750	£10,200
Oxford Brookes	41 / 38	48%	4	17.7	90%	94%	£3,990–£7,900	£10,590
Plymouth	59 / 26	7%	4	21.0	11%		£3,950	£9,850
Queen's, Belfast	47 / 109	21%	3	21.3	100%	100%	£3,319	£10,990
Robert Gordon	25 / 31	64%	4	19.5	79%	90%	£3,315–£7,712	£13,800
Royal College of Art	44 / 0	16%	10	11.2	95%		£4,780	£22,850
Strathclyde	43 / 29	28%	5	22.2	96%		£3,235	£11,465
UCL	169 / 127	55%	9	12.2	96%	94%	£3,300	£16,870
Westminster	24 / 253	25%	4	17.9	93%	98%	£3,800–£13,750	£13,750
Art and design								
Anglia Ruskin	22 / 88	15%	5	19.4	93%	60%	£1,550–£7,800	£9,300
University of the Arts, London	1,034 / 283	51%	8	22.2	96%	97%	£3,300	£10,400
Bath Spa	24 / 42	12%	5	18.3	80%	67%	£3,970	£9,000
Birmingham City	149 / 115	50%	7	13.2	82%	51%	£4,700	£9,400
Brighton	51 / 87	33%	7	18.4	93%	78%	£3,630	£9,500
Central Lancashire	40 / 106	29%	4	21.1	100%	58%	£3,300	£8,950
Coventry	49 / 29	40%	5	31.8	88%	75%	£3,420–£4,230	£8,600
University College for the Creative Arts	105 / 46	52%	3	22.4	97%	94%	£3,360	£9,125
De Montfort	62 / 54	46%	4	17.6	91%	92%	£3,315	£7,990
Derby	19 / 37	14%	6	17.9		93%	modular	£8,200
Dundee	33 / 29	42%	7	13.1	92%		£3,250	£8,000
East London	20 / 50	41%	4	21.3	94%	83%	£4,560–£9,600	£8,400
Edinburgh College of Art	135 / 0	58%	4	18.5	99%		£3,315–£4,975	£9,630
UC Falmouth	51 / 59	20%	4	16.6	65%	43%	£3,440–£4,655	£10,145
Glamorgan	18 / 32	2%	6	10.2	100%	100%	£3,300	£9,980
Glasgow School of Art	109 / 3	49%	6	13.6	98%		£3,315	£10,440

	Full-time/ part-time	% students from outside the UK	Expenditure per student (FTE)	Student:staff ratio	Full-time completion rate	Part-time completion rate	Tuition fees: home/EU students	Tuition fees: international students
Goldsmiths	149 / 51	58%	4	15.2	94%	88%	£3,300–£6,320	£9,580
Heriot-Watt	19 / 32	80%	5	21.7	83%		£3,790	£9,450
Kingston	124 / 36	53%	4	17.7	87%		£3,400	£9,000
Leeds	88 / 22	50%	5	20.9	90%		£3,300	£9,700
Lincoln	51 / 61	14%	4	25.9	64%	55%	£3,338	£8,730
Loughborough	35 / 8	40%	5	15.6	96%		£3,350	£9,850
Manchester Met	32 / 18	37%	4	18.1	19%		£3,320–£3,890	£8,420
Middlesex	45 / 74	58%	9	23.5		88%	£4,600–£6,870	£9,400
Newport	21 / 29	12%	4	23.2		78%	£4,350	£8,450
Northumbria	142 / 115	46%	5	17.7	88%	81%	£3,996	£8,300
Norwich School of Art	12 / 71	10%	3	29.0		81%	£3,300	£8,750
Nottingham Trent	149 / 13	52%	5	20.4	98%		£3,145–£6,900	£7,550
Oxford Brookes	59 / 38	46%	3	26.8	90%		£3,990–£7,900	£9,570
Plymouth	13 / 37	42%	10	18.5		60%	£3,950	£8,950
Queen Margaret	67 / 39	19%	3	20.2	94%	75%	£3,315	£8,800
Reading	36 / 5	61%	5	15.5	94%		£3,575–£15,750	£9,350
Royal College of Art	674 / 18	43%	10	10.7	99%		£4,780	£22,850
Salford	48 / 69	23%	3	27.9	85%	67%	£3,300	£8,400
Sheffield Hallam	82 / 52	38%	4	18.6	83%	61%	£3,300–£7,800	£8,100
Southampton	89 / 34	53%	8	20.1	88%		£3,300	£9,380
Staffordshire	38 / 50	31%	7	17.7	90%	79%		£9,395
Sunderland	83 / 43	28%	4	13.1	100%	77%	£3,965	£8,600
Swansea Met	18 / 30	8%	3	20.2		53%	£3,160	£7,550
UCL	124 / 0	55%	9	12.2	100%		£3,300	£12,940
Ulster	30 / 8	37%	4	13.6	84%		£3,420	£8,649
UWIC	12 / 49	18%	5	20.4	100%	64%	£3,330	£8,800
UWE Bristol	44 / 128	13%	5	19.8	94%	73%		£8,250
Westminster	44 / 24	54%	5	18.7	86%		£3,800–£13,750	£9,750
Wolverhampton	22 / 54	38%	4	22.5	81%	80%	£3,418–£4,400	£8,200

Building and town and country planning

	Full-time/ part-time	% students from outside the UK	Expenditure per student (FTE)	Student:staff ratio	Full-time completion rate	Part-time completion rate	Tuition fees: home/EU students	Tuition fees: international students
Anglia Ruskin	8 / 76	1%	4	27.1		89%	£1,550–£7,800	£9,300
Bath	0 / 70	66%	5	19.9		85%	£4,000	£10,300
Birmingham	14 / 29	12%	6	17.4	91%		£4,200	£9,450
Birmingham City	54 / 339	4%	3	23.2	28%	28%	£4,700	£9,400
Cambridge	55 / 7	84%	6	12.6	100%		£5,434	£11,371
Cardiff	189 / 139	29%	5	15.2	93%	84%	£3,300–£11,130	£9,100
Central Lancashire	22 / 212	17%	5	24.0	100%	52%	£3,300	£8,950
De Montfort	18 / 202	0%	3	22.9	93%	92%	£3,315	£7,990
Dundee	12 / 98	9%	4	17.2		39%	£3,250	£8,000
Edinburgh College of Art	39 / 1	68%	3	19.8	95%		£3,315–£4,975	£9,630
Glasgow Caledonian	67 / 43	48%	5	18.4	67%		£3,315	£9,000
Gloucestershire	33 / 22	7%	6	17.3	96%		£3,445–£8,725	£8,720
Greenwich	127 / 189	50%	5	23.3	75%	84%	£3,600–£7,410	£8,900
Heriot-Watt	152 / 432	33%	4	15.1	88%	89%	£3,790	£9,450
Kingston	86 / 62	22%	3	27.6	93%	71%	£3,400	£9,000
Leeds	48 / 38	37%	10	6.6	94%	74%	£3,300	£9,700
Leeds Met	68 / 212	5%	5	25.8	93%	79%	£3,400	£8,000
Liverpool	40 / 44	15%	5	16.9	94%	97%	£3,300	£9,100

	Full-time/ part-time	% students from outside the UK	Expenditure per student (FTE)	Student:staff ratio	Full-time completion rate	Part-time completion rate	Tuition fees: home/EU students	Tuition fees: international students
Liverpool John Moores	70 / 193	4%	2	32.1	93%	82%	£3,145	£8,320
London South Bank	89 / 760	6%	3	34.1	61%	49%	£3,890	£8,845
Loughborough	107 / 64	63%	6	9.8	95%	93%	£3,350	£9,850
Napier	39 / 90	42%	3	24.4	72%	46%	£3,675–£5,020	£9,180
Newcastle	75 / 50	19%	4	19.2	91%	96%	£4,070	£9,915
Northumbria	162 / 119	44%	3	22.9	84%	68%	£3,996	£8,300
Nottingham Trent	43 / 127	28%	4	20.2	94%	86%	£3,145–£6,900	£7,550
Oxford Brookes	164 / 308	22%	3	17.7	93%	89%	£3,990–£7,900	£9,570
Plymouth	5 / 42	9%	4	15.7		88%	£3,950	£8,950
Portsmouth	44 / 353	19%	3	27.6	93%	23%	£3,300	£8,350
Queen's, Belfast	58 / 74	23%	3	21.3	97%		£3,319	£8,970
Reading	57 / 210	22%	4	20.7	100%	90%	£3,575–£15,750	£9,350
Robert Gordon	16 / 32	56%	3	19.5	55%		£3,315–£7,712	£9,200
Salford	11 / 234	8%	6	14.5		87%	£3,300	£8,400
Sheffield	215 / 5	41%	4	15.1	98%		£3,300	£9,920
Sheffield Hallam	155 / 266	22%	3	27.5	76%	86%	£3,300–£7,800	£8,100
UCL	154 / 115	39%	6	12.2	95%	95%	£3,300	£12,940
UWE Bristol	208 / 628	14%	3	23.0	82%	54%		£8,250
Westminster	76 / 472	21%	3	17.9	89%	73%	£3,800–£13,750	£9,750
Wolverhampton	53 / 131	39%	3	27.3	72%	59%	£3,418–£4,400	£8,200

Drama and dance

	Full-time/ part-time	% students from outside the UK	Expenditure per student (FTE)	Student:staff ratio	Full-time completion rate	Part-time completion rate	Tuition fees: home/EU students	Tuition fees: international students
Aberystwyth	22 / 34	36%	3	27.2		95%	£3,300	£8,475
University of the Arts, London	149 / 98	36%	9	22.2	98%	98%	£3,300	£10,400
Bedfordshire	34 / 30	94%	4	22.6	93%		£4,150–£4,450	£8,200
Bolton	58 / 3	2%	3	22.6	89%		£3,717–£4,755	£7,800
Bristol	41 / 54	64%	8	22.3	94%		£3,950	£10,200
Central School of Speech and Drama	176 / 22	24%	4	18.3	95%	95%	£6,772	£12,937
Conservatoire for Dance and Drama	48 / 17	45%		11.1	96%	100%	£4,000	£13,340
University College for the Creative Arts	14 / 21	40%	3	22.4	90%		£3,360	£9,125
UEA	70 / 8	40%	10	19.5	97%		£3,300	£9,500
Essex	55 / 3	28%	7	20.2	90%		£3,500–£7,000	£9,990
Exeter	49 / 75	56%	5	17.6	100%		£4,000–£8,250	£9,600
Glamorgan	36 / 0	8%	7	10.2	100%		£3,300	£9,980
Goldsmiths	89 / 24	45%	4	15.2	99%		£3,300–£6,320	£9,580
Leeds	38 / 6	34%	5	20.9	89%		£3,300	£9,700
The Liverpool Institute for Performing Arts	21 / 23	23%	2	13.1	18%			
Middlesex	25 / 46	62%	10	23.5		80%	£4,600–£6,870	£9,400
Napier	49 / 47	17%	6	19.0	73%		£3,675–£5,020	£9,180
Newport	48 / 20	26%	3	23.2	87%		£4,350	£8,450
Northumbria	8 / 31	8%	5	17.7	56%		£3,996	£8,300
Rose Bruford College	18 / 37	27%	5	20.9	93%	38%	£6,000	£11,025
Trinity Laban	64 / 23	41%		7.7	97%	92%	£4,850–£6,600	£12,950 –£13,950

	Full-time/ part-time	% students from outside the UK	Expenditure per student (FTE)	Student:staff ratio	Full-time completion rate	Part-time completion rate	Tuition fees: home/EU students	Tuition fees: international students
Music								
Birmingham City	36 / 41	40%	7	13.2	89%	80%	£4,700	£9,400
Bristol	17 / 35	56%	8	22.3	100%		£3,950	£10,200
City	8 / 27	26%	9	10.4	100%	100%	£3,300	£7,950
Glamorgan	7 / 78	21%	7	10.2		88%	£3,300	£9,980
Goldsmiths	35 / 54	25%	4	15.2	100%	95%	£3,300-£6,320	£9,580
Guildhall School of Music and Drama	186 / 173	50%	7	8.0	92%	100%	£6,600	£14,500
Kingston	28 / 20	46%	3	17.7	63%		£3,400	£9,000
The Open University	0 / 101	0%	2	28.4		100%		
Queen's, Belfast	19 / 17	31%	3	31.0	100%		£3,319	£8,970
Royal Academy of Music	363 / 0	51%	8	8.2	85%		£7,600-£10,000	£16,200 -£18,500
Royal College of Music	269 / 14	53%	8	10.9	37%		£6,552-£8,726	£15,280 -£16,545
Royal Northern College of Music	187 / 4	45%	3	10.2	92%		£6,000-£7,150	£13,150 -£14,300
Royal Scottish Academy of Music and Drama	93 / 0	46%	9	5.6	100%		£5,226-£9,000	£11,499 -£12,498
Salford	78 / 17	11%	3	27.9	62%		£3,300	£8,400
Thames Valley	46 / 28	36%	4		92%	91%	£4,350	£8,650
Trinity Laban	65 / 74	37%		7.7	58%	92%	£4,850	£12,950 -£13,950
York	62 / 26	29%	7	17.2	97%		£3,300	£9,510

● Engineering

	Full-time/ part-time	% students from outside the UK	Expenditure per student (FTE)	Student:staff ratio	Full-time completion rate	Part-time completion rate	Tuition fees: home/EU students	Tuition fees: international students
Engineering: general								
Aberdeen	51 / 173	38%	3	16.8	92%	100%	£3,315	£11,250
Birmingham	32 / 9	71%	5	15.5	94%		£4,200	£12,250
Birmingham City	30 / 18	33%	4	11.7	19%		£4,700	£9,400
Brighton	74 / 29	73%	4	18.1	80%		£3,630	£11,000
Brunel	156 / 245	74%	4	15.0	91%	71%	£3,315–£5,130	£8,750
Cambridge	126 / 63	68%	6	13.5	97%	100%	£5,434	£14,353
Cranfield University	168 / 267	29%	10	7.7	81%	67%		
East London	115 / 27	70%	10	4.8	88%	55%	£4,560–£9,600	£14,220
Greenwich	73 / 20	74%	3	22.4	92%	87%	£3,600–£7,410	£10,600
Hull	26 / 9	94%	6	14.9	82%		£3,300	£10,500
Imperial College	55 / 1	73%	7	8.5	100%		£3,300	£24,250
Lancaster	13 / 61	11%	6	8.0		100%	£3,530	£11,100
Leicester	50 / 2	92%	7	10.0	77%		£3,300	£12,100
Napier	134 / 77	91%	2	19.2	71%		£3,675–£5,020	£10,665
The Open University	0 / 147	0%	2	20.0		97%		
Sheffield Hallam	75 / 70	49%	3	17.5	93%	92%	£3,300–£7,800	£11,900
Sunderland	49 / 7	89%	4	14.7	95%		£3,965	£8,600
Warwick	429 / 376	71%	7	13.7	95%	80%	£5,330	£13,350
Engineering: civil								
Abertay Dundee	21 / 22	49%	4	6.9	100%	73%	£3,315	£8,650
Birmingham	117 / 66	49%	8	15.5	97%		£4,200	£12,250
Brighton	33 / 10	87%	3	14.0	86%		£3,630	£11,000
City	22 / 52	65%	5	20.9	70%		£7,500	£9,750
Coventry	36 / 60	33%	3	20.7	85%		£3,420–£4,230	£9,100
Dundee	49 / 28	58%	5	13.6	96%		£3,250	£13,500
East London	180 / 170	22%		26.3	78%	49%	£4,560–£9,600	£14,220
Edinburgh	51 / 0	47%	8	16.4	91%		£4,600	£14,000
Glasgow	54 / 4	59%	4	20.9	100%		£3,750	£9,400
Heriot-Watt	67 / 109	51%	4	12.9	79%		£3,790	£11,810
Imperial College	184 / 55	60%	10	11.8	100%	92%	£3,300	£24,250
Kingston	24 / 87	52%	4	21.0		61%	£3,400	£11,000
Leeds	158 / 113	48%	6	22.6	99%	82%	£3,300	£12,600
Loughborough	52 / 163	66%	4	25.9	100%	97%	£3,350	£12,800
Manchester	115 / 195	34%	10	13.8	97%	88%	£3,300	£12,900
Napier	41 / 152	30%	3	23.1	83%	54%	£3,675–£5,020	£10,665
Newcastle	158 / 68	61%	5	14.4	97%		£4,070	£12,970
Nottingham	79 / 51	77%	8	12.9	91%	67%	£3,750	£10,200
Nottingham Trent	14 / 80	20%	4	20.7	100%	61%	£3,145–£6,900	£10,800
Portsmouth	68 / 9	90%	3	21.1	97%		£3,300	£9,650
Salford	33 / 74	35%	3	24.1	87%	94%	£3,300	£10,500
Sheffield	94 / 17	75%	4	12.2	95%		£3,300	£13,050
Southampton	140 / 77	35%	4	22.8	99%	90%	£3,300	£12,000
Surrey	113 / 294	43%	6	15.4	89%	49%	£3,600–£8,600	£13,300

	Full-time/ part-time	% students from outside the UK	Expenditure per student (FTE)	Student:staff ratio	Full-time completion rate	Part-time completion rate	Tuition fees: home/EU students	Tuition fees: international students
Engineering: chemical								
Birmingham	35 / 1	75%	6	14.1	79%		£4,200	£12,250
Heriot-Watt	130 / 371	55%	2	15.8	93%	82%	£3,790	£11,810
Imperial College	95 / 0	78%	7	15.0	98%		£3,300	£24,250
Leeds	59 / 74	34%	6	14.8	90%	100%	£3,300	£12,600
Manchester	54 / 120	43%	8	14.7	96%	64%	£3,300	£12,900
Newcastle	31 / 26	31%	9	10.2	100%		£4,070	£12,970
Sheffield	49 / 3	77%	3	13.9	100%		£3,300	£13,050
UCL	48 / 3	63%	3	13.1	94%		£3,300	£16,870
Engineering: electronic and electrical								
Bath	24 / 101	58%	6	9.9	93%	100%	£4,000	£13,150
Birmingham	27 / 13	53%	9	14.4	89%		£4,200	£12,250
Birmingham City	111 / 37	60%	5	11.7	33%	41%	£4,700	£9,400
Bradford	81 / 82	91%	4	18.5	85%		£3,960	£11,000
Bristol	36 / 43	86%	6	13.7	98%		£3,950	£13,100
Brunel	147 / 158	91%	4	13.5	91%		£3,315-£5,130	£8,750
City	33 / 17	76%	3	19.1	67%		£7,500	£9,750
Dundee	16 / 33	78%	3	15.0	84%		£3,250	£13,500
Essex	39 / 2	90%	5	7.9	98%		£3,500-£7,000	£9,990
Glasgow	42 / 6	79%	10	10.7	100%		£3,750	£9,400
Glasgow Caledonian	59 / 0	66%	3	21.6	0%		£3,315	£10,500
Greenwich	107 / 43	87%	3	22.4	36%	89%	£3,600-£7,410	£10,600
Heriot-Watt	74 / 44	85%	3	16.7	73%		£3,790	£11,810
Hertfordshire	109 / 4	94%	3	20.2	76%		£3,833	£9,500
Huddersfield	39 / 0	84%	3	24.7	86%		£3,900	£9,500
Imperial College	120 / 0	93%	10	14.2	99%		£3,300	£24,250
King's College London	69 / 5	69%	5	15.8	89%		£3,900-£5,900	£17,750
Lancaster	33 / 18	53%	8	8.0	85%		£3,530	£11,100
Leeds	95 / 0	97%	10	13.8	96%		£3,300	£12,600
Liverpool	48 / 14	85%	6	13.1	93%		£3,300	£11,650
Liverpool John Moores	45 / 54	90%	3	17.9		87%	£3,145	£8,950
London South Bank	104 / 43	80%		19.4	91%	57%	£3,890	£9,355
Loughborough	118 / 325	41%	6	15.1	90%	61%	£3,350	£12,800
Manchester	109 / 26	75%	10	9.7	93%		£3,300	£12,900
Newcastle	136 / 19	75%	6	14.4	94%		£4,070	£12,970
Northumbria	324 / 13	91%	3	20.1	60%		£3,996	£9,950
Nottingham	92 / 18	91%	8	12.2	84%		£3,750	£10,200
Oxford Brookes	45 / 12	84%	3	19.1	92%		£3,990-£7,900	£10,590
Portsmouth	71 / 16	87%	3	19.3	78%		£3,300	£9,650
Queen Mary	61 / 14	68%	9	14.6	96%	100%	£3,964	£11,100
Queen's, Belfast	15 / 36	76%	8	9.9	100%		£3,319	£10,990
Reading	35 / 14	53%	4	19.0	78%		£3,575-£15,750	£15,750
Salford	65 / 26	84%	4	20.5	84%		£3,300	£10,500
Sheffield	200 / 6	87%	5	10.1	89%		£3,300	£13,050
Sheffield Hallam	122 / 12	87%	4	19.3	98%		£3,300-£7,800	£11,900
Southampton	182 / 3	94%	6	15.1	98%		£3,300	£12,000
Southampton Solent	0 / 36	0%	3	13.7		100%	£2,675-£3,400	£8,495
Staffordshire	44 / 41	94%	5	18.6	71%			£9,875

	Full-time/ part-time	% students from outside the UK	Expenditure per student (FTE)	Student:staff ratio	Full-time completion rate	Part-time completion rate	Tuition fees: home/EU students	Tuition fees: international students
Strathclyde	64 / 78	69%	8	10.1	75%	35%	£3,235	£11,465
Surrey	194 / 116	73%	8	14.0	90%	66%	£3,600–£8,600	£13,300
Sussex	53 / 5	82%	4	15.7	94%		£4,100	£12,150
UCL	50 / 121	57%	8	8.8	100%	100%	£3,300	£16,870
UWE Bristol	37 / 6	74%	3	19.1	82%			£8,700
Westminster	75 / 42	79%	2	17.3	90%	75%	£3,800–£13,750	£13,750
York	51 / 15	78%	6	10.3	98%		£3,300	£12,555

Engineering: materials and mineral

	Full-time/ part-time	% students from outside the UK	Expenditure per student (FTE)	Student:staff ratio	Full-time completion rate	Part-time completion rate	Tuition fees: home/EU students	Tuition fees: international students
Exeter	24 / 20	16%	3	17.2	88%		£4,000–£8,250	£12,240
Leeds	25 / 15	66%	8	10.9	100%		£3,300	£12,600
Loughborough	42 / 80	44%	5	12.4	75%	59%	£3,350	£12,800
Manchester	86 / 37	74%	8	11.6	95%		£3,300	£12,900
Manchester Met	67 / 4	75%	2	23.9	62%		£3,320–£3,890	£8,420
Queen Mary	45 / 0	91%	7	18.1	93%		£3,964	£11,100
Sheffield	70 / 0	87%	5	9.7	87%		£3,300	£13,050

Engineering: mechanical

	Full-time/ part-time	% students from outside the UK	Expenditure per student (FTE)	Student:staff ratio	Full-time completion rate	Part-time completion rate	Tuition fees: home/EU students	Tuition fees: international students
Bath	51 / 28	72%	4	20.7	85%		£4,000	£13,150
Birmingham	39 / 1	93%	6	16.9	71%		£4,200	£12,250
Birmingham City	87 / 67	58%	5	11.7	35%	33%	£4,700	£9,400
Bradford	21 / 23	84%	4	13.4	67%		£3,960	£11,000
Bristol	12 / 192	21%	4	16.0	93%	83%	£3,950	£13,100
Brunel	56 / 329	57%	4	15.1	91%	64%	£3,315–£5,130	£8,750
City	50 / 330	73%	5	24.4	73%	83%	£7,500	£9,750
Coventry	360 / 105	77%	3	31.8	92%	58%	£3,420–£4,230	£10,200
Cranfield University	759 / 218	59%	10	4.6	94%	83%		
Glasgow	39 / 1	68%	6	14.1	92%		£3,750	£9,400
Greenwich	40 / 26	86%	3	22.4		100%	£3,600–£7,410	£10,600
Hertfordshire	97 / 13	87%	3	21.6	70%	90%	£3,833	£9,500
Huddersfield	66 / 7	87%	3	25.4	93%		£3,900	£9,500
Kingston	84 / 111	46%	7	18.0	92%	73%	£3,400	£11,000
Leeds	40 / 11	49%	8	17.1	100%		£3,300	£12,600
Liverpool	34 / 2	92%	6	19.9	95%		£3,300	£11,650
Liverpool John Moores	31 / 72	67%	3	14.4		76%	£3,145	£8,950
Loughborough	58 / 154	42%	6	12.2	91%	90%	£3,350	£12,800
Manchester	48 / 0	81%	8	19.3	93%		£3,300	£12,900
Newcastle	137 / 70	65%	6	16.6	99%		£4,070	£12,970
Northumbria	162 / 22	80%	3	23.4	80%		£3,996	£9,950
Nottingham	70 / 9	89%	7	14.5	94%		£3,750	£10,200
Plymouth	61 / 9	60%	4	15.8	95%		£3,950	£9,850
Portsmouth	60 / 11	79%	5	21.5	97%		£3,300	£9,650
Southampton	117 / 38	63%	5	11.5			£3,300	£12,000
Southampton Solent	39 / 8	77%	4	29.1	66%		£2,675–£3,400	£8,495
Strathclyde	61 / 100	50%	5	15.9	79%		£3,235	£11,465
Sussex	45 / 7	88%	4	15.7	86%		£4,100	£12,150
Teesside	65 / 9	74%	6	16.5	88%		£3,950	£8,750
UCL	69 / 41	37%	7	12.0	92%		£3,300	£16,870
UWE Bristol	1 / 244	7%	3	14.6		2%		£8,700
Wolverhampton	71 / 63	92%	3	11.8	98%	50%	£3,418–£4,400	£8,350

● Humanities

	Full-time/ part-time	% students from outside the UK	Expenditure per student (FTE)	Student:staff ratio	Full-time completion rate	Part-time completion rate	Tuition fees: home/EU students	Tuition fees: international students
Anthropology								
Brunel	28 / 58	38%	3	16.9	93%	83%	£3,315–£5,130	£8,500
Goldsmiths	39 / 32	32%	3	15.4	99%	100%	£3,300–£6,320	£9,580
Lampeter	1 / 47	52%	3	50.5			£3,300	£9,744
London School of Economics	88 / 8	84%	6	12.6	99%		£9,144–£17,352	£13,452
Manchester	42 / 9	53%	5	19.1	97%		£3,300	£12,900
Oxford	83 / 0	73%	10	11.4	97%		£5,200	£13,105
SOAS	45 / 22	52%	5	14.1	98%	100%	£4,090	£11,460
Sussex	45 / 11	55%	3	18.0	94%		£4,100	£9,500
UCL	33 / 10	44%	7	15.9	98%		£3,300	£12,940
Archaeology								
Birmingham	26 / 19	9%	3	11.2	71%		£4,200	£9,450
Bournemouth	78 / 23	35%	9	9.0	95%		£3,800–£8,000	£7,500
Bradford	45 / 80	30%	6	11.7	93%		£3,960	£8,500
Bristol	36 / 64	51%	4	22.2	97%		£3,950	£10,200
Durham	65 / 4	36%	4	9.5	98%		£3,996	£10,150
Lampeter	6 / 35	2%	3		62%		£3,300	£9,744
Leicester	3 / 68	4%	5	11.7		67%	£3,300	£9,050
Liverpool	18 / 21	20%	4	11.9	88%	100%	£3,300	£9,100
Oxford	36 / 20	46%	10	14.7	100%		£5,200	£13,105
Sheffield	96 / 19	38%	4	11.1	98%		£3,300	£9,920
Southampton	93 / 28	43%	3	12.7	96%	100%	£3,300	£9,380
Teesside	150 / 5	15%	6	19.7	90%	10%	£3,950	£8,250
UCL	207 / 55	49%	10	8.1	99%	94%	£3,300	£12,940
York	43 / 7	42%	4	12.6	100%		£3,300	£9,510
English								
Aberystwyth	9 / 34	19%	3	13.5		92%	£3,300	£8,475
Bath Spa	61 / 0	16%	3	22.3	100%		£3,970	£9,000
Birkbeck College	22 / 89	6%	3	13.7	100%	90%	£3,330	£12,336
Birmingham	44 / 89	29%	8	17.5	87%	76%	£4,200	£9,450
Birmingham City	5 / 33	11%	4	17.2		7%	£4,700	£9,400
Bristol	16 / 26	14%	6	18.9	94%		£3,950	£10,200
Central Lancashire	95 / 19	82%	7	25.8	90%	89%	£3,300	£8,950
Chichester	8 / 36	5%	4	16.2		90%	£3,125–£3,825	£7,400
De Montfort	9 / 35	21%	3	17.0		78%	£3,315	£7,990
Dundee	53 / 42	83%	6	14.6	70%		£3,250	£8,000
Durham	59 / 1	28%	3	16.1	100%		£3,996	£10,150
UEA	49 / 18	29%	7	22.9	95%	90%	£3,300	£9,500
Exeter	44 / 72	18%	5	15.5	100%		£4,000–£8,250	£9,600
Glasgow	49 / 13	28%	7	17.3	100%		£3,750	£9,400
Goldsmiths	21 / 14	23%	3	16.8	100%		£3,300–£6,320	£9,580
Hull	24 / 41	32%	3	20.6	94%		£3,300	£8,500
Kent	13 / 113	70%	4	17.6	91%		£3,500	£9,870

	Full-time/ part-time	% students from outside the UK	Expenditure per student (FTE)	Student:staff ratio	Full-time completion rate	Part-time completion rate	Tuition fees: home/EU students	Tuition fees: international students
King's College London	46 / 21	24%	8	11.9	100%		£3,900–£5,900	£9,100
Lancaster	59 / 29	53%	4	15.5	98%		£3,530	£9,200
Leeds	44 / 17	48%	6	15.8	97%		£3,300	£9,700
Liverpool	25 / 19	30%	6	16.7	97%		£3,300	£9,100
Loughborough	55 / 14	20%	6	21.2	100%		£3,350	£9,850
Manchester	46 / 23	17%	8	13.8	81%		£3,300	£12,900
Manchester Met	40 / 98	8%	3	25.5	95%	73%	£3,320–£3,890	£8,420
Newcastle	125 / 12	81%	4	25.4	95%		£4,070	£9,915
Northumbria	8 / 42	12%	6	19.4		93%	£3,996	£8,300
Nottingham	43 / 125	79%	5	20.3	87%		£3,750	£10,200
Nottingham Trent	53 / 34	36%	8	15.1	88%		£3,145–£6,900	£7,550
The Open University	0 / 278	0%	2	34.0		100%		
Oxford	68 / 0	54%	10	14.7	98%		£5,200	£13,105
Oxford Brookes	14 / 23	22%	4	15.3	100%		£3,990–£7,900	£9,570
Queen Mary	35 / 5	28%	8	19.0	100%		£3,964	£9,000
Queen's, Belfast	41 / 63	26%	5	15.7	98%		£3,319	£8,970
Reading	24 / 12	39%	4	16.7	100%		£3,575–£15,750	£9,350
Roehampton	14 / 69	18%	4	17.7	87%	67%	£3,700–£6,500	£9,000
Royal Holloway	95 / 21	61%	6	15.2	79%		£3,300	£11,555
Sheffield	54 / 11	14%	4	20.2	97%	80%	£3,300	£9,920
Southampton	22 / 16	21%	3	26.4	92%		£3,300	£9,380
St Andrews	106 / 1	73%	7	14.0	89%		£3,315–£5,800	£11,000 –£11,300
Strathclyde	40 / 9	62%	4	18.6	82%		£3,235	£8,930
Sunderland	36 / 37	47%	6	15.0	85%	81%	£3,965	£8,600
Sussex	34 / 34	25%	5	20.1	100%	100%	£4,100	£9,500
UCL	51 / 5	39%	9	12.2	100%		£3,300	£12,940
Warwick	43 / 18	50%	10	13.7	98%		£5,330	£10,250
Winchester	12 / 83	2%	2	20.2	90%	82%	£3,883	£8,070
York	122 / 5	36%	6	17.0	93%		£3,300	£9,510
York St John	29 / 32	21%	5	23.4	94%	65%	£3,833	£7,800

History and history of art

	Full-time/ part-time	% students from outside the UK	Expenditure per student (FTE)	Student:staff ratio	Full-time completion rate	Part-time completion rate	Tuition fees: home/EU students	Tuition fees: international students
Birkbeck College	49 / 232	4%	2	13.7	97%	88%	£3,330	£12,336
Birmingham	49 / 90	13%	3	17.5	91%	80%	£4,200	£9,450
Bristol	35 / 130	15%	3	18.9	90%	89%	£3,950	£10,200
Cardiff	34 / 4	28%	3	21.0	92%		£3,300–£11,130	£9,100
Chester	1 / 50	0%	2	22.9		32%	£3,510	£7,182
Courtauld Institute	155 / 14	46%	6	13.3	92%		£3,400–£4,745	£11,894 –£14,437
Durham	42 / 2	16%	2	16.1	100%		£3,996	£10,150
UEA	75 / 37	13%	3	22.9	89%		£3,300	£9,500
Edinburgh	34 / 2	53%	3	16.2	100%		£4,600	£10,650
Essex	32 / 25	42%	2	12.4	93%	91%	£3,500–£7,000	£9,990
Exeter	22 / 51	14%	3	15.5	90%	85%	£4,000–£8,250	£9,600
Glasgow	65 / 16	34%	3	17.3	98%		£3,750	£9,400
Goldsmiths	50 / 24	39%	2	16.8	100%	100%	£3,300–£6,320	£9,580
King's College London	39 / 13	23%	3	11.9	96%	90%	£3,900–£5,900	£9,100
Lancaster	13 / 47	3%	2	15.5	90%	91%	£3,530	£9,200
Leeds	72 / 36	20%	3	15.8	96%	92%	£3,300	£9,700
Leicester	33 / 53	13%	3	14.8	94%	83%	£3,300	£9,050

	Full-time/ part-time	% students from outside the UK	Expenditure per student (FTE)	Student:staff ratio	Full-time completion rate	Part-time completion rate	Tuition fees: home/EU students	Tuition fees: international students
Liverpool	33 / 16	10%	3	16.7	94%		£3,300	£9,100
University of London (Institutes and activities)	36 / 16	36%	10	3.7	90%			
London School of Economics	183 / 14	78%	4	12.6	99%		£9,144–£17,352	£13,452
Manchester	90 / 49	14%	3	13.8	90%	95%	£3,300	£12,900
Manchester Met	37 / 37	22%	2	25.5	95%	75%	£3,320–£3,890	£8,420
The Open University	0 / 322	0%	2	34.0		99%		
Oxford	167 / 29	51%	6	14.7	98%		£5,200	£13,105
Oxford Brookes	25 / 12	11%	2	15.3		90%	£3,990–£7,900	£9,570
Queen's, Belfast	22 / 30	25%	2	15.7	95%		£3,319	£8,970
Reading	15 / 29	16%	2	16.7	100%		£3,575–£15,750	£9,350
Royal Holloway	44 / 19	30%	3	15.2	100%	100%	£3,300	£11,555
Sheffield	52 / 1	13%	2	20.2	96%		£3,300	£9,920
SOAS	55 / 36	37%	3	10.0	100%	90%	£4,090	£11,460
Southampton	27 / 9	22%	2	26.4	100%		£3,300	£9,380
St Andrews	85 / 15	44%	3	14.0	90%	100%	£3,315–£5,800	£11,000 –£11,300
Sussex	15 / 47	11%	2	20.1	100%	82%	£4,100	£9,500
Swansea	14 / 28	9%	2	23.0	88%		£3,300	£9,010
UCL	111 / 38	38%	3	12.2	96%	75%	£3,300	£12,940
Warwick	24 / 26	12%	4	13.7	93%		£5,330	£10,250
Worcester	0 / 37	3%	2	14.8		40%	£3,600	£8,000
York	135 / 19	29%	3	17.0	99%	90%	£3,300	£9,510

Philosophy

Birkbeck College	14 / 64	5%	3	13.7	100%	89%	£3,330	£12,336
Bristol	14 / 24	18%	4	18.9	75%		£3,950	£10,200
London School of Economics	50 / 6	68%	7	12.6	96%		£9,144–£17,352	£13,452
The Open University	0 / 142	0%	2	34.0		94%		
Oxford	35 / 0	51%	9	14.7	100%		£5,200	£13,105
Warwick	23 / 38	26%	7	13.7	97%	67%	£5,330	£10,250
York	31 / 5	25%	4	17.0	100%		£3,300	£9,510

Religious studies and theology

Anglia Ruskin	20 / 233	9%	9	11.6	71%	38%	£1,550–£7,800	£9,300
Bangor	21 / 153	43%	4	20.1	89%	80%	£3,400	£8,500
Birmingham	14 / 32	11%	7	17.5		46%	£4,200	£9,450
Cardiff	11 / 35	15%	5	21.0		69%	£3,300–£11,130	£9,100
Chester	0 / 51	2%	3	22.9		65%	£3,510	£7,182
Durham	56 / 118	13%	3	16.1	89%	79%	£3,996	£10,150
Edinburgh	26 / 11	46%	7	16.2	93%	92%	£4,600	£10,650
Heythrop College	24 / 434	13%	3	16.8	94%	80%	£3,453	£8,680
Kent	5 / 49	11%	4	17.6		79%	£3,500	£9,870
Lampeter	77 / 807	41%	3	27.5	97%	55%	£3,300	£9,744
Manchester	18 / 22	22%	7	13.8	85%		£3,300	£12,900
Nottingham	10 / 33	5%	5	20.3	100%	91%	£3,750	£10,200
Oxford	81 / 30	38%	10	14.7	98%	91%	£5,200	£13,105
Queen's, Belfast	27 / 71	11%	4	15.7	100%	100%	£3,319	£8,970
SOAS	17 / 23	14%	7	10.0	100%		£4,090	£11,460
St Mary's UC, Twickenham	10 / 39	4%	3	20.9		77%	£3,090	£7,200
York St John	5 / 103	5%	5	23.4		73%	£3,833	£7,800

● Medical sciences

	Full-time/ part-time	% students from outside the UK	Expenditure per student (FTE)	Student:staff ratio	Full-time completion rate	Part-time completion rate	Tuition fees: home/EU students	Tuition fees: international students
Anatomy and physiology								
Birmingham	52 / 50	9%	4	13.4	100%		£4,200	£12,250
Bradford	0 / 120	6%	4	11.8		50%	£3,960	£11,000
Bristol	29 / 38	33%	7	13.5	94%		£3,950	£13,100
Cardiff	18 / 67	20%	10	10.5		91%	£3,300–£11,130	£11,700
City	315 / 148	14%	7	13.9	72%	66%	£3,300	£19,500
Cumbria	0 / 141	6%	2	20.5		75%	£3,330	£8,250
Glasgow Caledonian	74 / 113	12%	5	15.5	91%	36%	£3,315	£10,500
Hertfordshire	8 / 138	7%	4	12.1		15%	£3,833	£9,500
King's College London	99 / 16	23%	8	15.2	93%		£3,900–£5,900	£17,750
Manchester Met	53 / 83	16%	3	17.8		93%	£3,320–£3,890	£8,420
Newcastle	58 / 0	35%	5	16.1	96%		£4,070	£12,970
Robert Gordon	95 / 9	47%	3	18.4	9%		£3,315–£7,712	£13,800
UCL	58 / 97	17%	8	11.5	94%	73%	£3,300	£16,870
Dentistry								
Bristol	5 / 205	10%	6	16.8		84%	£3,950	£13,100
King's College London	121 / 0	40%	8	6.8	100%		£3,900–£5,900	£17,750
Manchester	19 / 20	56%	8	7.6	100%		£3,300	£12,900
Newcastle	6 / 47	19%	2	12.1		100%	£4,070	£12,970
Queen Mary	63 / 37	49%	5	8.8	95%		£3,964	£11,100
Medicine								
Aberdeen	40 / 62	43%	4	6.9	100%	100%	£3,315	£11,250
Birmingham	8 / 297	12%	4	9.5		72%	£4,200	£12,250
Brighton Sussex Medical School	12 / 266	8%	4	16.6		48%	£3,865	£11,575
Bristol	13 / 96	27%	4	12.5		71%	£3,950	£13,100
Cambridge	1 / 67	3%	8	7.4		100%	£5,434	£14,353
Cardiff	102 / 1,426	35%	3	7.7	93%	87%	£3,300–£11,130	£11,700
Edinburgh	104 / 100	3%		6.2	100%		£4,600	£14,000
Glasgow	218 / 179	32%	5	7.3	100%	100%	£3,750	£9,400
Imperial College	217 / 161	25%	7	6.7	92%	93%	£3,300	£24,250
The Institute of Cancer Research	0 / 113	8%	10	3.6				
King's College London	240 / 540	21%	7	6.8	97%	93%	£3,900–£5,900	£17,750
Leeds	0 / 320	41%	6	8.0	100%	76%	£3,300	£12,600
Leicester	2 / 198	12%	4	7.1		95%	£3,300	£12,100
Liverpool	22 / 313	30%	3	9.8	100%	96%	£3,300	£11,650
London School of Hygiene and Tropical Medicine	442 / 344	46%	8	2.2	99%	83%	£4,640	£16,440
Manchester	44 / 515	10%	7	8.9	88%	85%	£3,300	£12,900
Newcastle	12 / 162	9%	4	7.5		90%	£4,070	£12,970
Nottingham	98 / 282	34%	4	6.7	95%	81%	£3,750	£10,200
Queen Mary	103 / 251	21%	5	8.8	83%	83%	£3,964	£11,100
Sheffield	44 / 0	77%	3	7.9	93%		£3,300	£13,050
Strathclyde	9 / 53	45%	3	9.8			£3,235	£11,465
UCL	139 / 232	29%	6	4.3	98%	97%	£3,300	£16,870

	Full-time/ part-time	% students from outside the UK	Expenditure per student (FTE)	Student:staff ratio	Full-time completion rate	Part-time completion rate	Tuition fees: home/EU students	Tuition fees: international students
Nursing and paramedical studies								
Abertay Dundee	4 / 33	14%	4	17.2		31%	£3,315	£8,650
Anglia Ruskin	47 / 342	20%	6	21.3	48%	51%	£1,550–£7,800	£10,925
Bangor	30 / 47	8%	5	12.7	94%		£3,400	£9,850
Bedfordshire	45 / 189	12%	4	20.7	91%	63%	£4,150–£4,450	£8,700
Birmingham	99 / 355	16%	5	13.4	95%	81%	£4,200	£12,250
Birmingham City	4 / 351	2%	4	17.4		39%	£4,700	£9,400
Bournemouth	2 / 88	0%	5	19.3		56%	£3,800–£8,000	£11,000
Bradford	18 / 449	18%	5	11.9	63%	27%	£3,960	£11,000
Brighton	193 / 437	7%	4	15.7	65%	73%	£3,630	£11,000
Brunel	51 / 286	15%	4	18.3	84%	14%	£3,315–£5,130	£8,750
Bucks New University	5 / 91	16%	4	17.9		93%	£3,840	£9,900
Canterbury Christ Church	6 / 341	4%	4	17.2	83%	74%	£4,050	£8,355
Cardiff	66 / 135	22%	6	11.0	83%	85%	£3,300–£11,130	£11,700
Central Lancashire	26 / 180	6%	4	20.5	83%	71%	£3,300	£9,450
Chester	65 / 389	11%	2	18.2	88%	54%	£3,510	£9,540
City	119 / 409	7%	6	14.4	89%	74%	£3,300	£19,500
Coventry	7 / 159	15%	4	15.8		53%	£3,420–£4,230	£9,100
Cumbria	8 / 415	1%	3	18.9		89%	£3,330	£8,250
De Montfort	1 / 149	2%	4	17.1		68%	£3,315	£8,955
Derby	106 / 693	5%	4	12.4	96%	74%	modular	£12,290
Dundee	107 / 565	34%	4	19.0	89%	35%	£3,250	£13,500
UEA	56 / 170	9%	7	11.6	71%	79%	£3,300	£11,800
Edge Hill	0 / 126	2%	4	17.3		45%	£1,600–£3,600	£7,900
Edinburgh	61 / 145	22%	9		82%	59%	£4,600	£14,000
Essex	139 / 368	5%	4	15.3	85%	72%	£3,500–£7,000	£9,990
Glamorgan	8 / 192	6%	5	13.4		78%	£3,300	£9,980
Glasgow	34 / 46	0%	4	11.0	100%	100%	£3,750	£9,400
Glasgow Caledonian	91 / 829	8%	3	20.4	89%	49%	£3,315	£10,500
Greenwich	35 / 256	17%	3	18.8		40%	£3,600–£7,410	£10,600
Hertfordshire	71 / 425	7%	4	13.8	82%	64%	£3,833	£9,500
Huddersfield	2 / 223	2%	4	16.1		36%	£3,900	£9,500
Hull	3 / 129	1%	4	15.7		70%	£3,300	£10,500
Kent	22 / 226	6%	7	10.5		91%	£3,500	£12,000
King's College London	19 / 282	4%	6	15.4	85%	87%	£3,900–£5,900	£17,750
Kingston	22 / 262	19%	4	21.1	77%	50%	£3,400	£11,000
Leeds	134 / 429	16%	9	15.7	95%	91%	£3,300	£12,600
Leeds Met	135 / 332	4%	7	15.5	90%	78%	£3,400	£8,300
Lincoln	17 / 34	4%	3	18.3		100%	£3,338	£9,243
Liverpool	35 / 126	17%	6	11.5	93%	76%	£3,300	£11,650
Liverpool John Moores	77 / 344	4%	4	17.8	98%	88%	£3,145	£8,950
London South Bank	177 / 362	2%	4	17.8	92%	60%	£3,890	£9,355
Manchester	25 / 338	7%	6	17.9	100%	84%	£3,300	£12,900
Manchester Met	17 / 173	6%	3	17.8		69%	£3,320–£3,890	£8,420
Middlesex	16 / 212	15%	7	11.2		74%	£4,600–£6,870	£10,720
Napier	1 / 413	8%	3	15.0		30%	£3,675–£5,020	£10,665
Northampton	7 / 133	1%	3	11.8		69%	£3,600–£4,500	£8,700
Northumbria	123 / 352	9%	4	18.9	78%	53%	£3,996	£9,950
Nottingham	19 / 116	16%	6	14.6	81%	69%	£3,750	£10,200

	Full-time/ part-time	% students from outside the UK	Expenditure per student (FTE)	Student:staff ratio	Full-time completion rate	Part-time completion rate	Tuition fees: home/EU students	Tuition fees: international students
Oxford Brookes	52 / 337	17%	4	14.7	50%	82%	£3,990–£7,900	£10,590
Queen Margaret	159 / 364	22%	3	16.5	75%	65%	£3,315	£9,700
Queen's, Belfast	12 / 316	24%	3	17.8	100%	95%	£3,319	£10,990
Robert Gordon	0 / 55	2%	4	16.6		54%	£3,315–£7,712	£13,800
Roehampton	53 / 100	12%	4	10.4	96%	88%	£3,700–£6,500	£9,000
The Royal College of Nursing	0 / 177	3%	10	8.9		66%		
Salford	22 / 409	5%	5	14.1	73%	95%	£3,300	£10,500
Sheffield Hallam	95 / 822	3%	4	11.3	67%	58%	£3,300–£7,800	£11,900
Southampton	286 / 385	7%	6	17.3	95%	80%	£3,300	£12,000
Staffordshire	2 / 398	0%	6	14.3		76%		£9,875
Sunderland	0 / 38	3%	4	20.2		87%	£3,965	£8,600
Surrey	41 / 506	11%	5	20.5	74%	82%	£3,600–£8,600	£13,300
Swansea	42 / 418	9%	7	12.3	79%	49%	£3,300	£11,460
Teesside	453 / 422	5%	3	18.9	66%	44%	£3,950	£8,750
Thames Valley	0 / 343	2%	4	15.2		60%	£4,350	£10,150
Ulster	42 / 467	10%	5	14.4	91%	85%	£3,420	£8,649
UWE Bristol	102 / 479	6%	4	13.6	80%	38%		£8,700
Wolverhampton	47 / 242	39%	4	15.5	65%	52%	£3,418–£4,400	£8,350
Worcester	2 / 77	3%	3	16.4		44%	£3,600	£8,000
York	45 / 83	10%	6	12.5	93%	93%	£3,300	£12,555
York St John	5 / 233	1%	3	18.9		58%	£3,833	£7,800

Pharmacy and pharmacology

	Full-time/ part-time	% students from outside the UK	Expenditure per student (FTE)	Student:staff ratio	Full-time completion rate	Part-time completion rate	Tuition fees: home/EU students	Tuition fees: international students
Aston	68 / 199	9%	5	13.6	95%	97%	£3,325–£8,950	£12,950
Bath	0 / 106	2%	5	16.5		100%	£4,000	£13,150
Birmingham	59 / 0	17%	3	16.3	100%		£4,200	£12,250
Bradford	21 / 169	27%	5	18.8	100%	34%	£3,960	£11,000
Brighton	31 / 104	18%	5	17.8	100%	95%	£3,630	£11,000
Cardiff	1 / 238	10%	10	15.5		84%	£3,300–£11,130	£11,700
De Montfort	0 / 73	0%	4	14.0		77%	£3,315	£8,955
Derby	0 / 142	7%	4	21.7	100%	93%	modular	£12,290
Greenwich	233 / 1,134	23%	9	22.4	86%	71%	£3,600–£7,410	£10,600
Hertfordshire	116 / 72	75%	8		78%	75%	£3,833	£9,500
King's College London	45 / 55	31%	5	16.6	100%	88%	£3,900–£5,900	£17,750
Kingston	121 / 9	81%	3	21.3	83%		£3,400	£11,000
Leeds	0 / 40	0%	10	11.3		85%	£3,300	£12,600
Liverpool John Moores	0 / 116	5%	2	28.2		94%	£3,145	£8,950
Queen's, Belfast	0 / 271	13%	4	20.0		98%	£3,319	£10,990
Robert Gordon	15 / 348	13%	3	19.8	100%	44%	£3,315–£7,712	£13,800
School of Pharmacy	55 / 446	10%	7	18.1	92%	97%	£4,400	£13,370
Strathclyde	17 / 132	24%	7	13.5	100%	67%	£3,235	£11,465
Sunderland	82 / 139	37%	3	15.4	99%	94%	£3,965	£8,600

Psychology

	Full-time/ part-time	% students from outside the UK	Expenditure per student (FTE)	Student:staff ratio	Full-time completion rate	Part-time completion rate	Tuition fees: home/EU students	Tuition fees: international students
Aston	31 / 9	22%	3	18.7	100%		£3,325–£8,950	£12,950
Bangor	78 / 107	27%	8	19.9	98%	94%	£3,400	£9,850
Bath	25 / 28	13%	6	15.6	100%		£4,000	£13,150
Bedfordshire	33 / 28	34%	3	24.6	65%	77%	£4,150–£4,450	£8,700

	Full-time/ part-time	% students from outside the UK	Expenditure per student (FTE)	Student:staff ratio	Full-time completion rate	Part-time completion rate	Tuition fees: home/EU students	Tuition fees: international students
Birkbeck College	12 / 500	5%	4	22.0	100%	86%	£3,330	£15,534
Birmingham	32 / 35	1%	9	14.8	95%	90%	£4,200	£12,250
Bristol	37 / 76	31%	6	14.2	100%		£3,950	£13,100
Brunel	23 / 53	49%	3	20.0	89%		£3,315–£5,130	£8,750
Canterbury Christ Church	105 / 46	0%	10	11.1	95%	45%	£4,050	£8,355
Central Lancashire	75 / 49	10%	5	22.7	95%	87%	£3,300	£9,450
Chester	19 / 80	2%	3	20.9		31%	£3,510	£9,540
City	65 / 101	36%	4	19.7	89%	85%	£3,300	£19,500
Coventry	67 / 50	3%	5	18.8	88%	70%	£3,420–£4,230	£9,100
Dundee	37 / 66	10%	3	21.0	94%	96%	£3,250	£13,500
Durham	48 / 10	21%	4	18.8	96%		£3,996	£11,025
East London	127 / 1,064	8%	5	16.5	73%	41%	£4,560–£9,600	£14,220
Essex	45 / 86	31%	4	15.8	88%	65%	£3,500–£7,000	£9,990
Exeter	92 / 116	15%	8	13.8	97%		£4,000–£8,250	£12,240
Glasgow Caledonian	27 / 63	6%	3	16.4	63%		£3,315	£10,500
Goldsmiths	77 / 132	15%	3	11.9	100%	97%	£3,300–£6,320	£13,290
Hertfordshire	60 / 19	18%	2	15.3	83%		£3,833	£9,500
Kent	47 / 87	22%	5	14.9	57%	68%	£3,500	£12,000
Lancaster	48 / 8	41%	5	17.1	96%		£3,530	£11,100
Leeds	32 / 57	10%	7	19.6	100%	92%	£3,300	£12,600
Leeds Met	21 / 83	1%	3	35.9		91%	£3,400	£8,300
Leicester	19 / 297	4%	7	15.9	100%	52%	£3,300–£4,525	£12,100
Liverpool	152 / 12	15%	5	16.4	93%		£3,300	£11,650
Liverpool John Moores	20 / 91	18%	3	21.7		56%	£3,145	£8,950
London School of Economics	101 / 16	80%	9	11.9	100%		£9,144–£17,352	£21,600
Manchester	54 / 77	10%	8	14.2	95%	81%	£3,300	£12,900
Middlesex	21 / 51	21%	8	20.3		67%	£4,600–£6,870	£10,720
Nottingham	157 / 212	33%	9	14.9	93%	59%	£3,750	£10,200
Nottingham Trent	51 / 2	25%	5	13.1	92%		£3,145–£6,900	£10,800
The Open University	0 / 608	0%	2	39.4		99%		
Oxford	17 / 65	16%	10	15.0	100%		£5,200	£14,710
Portsmouth	24 / 87	9%	4	17.8	100%	50%	£3,300	£9,650
Queen's, Belfast	48 / 46	13%	7	19.4	100%		£3,319	£10,990
Roehampton	151 / 63	7%	5	24.9	69%	77%	£3700–£6500	£9,000
Royal Holloway	98 / 51	2%	5	12.8	100%	89%	£3,300	£12,785
Sheffield	169 / 30	13%	5	14.9	98%	87%	£3,300	£13,050
Southampton	135 / 166	10%	6	16.1	96%	92%	£3,300	£12,000
St Andrews	1 / 58	10%	8	12.5		50%	£3,315–£5,800	£11,000 –£11,300
Staffordshire	48 / 35	0%	5	16.6	100%			£9,875
Stirling	28 / 8	19%	5	12.1	100%		£4,200	£9,200
Strathclyde	24 / 53	0%	4	17.3	100%		£3,235	£11,465
Sunderland	43 / 7	42%	3	18.2	85%		£3,965	£8,600
Surrey	132 / 47	20%	7	14.9	93%	92%	£3,600–£8,600	£13,300
Sussex	35 / 20	20%	4	15.7	95%	75%	£4,100	£12,150
Swansea	28 / 54	13%	3	27.0	93%		£3,300	£11,460
Teesside	60 / 21	9%	4	15.7	42%		£3,950	£8,750
UCL	88 / 59	41%	9	11.4	100%	96%	£3,300	£16,870
UWE Bristol	23 / 16	0%	3	25.9	100%			£8,700
Westminster	20 / 38	29%	3	18.2	95%	93%	£3,800–£13,750	£13,750
Wolverhampton	40 / 36	16%	6	16.3	55%		£3,418–£4,400	£8,350
York	46 / 32	14%	8	13.2	98%	100%	£3,300	£12,555

	Full-time/part-time	% students from outside the UK	Expenditure per student (FTE)	Student:staff ratio	Full-time completion rate	Part-time completion rate	Tuition fees: home/EU students	Tuition fees: international students
Sports science								
Bangor	41 / 1	26%	10	19.9	93%		£3,400	£8,500
Brunel	14 / 80	17%	7	14.7	86%	75%	£3,315–£5,130	£8,500
Exeter	27 / 41	28%	5	20.6	97%		£4,000–£8,250	£9,600
Leeds Met	23 / 26	8%	7	30.1			£3,400	£8,000
Liverpool John Moores	16 / 29	29%	3	30.9		89%	£3,145	£8,320
Loughborough	170 / 110	34%	9	17.2	95%	82%	£3,350	£9,850
Manchester Met	19 / 34	11%	5	13.9	83%	67%	£3,320–£3,890	£8,420
Northumbria	35 / 27	40%	3	22.3	74%		£3,996	£8,300
Sheffield Hallam	54 / 30	23%	5	22.8	72%		£3,300–£7,800	£8,100
UWIC	49 / 170	4%	3	23.1	96%	83%	£3,330	£8,800
Wolverhampton	19 / 32	49%	3	32.3	23%	29%	£3,418–£4,400	£8,200

● Modern languages

	Full-time/ part-time	% students from outside the UK	Expenditure per student (FTE)	Student:staff ratio	Full-time completion rate	Part-time completion rate	Tuition fees: home/EU students	Tuition fees: international students
Anglia Ruskin	23 / 38	38%	4	9.7	79%	69%	£1,550–£7,800	£9,300
Bath	122 / 221	64%	7	15.8	99%		£4,000	£10,300
Birkbeck College	8 / 48	20%	6	10.9		93%	£3,330	£12,336
Birmingham	115 / 159	82%	7	12.7	89%	81%	£4,200	£9,450
Bristol	19 / 22	32%	7	21.9			£3,950	£10,200
Coventry	0 / 62	5%	5	15.8		11%	£3,420–£4,230	£8,600
Durham	34 / 4	53%	3	15.1	95%		£3,996	£10,150
Edinburgh	81 / 8	73%	7	16.2	91%		£4,600	£10,650
Essex	124 / 28	89%	3	12.8	92%		£3,500–£7,000	£9,990
Exeter	43 / 81	44%	4	16.9	100%	80%	£4,000–£8,250	£9,600
Greenwich	15 / 20	63%	2	18.1		77%	£3,600–£7,410	£8,900
Heriot-Watt	49 / 0	82%	9	10.7	88%	96%	£3,790	£9,450
King's College London	79 / 54	32%	7	13.4	98%	69%	£3,900–£5,900	£9,100
Leeds	57 / 7	64%	8	12.5	100%		£3,300	£9,700
Manchester	34 / 15	35%		15.1	88%		£3,300	£12,900
Newcastle	135 / 8	85%	4	19.1	99%		£4,070	£9,915
Northumbria	36 / 27	87%	3	23.1	96%		£3,996	£8,300
Oxford	187 / 5	60%	10	10.4	98%		£5,200	£13,105
Reading	29 / 40	62%	3	13.6	94%		£3,575–£15,750	£9,350
Royal Holloway	7 / 74	59%	3	12.9		94%	£3,300	£11,555
Salford	61 / 29	58%	8	11.2	91%		£3,300	£8,400
Sheffield	131 / 129	61%	4	13.0	93%	73%	£3,300	£9,920
SOAS	197 / 68	47%	6	10.0	99%	95%	£4,090	£11,460
Southampton	56 / 25	60%	9	10.3	95%	92%	£3,300	£9,380
St Andrews	37 / 1	79%	4	12.4	73%		£3,315–£5,800	£11,000 –£11,300
Sussex	42 / 17	63%	3	8.8	98%		£4,100	£9,500
Swansea	69 / 62	64%	3	13.0	91%		£3,300	£9,010
UCL	115 / 41	48%	9	10.5	97%	90%	£3,300	£12,940
Westminster	152 / 151	51%	5	11.4	91%	93%	£3,800–£13,750	£9,750

● Physical sciences

	Full-time/ part-time	% students from outside the UK	Expenditure per student (FTE)	Student:staff ratio	Full-time completion rate	Part-time completion rate	Tuition fees: home/EU students	Tuition fees: international students
Agriculture and forestry								
Bangor	32 / 26	43%	8	15.3	100%		£3,400	£9,850
Harper Adams UC	28 / 54	21%	3	19.7	83%	75%	£4,315	£8,730
Newcastle	68 / 12	40%	5	11.1	98%		£4,070	£12,970
Nottingham	40 / 38	74%		8.2	96%	67%	£3,750	£10,200
Queen's, Belfast	26 / 52	17%	2	10.7	100%	100%	£3,319	£10,990
Reading	63 / 6	80%	8	10.6	99%		£3,575–£15,750	£15,750
Royal Agricultural College	58 / 97	14%	7	12.2	75%	67%	£5,125–£6,650	£8,700
Biosciences								
Aberdeen	58 / 0	64%	6	10.8	94%		£3,315	£11,250
Aberystwyth	17 / 33	22%	5	19.4		100%	£3,300	£10,750
Birkbeck College	15 / 51	8%	8	13.8	95%	96%	£3,330	£15,534
Birmingham	45 / 92	13%	7	18.2	100%	43%	£4,200	£12,250
Brunel	33 / 24	40%	4	15.5	74%		£3,315–£5,130	£8,750
Central Lancashire	11 / 32	14%	4	17.9		77%	£3,300	£9,450
Chester	141 / 182	9%	6	13.7	81%	44%	£3,510	£9,540
Coventry	14 / 48	34%	2	21.8		71%	£3,420–£4,230	£9,100
Cranfield University	115 / 40	50%	10	9.3	94%			
UEA	50 / 1	50%	6	15.7	89%		£3,300	£11,800
East London	121 / 46	63%	3	12.5	64%	60%	£4,560–£9,600	£14,220
Essex	29 / 12	73%	4	16.7	82%		£3,500–£7,000	£9,990
Exeter	50 / 54	30%	5	16.2	96%		£4,000–£8,250	£12,240
Glasgow	99 / 4	60%	6	15.2	100%		£3,750	£9,400
Glasgow Caledonian	69 / 51	44%	4	18.1	81%	76%	£3,315	£10,500
Heriot-Watt	36 / 61	55%	5	23.9	89%		£3,790	£11,810
Hertfordshire	74 / 3	95%	2	21.9	39%		£3,833	£9,500
Hull	30 / 10	48%	6	20.9	100%		£3,300	£10,500
Imperial College	129 / 0	30%	9	11.4	99%		£3,300	£16,750
Kent	26 / 23	61%	5	13.5	96%		£3,500	£12,000
King's College London	87 / 0	24%	4	16.8	97%		£3,900–£5,900	£17,750
Leeds	168 / 48	41%	9	12.9	94%		£3,300	£12,600
Leicester	48 / 0	83%	10	8.3	93%		£3,300–£4,000	£10,175
Liverpool	34 / 10	40%	5	14.4	95%		£3,300	£11,650
Liverpool John Moores	13 / 89	30%	3	18.6		88%	£3,145	£8,950
Loughborough	2 / 267	9%	4	12.7		96%	£3,350	£12,800
Manchester	78 / 64	34%	9	14.7	93%	56%	£3,300	£12,900
Manchester Met	54 / 163	12%	3	17.0		92%	£3,320–£3,890	£8,420
Napier	77 / 111	48%	4	16.6	89%	20%	£3,675–£5,020	£10,665
Newcastle	25 / 92	35%	7	14.8	92%	79%	£4,070	£12,970
Northumbria	10 / 84	2%	2	19.3		86%	£3,996	£9,950
Nottingham	115 / 104	51%	6	13.8	96%	88%	£3,750	£10,200
Nottingham Trent	79 / 0	89%	3	9.9	72%		£3,145–£6,900	£10,800
Oxford Brookes	45 / 14	54%	4	17.0	97%		£3,990–£7,900	£10,590
Plymouth	43 / 2	20%	3	19.7	83%		£3,950	£9,850

	Full-time/ part-time	% students from outside the UK	Expenditure per student (FTE)	Student:staff ratio	Full-time completion rate	Part-time completion rate	Tuition fees: home/EU students	Tuition fees: international students
Queen Margaret	34 / 2	36%	3	14.6	65%		£3,315	£9,700
Queen's, Belfast	25 / 19	30%	6	14.4	100%		£3,319	£10,990
Reading	54 / 13	25%		14.1	96%		£3,575-£15,750	£15,750
Roehampton	20 / 44	34%	3	25.8	92%	95%	£3,700-£6,500	£9,000
Salford	47 / 34	41%	4	16.5	98%		£3,300	£10,500
Sheffield	101 / 13	53%	5	13.3	92%	64%	£3,300	£13,050
Sheffield Hallam	286 / 234	51%	4	21.2	86%	43%	£3,300-£7,800	£11,900
Southampton	35 / 2	46%	5	21.0	100%		£3,300	£12,000
St Andrews	45 / 0	53%	7	9.3	100%		£3,315-£5,800	£11,000 -£11,300
Surrey	22 / 333	35%	9	10.9		77%	£3,600-£8,600	£13,300
Sussex	52 / 2	70%	7	10.6	88%		£4,100	£12,150
Swansea	12 / 23	23%	4	13.7	100%		£3,300	£11,460
Teesside	28 / 20	27%	4	24.9	85%	64%	£3,950	£8,750
UCL	63 / 2	60%	7	13.3	96%		£3,300	£16,870
Ulster	62 / 498	44%	5	10.1	80%	86%	£3,420	£8,649
UWIC	53 / 150	13%	3	16.7	0%	2%	£3,330	£8,800
Westminster	42 / 172	25%	4	19.3	96%	95%	£3,800-£13,750	£13,750
Wolverhampton	56 / 136	56%	4	18.1	61%	59%	£3,418-£4,400	£8,350
York	44 / 0	54%	9	9.2	97%		£3,300	£12,555

Chemistry

	Full-time/ part-time	% students from outside the UK	Expenditure per student (FTE)	Student:staff ratio	Full-time completion rate	Part-time completion rate	Tuition fees: home/EU students	Tuition fees: international students
Huddersfield	22 / 24	20%	5	14.4	100%	90%	£3,900	£9,500
Loughborough	69 / 18	66%	7	14.7	95%	64%	£3,350	£12,800
Robert Gordon	37 / 20	58%	2	19.0	100%		£3,315-£7,712	£13,800
Strathclyde	47 / 11	79%	8	16.5	93%		£3,235	£11,465

Computer sciences and IT

	Full-time/ part-time	% students from outside the UK	Expenditure per student (FTE)	Student:staff ratio	Full-time completion rate	Part-time completion rate	Tuition fees: home/EU students	Tuition fees: international students
Aberdeen	45 / 5	47%	5	12.0	88%		£3,315	£11,250
Abertay Dundee	164 / 79	86%	3	26.1	71%	81%	£3,315	£8,650
Anglia Ruskin	34 / 45	43%	5	9.7	63%	40%	£1,550-£7,800	£10,925
Aston	54 / 15	69%	3	19.1	88%		£3,325-£8,950	£12,950
Bath	31 / 202	49%	6	17.0	95%	59%	£4,000	£13,150
Bedfordshire	138 / 74	83%	3	18.4	79%	64%	£4,150-£4,450	£8,700
Birkbeck College	19 / 116	4%	6	11.3		80%	£3,330	£15,534
Birmingham	213 / 4	50%	8	13.4	82%		£4,200	£12,250
Birmingham City	23 / 73	23%	4	15.5	31%	83%	£4,700	£9,400
Bournemouth	66 / 19	59%	7	13.9	83%		£3,800-£8,000	£11,000
Bradford	137 / 142	82%	4	17.1	85%		£3,960	£11,000
Brighton	85 / 93	33%	3	16.2	83%	66%	£3,630	£11,000
Bristol	113 / 99	74%	5	15.9	88%		£3,950	£13,100
Brunel	85 / 177	63%	4	15.7	88%	78%	£3,315-£5,130	£8,750
Canterbury Christ Church	34 / 13	28%	5	16.7	70%		£4,050	£8,355
Cardiff	32 / 14	43%	5	15.1	77%		£3,300-£11,130	£11,700
Central Lancashire	153 / 57	54%	4	20.3	79%	67%	£3,300	£9,450
Chester	4 / 107	4%	4	15.8		28%	£3,510	£9,540
City	170 / 487	33%	5	19.4	75%	57%	£3,300	£19,500
Coventry	226 / 130	58%	4	16.6	87%	48%	£3,420-£4,230	£9,100
De Montfort	59 / 29	32%	4	20.5	87%		£3,315	£8,955

	Full-time/ part-time	% students from outside the UK	Expenditure per student (FTE)	Student:staff ratio	Full-time completion rate	Part-time completion rate	Tuition fees: home/EU students	Tuition fees: international students
Derby	22 / 51	48%	3	15.2	100%		modular	£12,290
Durham	68 / 11	72%	4		100%		£3,996	£11,025
UEA	100 / 15	59%	6	17.9	84%		£3,300	£11,800
East London	288 / 66	60%	4	17.5	89%	56%	£4,560-£9,600	£14,220
Edinburgh	163 / 17	68%		8.7	80%		£4,600	£14,000
Glamorgan	219 / 81	60%	4		82%	80%	£3,300	£9,980
Glasgow	120 / 9	43%	7	7.8	100%		£3,750	£9,400
Glasgow Caledonian	184 / 31	70%	3	18.5	37%	86%	£3,315	£10,500
Gloucestershire	32 / 21	42%	5	17.4	86%		£3,445-£8,725	£8,720
Greenwich	467 / 211	83%	4	27.1	65%	65%	£3,600-£7,410	£10,600
Heriot-Watt	69 / 77	74%	4	11.7	77%		£3,790	£11,810
Hertfordshire	280 / 39	78%	4	12.9	75%	62%	£3,833	£9,500
Huddersfield	54 / 71	36%	4	20.5	78%	51%	£3,900	£9,500
Hull	96 / 39	51%	6	16.3	91%		£3,300	£10,500
Imperial College	110 / 5	68%	10	14.2	95%		£3,300	£19,500
Kent	46 / 35	39%	7	11.7	90%		£3,500	£12,000
King's College London	97 / 16	52%	8	15.2	91%	74%	£3,900-£5,900	£17,750
Kingston	96 / 128	50%	5	15.9	71%	56%	£3,400	£11,000
Lancaster	39 / 10	45%	10		92%		£3,530	£11,100
Leeds	36 / 1	40%	9	15.8	95%		£3,300	£12,600
Leeds Met	133 / 40	65%	3	36.9	96%	55%	£3,400	£8,300
Liverpool John Moores	74 / 75	47%	3	19.5	93%	77%	£3,145	£8,950
London School of Economics	155 / 3	91%	6	10.2	100%		£9,144-£17,352	£21,600
London South Bank	87 / 119	61%		21.1	84%	57%	£3,890	£9,355
Loughborough	221 / 46	57%	5	17.7	90%	83%	£3,350	£12,800
Manchester	284 / 43	73%	9	14.9	91%	82%	£3,300	£12,900
Manchester Met	62 / 18	41%	3	22.0	9%		£3,320-£3,890	£8,420
Middlesex	175 / 260	90%	4	19.5	96%	75%	£4,600-£6,870	£10,720
Napier	155 / 175	59%	3	13.6	39%	9%	£3,675-£5,020	£10,665
Newcastle	60 / 6	60%	8	10.0	98%		£4,070	£12,970
Newport	23 / 30	45%	2		84%	79%	£4,350	£8,450
Northampton	28 / 19	77%	2	17.8	36%		£3,600-£4,500	£8,700
Northumbria	243 / 265	45%	3	21.7	68%	62%	£3,996	£9,950
Nottingham	91 / 91	76%	8	11.8	86%		£3,750	£10,200
Nottingham Trent	83 / 7	50%	4	21.1	64%		£3,145-£6,900	£10,800
The Open University	0 / 1015	0%	3	19.1		99%		
Oxford	57 / 233	34%	10	11.7	100%	92%	£5,200	£14,710
Oxford Brookes	78 / 25	73%	5	14.7	93%	89%	£3,990-£7,900	£10,590
Plymouth	92 / 33	80%	8	16.4	78%	52%	£3,950	£9,850
Portsmouth	56 / 102	36%	4	21.6	81%	34%	£3,300	£9,650
Queen Mary	66 / 2	69%	9	9.3	75%		£3,964	£11,100
Queen's, Belfast	7 / 54	16%	6	15.7		100%	£3,319	£10,990
Reading	48 / 15	63%	7	11.9	96%		£3,575-£15,750	£15,750
Robert Gordon	97 / 38	79%	3	14.4	89%		£3,315-£7,712	£13,800
Royal Holloway	96 / 36	57%	4		99%	90%	£3,300	£12,785
Salford	78 / 68	53%	5	24.8	89%		£3,300	£10,500
Sheffield	124 / 60	55%	7	10.1	93%	100%	£3,300	£13,050
Sheffield Hallam	221 / 157	54%	3	18.3	62%	58%	£3,300-£7,800	£11,900
Southampton	50 / 1	69%	10	9.6	100%		£3,300	£12,000

	Full-time/part-time	% students from outside the UK	Expenditure per student (FTE)	Student:staff ratio	Full-time completion rate	Part-time completion rate	Tuition fees: home/EU students	Tuition fees: international students
Staffordshire	428 / 161	79%	5	18.2	74%	82%		£9,875
Stirling	57 / 2	59%	5	14.0	87%		£4,200	£9,200
Strathclyde	92 / 169	31%	5	13.4	90%	82%	£3,235	£11,465
Sunderland	415 / 176	74%	7	14.6	79%	56%	£3,965	£8,600
Surrey	88 / 31	72%	8	16.9	81%		£3,600-£8,600	£13,300
Sussex	51 / 74	40%	8	11.0	94%	93%	£4,100	£12,150
Swansea	29 / 32	72%	5	10.7	75%		£3,300	£11,460
Teesside	104 / 29	34%	4	20.2	72%	52%	£3,950	£8,750
Thames Valley	31 / 34	31%	2	26.3		67%	£4,350	£10,150
UCL	119 / 48	51%	8	9.4	95%	79%	£3,300	£16,870
Ulster	42 / 74	25%	4	13.5		61%	£3,420	£8,649
UWE Bristol	97 / 89	39%	4	15.6	59%	44%		£8,700
Westminster	190 / 321	41%	3	12.5	89%	73%	£3,800-£13,750	£13,750
Wolverhampton	38 / 191	54%	3	18.2	29%	35%	£3,418-£4,400	£8,350
York	125 / 72	52%	10	10.4	90%	100%	£3,300	£12,555

Earth and marine sciences

	Full-time/part-time	% students from outside the UK	Expenditure per student (FTE)	Student:staff ratio	Full-time completion rate	Part-time completion rate	Tuition fees: home/EU students	Tuition fees: international students
Aberdeen	37 / 0	57%	3	10.7	100%		£3,315	£11,250
Bangor	116 / 0	22%	6	14.3	91%		£3,400	£9,850
Birmingham	43 / 6	12%	5	16.2	95%		£4,200	£12,250
Bristol	20 / 16	25%	4	12.2	100%		£3,950	£13,100
Cardiff	30 / 5	11%	4	13.9	83%		£3,300-£11,130	£11,700
Edinburgh	46 / 3	60%	9	15.1	97%		£4,600	£14,000
Hertfordshire	10 / 47	30%	3	8.6	82%	64%	£3,833	£9,500
Leeds	143 / 5	33%	7	12.2	98%		£3,300	£12,600
Manchester	43 / 3	70%	10	8.7	100%		£3,300	£12,900
Plymouth	29 / 6	34%	5	15.6	61%		£3,950	£9,850
Portsmouth	31 / 24	31%	3	16.9	94%		£3,300	£9,650
Royal Holloway	39 / 3	40%	5	10.7	100%		£3,300	£12,785
Southampton	189 / 19	51%	7	15.8	98%		£3,300	£12,000
UCL	37 / 19	11%	8	8.1	100%		£3,300	£16,870
York	62 / 1	44%	3	12.1	98%		£3,300	£12,555

Geography and environmental studies

	Full-time/part-time	% students from outside the UK	Expenditure per student (FTE)	Student:staff ratio	Full-time completion rate	Part-time completion rate	Tuition fees: home/EU students	Tuition fees: international students
Aberdeen	43 / 4	62%	6	15.7	92%		£3,315	£9,000
Aberystwyth	25 / 24	6%	6	15.2		100%	£3,300	£8,475
Birkbeck College	1 / 41	4%	3	16.1		96%	£3,330	£12,336
Birmingham	44 / 7	14%	6	20.3	82%		£4,200	£9,450
Coventry	57 / 10	73%	3	17.5	78%		£3,420-£4,230	£8,600
Derby	6 / 64	13%	8	17.1	91%		modular	£8,200
Dundee	13 / 24	46%	3	15.8	81%		£3,250	£8,000
UEA	198 / 5	50%	5	15.3	94%		£3,300	£9,500
Edinburgh	93 / 7	49%	10	10.1	94%		£4,600	£10,650
Exeter	16 / 21	12%	4	22.5	83%		£4,000-£8,250	£9,600
Glamorgan	23 / 32	11%	3	9.3	83%	90%	£3,300	£9,980
Greenwich	47 / 101	51%	4	20.6		90%	£3,600-£7,410	£8,900
King's College London	104 / 36	33%	5	18.0	91%	94%	£3,900-£5,900	£9,100
Lancaster	41 / 1	26%	5	18.6	95%		£3,530	£9,200
Leeds	145 / 70	36%	6	18.2	98%	89%	£3,300	£9,700

	Full-time/ part-time	% students from outside the UK	Expenditure per student (FTE)	Student:staff ratio	Full-time completion rate	Part-time completion rate	Tuition fees: home/EU students	Tuition fees: international students
London School of Economics	193 / 16	84%	4	13.0	99%	100%	£9,144–£17,352	£13,452
Manchester	34 / 3	38%	5	22.4	100%		£3,300	£12,900
Manchester Met	34 / 195	42%	4	15.2		38%	£3,320–£3,890	£8,420
Northumbria	39 / 0	28%	4	16.2	92%		£3,996	£8,300
Nottingham	31 / 48	36%	5	16.6	93%		£3,750	£10,200
Oxford	105 / 0	79%	10	14.0	100%		£5,200	£13,105
Reading	43 / 8	16%	8	20.8	99%		£3,575–£15,750	£9,350
Royal Holloway	35 / 3	30%	6	11.0	98%		£3,300	£11,555
Staffordshire	0 / 56	4%	8	9.1		91%		£9,395
Stirling	55 / 15	17%	4	27.0	71%		£4,200	£9,200
Strathclyde	15 / 33	19%	3	20.1	90%		£3,235	£8,930
Sussex	43 / 9	54%	4	16.3	93%		£4,100	£9,500
UCL	45 / 16	43%	9	13.1	99%	90%	£3,300	£12,940
Ulster	15 / 135	29%	3	22.9		59%	£3,420	£8,649
UWE Bristol	26 / 33	16%	4	15.5	77%			£8,250

Mathematics

	Full-time/ part-time	% students from outside the UK	Expenditure per student (FTE)	Student:staff ratio	Full-time completion rate	Part-time completion rate	Tuition fees: home/EU students	Tuition fees: international students
Aston	28 / 7	66%	3	19.1	81%		£3,325–£8,950	£12,950
Birkbeck College	8 / 106	12%	2	11.2		81%	£3,330	£15,534
Brunel	36 / 25	82%	5	14.1	86%		£3,315–£5,130	£8,750
Cambridge	71 / 1	86%	10	13.8	93%		£5,434	£14,353
City	4 / 32	37%	4	21.0			£3,300	£19,500
Edinburgh	41 / 1	79%	7	17.2	73%		£4,600	£14,000
Heriot-Watt	79 / 95	80%	4	15.7	88%		£3,790	£11,810
King's College London	48 / 50	41%	5	14.5	96%	89%	£3,900–£5,900	£17,750
London School of Economics	169 / 14	85%	5	19.6	98%		£9,144–£17,352	£21,600
Manchester	78 / 6	57%	7	16.7	82%		£3,300	£12,900
Napier	20 / 72	16%	4	11.0	41%	31%	£3,675–£5,020	£10,665
The Open University	0 / 481	0%	2	27.4		100%		
Oxford	81 / 149	63%	10	14.7	95%	92%	£5,200	£14,710
Royal Holloway	63 / 34	46%	7	11.5	100%	97%	£3,300	£12,785
Sheffield	20 / 30	30%	4	14.5	100%		£3,300	£13,050
Sheffield Hallam	0 / 144	29%	4	18.3		45%	£3,300–£7,800	£11,900
Southampton	121 / 57	32%	5	14.2	100%	100%	£3,300	£12,000
Strathclyde	26 / 30	48%	3	18.7	74%		£3,235	£11,465
UCL	41 / 3	55%	6	16.7	88%		£3,300	£16,870
Warwick	78 / 30	59%	8	12.8	95%		£5,330	£13,350
York	90 / 2	85%	4	15.4	91%		£3,300	£12,555

Physics

	Full-time/ part-time	% students from outside the UK	Expenditure per student (FTE)	Student:staff ratio	Full-time completion rate	Part-time completion rate	Tuition fees: home/EU students	Tuition fees: international students
Birmingham	72 / 17	15%	4	11.7	96%		£4,200	£12,250
Heriot-Watt	42 / 13	51%	3	10.8	86%		£3,790	£11,810
Imperial College	40 / 5	60%	7	8.2	97%		£3,300	£16,750
Leeds	41 / 8	26%	9	9.0	100%		£3,300	£12,600
Surrey	102 / 30	39%	3	11.6	96%		£3,600–£8,600	£13,300
UCL	51 / 32	37%	6	7.5	100%	100%	£3,300	£16,870

● Social sciences

	Full-time/ part-time	% students from outside the UK	Expenditure per student (FTE)	Student:staff ratio	Full-time completion rate	Part-time completion rate	Tuition fees: home/EU students	Tuition fees: international students
Business and management studies								
Aberdeen	292 / 10	89%	4	18.4	97%		£3,315	£9,000
Abertay Dundee	67 / 27	61%	4	20.0	67%	85%	£3,315	£8,650
Aberystwyth	74 / 112	83%	3	23.9		91%	£4,150	£8,475
Anglia Ruskin	161 / 630	27%	4	19.8	66%	83%	£1,550-£7,800	£9,300
University of the Arts, London	232 / 113	53%	4	23.0	97%	100%	£3,300	£10,400
Aston	825 / 506	57%	6	26.5	94%	88%	£3,325-£8,950	£8,570
Bangor	115 / 14	62%	3	12.7	81%		£3,400	£8,500
Bath	319 / 943	37%	6	24.9	97%	88%	£4,000	£10,300
Bedfordshire	383 / 322	78%	3	32.4	88%	81%	£4,150-£4,450	£8,200
Birkbeck College	67 / 152	22%	4	16.2	91%	83%	£3,330	£12,336
Birmingham	1,177 / 573	66%	6	20.8	93%	92%	£4,200	£9,450
Birmingham City	454 / 447	44%	4	24.1	56%	72%	£4,700	£9,400
Bolton	142 / 142	45%	3	21.8	92%	72%	£3,717-£4,755	£7,800
Bournemouth	578 / 210	68%	4	28.0	89%	70%	£3,800-£8,000	£7,500
Bradford	514 / 963	60%	6	19.7	85%	82%	£3,960	£8,500
Brighton	187 / 224	40%	3	25.7	87%	80%	£3,630	£9,500
Brunel	254 / 263	79%	4	25.2	90%		£3,315-£5,130	£8,500
Bucks New University	72 / 179	29%	3	27.0	70%	90%	£3,840	£7,700
Cambridge	220 / 106	83%	9	9.3	67%		£5,434	£11,371
Canterbury Christ Church	72 / 325	15%	2	20.4	74%	71%	£4,050	£8,355
Cardiff	540 / 133	77%	4	19.4	73%	85%	£12,060	£9,100
Central Lancashire	471 / 538	35%	5	16.4	71%	59%	£3,300	£8,950
Chester	21 / 243	4%	3	20.8	82%	56%	£3,510	£7,182
Chichester	0 / 55	0%	2	35.2		100%	£3,125-£3,825	£7,400
City	1,160 / 2,092	61%	8	21.8	92%	88%	£19,500	£19,500
Coventry	317 / 510	36%	3	32.8	71%	75%	£3,420-£4,230	£8,600
Cranfield University	457 / 623	42%	10	7.9	97%	83%		
De Montfort	249 / 717	21%	3	22.9	76%	90%	£3,315	£7,990
Derby	140 / 423	23%	3	24.2	90%	84%	modular	£8,200
Dundee	102 / 110	80%	3	15.3	84%		£3,250	£8,000
Durham	787 / 748	46%	6	22.4	97%	67%	£12,000	£10,150
UEA	303 / 91	69%	6	31.0	89%	76%	£3,300	£9,500
East London	335 / 242	59%	4	24.7	82%	77%	£4,560-£9,600	£8,400
Edge Hill	0 / 116	0%	3	20.4		70%	£1,600-£3,600	£7,900
Edinburgh	271 / 125	54%	6	26.5	91%	93%	£4,600	£10,650
Essex	188 / 77	77%	3	19.8	87%	83%	£3,500-£7,000	£9,990
Exeter	330 / 227	77%	6	19.3	94%	90%	£4,000-£8,250	£9,600
Glamorgan	426 / 955	28%	7	15.8	90%	94%	£3,300	£9,980
Glasgow	629 / 67	86%	6	19.6	100%	100%	£3,750	£9,400
Glasgow Caledonian	386 / 455	36%	3	23.8	42%	48%	£3,315	£9,000
Gloucestershire	50 / 368	14%	4	23.2	76%	71%	£3,445-£8,725	£8,720
Glyndŵr University	75 / 99	45%	3	23.6	76%	63%	£3,300	£8,300
Greenwich	398 / 470	63%	3	26.9	59%	72%	£3,600-£7,410	£8,900
Heriot-Watt	334 / 1,964	26%	6	27.9	88%	96%	£3,790	£9,450

	Full-time/ part-time	% students from outside the UK	Expenditure per student (FTE)	Student:staff ratio	Full-time completion rate	Part-time completion rate	Tuition fees: home/EU students	Tuition fees: international students
Hertfordshire	554 / 252	67%	3	26.2	71%	80%	£3,833	£9,500
Huddersfield	215 / 399	38%	3	20.3	90%	81%	£3,900	£8,500
Hull	371 / 408	60%	4	28.0	86%	84%	£3,300	£8,500
Imperial College	462 / 255	54%	9	21.4	99%	91%	£3,300	£24,250
Kent	190 / 129	58%	4	20.3	98%		£3,500	£9,870
King's College London	145 / 26	64%	5	21.8	99%		£3,900–£5,900	£9,100
Kingston	480 / 844	32%	4	25.5	84%	84%	£3,400	£9,000
Lancaster	474 / 591	44%	7	16.4	95%	94%	£4,400	£9,200
Leeds	844 / 136	73%	6	17.0	98%	97%	£3,300	£9,700
Leeds Met	385 / 670	37%	4	22.8	83%	78%	£3,400	£8,000
Leicester	275 / 1,221	23%	7	26.0	89%	43%	£3,300–£6,450	£11,250
Lincoln	172 / 379	29%	2	22.6	91%	68%	£3,338	£8,730
Liverpool	252 / 37	82%	6	21.6	93%	84%	£3,300	£9,100
Liverpool John Moores	317 / 536	51%	3	27.0	76%	83%	£3,145	£8,320
London Business School	824 / 601	69%	10	14.9	100%	100%	£29,700	£29,700
London School of Economics	636 / 56	89%	5	16.2	99%		£13,452–£21,600	£13,452 -£21,600
London South Bank	932 / 950	44%	3		75%	49%	£3,890	£8,845
Loughborough	691 / 605	48%	5	24.6	95%	84%	£3,350	£9,850
Manchester	786 / 882	46%	8	16.2	96%	87%	£3,300	£12,900
Manchester Met	252 / 737	23%	3	23.8	73%	83%	£3,320–£3,890	£8,420
Middlesex	492 / 1,196	63%	4	38.0	77%	80%	£4,600–£6,870	£9,400
Napier	292 / 745	42%	3	25.9	65%	47%	£3,675–£5,020	£9,180
Newcastle	259 / 88	66%	4	25.1	95%	95%	£4,070	£9,915
Newport	180 / 454	25%	3	26.4	79%	76%	£4,350	£8,450
Northampton	234 / 509	43%	2	25.7	73%	69%	£3,600–£4,500	£7,950
Northumbria	869 / 510	65%	4	23.5	78%	75%	£3,996	£8,300
Nottingham	467 / 533	78%	6	21.0	95%	90%	£3,750	£10,200
Nottingham Trent	247 / 936	28%	5	21.3	82%	78%	£3,145–£6,900	£7,550
The Open University	0 / 4,088	0%	4	28.3		99%		
Oxford	280 / 83	82%		8.3	99%	100%	£5,200	£13,105
Oxford Brookes	323 / 559	47%	4	22.1	90%	93%	£3,990–£7,900	£9,570
Plymouth	89 / 164	34%	6	18.7	91%	84%	£3,950	£8,950
Portsmouth	415 / 592	43%	3	28.4	90%	81%	£3,300	£8,350
Queen Mary	246 / 33	78%	4	30.1	98%		£3,964	£9,000
Queen's, Belfast	60 / 233	16%	3	13.4	95%	98%	£3,319	£8,970
Reading	363 / 271	54%	5	17.8	86%	77%	£3,575–£15,750	£9,350
Robert Gordon	426 / 976	54%	3	22.7	54%	58%	£3,315–£7,712	£9,200
Royal Agricultural College	43 / 46	88%	4	23.4	78%	70%	£5,125–£6,650	£7,650
Royal Holloway	273 / 5	87%	4	23.4	94%		£3,300	£11,555
Salford	398 / 918	44%	3	17.8	89%	89%	£3,300	£8,400
Sheffield	280 / 5	81%	3	21.6	91%	100%	£3,300	£9,920
Sheffield Hallam	509 / 872	41%	3	27.3	84%	52%	£3,300–£7,800	£8,100
SOAS	36 / 4	83%	4	14.1	100%		£4,090	£11,460
Southampton	787 / 212	68%	4	30.6	98%	93%	£3,300	£9,380
Southampton Solent	144 / 188	36%	3	33.2	76%	86%	£2,675–£3,400	£8,495
St Andrews	339 / 25	90%	4	15.5	94%		£3,315–£5,800	£13,250
Staffordshire	259 / 450	51%	6	19.5	94%	92%		£9,395
Stirling	587 / 300	75%	3	15.0	84%	75%	£4,200	£9,200
Strathclyde	432 / 1,324	27%	7	18.9	86%	70%	£3,235	£8,930

	Full-time/part-time	% students from outside the UK	Expenditure per student (FTE)	Student:staff ratio	Full-time completion rate	Part-time completion rate	Tuition fees: home/EU students	Tuition fees: international students
Sunderland	539 / 200	67%	3	31.2	95%	81%	£3,965	£8,600
Surrey	884 / 467	69%	5	23.8	90%	72%	£3,600-£8,600	£8,600
Sussex	72 / 9	80%	3	18.0	92%		£4,100	£9,500
Swansea	166 / 52	82%	3	26.3	62%		£3,300	£9,010
Teesside	80 / 419	7%	6	18.0	82%	73%	£3,950	£8,250
Thames Valley	386 / 597	34%	3	24.9	77%	83%	£4,350	£8,650
Trinity College, Carmarthen	0 / 85	0%	3	5.4		100%	£3,150	£6,500
UCL	80 / 76	13%	6	14.9	97%	89%	£3,300	£24,740
Ulster	231 / 567	26%	3	25.5	83%	86%	£3,420	£8,649
UWIC	458 / 1,238	74%	3	17.7	93%	99%	£3,330	£8,800
Warwick	566 / 3,385	42%	8	16.2	96%	78%	£5,330	£10,250
UWE Bristol	281 / 559	21%	3	22.9	74%	29%		£8,250
Westminster	946 / 1,547	42%	3	24.9	81%	77%	£3,800-£13,750	£9,750
Wolverhampton	94 / 768	26%	3	17.0	68%	61%	£3,418-£4,400	£8,200
Worcester	40 / 86	36%	3	22.3	77%	80%	£3,600	£8,000
York	161 / 2	93%	4	14.9	97%	100%	£3,300	£9,510
York St John	17 / 33	32%	3	28.6	100%	83%	£3,833	£7,800

Economics

	Full-time/part-time	% students from outside the UK	Expenditure per student (FTE)	Student:staff ratio	Full-time completion rate	Part-time completion rate	Tuition fees: home/EU students	Tuition fees: international students
Bath	65 / 85	52%	4	16.5	93%	100%	£4,000	£10,300
Birkbeck College	71 / 153	27%	3	23.9	90%	86%	£3,330	£12,336
Birmingham	56 / 13	68%	8	17.4	92%		£4,200	£9,450
Bradford	41 / 41	89%	5	11.8	83%		£3,960	£8,500
Bristol	115 / 91	77%	5	20.2	95%		£3,950	£10,200
Brunel	104 / 39	87%	3	16.9	82%		£3,315-£5,130	£8,500
Cambridge	71 / 7	77%	8	16.2	100%		£5,434	£11,371
Cardiff	132 / 0	92%	5	19.4	84%		£3,300-£11,130	£9,100
City	85 / 93	70%	4	17.7	88%		£3,300	£7,950
UEA	58 / 9	80%	3	27.4			£3,300	£9,500
Edinburgh	85 / 3	70%	8	15.9	85%		£4,600	£10,650
Essex	73 / 7	96%	4	15.2	86%		£3,500-£7,000	£9,990
Glasgow	172 / 79	60%	3	17.6	100%	100%	£3,750	£9,400
Greenwich	28 / 37	82%	2	30.5		80%	£3,600-£7,410	£8,900
Kent	22 / 26	78%	4	17.2	96%		£3,500	£9,870
Lancaster	60 / 0	88%	10	16.4	95%		£3,530	£9,200
Leeds Met	37 / 20	100%	9	20.4	100%	85%	£3,400	£8,000
Leicester	70 / 0	86%	4	22.4	92%		£3,300-£6,995	£9,475
London School of Economics	232 / 4	85%	7	12.6	99%		£13,452-£17,352	£13,452-£17,352
Loughborough	229 / 2	96%	5	20.4	93%		£3,350	£9,850
Manchester	120 / 9	77%	6	19.1	89%		£3,300	£12,900
Middlesex	18 / 18	88%	4	39.7		84%	£4,600-£6,870	£9,400
Newcastle	36 / 3	82%	4	23.1	91%		£4,070	£9,915
Nottingham	84 / 115	68%	5	17.2	89%		£3,750	£10,200
Oxford	282 / 0	77%	10	11.4	99%		£5,200	£13,105
Portsmouth	95 / 4	91%	4	17.4	79%		£3,300	£8,350
Sheffield	90 / 10	70%	3	21.6	90%		£3,300	£9,920
SOAS	68 / 5	53%	5	14.1	98%		£4,090-£11,740	£11,460
Southampton	63 / 0	77%	3	22.6	96%		£3,300	£9,380

	Full-time/ part-time	% students from outside the UK	Expenditure per student (FTE)	Student:staff ratio	Full-time completion rate	Part-time completion rate	Tuition fees: home/EU students	Tuition fees: international students
St Andrews	128 / 0	91%	5	15.5	92%		£3,315–£5,800	£11,000 –£11,300
Strathclyde	24 / 73	62%	7	22.0	90%		£3,235	£8,930
Surrey	58 / 28	77%	4	19.9	100%		£3,600–£8,600	£8,600
Sussex	62 / 2	77%	3	18.0	95%		£4,100	£9,500
UCL	98 / 8	67%	8	15.9	98%		£3,300	£12,940
Warwick	139 / 17	79%	8	14.0	96%		£5,330	£10,250
York	322 / 24	81%	6	13.8	96%		£3,300	£9,510

Education

	Full-time/ part-time	% students from outside the UK	Expenditure per student (FTE)	Student:staff ratio	Full-time completion rate	Part-time completion rate	Tuition fees: home/EU students	Tuition fees: international students
Aberdeen	400 / 728	4%	7	14.9	85%	77%	£3,315	£9,000
Aberystwyth	248 / 99	16%	4	24.1	96%	81%	£3,300	£8,475
Anglia Ruskin	190 / 590	4%	6	19.4	90%	70%	£1,550–£7,800	£9,300
University of the Arts, London	0 / 149	2%	10	5.7		90%	£3,300	£10,400
Bangor	265 / 263	6%	3	23.7	100%	50%	£3,400	£8,500
Bath	196 / 448	39%	5	16.9	93%	100%	£4,000	£10,300
Bath Spa	495 / 1,834	1%	3	27.6	92%	15%	£3,970	£9,000
Bedfordshire	200 / 370	4%	4	15.9	89%	58%	£4,150–£4,450	£8,200
Birmingham	498 / 1,355	10%	5	25.6	92%	67%	£4,200	£9,450
Birmingham City	328 / 902	1%	4	19.3	94%	44%	£4,700	£9,400
Bishop Grosseteste UC	288 / 430	1%	2	25.1	99%	34%	£2,310	£7,725
Bolton	275 / 303	2%	4	15.9	90%	86%	£3,717–£4,755	£7,800
Bradford	5 / 57	18%	7	20.7		78%	£3,960	£8,500
Brighton	440 / 446	14%	3	22.6	84%	88%	£3,630	£9,500
Bristol	352 / 705	27%	7	12.7	92%	87%	£3,950	£10,200
Brunel	334 / 400	15%	4	15.0	88%	78%	£3,315–£5,130	£8,500
Buckingham	60 / 0	15%	4		98%		£8,800–£12,200	£8,800 –£12,200
Bucks New University	0 / 124	2%	10	4.7		92%	£3,840	£7,700
Cambridge	508 / 2,246	1%	6	13.6	94%	95%	£5,434	£11,371
Canterbury Christ Church	696 / 1,304	6%	4	16.7	79%	52%	£4,050	£8,355
Central Lancashire	45 / 321	2%			98%	65%	£3,300	£8,950
Central School of Speech and Drama	62 / 13	3%	3	30.2	92%	67%	£6,772	£12,937
Chester	245 / 1,089	1%	4	25.9	90%	68%	£3,510	£7,182
Chichester	269 / 576	0%	3	23.8	94%	33%	£3,125–£3,825	£7,400
Cumbria	1,110 / 818	5%	3	20.3	89%	82%	£3,330	£8,250
Derby	121 / 365	2%	3	20.0	90%	67%	modular	£8,200
Dundee	296 / 2,258	21%	3	18.2	84%	82%	£3,250	£8,000
Durham	366 / 501	8%	5	18.3	89%	75%	£3,996	£10,150
UEA	433 / 233	6%	9	8.1	88%	54%	£3,300	£9,500
East London	527 / 96	8%	4	18.1	93%	73%	£4,560–£9,600	£8,400
Edge Hill	668 / 5,388	1%	3	27.3	93%	52%	£1,600–£3,600	£7,900
Edinburgh	766 / 555	11%	6	17.3	93%	85%	£4,600	£10,650
Exeter	698 / 374	18%	6	18.9	93%	62%	£4,000–£8,250	£9,600
Glamorgan	11 / 31	40%	3		73%	100%	£3,300	£9,980
Glasgow	653 / 1,045	5%	3	19.3	100%	100%	£3,750	£9,400
Gloucestershire	245 / 582	6%	6	20.3	89%	82%	£3,445–£8,725	£8,720
Goldsmiths	537 / 39	5%	4	19.6	89%	92%	£3,300–£6,320	£9,580

	Full-time/ part-time	% students from outside the UK	Expenditure per student (FTE)	Student:staff ratio	Full-time completion rate	Part-time completion rate	Tuition fees: home/EU students	Tuition fees: international students
Greenwich	503 / 1,369	5%	4	24.2	87%	79%	£3,600–£7,410	£8,900
Hertfordshire	244 / 483	2%	4	12.9	91%	28%	£3,833	£9,500
Huddersfield	383 / 1,122	1%	6	17.1	92%	86%	£3,900	£8,500
Hull	313 / 695	25%	4	24.3	89%	93%	£3,300	£8,500
Institute of Education	1,648 / 2,909	16%	8	15.2	91%	88%		
King's College London	324 / 314	9%	6	14.4	91%	87%	£3,900–£5,900	£9,100
Kingston	236 / 531	4%	5	13.1	92%	88%	£3,400	£9,000
Leeds	606 / 597	19%	6	15.3	92%	89%	£3,300	£9,700
Leeds Met	64 / 399	6%	4	17.0	95%	83%	£3,400	£8,000
Leeds Trinity & All Saints	175 / 0	3%	3	21.0	91%		£1,590	£7,975
Leicester	338 / 350	10%	5	18.8	92%	62%	£3,300	£9,050
Liverpool John Moores	352 / 453	7%	4	17.6	91%	80%	£3,145	£8,320
London South Bank	255 / 746	8%	3	35.2	98%	73%	£3,890	£8,845
Manchester	409 / 287	12%		17.0	95%	82%	£3,300	£12,900
Manchester Met	905 / 1,207	3%	4	21.5	90%	72%	£3,320–£3,890	£8,420
Marjon (St Mark and St John)	255 / 1,067	2%	3	25.0	91%	67%	£3,320	£8,350
Middlesex	400 / 949	8%	6	19.5	99%	73%	£4,600–£6,870	£9,400
Newcastle	281 / 129	4%	4	16.7	93%	87%	£4,070	£9,915
Newman University College	262 / 62	3%	3	17.7	90%	87%	£3,145	
Newport	161 / 757	1%	7	12.1	91%	71%	£4,350	£8,450
Northampton	85 / 187	7%	3	22.8	95%	31%	£3,600–£4,500	£7,950
Northumbria	234 / 462	3%	5	19.9	94%	39%	£3,996	£8,300
Nottingham	485 / 719	20%	7	13.7	90%	80%	£3,750	£10,200
Nottingham Trent	318 / 500	3%	4	19.8	94%	81%	£3,145–£6,900	£7,550
The Open University	0 / 3,133	0%	3	23.3		97%		
Oxford	246 / 2	28%	8	10.8	97%		£5,200	£13,105
Oxford Brookes	475 / 1,460	4%	4	21.4	92%	65%	£3,990–£7,900	£9,570
Plymouth	310 / 3,447	2%	6	20.8	92%	79%	£3,950	£8,950
Portsmouth	214 / 182	12%	6	17.9	90%	96%	£3,300	£8,350
Queen's, Belfast	228 / 550	11%	6	13.7	98%	98%	£3,319	£8,970
Reading	376 / 522	13%	4	19.4	86%	55%	£3,575–£15,750	£9,350
Roehampton	574 / 270	21%	3	20.2	91%	90%	£3,700–£6,500	£9,000
Sheffield Hallam	596 / 1,280	9%	3	22.0	91%	76%	£3,300–£7,800	£8,100
Southampton Solent	0 / 54	6%	2	17.3		88%	£2,675–£3,400	£8,495
St Mary's UC, Belfast	16 / 95	2%	2	15.6	100%	88%		
St Mary's UC, Twickenham	439 / 240	17%	3	26.0	90%	80%	£3,090	£7,200
Staffordshire	52 / 124	1%	5	14.1	89%	88%		£9,395
Stirling	94 / 448	8%	4	10.6	97%	85%	£4,200	£9,200
Stranmillis UC	32 / 113	2%	2	17.1	97%	95%	£3,320	£8,970
Strathclyde	1,296 / 2,309	3%	4	18.2	92%	52%	£3,235	£8,930
Sunderland	289 / 186	6%	4	19.5	83%	48%	£3,965	£8,600
Sussex	207 / 244	6%	4	10.5	87%	90%	£4,100	£9,500
Swansea Met	420 / 321	4%	2	23.2	87%	57%	£3,160	£7,550
Teesside	22 / 201	2%	8	24.5	33%	68%	£3,950	£8,250
Thames Valley	31 / 81	5%	2	23.4	69%	70%	£4,350	£8,650
Trinity College, Carmarthen	111 / 45	6%	2	17.1	94%	54%	£3,150	£6,500
Ulster	198 / 435	19%	3	15.0	97%	87%	£3,420	£8,649
UWIC	405 / 183	4%	5	21.9	93%	75%	£3,330	£8,800
Warwick	574 / 400	18%	7	15.5	93%	72%	£5,330	£10,250

	Full-time/ part-time	% students from outside the UK	Expenditure per student (FTE)	Student:staff ratio	Full-time completion rate	Part-time completion rate	Tuition fees: home/EU students	Tuition fees: international students
UWE Bristol	361 / 217	4%	3	24.3	83%	47%		£8,250
Winchester	61 / 635	1%	2	22.0	92%	75%	£3,883	£8,070
Wolverhampton	384 / 1,252	7%	4	18.6	81%	32%	£3,418–£4,400	£8,200
Worcester	375 / 801	2%	4	18.6	90%	40%	£3,600	£8,000
York	294 / 101	44%	5	20.9	92%	93%	£3,300	£9,510
York St John	168 / 253	0%	4	18.9	90%	80%	£3,833	£7,800

Law

	Full-time/ part-time	% students from outside the UK	Expenditure per student (FTE)	Student:staff ratio	Full-time completion rate	Part-time completion rate	Tuition fees: home/EU students	Tuition fees: international students
Aberdeen	251 / 15	40%	4	20.7	100%		£3,315	£9,000
Aberystwyth	15 / 83	33%	3	20.5		65%	£8,100	£8,475
Anglia Ruskin	96 / 131	24%	6	19.5	83%	78%	£1,550–£7,800	£9,300
Bedfordshire	20 / 16	75%	3	28.0	86%		£4,150–£4,450	£8,200
Birkbeck College	21 / 43	9%	3	23.9		100%	£3,330	£12,336
Birmingham	159 / 16	37%	9	17.4	84%		£4,200	£9,450
Birmingham City	71 / 79	7%	5	18.5	77%	53%	£4,700	£9,400
Bournemouth	97 / 17	33%	4	38.0	21%		£3,800–£8,000	£7,500
Brighton	0 / 38	8%	3	30.8		69%	£3,630	£9,500
Bristol	143 / 294	40%	6	20.2	96%	91%	£3,950	£10,200
Brunel	71 / 77	52%	3	16.9	73%	96%	£3,315–£5,130	£8,500
Cambridge	108 / 0	86%	10	16.2	100%		£5,434	£11,371
Cardiff	426 / 149	24%	8	18.5	94%	88%	£9,600	£9,100
Central Lancashire	112 / 175	10%	4	28.1	84%	72%	£3,300	£8,950
City	1,079 / 377	33%	5	17.7	95%	80%	£3,300	£7,950
De Montfort	74 / 405	8%	2	24.1	90%	80%	£3,315	£7,990
Dundee	243 / 278	69%	5	19.8	93%		£3,250	£8,000
Durham	168 / 0	90%	7	18.6	96%		£3,996	£10,150
UEA	119 / 47	64%	4	27.4	97%	96%	£3,300	£9,500
East London	152 / 34	39%	5	21.5	93%	58%	£4,560–£9,600	£8,400
Edinburgh	266 / 21	35%	9	15.9	94%		£4,600	£10,650
Essex	153 / 22	81%	5	15.2	98%		£3,500–£7,000	£9,990
Exeter	85 / 99	83%	4	16.5	99%		£4,000–£8,250	£9,600
Glamorgan	128 / 152	8%	3		89%	46%	£3,300	£9,980
Glasgow	214 / 62	70%	4	17.6	100%	100%	£3,750	£9,400
Hertfordshire	90 / 119	28%	3	32.1	84%	86%	£3,833	£9,500
Huddersfield	41 / 179	5%	3	27.3	96%	82%	£3,900	£8,500
Hull	40 / 22	76%	4	16.0	94%		£3,300	£8,500
Kent	139 / 152	65%	5	17.2	97%	95%	£3,500	£9,870
King's College London	349 / 400	37%	7	14.3	99%	92%	£3,900–£5,900	£9,100
Kingston	54 / 36	51%	3	27.0	100%	79%	£3,400–£5,700	£9,000
Leeds	139 / 23	51%	5	19.0	94%		£3,300	£9,700
Leeds Met	82 / 158	2%	10	20.4	69%	68%	£3,400	£8,000
Leicester	50 / 150	23%	5	22.4	93%	73%	£3,300	£9,050
Liverpool	32 / 10	50%	5	21.7	100%		£3,300	£9,100
Liverpool John Moores	73 / 96	6%	3	28.5	96%	96%	£3,145	£8,320
London School of Economics	298 / 31	80%	8	12.6	99%	93%	£9,144–£17,352	£13,452
Manchester	229 / 128	58%	7	19.1	97%	87%	£3,300	£12,900
Manchester Met	324 / 197	4%	4	19.8	76%	48%	£3,320–£3,890	£8,420
Middlesex	42 / 70	21%	5	39.7		83%	£4,600–£6,870	£9,400
Northumbria	319 / 1,206	34%	4	27.4	65%	60%	£3,996	£8,300

	Full-time/ part-time	% students from outside the UK	Expenditure per student (FTE)	Student:staff ratio	Full-time completion rate	Part-time completion rate	Tuition fees: home/EU students	Tuition fees: international students
Nottingham	124 / 32	71%	6	17.2	92%		£3,750	£10,200
Nottingham Trent	1,082 / 625	10%	7	16.7	83%	85%	£3,145-£6,900	£7,550
Oxford	168 / 72	80%	10	11.4	100%	100%	£5,200	£13,105
Oxford Brookes	203 / 12	20%	4	19.2	8%		£3,990-£7,900	£9,570
Plymouth	56 / 4	3%	7	16.4	89%		£3,950	£8,950
Portsmouth	41 / 33	69%	5	17.4	94%		£3,300	£8,350
Queen Mary	334 / 157	56%	8	17.0	97%	96%	£3,964	£9,000
Queen's, Belfast	292 / 147	12%	4	19.5	97%	97%	£3,319	£8,970
Robert Gordon	115 / 236	39%	3	24.2	78%	52%	£3,315-£7,712	£9,200
Salford	9 / 97	3%	6	22.1		83%	£3,300	£8,400
Sheffield	290 / 3	27%	3	23.7	91%		£3,300	£9,920
SOAS	102 / 23	66%	7	14.1	100%		£4,090	£11,460
Southampton	188 / 5	84%	4	22.6	98%		£3,300	£9,380
Staffordshire	127 / 472	23%	5	24.6	89%	52%		£9,395
Strathclyde	343 / 270	17%	8	22.0	99%	86%	£3,235	£8,930
Sussex	73 / 13	50%	4	18.0	93%		£4,100	£9,500
Swansea	206 / 6	47%	4	24.0	93%		£3,300	£9,010
UCL	346 / 102	59%	9	15.9	99%	96%	£3,300	£12,940
Warwick	105 / 42	61%	10	14.0	92%		£5,330	£10,250
UWE Bristol	548 / 340	9%	4	20.2	85%	62%		£8,250
Westminster	317 / 151	35%	3	20.5	97%	84%	£3,800-£13,750	£9,750
Wolverhampton	51 / 167	56%	4	26.9	73%	76%	£3,418-£4,400	£8,200

Media studies, communications and librarianship

	Full-time/ part-time	% students from outside the UK	Expenditure per student (FTE)	Student:staff ratio	Full-time completion rate	Part-time completion rate	Tuition fees: home/EU students	Tuition fees: international students
Aberystwyth	28 / 796	30%	7	27.8		40%	£3,300	£8,475
University of the Arts, London	142 / 27	42%	9	22.8	98%		£3,300	£10,400
Birmingham City	77 / 27	20%	9	15.1	83%	12%	£4,700	£9,400
Bournemouth	240 / 88	38%		15.7	88%	78%	£3,800-£8,000	£7,500
Brunel	15 / 37	46%	3	31.7	87%		£3,315-£5,130	£8,500
Cardiff	289 / 0	50%	9	18.9	95%		£3,300-£10,600	£9,100
Central Lancashire	136 / 36	25%	5	20.4	98%		£3,300	£8,950
City	275 / 220	40%	7	16.2	95%		£3,300	£7,950
De Montfort	49 / 14	29%	1	18.9	79%		£3,315	£7,990
East London	28 / 9	46%	7	37.2	83%		£4,560-£9,600	£8,400
UC Falmouth	72 / 8	10%	4	25.8	96%		£3,440-£4,655	£10,145
Goldsmiths	212 / 22	62%	6	25.9	97%		£3,300-£6,320	£9,580
King's College London	58 / 19	55%	10	13.2	100%		£3,900-£5,900	£9,100
Kingston	53 / 12	37%	5	16.3	94%		£3,400-£4,957	£9,000
Leeds	176 / 5	77%	9	18.7	99%		£3,300	£9,700
Leeds Met	72 / 61	34%	6	29.3	91%	50%	£3,400	£8,000
Leeds Trinity & All Saints	52 / 108	1%	2	29.1	0%	19%	£1,590	£7,975
Leicester	150 / 216	29%	8	13.3	92%	56%	£3,300	£9,050
Liverpool John Moores	38 / 58	6%	4	20.4	88%	95%	£3,145	£8,320
London School of Economics	160 / 21	83%	8	15.0	100%		£9144-£17,352	£13,452
Loughborough	86 / 0	97%	5	18.0	100%		£3,350	£9,850
Manchester Met	59 / 104	10%	7	18.6	65%	76%	£3,320-£3,890	£8,420
Middlesex	21 / 45	76%	8	16.6		90%	£4,600-£6,870	£9,400
Napier	57 / 83	21%	6	19.4	56%		£3,675-£5,020	£9,180

	Full-time/ part-time	% students from outside the UK	Expenditure per student (FTE)	Student:staff ratio	Full-time completion rate	Part-time completion rate	Tuition fees: home/EU students	Tuition fees: international students
Newcastle	92 / 18	44%	8	16.7	93%		£4,070	£9,915
Nottingham Trent	61 / 18	36%	8	14.4	89%	96%	£3,145–£6,900	£7,550
Portsmouth	34 / 13	45%	2	19.4	100%		£3,300	£8,350
Robert Gordon	78 / 322	28%	4	15.4	29%	39%	£3,315–£7,712	£9,200
Royal Holloway	43 / 40	41%	7	14.8	94%	91%	£3,300	£11,555
Salford	46 / 66	13%	3	22.8	85%	95%	£3,300	£8,400
Sheffield	272 / 30	36%	4	18.3	97%	80%	£3,300	£9,920
Sheffield Hallam	24 / 141	46%	5	18.7		23%	£3,300–£7,800	£8,100
Southampton Solent	27 / 9	25%	4	22.9	55%		£2,675–£3,400	£8,495
Staffordshire	26 / 9	14%	2	19.0	80%			£9,395
Stirling	128 / 51	73%	3	22.1	91%	80%	£4,200	£9,200
Sunderland	160 / 23	21%	4	16.2	94%		£3,965	£8,600
Sussex	30 / 22	52%	3	19.0	94%		£4,100	£9,500
Thames Valley	71 / 33	33%	5	17.4	81%	70%	£4,350	£8,650
Ulster	57 / 40	37%	5	19.7	84%	96%	£3,420	£8,649
UWE Bristol	44 / 48	19%	2	17.1	75%	55%		£8,250
Westminster	368 / 153	64%	6	12.8	96%	75%	£3,800–£13,750	£9,750

Politics

	Full-time/ part-time	% students from outside the UK	Expenditure per student (FTE)	Student:staff ratio	Full-time completion rate	Part-time completion rate	Tuition fees: home/EU students	Tuition fees: international students
Aberdeen	35 / 4	51%	4	20.7	100%		£3,315	£9,000
Aberystwyth	83 / 69	49%	3	20.5		93%	£3,700	£8,475
Birkbeck College	38 / 180	12%	3	23.9	100%	90%	£3,330	£12,336
Birmingham	111 / 40	44%	9	17.4	97%	75%	£4,200	£9,450
Birmingham City	42 / 31	15%	5	18.5	64%	50%	£4,700	£9,400
Bradford	95 / 140	74%	6	11.8	92%	55%	£3,960	£8,500
Bristol	100 / 128	50%	6	20.2	94%		£3,950	£10,200
Brunel	32 / 12	34%	4	16.9	50%		£3,315–£5,130	£8,500
Cardiff	45 / 40	31%	5	21.0	75%		£3,300–£11,130	£9,100
Coventry	33 / 21	52%	5	19.4	88%	19%	£3,420–£4,230	£8,600
Dundee	16 / 20	47%	5	19.8	63%		£3,250	£8,000
Durham	86 / 0	51%	7	18.6	95%		£3,996	£10,150
UEA	74 / 3	39%	4	27.4	44%		£3,300	£9,500
Edinburgh	57 / 7	64%	9	15.9	91%		£4,600	£10,650
Essex	69 / 31	84%	5	15.2	94%		£3,500–£7,000	£9,990
Exeter	42 / 52	41%	4	16.5	97%		£4,000–£8,250	£9,600
Glasgow	85 / 10	40%	4	17.6	100%		£3,750	£9,400
Goldsmiths	33 / 11	36%	3	15.4	95%		£3,300–£6,320	£9,580
Hull	19 / 26	49%	4	16.0	90%		£3,300	£8,500
Kent	79 / 32	84%	5	17.2	95%	55%	£3,500	£9,870
King's College London	546 / 121	31%	7	14.3	91%	64%	£3,900–£5,900	£9,100
Kingston	48 / 13	54%	3	27.0	93%	70%	£3,400	£9,000
Lancaster	29 / 9	47%	6	15.2	89%		£3,530	£9,200
Leeds	208 / 15	49%	5	19.0	100%		£3,300	£9,700
Leicester	34 / 4	47%	5	22.4	91%		£3,300	£9,050
London School of Economics	740 / 41	84%	8	12.6	99%	86%	£9,144–£17,352	£13,452
London South Bank	33 / 5	68%	2	37.2	93%		£3,890	£8,845
Loughborough	33 / 2	54%	6	20.4	100%		£3,350	£9,850
Manchester	138 / 43	48%	7	19.1	97%		£3,300	£12,900
Middlesex	15 / 62	53%	5	39.7		92%	£4,600–£6,870	£9,400

	Full-time/ part-time	% students from outside the UK	Expenditure per student (FTE)	Student:staff ratio	Full-time completion rate	Part-time completion rate	Tuition fees: home/EU students	Tuition fees: international students
Newcastle	48 / 10	36%	5	23.1	91%		£4,070	£9,915
Northumbria	9 / 86	21%	4	27.4	84%	78%	£3,996	£8,300
Nottingham	80 / 83	52%	7	17.2	90%		£3,750	£10,200
Oxford	189 / 0	76%	10	11.4	99%		£5,200	£13,105
Oxford Brookes	28 / 16	48%	4	19.2	91%		£3,990-£7,900	£9,570
Queen's, Belfast	38 / 69	34%	5	19.5	97%		£3,319	£8,970
Reading	28 / 22	62%	3	19.8	100%		£3,575-£15,750	£9,350
Robert Gordon	30 / 48	65%	3	24.2	26%	35%	£3,315-£7,712	£9,200
Royal Holloway	35 / 6	61%	4	20.1	92%		£3,300	£11,555
Salford	15 / 23	26%	7	22.1	67%		£3,300	£8,400
Sheffield	81 / 5	42%	3	23.7	97%		£3,300	£9,920
SOAS	143 / 43	54%	7	14.1	98%	100%	£4,090-£11,740	£11,460
Southampton	67 / 9	43%	4	22.6	91%		£3,300	£9,380
St Andrews	74 / 3	73%	4	18.5	94%		£3,315-£5,800	£11,000 -£11,300
Sussex	74 / 15	62%	4	18.0	100%		£4,100	£9,500
Swansea	27 / 16	37%	4	24.0	78%		£3,300	£9,010
UCL	66 / 17	42%	9	15.9	100%		£3,300	£12,940
Warwick	107 / 22	70%	10	14.0	93%		£5,330	£10,250
Westminster	206 / 61	72%	3	20.5	96%	92%	£3,800-£13,750	£9,750
York	176 / 10	54%	7	13.8	99%		£3,300	£9,510

Social policy and administration

	Full-time/ part-time	% students from outside the UK	Expenditure per student (FTE)	Student:staff ratio	Full-time completion rate	Part-time completion rate	Tuition fees: home/EU students	Tuition fees: international students
Bath	15 / 22	41%	4	16.5	100%		£4,000	£10,300
Birmingham	280 / 426	25%	8	17.4	92%	83%	£4,200	£9,450
Bristol	43 / 96	34%	9	13.5	93%	68%	£3,950	£10,200
Brunel	18 / 37	25%	3	16.9	92%		£3,315-£5,130	£8,500
Cardiff	4 / 32	3%	7	18.5		73%	£3,300-£11,130	£9,100
City	16 / 107	24%	4	17.7	64%	83%	£3,300	£7,950
East London	22 / 45	22%	4	21.5	92%	67%	£4,560-£9,600	£8,400
Edinburgh	37 / 9	50%	7	15.9	94%		£4,600	£10,650
Leeds	48 / 45	44%	4	19.0	96%	83%	£3,300	£9,700
London School of Economics	232 / 65	65%	7	12.6	100%	97%	£9,144-£17,352	£13,452
Manchester	46 / 27	29%	6	19.1	91%		£3,300	£12,900
Middlesex	15 / 47	44%	4	39.7		93%	£4,600-£6,870	£9,400
Nottingham	36 / 14	60%	5	17.2	94%		£3,750	£10,200
The Open University	0 / 290	0%	2	28.2		94%		
Oxford	58 / 0	82%	10	11.4	98%		£5,200	£13,105
Queen's, Belfast	9 / 81	74%	4	19.5	100%		£3,319	£8,970
Sheffield Hallam	14 / 54	23%	3	24.0		75%	£3,300-£7,800	£8,100
Ulster	0 / 67	10%	3	19.1		91%	£3,420	£8,649
Warwick	84 / 9	2%	8	14.0	92%		£5,330	£10,250
UWE Bristol	8 / 84	4%	3	20.2		53%		£8,250
York	21 / 141	10%	6	13.8	100%	90%	£3,300	£9,510

Social work

	Full-time/ part-time	% students from outside the UK	Expenditure per student (FTE)	Student:staff ratio	Full-time completion rate	Part-time completion rate	Tuition fees: home/EU students	Tuition fees: international students
Anglia Ruskin	49 / 86	4%	7			82%	74%	£1,550-£7,800	£9,300
Bath	1 / 38	0%	10	9.9		82%	£4,000	£10,300
Birmingham	0 / 268	3%	9	15.0		77%	£4,200	£9,450

	Full-time/ part-time	% students from outside the UK	Expenditure per student (FTE)	Student:staff ratio	Full-time completion rate	Part-time completion rate	Tuition fees: home/EU students	Tuition fees: international students
Bradford	78 / 4	7%	3	23.7	83%		£3,960	£8,500
Brighton	71 / 316	7%	3	25.5	61%	74%	£3,630	£9,500
Bristol	108 / 291	8%	8	13.5	94%	89%	£3,950	£10,200
Brunel	84 / 66	5%	7	12.6	53%	90%	£3,315–£5,130	£8,500
Canterbury Christ Church	63 / 250	7%	4	25.6	62%	61%	£4,050	£8,355
Cardiff	137 / 52	3%	8	7.7	47%		£3,300–£11,130	£9,100
Central Lancashire	167 / 477	5%	9	12.1	63%	61%	£3,300	£8,950
Chichester	0 / 45	4%	2	15.7		36%	£3,125–£3,825	£7,400
Cumbria	0 / 230	0%	8	20.5		85%	£3,330	£8,250
De Montfort	9 / 257	3%	4	14.2		67%	£3,315	£7,990
Dundee	80 / 76	1%	5		84%	96%	£3,250	£8,000
UEA	122 / 131	8%	6	29.4	88%	82%	£3,300	£9,500
East London	110 / 529	7%		15.2	78%	70%	£4560–£9,600	£8,400
Edinburgh	106 / 21	9%	6	22.8	83%		£4,600	£10,650
Glyndŵr University	16 / 34	2%	3	17.3	55%	75%	£3,300	£8,300
Goldsmiths	64 / 73	3%	3		99%	96%	£3,300–£6,320	£9,580
Hertfordshire	84 / 12	0%	5	10.4	84%		£3,833	£9,500
Huddersfield	25 / 75	2%	3	24.7	93%	92%	£3,900	£8,500
Hull	107 / 14	5%	4	23.6	94%		£3,300	£8,500
Lancaster	92 / 4	1%	4	15.2	74%		£3,530	£9,200
Leeds Met	78 / 208	6%	6	24.0	86%	53%	£3,400	£8,000
Liverpool John Moores	66 / 65	0%	6		97%	50%	£3,145	£8,320
London South Bank	96 / 52	3%	4		65%	65%	£3,890	£8,845
Manchester	64 / 34	2%	6	14.5	85%		£3,300	£12,900
Manchester Met	153 / 27	8%	4	15.7	53%	75%	£3,320–£3,890	£8,420
Middlesex	76 / 25	4%	8	17.4	100%	95%	£4,600–£6,870	£9,400
Napier	23 / 13	3%	3	12.9	91%		£3,675–£5,020	£9,180
Northumbria	27 / 27	0%	4	18.8	84%	69%	£3,996	£8,300
Nottingham	96 / 42	3%	9	20.4	93%		£3,750	£10,200
Queen's, Belfast	0 / 67	3%	3	18.5		93%	£3,319	£8,970
Reading	0 / 159	2%	3	24.7		93%	£3,575–£15,750	£9,350
Robert Gordon	77 / 42	5%	3	14.9	95%	74%	£3,315–£7,712	£9,200
Royal Holloway	115 / 128	1%	3	21.3	98%	80%	£3,300	£11,555
Salford	185 / 156	3%	4	19.1	92%	82%	£3,300	£8,400
Sheffield	93 / 0	1%	6	6.9	92%		£3,300	£9,920
Southampton	87 / 217	2%	8	22.2	98%	83%	£3,300	£9,380
Strathclyde	86 / 197	3%	10	11.9	31%	52%	£3,235	£8,930
Sunderland	21 / 21	10%	4	18.2	96%	83%	£3,965	£8,600
Sussex	57 / 122	2%	4	23.8	89%	85%	£4,100	£9,500
Thames Valley	0 / 76	0%	4	10.8		95%	£4,350	£8,650
Ulster	32 / 112	18%	4	20.0	57%	93%	£3,420	£8,649
Warwick	24 / 1,012	22%	5	26.8		57%	£5,330	£10,250
Westminster	41 / 310	17%	5	11.6	100%	92%	£3,800–£13,750	£9,750
Wolverhampton	13 / 28	2%	4	9.4		23%	£3,418–£4,400	£8,200
York	72 / 52	18%	7	10.0	100%	92%	£3,300	£9,510

	Full-time/part-time	% students from outside the UK	Expenditure per student (FTE)	Student:staff ratio	Full-time completion rate	Part-time completion rate	Tuition fees: home/EU students	Tuition fees: international students
Sociology								
Cambridge	0 / 152	4%	9	16.2		100%	£5,434	£11,371
Cardiff	47 / 11	28%	7	18.5	100%		£3,300–£11,130	£9,100
City	80 / 168	52%	4	17.7	88%	95%	£3,300	£7,950
Goldsmiths	36 / 21	37%	3	15.4	94%	86%	£3,300–£6,320	£9,580
Leeds	80 / 85	35%	4	19.0	97%	73%	£3,300	£9,700
Leicester	41 / 22	41%	4	22.4	79%	63%	£3,300	£9,050
London School of Economics	227 / 35	72%	7	12.6	97%	100%	£9,144–£17,352	£13,452
Loughborough	61 / 21	13%	5	20.4	91%		£3,350	£9,850
Manchester	50 / 49	33%	6	19.1	89%	96%	£3,300	£12,900
Middlesex	41 / 94	38%	4	39.7		88%	£4,600–£6,870	£9,400
Northumbria	11 / 56	7%	4	27.4		78%	£3,996	£8,300
Nottingham Trent	35 / 180	5%	6	16.7	75%	100%	£3,145–£6,900	£7,550
The Open University	0 / 100	0%	2	28.2		100%		
Oxford	44 / 0	69%	10	11.4	97%		£5,200	£13,105
Portsmouth	46 / 170	8%	4	17.4	90%	73%	£3,300	£8,350
Sheffield Hallam	20 / 71	22%	4	24.0		37%	£3,300–£7,800	£8,100
Staffordshire	2 / 43	38%	5	24.6		96%		£9,395
Surrey	31 / 52	21%	5	19.9	100%	57%	£3,600–£8,600	£8,600
Sussex	54 / 10	67%	4	18.0	94%		£4,100	£9,500
Swansea	24 / 24	25%	3	24.0	87%		£3,300	£9,010
Teesside	66 / 56	12%	4	26.9	61%	73%	£3,950	£8,250
Warwick	25 / 20	45%	9	14.0	93%		£5,330	£10,250
Westminster	12 / 45	39%	3	20.5		91%	£3,800–£13,750	£9,750
York	41 / 8	45%	6	13.8	100%		£3,300	£9,510
Tourism, transport and travel								
University College Birmingham	52 / 50	72%	2	24.2	14%		£2,200	£7,450
Leeds Met	39 / 8	55%	6	30.7	73%		£3,400	£8,000
Napier	56 / 25	68%	3	20.2	57%		£3,675–£5,020	£9,180
Oxford Brookes	97 / 22	86%	6	24.7	83%		£3,990–£7,900	£9,570
Plymouth	87 / 7	89%	9	18.7	97%		£3,950	£8,950
Robert Gordon	27 / 23	70%	4	14.9	10%		£3,315–£7,712	£9,200
Sheffield Hallam	98 / 31	72%	3	27.3	46%	19%	£3,300–£7,800	£8,100
Strathclyde	32 / 19	76%	9	34.4	76%		£3,235	£8,930
Sunderland	119 / 45	37%	7	13.3	92%	73%	£3,965	£8,600
Surrey	71 / 27	82%	8	23.3	87%		£3,600–£8,600	£8,600
Wolverhampton	43 / 95	60%	4		74%	76%	£3,418–£4,400	£8,200

PhD

PhD

Dr Elizabeth Cripps

Three years of intensely rewarding focus on a subject that fascinates you? Or four-plus years of frustrating slog? A PhD can be either, depending on the temperament, interests and motivations of the person doing it, their subject, and the department in which they study. For most, it will contain elements of both. That's why it is so important to think carefully before committing yourself.

There are huge positives. If you are truly fascinated by your subject, this is a chance to throw yourself into it. You will go into your chosen topic in far greater detail than there is scope for in an undergraduate or even a master's degree. You will come up with your own project and should expect to finish with something original to add to the field. Not only is this an opportunity to explore something which you believe to be genuinely worthwhile and interesting in its own right, but you will be constantly exercising your brain. You should also benefit from being surrounded by similarly motivated individuals (other students as well as lecturers and fellows) with ideas to exchange.

For some, a PhD is a shrewd or even a necessary step in pursuit of a certain career. This goes without saying for would-be academics, but is also, increasingly, the case for scientists pursuing industrial posts. For example, you would generally need a PhD to get a job as a geologist in an oil company.

There's a lot to be said for the lifestyle too. Especially in arts subjects, there is plenty of flexibility as to when and where you work. Rather than spend eight hours a day behind a desk, you might work some of the time at home or (if you are lucky enough to have one) in your office, some in a library, some even in cafes or a graduate common room. This will be interspersed with seminars and meetings with other students, as well as time spent teaching.

The teaching itself can be another advantage. Most PhD students will get the opportunity to lead undergraduate tutorials or seminars, and this is a valuable opportunity to work out how suited you are to an academic career, as well as to gain practice explaining your ideas – and pick up some extra cash.

However, there are also downsides. If you are not completely enthralled by your topic, then the constant devotion to one relatively narrow slice of one subject could prove very wearing after a couple of years. Postgraduate study requires a commitment and focus far beyond that of an undergraduate degree. Nor is it one constant stream of bright ideas: arts students can expect to spend hours upon hours making notes on heavy texts, while many scientists will have to devote long periods to the day-to-day routine of lab work. It can prove intensely frustrating when (as often happens) results are not as you would like, or you can't get results at all.

Moreover, essential as it is to some careers, and as useful as it can be to others, it is worth considering that there are some jobs in which a PhD will not be an asset. Some employers might consider it a disadvantage that you are starting on the graduate recruitment merry-go-round some four or so years later than usual, with only a thesis in Kantian ethics or Shakespearean tragedies to show for it.

The lifestyle also has its flipside. Freedom to develop your own timetable means finding the motivation to do so. Three or four years is a long time to be incentivising yourself. The work can be very hard, with no immediate pay-offs, and it can be lonely working by yourself for much of the time.

Moreover, unless you happen to have vast private wealth or very generous parents to draw on, you will be comparatively poor. Funding is notoriously hard to come by, especially in arts and humanities subjects, and even funded PhD students can expect to be living on rather less than most of their contemporaries who have graduated into the world of work.

Still keen? Then, before you can settle down with a cup of coffee and a pile of reading to fine tune your research proposal, you have to do some serious thinking about the practicalities. When? Where? And − sadly, often the most crucial of all − how to pay for it?

● When to do it

Before embarking on a PhD, you will be expected to have completed an undergraduate degree and a master's. (If your master's is an MA, rather than an MPhil, you might well have to start as an MPhil student with the option of upgrading after the first year, rather than as a fully fledged PhD candidate.) One option is to move straight on from these without a gap. This has the advantage that you are still completely involved with the subject when you resume study and, especially if you stay at the same institution, that you will already be in touch with potential supervisors and may find it easier to apply for funding.

That said, there are also advantages to coming into graduate research after spending some time outside the ivory (or indeed redbrick) towers. You will be committing yourself to academia from a more informed background, rather than drifting into it without examining the alternatives. You may well have acquired skills (in writing, communication or time management, for example) which will help you. You might have been able to save some money to help fund yourself.

If the interim period has involved slogging away from nine to five at a standard graduate office job, you will relish the PhD student lifestyle all the more. But having become accustomed to a non-student salary could make the lack of money even harder to deal with, especially if your friends are still earning a good wage and want to eat, drink and holiday accordingly.

An interim option is to take a year out, either between your master's and PhD or between your undergraduate and master's degree. This can be a welcome opportunity to clear your head and return refreshed to academia, rather than do seven or so years of uninterrupted study and risk burn-out in the middle of it. It can also be a chance to earn some extra money.

However, it is worth checking first whether your preferred institution has a view on this kind of gap year. Some like them, some don't. Also bear in mind that, if it's to be an asset rather than a liability on your CV, you should do something at least vaguely constructive with the time – charity work, volunteering or some kind of relatively serious, graduate level, job – rather than just lounging on a beach in Thailand, or working in the local corner shop.

● How to do it

The next question is whether to do your PhD full-time, which should take three or four years after finishing a master's, or part-time, which can take twice as long.

As well as taking a much smaller chunk of years out of your life, a full-time PhD will enable you to throw yourself more into the life of the department, benefiting from all the seminars, reading groups, research training and graduate conferences in a way that just isn't possible if you are constrained by the demands of a job outside your studying. However, if you are unsuccessful in finding funding, self-funding by part-time work is often impossible and invariably extremely difficult alongside a full-time PhD. In which case, the most sensible option may be to do your PhD part-time.

If you take the part-time route, you could maintain an existing job (or take up a new one) alongside studying for the PhD. Moreover, you would have a regular escape into the 'real world' and wouldn't be devoting all your time to focusing on one subject. However, as well as taking many years to complete, a part-time PhD requires great dedication and a lot of hard work. It is no mean feat to return from a day in the office, resist the lure of the pub, your friends or the TV, and spend the evening on intense academic thought. Students often flag and struggle to finish, or at least take longer than planned. And if you do succeed in juggling two demanding workloads, you can expect your family and social life to suffer.

If you do take the part-time route, it is worth considering doing so at an institution which specialises in part-time research students. This will be geared up to providing teaching outside office hours and your fellow graduate students are more likely to be in the same boat, so you can help motivate each other.

There is also the option of doing a PhD by distance learning. This, again, allows flexibility and opens the possibility of maintaining an existing job alongside your research. Again, however, it will take great self-discipline to put in the necessary hours, and it can be all the more lonely as you will generally not have immediate, physical access to a department or the same face-to-face contact with your supervisor. Nor can you expect to have other students close by, with whom to swap ideas or moral support over a coffee or beer.

● Where to do it

Your own efforts aside, the most important factors in determining how successful you are in your PhD will be your supervisor and department. This makes it crucial to research possible departments and individuals within them, to find out where will be the best for your particular field. Given the specificity of PhD topics, this is likely to be harder work than picking the best university for your undergraduate subject – although a quick hunt through undergraduate league tables (such as those published by the *Guardian*) for your subject will at least give you a starting point.

Once you've got a short list of universities that are strong in the relevant department, you can search those universities' websites for detailed information. Almost all of them will have staff profile pages linked to each department which will enable you to research individual specialisms and areas of research interests. Don't be afraid to seek advice from those in the field – starting with your current lecturers or tutors if you are an undergraduate or master's student, or your ex-tutors if you have been in another career since graduating. (Be aware, though, that they may be naturally biased towards their own institution.)

Getting the right department, academically, is necessary. But it is probably not enough. It may sound obvious, but it is worth remembering that you will have to live in this town or city for the next three or four years. If you hate it, you will be unhappy – and then you would have to be an incredibly strong-willed person with an almost superhuman devotion to your subject for your academic work not to suffer.

Ask yourself some basic questions. Do you hate big cities? Or do you want a change, having been on an out-of-town campus for the past four years? How expensive is the area you are considering? How would you cope with living in, say, London or Manchester, without the money to splash out on clothes or eat out expensively? Do you have friends or family you would struggle to do without for the length of a PhD? Are you an avid sailor who won't be able to survive four years out of reach of the sea, or a culture fiend who needs theatres and galleries to unwind?

It goes without saying that these shouldn't be the only factors in considering where to go, but don't neglect them altogether. You are committing yourself to a very demanding few years and there's no point setting out by making it harder than it has to be.

Often the easiest option is to stay where you are and certainly some students do remain in their undergraduate university through a master's and then a PhD. There are advantages (quite apart from being the low-effort option): you know the department and they know you, which can make it easier to apply for funding, and you don't have to uproot to another city. However, this short term ease can come at a price: when it comes to finding an academic job, many institutions will look less favourably on someone who has only experienced one university.

From the point of view of personal academic development, the chance to work in a different department, with different thinkers, is also an advantage. At a more basic level, you are likely, after seven or eight years in one place, to feel that you have stagnated. This is especially the case with institutions dominating small university cities, or campus-based universities. In a larger city, or an area where you have an extensive social life outside the university, you are less likely to find it claustrophobic.

Often, an MPhil and PhD will run naturally together, and in many subjects your MPhil dissertation is supposed to form the basis of part of your PhD thesis. Given this, the obvious time to change university will be before starting an MPhil. Moreover, you are likely to have become familiar with the department and your supervisor and to have established a circle of friends and colleagues.

However, some do move between MPhil and PhD. Often, it isn't until you are well into the MPhil course, working on your dissertation, that you will have a detailed idea of your PhD topic. At this stage, it might become apparent that there is another department – or an individual within another department – more suited to the subject than the one you are currently in. Moving institution during the PhD itself is relatively unusual and is likely to be because a supervisor has moved.

● How to apply

Different institutions will have different deadlines and some consider applications in batches throughout the year. Generally speaking, the earlier you start to think seriously about where you want to go, the better.

For funded PhD places on specific projects, which are more the norm in science subjects, departments will advertise positions via the university website, specialist academic recruitment websites (like www.jobs.ac.uk), or subject-specific mailing lists, and then conduct a selection process akin to that you go through to get a job.

If you are applying simply for a place, deadlines will probably be more flexible and you may not be required to attend an interview. However, because both the Arts and Humanities Research Council (AHRC) and the Economic and Social Research Council (ESRC) – two of the main funding bodies – tend to have funding application deadlines in May, it is worth establishing as soon as possible which institution you will be applying to them through. This means applying to that institution as early as possible in the calendar year in which you intend to start studying.

In either case, you will most likely have to fill in a detailed application form, specific to the university. You can expect to have to ask your current or previous university to supply a detailed academic record and you will have to produce academic references.

In addition, you should prepare a research proposal, which sets out what you aim to discover during your PhD and how you intend to do it, and provide samples of previous work. It is important to get the research proposal right. Enthusiasm is the key, but so is demonstrating that you are well-informed and have given the matter significant thought. If you are seeking to return to academia after a gap, brush up on your reading. If you did a final year undergraduate or master's dissertation, make sure you have re-read it thoroughly: you are likely to have to discuss it in detail at your interview.

● Funding

Research councils

Research councils are the first port of call for funding: the Arts and Humanities Research Council (www.ahrc.ac.uk); the Biotechnology and Biological Sciences Research Council (www.bbsrc.ac.uk); the Medical Research Council (www.mrc.ac.uk); the Engineering and Physical Sciences Research Council (www.epsrc.ac.uk); the Economic and Social Research Council (www.esrc.ac.uk); the Natural Environment Research Council (www.nerc.ac.uk); and the Particle Physics and Astronomy Research Council, which has now become part of the Science and Technology Facilities Council (www.scitech.ac.uk).

To qualify for a full grant, you need to be a UK citizen or to have been resident here for at least three years. Such grants, which are extremely oversubscribed and correspondingly competitive, include fees and a tax-free living grant of £12,000-£13,000 (more for London) and often specify a deadline for completing the PhD. EU students can be eligible for fees-only awards.

When it comes to research council funding, there is a major divide between science PhDs and those in the arts, humanities or social sciences. The norm with science subjects is for funding for particular projects to be allocated to departments, who then advertise funded PhD places within those projects.

Outside the sciences, there are some funded PhD places similarly available as part of research projects. However, it is more usual for students to apply directly to the AHRC or ESRC for a grant for their own research. This involves submitting a detailed research proposal, including academic references, and has to be done in collaboration with the institution where you will do your PhD. Both institutions have deadlines in early May, and you will need to allow your institution at least a month to fill in its part of the form.

Competition is extremely fierce, so it is impossible to overstate the work that should go into getting your proposal just right. There is an art to writing funding proposals. You need to demonstrate real enthusiasm for and familiarity with your field and show that what you are doing is both original and important. (Explaining your project in relation to existing theorists helps on both counts.) Between you, you and your supervisor will need to explain why the project is suited to the department and its existing research focus.

Most important of all, be specific. You have to show that you have planned your project in detail – that this is not something you vaguely fancy thinking about for a few years. Ideally, you would do the impossible: say exactly what you will find out before you have started. Try to get as close as you can. At the very least, provide a very detailed outline of the questions you will tackle at each stage of the project.

Some departments will provide coaching sessions for funding applications. If yours does, thank your lucky stars – and go. At the very least, ask your future supervisor or graduate tutor to read it through and give you some feedback.

Even after all the effort, you have to be realistic about the possibility of failure. A first class undergraduate degree is almost always necessary but is certainly not enough to ensure success. If you do succeed, bear in mind that there are likely to be other resources available to you through your research council, such as research training or travel grants to attend conferences or carry out field work. Don't expect these to be spoon fed to you: read the small print of your brochure, examine the website or, if you are unsure, phone them to find out.

Charity, industry or university scholarships

Another option for scientists is charity funding – for example from the Wellcome Trust (www.wellcome.ac.uk) or the Leverhulme Trust (www.leverhulme.ac.uk) – or industry funding, often as part of a job contract for after you finish. In arts, humanities and social sciences, this is less likely, although it is worth researching your particular field for subject-specific organisations, such as the Royal Institute of Philosophy (www.royalinstitutephilosophy.org), which provide grants. Your future supervisor or graduate tutor should be able to advise you on this.

In addition, many departments will have a limited number of places which are internally funded, perhaps through a subject-specific bequest to the university. These may not be as comprehensive as the research council grants, but will often at least cover fees.

Options for international students

There are a number of scholarships and awards available for international students, from an often bewildering variety of institutions. The British Council's Education UK website (www.educationuk.org) is an invaluable source of information, including a free downloadable booklet: Sources of Funding for International Students.

Limited funding, to bridge the gap between international and home/EU admission fees, is available at a total of 138 UK institutions through the Overseas Research Student Awards Scheme (www.orsas.ac.uk). These grants, which do not include maintenance or travel, are intended for those students who will make some valuable contribution both to academic research in the UK and some key aspect – economic, scientific or educational – of their own country.

Awards for international students are often country or region-specific. For example, US students should consider Fulbright Awards (www.fulbright.co.uk), which fund the first year of study, or, for under-26s only, Marshall Scholarships (www.marshallscholarship.org).

The Commonwealth Scholarship Commission (www.cscuk.org.uk) provides funding for residents of commonwealth countries, as part of the Commonwealth Scholarship and Fellowship Plan, while students from developing countries could be eligible for the Shared Scholarship Scheme (www.dfid.gov.uk). This targets high quality candidates for postgraduate studies in a subject relevant to development issues.

There are also likely to be options for funding from individual overseas governments. Some universities will contribute to the costs of a PhD at a reputable UK university, on the understanding that you return to take up a teaching post with them afterwards.

Self-funding

The final option is self-funding. If you are considering this, make sure you have done your sums right. However unappealing the prospect of hours spent in front of an Excel spreadsheet is, doing it now could prevent you getting into serious financial trouble a few years down the line.

The first thing to take into account is fees. These vary dramatically between UK/EU and international students. The UK government does not set research degree fees, so they are up to the individual institutions. UK/EU full-time fees start at £3,000-£4,000 a year at most universities, with some charging more for some scientific subjects. International students can expect to pay from £9,000 upwards – and it can be a lot upwards. Check with the relevant institution.

Then there are your living expenses. Again, these vary from place to place. Make a detailed note of all your essential expenses, from rent and bills down to beer money. Make sure you take into account any transport you will need to get into university. Will you need a car? A monthly travel card? Find out which student discounts are available on local transport. For example, London students can get a third off travel cards. (See www.tfl.gov.uk for details.) Ask yourself (realistically) which luxuries you can do without.

Generally speaking, the stipend allowed by the research councils is just enough to live on. Unless you can make a significant saving in day-to-day costs (say, by living with family) you will be unlikely to get by on less. If you have even remotely expensive tastes, and especially if you have been used to earning a reasonable salary, you might well need more. Indeed, it is worth doing these sums, and considering how you might supplement your grant, even if you are relying on research council funding. Bear in mind, however, that grants will often come with a requirement that you limit any non-academic work to a certain number of hours a week.

Then consider your sources of money. You are likely to be self-funding in one of two ways – or through a combination of the two. A fortunate or forward-thinking few will have access to a lump sum of saved or inherited money, or a private source of income. The other option is paid work alongside the PhD.

If you plan to fund yourself entirely by working, you will probably have to do a part-time PhD. Doing so whilst studying full-time is only plausible if you are moving into the PhD from a previous career which lends itself to well-paid consultancy or freelance work. You'd need to be able to put in relatively few hours at relatively high rates. Even then, it is likely to be extremely hard work. There simply wouldn't be adequate hours in the day for you to earn enough money through a low paid job in a bar or shop to pay fees, live, and still meet the demands of the course.

One way of earning extra money whilst boosting your academic CV is teaching work, usually either demonstrating in practicals, or giving tutorials, seminars, back-up classes or revision classes to undergraduates. Most universities encourage this and your own department will generally be your first port of call. You should earn upwards of £10 an hour and be paid for a couple of hours of preparation as well as for the classes themselves. Many departments will also have other work available for their graduate students, for example shifts in the library, but this may not be well advertised. Ask the departmental administrator.

Once you have embarked on your PhD, keeping a grip on your finances is (almost) as crucial as keeping control of your academic work. It might be a good idea, especially if you haven't been used to living on a limited student income, to work out exactly how much you can spend a week after your regular bills and keep a record of everything you buy, to keep it within limits. If things do slip and you end up in difficulties, tackle it straight away. Many universities have emergency hardship funds which they can draw on in extreme cases. Make sure you get in touch with them immediately.

● What it's like to do a PhD

Doing a PhD is significantly different from any academic work you will have done before.

As an undergraduate, you will have attended lectures, tutorials, seminars and other classes. You will have enrolled in a range of courses, some mandatory, some selected by you from a number of approved options. Those will have followed a detailed structure designed by the lecturer or teacher. You will have been told exactly what to read and given very detailed advice on how to succeed in exams and coursework. In short, you will have had your hand held. On a master's course, slightly more independence will have been required of you, but to nothing like the extent needed for a PhD.

A PhD is a huge project. Rather than having regular deadlines, weekly or monthly, for essays or other small scale projects, you will have three years (or longer if you are a part-time student) to produce the equivalent of a book. This is incredibly daunting. Most universities will now impose some kind of formal structure – at the very least they will require termly reports and regular formal progress meetings – and research councils will require progress reports, but this is a far cry from the detailed monitoring you will have had as an undergraduate. You will generally have to set your own deadlines and answer to yourself if you don't stick to them.

The standard PhD begins with a huge amount of reading, compiling a literature review, after which you carry out your own research, then write up the entire project over the last six months to a year.

However, for some arts subjects the structure is slightly different. If your research revolves entirely around engaging with the texts at a theoretical level then you can expect to be writing as you go along. You'll do some reading, think about it, develop your own arguments, turn them into a paper, try them out by discussing them with your supervisor or in seminars or graduate conferences, and end up with a chapter at a time.

Your day-to-day routine will also vary depending on your subject. Whatever your subject, you will have to spend some time in libraries and, increasingly, to use electronic resources. You will spend the bulk of the time in your own research, although you will be able to break up the day by attending reading groups, seminars and graduate conferences, and by teaching work.

Whether you emerge after three years with a passable PhD thesis could come down to something as simple as whether you establish a clear working routine from the outset. Before committing yourself, think carefully about how self-motivated you are. How will you manage this? Will you allow yourself weekends and evenings off, and work nine to five each day? Can you make yourself work without an immediate deadline? If you are a daytime TV addict with limited willpower, this may not be the career path for you.

Generally speaking, if you are restricted to working in a certain place, it will often be easier to establish a routine. Computer scientists, for example, may end up spending most of each day in front of a screen. Laboratory scientists will inevitably pass much of their time in the lab, but not necessarily in a settled routine. While an experiment is in progress, you could be working 18-hour days, but then taking some time off to recover. You will need to consider whether you could cope with this.

If you don't have access to an office or a lab, you will need to find somewhere that you can work, and it is even more crucial to get yourself into a pattern that works for you. You might work best in the university library, or you might hate libraries. You might have a study at home, or you might be constantly distracted by housemates, detective novels, or the innumerable household tasks that seem suddenly interesting when the alternative is getting on with your work. One option is to work in a graduate study area or common room if your university has one, or you may even find it productive (if pricey) to work in coffee shops. You may end up with some combination of them all.

You will also have regular meetings with your supervisor. About once every fortnight is standard, but it can vary between institutions. You may have some formal meetings, involving progress reports back to the university, and some informal ones – or your supervisor may simply fill in a termly report on your progress, and meet you as and when it suits you both. Generally, your supervision will revolve around discussion of a piece of work that you have sent to the supervisor in advance.

Your relationship will be very different from that you will have been used to

● PhD survival tips

1. Get into a routine

You need a timetable and a location that works for you. Work consistently rather than trying to pull off undergraduate-style all-nighters just before the deadline. You won't have the mental energy to get away with it at this level.

2. Keep on top of the reading

Do this from the very start. Search electronic databases, pursue references to other authors in useful texts. Ask for reading suggestions. Keep up-to-date on the journals. You don't want to find out two years down the line that someone has had exactly your idea, and that it didn't work.

3. Stay in contact with your supervisor

Chase them if necessary. Sit down together and lay out deadlines. Whenever you meet, set a time for the next meeting and a date before that for you to send some work. Avoid just agreeing vaguely to contact them when you have something to show them. A meeting in the diary will be an incentive to produce something.

4. Do the filing

Tedious but essential: organise your research. Whether electronically or on paper, make sure all your notes are where you can find them. Back up everything. The last thing you want is to lose your thesis to an opportunistic laptop thief two weeks before submission.

5. Exchange ideas

Go to seminars and reading groups in your department. If there aren't any in your particular field, set them up with fellow postgraduates. Attend graduate conferences and present papers as often as possible.

6. Start writing

Whether you are writing a paper, beginning a chapter in a chapter-by-chapter project, or embarking on the daunting 'write up' of your whole thesis, force yourself to sit down and get on with it. Set targets, in hours or words, for each day. Don't worry if it's nowhere near perfect: just get a first draft down as a base for improvement.

7. Have a life

Don't think about your PhD 24/7. It won't help. Make time for non-academic interests, such as sports, and keep in touch with friends from outside the university. If you reach a sticking point, do something else. Go for a walk, to the gym, or to meet a friend. Come back after a few hours when you feel more detached. Head in hands at your desk, frustration mounting, is the least likely place to come up with fresh ideas.

8. Troubleshoot

If things go wrong — financially, academically, health wise — don't wait for them to get out of control. Talk to somebody — your supervisor, another member of staff such as the graduate tutor, a fellow PhD student, even your partner or best friend. If you feel you are falling behind, alert the department and get them to help you establish achievable targets for catching up.

9. Get the viva right ...

Devote a few days before the viva to rereading your thesis. Be clear on all the arguments, inside out, and remind yourself of any literature that you have become unclear on. Use the advantage of coming back to it after a break to identify weak points or potential counterarguments. Consider how you would respond.

10. ... but admit your mistakes

If your examiner scores a hit, don't try to bluff your way out. Acknowledge it. Say if you'd need to think about it further, and try to outline how you might go about that. If it's something you didn't include for reasons of scope, say so. Remember that your PhD thesis doesn't need to be flawless. (What piece of academic work is?)

with undergraduate lecturers. A good supervisor will suggest some reading and offer constructive feedback on your project, both in terms of overall structure and when it comes to the fine detail. But they won't spoon feed you. It is up to you to define and carry out your own project. It is up to you to keep up to date with developments in the field. Even if your PhD is part of a wider funded project, led by your supervisor, you will still be expected to take responsibility for your part of it.

Bear in mind that your supervisor is a busy academic, most probably juggling teaching responsibilities on master's and undergraduate courses, supervising more than one PhD student, his or her own research, and an increasingly weighty administrative workload. If you think you are being forgotten, never be afraid to chase. But, equally, be aware that there are limits to what you can reasonably expect.

Finally, at the end of your PhD, you will have a viva. This is a grilling by two or more examiners, in which you are expected to demonstrate not only that you actually wrote your thesis and have a thorough grasp of the subject matter and relevant literature, but also that you are capable of responding thoughtfully to insightful and often unexpected criticisms.

Unsurprisingly, even the most confident students can find the prospect terrifying. However, viewed in a more positive light, and with less focus on its make-or-break aspect, the viva is a relatively unusual opportunity to discuss your entire project with two or more extremely intelligent people, both experts in this or a closely related field, who have actually read it from cover to cover. If all goes well, you should leave with some ideas of how to turn your project into something publishable.

● Making your PhD work for you

Your PhD, long and drawn out as it may seem at the time, is only the start. You might be taking the first step on the steep slope to an academic career, with a view to securing a post-doc or temporary lectureship after you gain your doctorate, then, eventually, a permanent post.

You might be intending to work outside academia but in a field (for example, in some industrial or financial areas) where a PhD is either necessary or desirable to get a job. You might be doing a PhD purely out of love for the subject, intending afterwards to take up or return to a career for which it is no help at all. Or you might not be quite sure, when you start, which of these categories you fall into.

Whichever turns out to be the case, you will need to think about how you can use the experience to boost your future career.

Academia

If you want to be an academic, there are various things you need to do. First, get your PhD finished. It may sound obvious, but it's absolutely crucial. You won't be taken seriously on the job market until you have handed in your thesis or can at least show that you are very close to doing so. No-one will want to pay you to finish an overdue PhD.

Second, get teaching experience. Bear in mind that pretty much everyone applying for the post-docs and (especially) temporary lectureships that you'll be going for will have at least tutorial and almost certainly class teaching experience. If you secure some lecturing work as well – for example as cover for a member of the department on sabbatical – then that could give you an extra edge.

Third, speak at conferences. This will not only give you crucial CV points but is also a very useful way of getting feedback on your ideas. Submit papers or abstracts whenever a relevant conference is advertised. Make sure you are signed up to the electronic mailing lists for calls for papers in your subject. Your supervisor should be able to advise you on which they are.

Of course, public speaking can be frightening, all the more for a relatively ill-informed newcomer surrounded by experts. But if you want a job in academia, you will have to get used to it – and there are ways to make it easier.

Let yourself in gently. Start off by attending as many graduate conferences as possible. Force yourself to ask questions. Consider applying to respond to others' papers first, then start submitting your own abstracts. Begin with seminars in your own department, then move on to graduate conferences and, in the final years of your PhD, to full blown academic conferences.

Always remember that everyone has had to start where you are, and that there will be others who are just as nervous even if they are hiding it. Practice presenting the paper and use slides or handouts to make it easier to follow.

Fourth, try to get published. This will put you in a much stronger position in the job market. Bear in mind that academic journals get an unbelievably long time to respond to submissions. If your paper is sent out by the journal to referees, you could be waiting for up to a year to hear back. Given that the etiquette is only to submit to one journal at a time, this is intensely frustrating, and makes it all the more important to start submitting papers sooner rather than later. Begin, if possible, in the penultimate year of your PhD.

If you haven't been accepted for publication, you will need to show that you have papers in the pipeline. Make it clear that you have a strategy for getting published. List your conference papers and make sure you have at least sent them off to journals. Then, so long as they haven't yet been returned, you can put them on your CV as 'under editorial review'.

Finally, prepare a good job talk. You will usually be expected to do one, especially for teaching posts. It might feel like an almost impossible task: you have at once to show how you would introduce students to your field and to demonstrate what your own research has added to it. And you have as little as 15 minutes in which to do so.

The key is not to cram too much in. It is better to say less clearly – so long as it is interesting and contains some new ideas – than to try to say more and lose your audience after five minutes. Use slides or at least handouts to help you. Each slide should make one or at most two clear points. Don't be afraid to use illustrations and everyday examples. Let your own enthusiasm show through. Practise on a friend or family member who is intelligent but not a specialist in your field, and see whether they can follow it.

Non-academic jobs

If you have your heart set on a particular career, you don't want your PhD to get in the way. If it is in an industry for which a PhD is helpful, make sure you've done your homework and know exactly what the PhD needs to be in. You might be able to fine tune it to the kind of companies to which you are applying. Use examples or case studies from the relevant sector. You might even be able to make your research immediately, practically useful to a future employer, for example a big drugs company. This is taken to its extreme when such companies sponsor PhD projects.

If a PhD – or at least one in the subject you are set on studying – isn't useful for your chosen career, make sure you have a very good explanation as to why you have done it. If you spend three years poring over classical mythology, then claim always to have wanted to go into investment banking, eyebrows will be raised.

However, there are things you can do to help yourself. Consider which of the many generic skills gained in graduate research would be useful in that job – public speaking, say, or teaching or intensive time management – and make sure you utilise them as much as possible during the PhD. Try to get some experience in the relevant field, perhaps by doing a summer internship.

Above all, work hard to show that you had a good reason for embarking on your PhD, that you have a good reason for choosing this particular career afterwards – and a genuine commitment to it – and that the two are, if not a perfect fit, then at least as close as possible to complementary.

CASE STUDY 1

The final year student

Nadine Elzein, final year PhD student in philosophy at University College London

I decided to do a PhD because I love philosophy. I had to either get a job and give up serious philosophy forever or do a PhD and try to make a career out of. If you do study at this level, it has to be because you really love your subject and genuinely want to do it. Otherwise, it would be a nightmare to get through it.

It's a different skill at this level. As an undergraduate, you can do very well if you have a basic understanding of the arguments and can write a reasonable exam essay. In the PhD, you study just one thing in incredible depth and you have to have a very clear idea of what you want to establish. You need a lot more originality and to be able to spend a lot of time on your own thinking very hard about one topic. It takes focus and perseverance.

It is very rewarding. You feel like you gain an in-depth understanding of the topic that you would never gain through any other method, and when you finally get a thesis you really feel like you've achieved something.

I did an undergraduate degree at UCL, then the MPhil, then the PhD. I'm glad I did it that way. I think if I had taken time out I would have lost some momentum. It's hard to think about philosophy seriously after a long break — it's enough of a struggle when I've just been on holiday.

I did think about going elsewhere but one main reason for staying at UCL was that I wanted to stay in London. I had other commitments that kept me here, and I like UCL. It also helped with applying for funding. They knew me and were familiar with my research project. They also give you a lot of help with funding applications — not a lot of places do.

I had AHRC [Arts and Humanities Research Council] funding for my MPhil. For the first year of the PhD I was relying on a UCL scholarship and for the next two years I had AHRC funding again. To get it, you have to write painstaking research proposals that take a really long time and numerous drafts, and almost induce a nervous breakdown. I applied for it for the first year of the PhD but didn't get it then. The departmental funding covered the fees. I still had a year of being really broke but without the fees being paid I couldn't have done it at all.

I would normally try to think about the topic independently and work out what I wanted to say, then do all the relevant background reading, which is probably not the wise way round to do it. I work in coffee shops! I don't like the silence of libraries and I need constant coffee. Lately I've also spent a lot of time working at home. I discuss deadlines with my supervisor and I set myself continuous tasks, which helps to keep me focused.

It's very important to meet up regularly with your supervisor and that he or she is someone you feel you can come to with ideas that are not as developed as you would like, and can give you constructive feedback. My supervisor is excellent at that.

Seminars can be quite mixed. In philosophy, people have very different research projects and a lot of stuff you attend will be on something that just goes over your head. But a good seminar series breaks up the time spent sitting on your own reading.

It's very good experience to speak at graduate conferences. It's something I found very frightening at first but it's remarkable how used to it you get. I've also done quite a lot of undergraduate teaching. I recommend that.

I like the lifestyle. Although in some ways you have this burden of work hanging over you all the time, you can decide how to go about your day yourself. You can have breaks when you want to and do other things too, and you do feel you are doing something you are passionate about.

The main difficulty has been trying to keep up the will power and self discipline required to work continuously on a difficult project for a number of years. I've had whole periods – sometimes months – where I just felt utterly disheartened and like I really wasn't getting anywhere. Normally, eventually, I would either find my attitude changed and I would stop moping and sort it out, or I would read something that gave me an idea or new direction.

I am about to hand in my thesis. I'm applying for academic jobs at the moment, and sending papers off to journals. I'm likely to do more part-time teaching next year. The fact that I'm constrained to living in London makes it very difficult. If you want an academic career it helps if you can just move to anywhere in the world.

If you want an academic job, I'd advise doing things that would help with that earlier in the degree than I did – conference papers, doing a job talk, trying to get published. If you leave it until the final year it will be quite stressful. Other than that, it's just a case of sitting down and making sure you spend the time every day working towards it and trying to stay focused.

CASE STUDY 2

The supervisor

Dr Giles Droop, senior lecturer in earth sciences at the School of Earth, Atmospheric and Environmental Sciences, University of Manchester

I've been supervising PhD students for more than 25 years. The main difference between a PhD and a master's or undergraduate degree is that there is much more reliance on private study. There is also greater reliance on the supervisor or supervisory team as the main point of contact. In our subject, there is also more emphasis on generating your own data.

PhD students here have formal and informal meetings with supervisors and are encouraged to meet informally with other academic staff and postgraduates. Then there are internal lab meetings, research group meetings and seminars, as well as external conferences. If they are using equipment, which most do, students receive guidance from technical staff. Many will go off and do fieldwork. We also ask most of our PhDs to demonstrate in undergraduate practical classes.

Many PhD students find it challenging adjusting to a regime dominated by private study. A few also find it difficult accepting ownership of their projects, particularly in the first year. Maintaining motivation can also be hard, particularly if things prove unexpectedly difficult, for example if results take a long time coming.

A lot of students find it difficult to develop a good work ethic. There's a freedom that comes with private study and sometimes not enough hours are put in during the early stages. Then there are financial problems, especially for part-time and self-funded students. For some mature students, there can be problems balancing the PhD and family life.

The main way to avoid pitfalls is to communicate with other people. Take the opportunities to talk to supervisors. Here, every PhD student is also assigned a member of staff as an adviser.

We try to get our students to set themselves targets and stick to them. Put in the hours and get organised. Keep up-to-date records, a lab book or a list of references. Set aside regular time slots for doing certain things, for example going to the library and checking journals.

It is important to keep communication channels open with your supervisors. A supervisor may well have several PhD students and will usually be snowed under with other teaching, research and administrative commitments. You might have to keep reminding him or her of your existence, so if you feel your supervisor hasn't seen you for a while, just go along or send an email and solicit a meeting.

For any formal meeting, make sure you have something new to show them. Be prepared to discuss ideas and strategies proactively rather than sitting there and expecting to be grilled. By the second and third years most students have built up a reasonable relationship with their supervisor. There's a two-way flow of ideas. It does happen sometimes that supervisors and students don't get on, and a student has to change supervisor, but very rarely. That's one of the reasons we recommend that there be two or more supervisors.

We have about 40 members of academic staff in the department and about 90 research students, mostly PhD students. About half are funded with research council money and 70 to 80 per cent of those by the NERC [Natural Environment Research Council]. Approximately 20 per cent of our PhDs are funded by industrial money and about the same by external scholarships, mainly from overseas governments. A small percentage is funded through the countrywide Overseas Research Students Awards Scheme [ORSAS] and a few are truly self-funded students.

Research Council PhD places are very competitive and the department only gets a few awards per year. We decide as a department which projects to go ahead with, mostly on the basis of which are the best students, but with some reference to the overall balance of research topics. We are looking not just for people who will do well, but for people who will be excellent.

Usually, candidates are called for interview on an open day. They are shown round and interviewed by potential supervisors but they also get an interview by a panel of senior staff. Obviously, we are looking for enthusiasm. The panel will have read the references: they will know who is academically very able. Often, they will ask candidates to explain any independent work they have done in the course of an undergraduate degree.

Students are generally applying for one or more projects on a list that we have published. It helps if you have a clear idea of which project you are most interested in — occasionally we get a student who applies for all the projects in one area, which doesn't give a terribly good impression — and if you have genned up on what the potential supervisors are interested in.

A PhD is an opportunity to pursue a subject that really interests you and to discover new truths, if that's something you enjoy doing. Obviously, there's the training side as well – training in how to do research, in design and implementation of a project, and general training in using your mind. Then there's a whole list of generic skills – communication skills, making sense of complex data, organising practical tasks, time management, working with people.

It can prepare you for a career in academia, research positions in industry or a teaching career. Then there are a large number of professions, some of which may be only fairly remotely connected to the PhD subject, where the generic skills acquired may be very useful.

A PhD is not suitable for people who want to get rich quick, who want something to fill in time between their undergraduate degree and getting a paid job, who are tired of learning, or who expect others to tell them what to do. You need a certain independence of mind.

You should be genuinely fired up by a subject and want to find out more. You should enjoy the prospect of finding out new things and like the idea of telling people what you have found. Initiative is crucial and you need a certain amount of resilience in the face of setbacks. Basically, you need enthusiasm, ability and dedication.

CASE STUDY 3

The recruiter for a non-academic job

Mike Sherwin, director, Huxley Associates Global Markets, recruitment consultancy specialising in front office finance professionals

Whether the pursuit of a PhD will help you to secure a job within another sector will depend entirely on the role you desire, the subject of your studies and the educational establishment you attend.

A common misconception is that the completion of any PhD will make you instantly more employable by serving as an indication of your intelligence and aptitude for hard work. While this may be true in some cases, it is also important to remember that staying in academia can also hinder your pursuit of a career.

It would be incorrect to suggest that there is a definitive answer to what financial institutions value in new recruits, as every hiring manager is different, but it is fair to say that there are general guidelines to consider when questioning whether to continue with higher education.

In finance, for example, if you wish to work within wealth management or as a private banker or trader, there is no real benefit in studying for a PhD. Indeed, the majority of banks or funds would question your motivation for staying in education for so long and whether you will cope in an extremely fast-paced, non-theoretical world. Academia is much slower paced with less immediate pressures. Students coming out of a doctorate are often entering the working world for the first time and this can be a massive shock to the system.

Even where PhDs are the norm, many hiring managers still question recruiters about candidate's motivations – about how long they have had this ambition. Candidates with a strong PhD in a related subject, coupled with evidence of their commitment to this career, fare much better than those who have shown no prior interest. Your ambition can be reflected if you have factored in a related element to your studies or have completed internships, for example.

Securing a job is always a question of convincing the employer that you are the right person for the team and for the business dynamic. If you do have a PhD, it won't necessarily stand against you, but you would need to justify why you completed it.

CASE STUDY 4

The recruiter for an academic job

Professor John Peterson, head of politics and international relations at Edinburgh University

By the time you are applying for full-time posts, those interviewing you will want evidence that you are on an upward curve in terms of publications. It's good to have a couple of things published. But if you can show that you have things in the pipeline (that is, under review or in press), that's even better. We all want to see our own institutions on articles authored by young, up-and-coming colleagues.

It is also important to show that you have been out to conferences — that you have been in situations where you are presenting your work and that you are able to respond to comments and criticism. You also need to show that you have teaching experience. In particular, it's beneficial if you can say to employees that you have given lectures, and can do more than lead tutorials and seminars.

Ultimately, however, the most important thing is to get your PhD done. The last thing in anyone's interest is to hire someone who is not really very close to finishing but says they are, then ends up getting so distracted by all their work planning new courses (and so on) that they end up not finishing. The PhD is always job one.

It is generally preferable, all else being equal, to show that you can cope with different institutions. If it can be avoided, having three degrees from one institution is probably undesirable.

My personal view is that it can be an advantage to have spent some time outside academia. For one thing, people who have done other sorts of work tend to appreciate all the virtues of working in a university environment — working with young people and having the privilege of ideas, debates and books being part of their work. It can happen that people who do three degrees consecutively and then go straight into an academic job, never experiencing other kinds of work, have a problem with burn out.

When it comes to applying for jobs, it is worth researching the department. Spend some time on their website, looking at how you could add value. It always helps when someone says in a covering letter that they could contribute to teaching a particular course, that they have research interests that overlap with those of individual colleagues, or that they could contribute actively to an established research group.

It is always helpful to send writing samples. Most good departments will ask for those anyway. A research plan also helps — if you have a clear idea what work you will do in the future and how it relates to what you have done in the past. If you have a good idea of what you will do with your PhD in terms of spinning out publications from individual chapters, that will help a lot.

Coach your referees. If you have done your homework on the department, you shouldn't be afraid to say to your referees: 'I hope you will be asked for a letter of reference from this university, can I just tell you three or four things about the department and what they want for this job?' Generic references often don't help much. If a referee can show that they know about the department and know about the candidate, and can demonstrate how they would match up, that's gold dust.

It has also become crucially important to show that you are fundable: that you have ideas for applying for grants, that you have external money in mind that could help you develop your own projects and research interests.

At interviews, it helps if you can show that you are capable of mounting your own course, what it would be about and how it would hang together. Your job talk should balance two things. First, you want to talk about your own work and demonstrate deep knowledge of your subject, all the while thinking to yourself: 'If I didn't know anything about this, what would I ask me?' Second, you want to show how you would connect to the institution that is interviewing you.

RAE 2008

For any student looking to undertake postgraduate research and eventually add the coveted title of 'doctor' to their name, the newly published results of the Research Assessment Exercise (RAE) are invaluable.

For this unique British event the research of academics in every university in the UK in all subjects was assessed by their fellow specialists in the field.

Panels of experts in 67 subject areas rank this work as either 4* (world-leading), 3* (internationally excellent), 2* (internationally recognised), 1* (nationally recognised) or 0 (sub-standard/unclassified).

Each piece of research submitted by universities – a maximum of four per full-time academic – has been ranked to reveal the percentages of research within departments that are 4*, 3* and so on. These judgments lead to a 'quality profile', giving a clearer idea of where the universities' research strengths lie and what proportion of their work is world-beating or, alternatively, below-standard.

The *Guardian* tables for each subject show the number of staff whose work was submitted to RAE 2008, expressed as full-time equivalents (FTEs); the percentage of the work submitted (not the individuals involved) graded 4*, 3* and so on. We also give a grade point average – institutions with the same average score are sorted alphabetically in the tables.

Potential students will be interested in the proportion of the best research – 4* and 3* – in a department and want to follow up with inquiries about the exact areas of strength when considering where to apply.

The 67 panels of experts involved in the RAE worked under the guidance of 15 main panels. Over the following pages, subjects are grouped with other subjects overseen by the same main panel. These groups are labelled A-O. An alphabetical index of subjects is given opposite.

An asterisk beside an institution name indicates that two or more submissions were included for that institution in that subject area. In these instances we have kept just the highest score. For the other scores, see the RAE tables published online at www.guardian.co.uk/education/rae

Students should bear in mind that one of the surprises of the latest RAE was that pockets of very good research were scattered across a large number of universities. The choice may be wider than you think – use the tables to help you track down the cutting-edge research in your chosen field.

	Group	Page
Accounting and finance	I	164
Agriculture, veterinary and food science	D	150
Allied health professions and studies	C	147
American studies and anglophone area studies	L	176
Anthropology	J	171
Applied mathematics	F	153
Archaeology	H	162
Architecture and the built environment	H	160
Art and design	O	186
Asian studies	L	176
Biological sciences	D	148
Business and management studies	I	164
Cancer studies	A	142
Cardiovascular medicine	A	142
Celtic studies	M	179
Chemical engineering	G	158
Chemistry	E	151
Civil engineering	G	159
Classics, ancient history, Byzantine and modern Greek studies	N	182
Communication, culture and media studies	O	189
Computer science and informatics	F	155
Dentistry	C	146
Development studies	J	171
Drama, dance and performing arts	O	188
Earth systems and environmental sciences	E	150
Economics and econometrics	I	163
Education	K	173
Electrical and electronic engineering	G	157
English language and literature	M	180
Epidemiology and public health	B	144
European studies	L	176
French	M	177
General engineering and mineral & mining engineering	G	157
Geography and environmental studies	H	161
German, Dutch and Scandinavian languages	M	178
Health services research	B	144
History	N	184
History of art, architecture and design	O	187
Iberian and Latin American languages	M	179
Infection and immunology	A	142
Italian	M	178
Law	J	166
Library and information management	I	166
Linguistics	M	181
Mechanical, aeronautical and manufacturing engineering	G	159
Metallurgy and materials	G	160
Middle Eastern and African studies	L	176
Music	O	190
Nursing and midwifery	C	146
Other hospital based clinical subjects	A	143
Other laboratory based clinical subjects	A	143
Pharmacy	C	148
Philosophy	N	183
Physics	E	152
Politics and international studies	J	168
Pre-clinical and human biological sciences	D	149
Primary care and other community based clinical subjects	B	145
Psychiatry, neuroscience and clinical psychology	B	145
Psychology	K	172
Pure mathematics	F	153
Russian, Slavonic and East European languages	M	177
Social work and social policy & administration	J	169
Sociology	J	170
Sports-related studies	K	175
Statistics and operational research	F	154
Theology, divinity and religious studies	N	183
Town and country planning	H	161

	Staff submitted (FTE)	4*	3*	2*	1*	Unclassified	Average ranking

● Group A

Cardiovascular medicine

	Staff submitted (FTE)	4*	3*	2*	1*	Unclassified	Average ranking
Oxford	18.60	45	40	15	0	0	3.30
Cambridge	14.00	35	50	10	5	0	3.15
King's College London	32.40	20	60	20	0	0	3.00
Manchester	24.20	15	60	25	0	0	2.90
Imperial College	64.27	20	45	30	5	0	2.80
Glasgow	50.60	15	50	30	5	0	2.75
Bristol	20.00	10	45	45	0	0	2.65
Leicester	21.00	10	45	40	5	0	2.60
Leeds	30.00	5	40	55	0	0	2.50
Birmingham	25.70	5	35	60	0	0	2.45
St George's Hospital Medical School	16.86	5	45	40	5	5	2.40
Cardiff	19.40	5	35	40	20	0	2.25
Sheffield	22.00	0	25	65	10	0	2.15

Cancer studies

	Staff submitted (FTE)	4*	3*	2*	1*	Unclassified	Average ranking
Manchester	38.70	30	60	10	0	0	3.20
Cambridge	33.50	35	45	15	5	0	3.10
Institute of Cancer Research	65.51	35	40	25	0	0	3.10
Newcastle upon Tyne	32.93	15	75	10	0	0	3.05
Glasgow	42.05	25	50	25	0	0	3.00
Queen Mary	33.30	15	70	15	0	0	3.00
Leeds	48.70	15	65	20	0	0	2.95
Oxford	38.75	25	50	20	5	0	2.95
Birmingham	50.70	15	65	15	5	0	2.90
Imperial College	51.55	15	60	20	5	0	2.85
Southampton	24.79	15	60	20	5	0	2.85
UCL	40.40	25	50	15	5	5	2.85
Cardiff	26.60	10	55	30	5	0	2.70
Sheffield	34.85	5	55	40	0	0	2.65
King's College London	30.00	5	50	45	0	0	2.60
Queen's, Belfast	37.00	10	40	45	5	0	2.55
Leicester	27.05	5	50	40	0	5	2.50
Liverpool	22.00	10	30	50	5	5	2.35

Infection and immunology

	Staff submitted (FTE)	4*	3*	2*	1*	Unclassified	Average ranking
Oxford	91.00	45	40	10	5	0	3.25
Cambridge	46.00	35	45	15	0	5	3.05
Imperial College	102.40	30	40	25	5	0	2.95
London School of Hygiene & Tropical Medicine	30.80	20	60	15	5	0	2.95
UCL	44.36	20	60	15	5	0	2.95
King's College London	41.80	15	55	25	5	0	2.80
Glasgow	39.00	5	65	25	5	0	2.70
Liverpool	47.30	20	45	25	5	5	2.70
Bristol	28.00	5	45	50	0	0	2.55
Cardiff	42.60	10	40	45	5	0	2.55
Birmingham	50.00	10	40	40	5	5	2.45
Sheffield	18.00	5	40	50	5	0	2.45

	Staff submitted (FTE)	4*	3*	2*	1*	Unclassified	Average ranking
St George's Hospital Medical School	22.00	5	40	45	10	0	2.40
Leicester	29.00	5	25	65	5	0	2.30
Nottingham	18.00	0	25	75	0	0	2.25

Other hospital based clinical subjects

	Staff submitted (FTE)	4*	3*	2*	1*	Unclassified	Average ranking
Edinburgh	158.47	40	40	20	0	0	3.20
Cambridge	53.70	35	45	20	0	0	3.15
UCL	296.56	40	30	25	5	0	3.05
Imperial College	174.10	30	45	20	5	0	3.00
King's College London	47.00	25	50	25	0	0	3.00
Oxford	62.84	35	35	25	5	0	3.00
Birmingham	30.65	20	55	25	0	0	2.95
Queen Mary	61.76	15	65	20	0	0	2.95
Aberdeen	47.00	15	60	20	5	0	2.85
Manchester	39.13	10	60	30	0	0	2.80
Newcastle upon Tyne	92.84	15	50	30	5	0	2.75
Bristol	21.00	5	55	40	0	0	2.65
Southampton	105.65	10	50	35	5	0	2.65
Exeter	20.96	5	60	25	10	0	2.60
Liverpool	54.80	5	55	35	5	0	2.60
Plymouth	10.60	5	60	25	10	0	2.60
Sheffield	54.36	5	55	30	10	0	2.55
Queen's, Belfast	13.00	10	35	45	10	0	2.45
Warwick	38.00	5	35	55	5	0	2.40
Nottingham	71.70	5	30	55	10	0	2.30
Glasgow	35.20	10	25	45	20	0	2.25
Leeds	35.05	5	25	60	10	0	2.25
Leicester	17.00	5	25	60	10	0	2.25
St George's Hospital Medical School	11.00	0	35	55	10	0	2.25
Brighton/Sussex Medical School	34.50	5	30	45	20	0	2.20
Cardiff	31.42	0	25	60	15	0	2.10
Bournemouth	5.70	0	20	30	35	15	1.55

Other laboratory based clinical subjects

	Staff submitted (FTE)	4*	3*	2*	1*	Unclassified	Average ranking
Edinburgh	158.47	40	40	20	0	0	3.20
Cambridge	53.70	35	45	20	0	0	3.15
UCL	296.56	40	30	25	5	0	3.05
Imperial College	174.10	30	45	20	5	0	3.00
King's College London	47.00	25	50	25	0	0	3.00
Oxford	62.84	35	35	25	5	0	3.00
Birmingham	30.65	20	55	25	0	0	2.95
Queen Mary	61.76	15	65	20	0	0	2.95
Aberdeen	47.00	15	60	20	5	0	2.85
Manchester	39.13	10	60	30	0	0	2.80
Newcastle upon Tyne	92.84	15	50	30	5	0	2.75
Bristol	21.00	5	55	40	0	0	2.65
Southampton	105.65	10	50	35	5	0	2.65
Exeter	20.96	5	60	25	10	0	2.60
Liverpool	54.80	5	55	35	5	0	2.60
Plymouth	10.60	5	60	25	10	0	2.60
Sheffield	54.36	5	55	30	10	0	2.55

	Staff submitted (FTE)	4*	3*	2*	1*	Unclassified	Average ranking
Queen's, Belfast	13.00	10	35	45	10	0	2.45
Warwick	38.00	5	35	55	5	0	2.40
Nottingham	71.70	5	30	55	10	0	2.30
Glasgow	35.20	10	25	45	20	0	2.25
Leeds	35.05	5	25	60	10	0	2.25
Leicester	17.00	5	25	60	10	0	2.25
St George's Hospital Medical School	11.00	0	35	55	10	0	2.25
Brighton/Sussex Medical School	34.50	5	30	45	20	0	2.20
Cardiff	31.42	0	25	60	15	0	2.10
Bournemouth	5.70	0	20	30	35	15	1.55

● Group B

Epidemiology and public health

	Staff submitted (FTE)	4*	3*	2*	1*	Unclassified	Average ranking
University of Cambridge	10.00	40	45	15	0	0	3.25
Imperial College	32.95	40	30	30	0	0	3.10
Queen Mary	10.60	30	50	15	5	0	3.05
Bristol	19.10	35	35	25	5	0	3.00
London School of Hygiene & Tropical Medicine	135.37	35	35	25	5	0	3.00
Oxford	19.40	40	25	30	0	5	2.95
UCL	58.92	25	35	35	5	0	2.80
Manchester	20.70	15	45	40	0	0	2.75
St George's Hospital Medical School	10.94	10	55	30	5	0	2.70
Aberdeen	18.80	10	50	35	5	0	2.65
Birmingham	11.00	10	50	35	5	0	2.65
Leeds	24.90	10	50	35	5	0	2.65
Leicester	24.40	10	50	35	5	0	2.65
Glasgow	22.70	10	45	40	5	0	2.60
UEA	16.30	5	40	40	15	0	2.35
Nottingham	24.20	5	35	50	10	0	2.35
Queen's, Belfast	23.50	5	35	50	10	0	2.35
Newcastle upon Tyne	16.77	0	40	45	15	0	2.25
York	20.00	0	30	60	10	0	2.20
Plymouth	5.00	5	20	55	15	5	2.05
Loughborough	19.00	0	15	45	40	0	1.75

Health services research

	Staff submitted (FTE)	4*	3*	2*	1*	Unclassified	Average ranking
Aberdeen	29.40	25	55	20	0	0	3.05
York	25.88	35	40	20	5	0	3.05
Bristol	20.41	20	60	20	0	0	3.00
Queen Mary	6.20	30	35	35	0	0	2.95
London School of Hygiene & Tropical Medicine	43.65	30	35	30	5	0	2.90
Oxford	22.30	20	45	30	5	0	2.80
Birmingham	23.10	15	50	30	5	0	2.75
Brunel	5.40	15	50	30	5	0	2.75
Leeds	11.50	20	40	35	5	0	2.75
Warwick	30.90	10	55	30	5	0	2.70
Sheffield*	56.17	20	35	35	10	0	2.65

	Staff submitted (FTE)	4*	3*	2*	1*	Unclassified	Average ranking
Liverpool	36.60	10	45	35	10	0	2.55
Newcastle upon Tyne	18.25	10	40	45	5	0	2.55
Exeter	16.10	5	45	45	5	0	2.50
King's College London	38.50	10	40	40	10	0	2.50
Plymouth	7.95	5	45	45	5	0	2.50
UEA	21.20	5	40	45	10	0	2.40
Swansea	14.65	0	35	45	20	0	2.15
UCL	12.08	5	25	40	25	5	2.00
Bangor	16.10	5	20	35	40	0	1.90
West of Scotland	7.40	0	15	30	55	0	1.60
Surrey	31.03	0	5	50	40	5	1.55
City	5.75	0	5	45	45	5	1.50

Primary care and other community based clinical subjects

Oxford	10.90	45	40	10	5	0	3.25
Manchester	12.90	40	40	15	5	0	3.15
Southampton	5.55	25	60	15	0	0	3.10
Birmingham	16.40	35	30	30	5	0	2.95
Nottingham	6.56	30	40	25	5	0	2.95
Bristol	10.25	25	45	25	5	0	2.90
Aberdeen	12.30	25	40	25	10	0	2.80
Cambridge	5.20	20	45	30	5	0	2.80
Cardiff	11.90	5	60	30	5	0	2.65
Keele	16.50	15	25	45	15	0	2.40
UCL	17.80	10	40	30	15	5	2.35
Dundee	12.50	5	40	40	10	5	2.30
Westminster	7.95	10	15	30	45	0	1.90
Sunderland	4.60	0	15	25	50	10	1.45

Psychiatry, neuroscience and clinical psychology

Cambridge	40.80	40	40	15	5	0	3.15
Cardiff	21.30	20	60	15	5	0	2.95
UCL	99.20	15	55	25	5	0	2.80
King's College London	214.59	15	40	40	5	0	2.65
Oxford	46.40	15	45	30	10	0	2.65
Bristol	20.76	5	55	35	5	0	2.60
Edinburgh	89.86	10	55	25	5	5	2.60
Imperial College	55.10	10	50	30	10	0	2.60
Manchester	39.50	10	45	40	10	0	2.45
Sheffield	20.00	10	30	50	10	0	2.40
Newcastle upon Tyne	46.90	5	35	50	10	0	2.35
Queen Mary	8.65	10	30	40	20	0	2.30
Nottingham	31.50	5	30	50	15	0	2.25
Glasgow	13.90	0	25	55	20	0	2.05
Kent	8.10	10	20	30	35	5	1.95
Birmingham	18.20	5	20	40	25	10	1.85
St George's Hospital Medical School	3.83	5	10	45	20	20	1.60

● Group C

Dentistry

	Staff submitted (FTE)	4*	3*	2*	1*	Unclassified	Average ranking
Manchester	20.30	30	45	25	0	0	3.05
Queen Mary	33.70	25	50	25	0	0	3.00
King's College London	68.46	30	40	25	5	0	2.95
Sheffield	31.40	15	55	25	5	0	2.80
Bristol	19.41	20	40	35	5	0	2.75
Cardiff	27.60	15	50	30	5	0	2.75
Leeds	24.20	20	40	30	10	0	2.70
Newcastle upon Tyne	27.00	15	45	35	5	0	2.70
UCL	42.40	15	45	35	5	0	2.70
Glasgow	17.60	15	45	30	10	0	2.65
Queen's, Belfast	13.00	5	60	30	5	0	2.65
Birmingham	24.50	10	50	30	10	0	2.60
Dundee	29.92	10	40	40	10	0	2.50
Liverpool	19.40	10	30	55	5	0	2.45

Nursing and midwifery

	Staff submitted (FTE)	4*	3*	2*	1*	Unclassified	Average ranking
Manchester	57.92	50	35	10	5	0	3.30
Southampton	25.00	45	40	10	5	0	3.25
Ulster	25.90	40	40	20	0	0	3.20
York	22.16	35	35	25	5	0	3.00
City	48.60	30	40	15	5	10	2.75
Hertfordshire	15.00	25	30	35	5	5	2.65
Leeds	17.80	25	35	25	10	5	2.65
Nottingham	34.23	20	35	35	10	0	2.65
Stirling	16.60	20	30	35	10	5	2.50
Northumbria	15.55	15	35	35	10	5	2.45
Sheffield	13.00	15	35	35	10	5	2.45
Central Lancashire	23.40	10	40	35	10	5	2.40
Dundee	16.00	10	40	35	10	5	2.40
Cardiff	11.50	15	30	35	15	5	2.35
Salford	24.00	10	30	50	5	5	2.35
UCL	4.00	5	40	35	20	0	2.30
UWE Bristol	29.90	5	35	40	20	0	2.25
Bournemouth	9.20	10	30	35	20	5	2.20
Kingston	6.50	15	30	25	20	10	2.20
Liverpool John Moores	16.20	5	35	40	15	5	2.20
St George's Hospital Medical School	7.00	15	30	25	20	10	2.20
Thames Valley	17.63	10	30	35	20	5	2.20
Bradford	13.75	10	25	40	20	5	2.15
UEA	5.00	10	30	30	25	5	2.15
Glamorgan	22.60	10	25	40	20	5	2.15
London South Bank	11.50	5	30	45	15	5	2.15
Queen's, Belfast	10.68	10	30	30	25	5	2.15
Middlesex	7.90	5	30	40	20	5	2.10
Napier	11.80	5	35	35	15	10	2.10
Swansea	33.65	10	25	35	25	5	2.10
De Montfort	8.00	10	20	40	20	10	2.00
Plymouth	16.00	10	20	35	30	5	2.00

	Staff submitted (FTE)	4*	3*	2*	1*	Unclassified	Average ranking
Edge Hill	5.60	5	25	35	30	5	1.95
Greenwich	3.80	5	25	35	25	10	1.90
Sheffield Hallam	28.50	10	25	25	25	15	1.90
Glyndŵr	5.80	0	25	30	30	15	1.65

Allied health professions and studies

	Staff submitted (FTE)	4*	3*	2*	1*	Unclassified	Average ranking
King's College London*	18.70	30	35	25	10	0	2.85
Ulster*	60.75	25	35	35	5	0	2.80
Lancaster	18.00	20	40	35	5	0	2.75
Surrey	61.65	20	40	35	5	0	2.75
UCL	20.10	25	35	30	10	0	2.75
UWE Bristol	13.00	15	50	25	10	0	2.70
Cardiff	21.70	20	35	35	10	0	2.65
Glasgow	2.00	15	45	30	10	0	2.65
Glasgow Caledonian*	14.20	15	45	30	10	0	2.65
Hull	30.60	20	40	30	5	5	2.65
Queen's, Belfast	14.00	15	45	30	10	0	2.65
Strathclyde	2.00	15	45	30	10	0	2.65
Swansea	35.50	20	35	35	10	0	2.65
Manchester	23.50	20	30	35	15	0	2.55
Nottingham Trent	14.00	20	30	40	5	5	2.55
Aston	56.40	15	35	35	15	0	2.50
Portsmouth	35.70	15	40	30	10	5	2.50
Sheffield	12.90	20	30	25	20	5	2.40
Bradford*	40.40	5	35	40	20	0	2.25
Manchester Met*	29.80	5	30	50	15	0	2.25
Brighton*	35.40	10	25	45	15	5	2.20
Liverpool	37.00	10	30	35	20	5	2.20
Salford	32.93	5	30	45	20	0	2.20
West of Scotland	6.00	15	25	30	25	5	2.20
Nottingham	9.20	10	30	35	15	10	2.15
Westminster	20.00	10	25	40	15	10	2.10
City*	21.75	10	20	45	15	10	2.05
East London	12.50	10	20	35	35	0	2.05
Oxford Brookes	14.30	10	20	40	25	5	2.05
Liverpool John Moores	45.40	5	20	45	30	0	2.00
Middlesex	10.10	5	25	35	30	5	1.95
Northumbria	17.00	5	25	40	20	10	1.95
De Montfort	9.60	5	20	40	30	5	1.90
London Met	10.00	5	25	35	25	10	1.90
Robert Gordon	37.80	5	15	50	25	5	1.90
Central Lancashire	17.80	10	10	45	25	10	1.85
Kingston	28.30	5	20	40	25	10	1.85
Sheffield Hallam	24.00	0	25	40	25	10	1.80
Southampton	19.30	0	25	35	30	10	1.75
Anglia Ruskin	8.40	5	10	40	35	10	1.65
Roehampton	3.80	0	20	35	35	10	1.65
Teesside	21.53	0	20	35	35	10	1.65
Napier	17.80	5	5	40	45	5	1.60
Wolverhampton	33.72	5	15	30	35	15	1.60
Brunel	55.60	10	15	20	30	25	1.55
UEA	12.60	0	15	35	40	10	1.55

	Staff submitted (FTE)	4*	3*	2*	1*	Unclassified	Average ranking
UWIC	28.70	5	10	35	35	15	1.55
Chester	13.80	0	15	30	45	10	1.50
Coventry	14.20	5	5	25	55	10	1.40
Northampton	10.60	5	5	30	45	15	1.40
Worcester	8.20	0	5	40	45	10	1.40
Abertay Dundee	9.70	0	10	35	35	20	1.35
Leeds Met	16.20	0	10	25	55	10	1.35
Plymouth	15.30	0	10	20	45	25	1.15
Canterbury Christ Church	10.60	0	5	25	45	25	1.10
Queen Margaret	51.80	0	5	30	35	30	1.10
Bucks New University	5.60	0	10	15	45	30	1.05
Lincoln	9.00	0	10	15	40	35	1.00
York St John	6.10	0	5	15	55	25	1.00
Staffordshire	12.80	0	5	10	45	40	0.80
Cumbria	12.60	0	0	10	55	35	0.75
Goldsmiths	4.50	0	0	15	40	45	0.70
Glamorgan	4.00	0	0	5	55	40	0.65

Pharmacy

	Staff submitted (FTE)	4*	3*	2*	1*	Unclassified	Average ranking
Nottingham	39.60	35	45	15	5	0	3.10
Manchester	31.60	30	40	25	5	0	2.95
School of Pharmacy	55.00	25	40	25	10	0	2.80
Bath	40.70	20	40	30	10	0	2.70
Queen's, Belfast	23.00	15	40	40	5	0	2.65
UEA	19.00	15	40	30	15	0	2.55
King's College London	44.25	15	40	30	15	0	2.55
Strathclyde	59.50	15	40	30	15	0	2.55
Bradford	20.00	15	40	30	10	5	2.50
Cardiff	26.87	15	40	30	10	5	2.50
Reading	17.50	10	35	35	20	0	2.35
De Montfort	13.40	5	40	40	10	5	2.30
Hertfordshire	12.22	5	30	40	25	0	2.15
Greenwich	12.30	5	20	30	35	10	1.75
Sunderland	25.00	0	20	25	40	15	1.50

● Group D

Biological sciences

	Staff submitted (FTE)	4*	3*	2*	1*	Unclassified	Average ranking
Institute of Cancer Research	31.00	40	45	15	0	0	3.25
Oxford*	37.38	35	40	20	0	5	3.00
Manchester	107.20	25	40	30	5	0	2.85
Sheffield	70.50	20	50	25	5	0	2.85
Bristol*	30.50	20	45	30	5	0	2.80
Dundee	65.00	25	40	25	10	0	2.80
Royal Holloway	22.00	15	55	25	5	0	2.80
Imperial College	92.30	20	45	25	10	0	2.75
King's College London	18.20	20	45	25	10	0	2.75
York	57.51	25	35	30	10	0	2.75
Leeds	113.80	15	45	35	5	0	2.70
Cambridge	213.69	20	40	30	5	5	2.65

	Staff submitted (FTE)	4*	3*	2*	1*	Unclassified	Average ranking
Edinburgh	122.71	15	45	30	10	0	2.65
Aberdeen	46.80	15	40	35	10	0	2.60
Cardiff	53.90	15	40	35	10	0	2.60
Glasgow	78.60	15	40	35	10	0	2.60
Newcastle upon Tyne	44.00	15	45	30	5	5	2.60
Institute of Zoology	21.00	10	40	45	5	0	2.55
St Andrews	45.50	10	40	45	5	0	2.55
Bath	36.70	10	40	40	10	0	2.50
Birkbeck College	22.95	15	40	30	10	5	2.50
Durham	36.00	10	40	40	10	0	2.50
UEA	58.70	10	40	40	10	0	2.50
Exeter	48.83	10	40	40	10	0	2.50
UCL	79.05	15	40	30	10	5	2.50
Birmingham	58.30	10	40	40	5	5	2.45
Nottingham	36.90	10	40	40	5	5	2.45
Southampton	41.66	10	40	35	15	0	2.45
Warwick	57.57	10	40	35	15	0	2.45
Leicester	79.33	10	35	40	15	0	2.40
Liverpool	65.00	10	30	45	15	0	2.35
Essex	30.90	5	35	45	10	5	2.25
Queen Mary	51.80	5	35	45	10	5	2.25
Sussex	27.30	5	30	45	20	0	2.20
Queen's, Belfast	35.00	5	25	50	20	0	2.15
Reading	34.70	5	30	45	15	5	2.15
Bangor	16.56	5	20	55	20	0	2.10
Kent	19.40	5	30	40	20	5	2.10
Plymouth	30.80	0	25	50	25	0	2.00
Open University	18.80	5	20	45	25	5	1.95
Hull	11.80	5	10	55	30	0	1.90
Swansea	16.00	0	20	55	20	5	1.90
Oxford Brookes	12.00	5	15	45	30	5	1.85
Cranfield	23.20	5	15	35	35	10	1.70
Liverpool John Moores	7.00	0	10	50	40	0	1.70
Derby	6.00	0	15	35	50	0	1.65
Glamorgan	4.00	0	10	30	55	5	1.45
Roehampton	4.00	0	5	35	55	5	1.40
Bath Spa	3.00	0	0	15	80	5	1.10

Pre-clinical and human biological sciences

	Staff submitted (FTE)	4*	3*	2*	1*	Unclassified	Average ranking
Oxford	54.00	30	50	15	0	5	3.00
Manchester	72.70	20	45	35	0	0	2.85
UCL	46.31	35	35	20	0	10	2.85
Queen Mary	28.60	20	45	25	10	0	2.75
Bristol	80.18	15	40	35	10	0	2.60
King's College London	70.90	20	35	35	5	5	2.60
Liverpool	44.00	10	45	35	10	0	2.55
Sussex	35.60	20	35	30	5	10	2.50
Nottingham	56.44	5	35	45	10	5	2.25
St George's Hospital Medical School	46.40	5	35	45	5	10	2.20
Aberdeen	35.00	5	35	35	15	10	2.10
UHI Millennium Institute	2.00	0	10	55	35	0	1.75
London Met	8.00	0	5	25	45	25	1.10

	Staff submitted (FTE)	4*	3*	2*	1*	Unclassified	Average ranking

Agriculture, veterinary and food science

	Staff submitted (FTE)	4*	3*	2*	1*	Unclassified	Average ranking
Warwick	33.52	20	40	35	5	0	2.75
Aberdeen	20.00	20	35	40	5	0	2.70
Nottingham	104.30	15	45	35	5	0	2.70
Leeds	9.80	20	35	35	5	5	2.60
Reading*	31.10	15	40	35	10	0	2.60
Aberystwyth	46.50	10	35	50	5	0	2.50
Glasgow	74.90	5	50	35	10	0	2.50
Royal Veterinary College	102.97	10	45	35	5	5	2.50
Edinburgh	107.24	20	35	25	10	10	2.45
Stirling	32.90	5	45	40	10	0	2.45
Bangor	35.00	5	40	45	10	0	2.40
Cambridge	38.60	5	40	45	10	0	2.40
Liverpool	62.60	5	40	45	10	0	2.40
Newcastle upon Tyne	39.00	5	40	45	10	0	2.40
UWE Bristol	6.00	5	40	45	10	0	2.40
Bristol	55.38	0	40	45	15	0	2.25
Cranfield	27.40	0	40	45	15	0	2.25
Ulster	7.00	0	35	55	10	0	2.25
Heriot-Watt	12.70	5	35	35	25	0	2.20
Queen's, Belfast	13.00	5	25	55	15	0	2.20
Greenwich	24.45	5	25	50	20	0	2.15
Harper Adams UC	18.40	0	25	45	30	0	1.95
Plymouth	19.00	0	10	55	30	5	1.70
Lincoln	8.45	5	5	45	40	5	1.65
Royal Agricultural College	8.20	0	15	25	55	5	1.50
University Marine Biological Station, Millport	4.00	5	10	15	70	0	1.50
London Met	3.00	0	5	50	30	15	1.45
UHI Millennium Institute	3.00	0	5	35	60	0	1.45
Cumbria	5.00	0	0	35	55	10	1.25

● Group E

Earth systems and environmental sciences

	Staff submitted (FTE)	4*	3*	2*	1*	Unclassified	Average ranking
Cambridge	44.90	40	50	10	0	0	3.30
Oxford	32.08	35	50	15	0	0	3.20
Birkbeck College	9.00	25	55	20	0	0	3.05
UCL	31.50	25	55	20	0	0	3.05
Reading	40.70	30	45	20	5	0	3.00
Bristol	47.70	25	50	20	5	0	2.95
UEA	71.67	25	45	25	5	0	2.90
Royal Holloway	22.30	20	50	30	0	0	2.90
Liverpool	25.00	15	60	20	5	0	2.85
Manchester	37.10	20	50	25	5	0	2.85
Southampton	62.83	20	50	25	5	0	2.85
Cardiff	37.00	15	55	25	5	0	2.80
Durham	32.20	15	55	25	5	0	2.80
Edinburgh	77.14	15	55	25	5	0	2.80
Lancaster	55.25	15	55	25	5	0	2.80

	Staff submitted (FTE)	4*	3*	2*	1*	Unclassified	Average ranking
Leeds	74.30	15	55	25	5	0	2.80
Open University	52.80	15	55	25	5	0	2.80
Birmingham	17.48	15	50	30	5	0	2.75
Newcastle upon Tyne	26.20	15	50	30	5	0	2.75
Sheffield	19.20	15	50	30	5	0	2.75
Leicester	17.20	10	55	30	5	0	2.70
Aberdeen	14.53	10	50	35	5	0	2.65
York	16.80	10	50	35	5	0	2.65
Bangor	28.40	10	50	30	10	0	2.60
Glasgow	36.00	5	50	35	10	0	2.50
Kent	8.41	5	50	35	10	0	2.50
Plymouth	36.50	5	45	45	5	0	2.50
Abertay Dundee	12.00	10	35	40	15	0	2.40
Brunel	8.60	10	30	50	10	0	2.40
Portsmouth	13.20	5	40	45	10	0	2.40
Manchester Met	17.91	5	40	40	15	0	2.35
Stirling	19.80	5	35	50	10	0	2.35
Ulster	24.00	5	35	50	10	0	2.35
Brighton	17.00	0	40	50	10	0	2.30
UHI Millennium Institute	42.00	5	35	45	15	0	2.30
Westminster	4.20	5	30	45	20	0	2.20
Heriot-Watt	10.90	0	25	55	20	0	2.05
Bedfordshire	8.40	5	10	55	30	0	1.90
Napier	13.00	0	20	45	30	5	1.80
West of Scotland	7.00	0	15	50	35	0	1.80
Sunderland	5.00	0	10	50	40	0	1.70
Nottingham Trent	2.00	0	5	50	45	0	1.60

Chemistry

	Staff submitted (FTE)	4*	3*	2*	1*	Unclassified	Average ranking
Cambridge	62.95	40	40	20	0	0	3.20
Nottingham	35.00	30	55	15	0	0	3.15
Oxford	73.90	30	45	25	0	0	3.05
Bristol	67.00	25	50	25	0	0	3.00
Edinburgh	43.89	30	40	30	0	0	3.00
St Andrews	33.00	30	40	30	0	0	3.00
Imperial College	53.10	20	55	25	0	0	2.95
Leeds	37.20	20	50	30	0	0	2.90
Warwick	32.80	15	60	25	0	0	2.90
York	46.71	15	60	25	0	0	2.90
Liverpool	37.10	20	50	25	5	0	2.85
Manchester	58.30	20	45	35	0	0	2.85
Sheffield	33.70	15	55	30	0	0	2.85
Durham	42.60	20	45	30	5	0	2.80
UCL	53.75	15	50	35	0	0	2.80
Glasgow	25.00	10	60	25	5	0	2.75
Strathclyde	26.40	10	60	25	5	0	2.75
Cardiff	36.57	10	50	40	0	0	2.70
Bath	28.00	5	55	40	0	0	2.65
Birmingham	22.00	10	50	35	5	0	2.65
Southampton	41.20	10	50	35	5	0	2.65
UEA	30.00	5	50	45	0	0	2.60
Heriot-Watt	19.00	10	40	50	0	0	2.60
Sussex	21.00	10	40	45	5	0	2.55

	Staff submitted (FTE)	4*	3*	2*	1*	Unclassified	Average ranking
Hull	26.00	5	45	45	5	0	2.50
Bangor	12.00	10	35	45	10	0	2.45
Newcastle upon Tyne	23.00	5	40	50	5	0	2.45
Queen's, Belfast	32.60	5	40	50	5	0	2.45
Aberdeen	12.00	5	35	55	5	0	2.40
Leicester	21.80	5	35	55	5	0	2.40
Loughborough	25.33	0	25	70	5	0	2.20
Reading	28.00	0	25	65	10	0	2.15
Huddersfield	10.00	0	25	50	25	0	2.00

Physics

	Staff submitted (FTE)	4*	3*	2*	1*	Unclassified	Average ranking
Lancaster	26.40	25	45	25	5	0	2.90
Bath	20.20	20	50	25	5	0	2.85
Cambridge	141.25	25	40	30	5	0	2.85
Nottingham	44.45	25	40	30	5	0	2.85
St Andrews	32.20	25	40	30	5	0	2.85
Edinburgh	60.50	20	45	30	5	0	2.80
Durham	69.50	20	40	35	5	0	2.75
Glasgow	45.75	20	40	35	5	0	2.75
Imperial College	126.80	20	45	25	10	0	2.75
Sheffield	31.50	20	40	35	5	0	2.75
UCL	101.03	20	40	35	5	0	2.75
Birmingham	43.60	20	40	30	10	0	2.70
Exeter	28.00	15	45	35	5	0	2.70
Sussex	20.00	15	45	35	5	0	2.70
Bristol	46.00	20	35	35	10	0	2.65
Heriot-Watt	19.50	15	40	40	5	0	2.65
Liverpool	34.60	20	35	35	10	0	2.65
Oxford	140.10	20	35	35	10	0	2.65
Southampton	45.30	15	40	40	5	0	2.65
Hertfordshire	28.00	15	40	35	10	0	2.60
Manchester	82.80	20	35	30	15	0	2.60
Warwick	51.00	15	35	45	5	0	2.60
York	26.00	15	40	35	10	0	2.60
King's College London	16.40	10	40	45	5	0	2.55
Leeds	35.50	15	35	40	10	0	2.55
Leicester	45.00	15	40	30	15	0	2.55
Royal Holloway	27.96	10	45	35	10	0	2.55
Surrey	27.20	10	45	35	10	0	2.55
Swansea	20.75	10	40	45	5	0	2.55
Queen Mary	34.98	15	35	35	15	0	2.50
Queen's, Belfast	50.00	10	40	40	10	0	2.50
Loughborough	17.10	15	35	35	10	5	2.45
Liverpool John Moores	16.50	10	35	40	15	0	2.40
Cardiff	32.30	5	45	30	20	0	2.35
Strathclyde	31.67	5	35	50	10	0	2.35
Brighton	1.00	0	45	45	5	5	2.30
Central Lancashire	22.20	5	35	45	15	0	2.30
Armagh Observatory	7.50	5	30	50	15	0	2.25
Keele	10.00	5	35	40	20	0	2.25
Kent	3.00	0	30	60	10	0	2.20
Aberystwyth	18.33	5	15	50	30	0	1.95
West of Scotland	3.70	0	20	50	20	10	1.80

● Group F

Pure mathematics

	Staff submitted (FTE)	4*	3*	2*	1*	Unclassified	Average ranking
Imperial College	21.80	40	45	15	0	0	3.25
Warwick	32.00	35	45	20	0	0	3.15
Oxford	55.16	35	40	25	0	0	3.10
Cambridge	55.00	30	45	25	0	0	3.05
Bristol	34.53	30	40	25	5	0	2.95
Edinburgh	31.00	25	45	30	0	0	2.95
Heriot-Watt	10.00	25	45	30	0	0	2.95
Aberdeen	14.00	20	45	35	0	0	2.85
Bath	10.00	25	35	40	0	0	2.85
King's College London	13.00	20	50	25	0	5	2.80
Manchester	27.00	20	40	35	5	0	2.75
UCL	15.25	20	40	35	5	0	2.75
Durham	15.00	20	40	35	0	5	2.70
UEA	7.00	15	45	35	5	0	2.70
Queen Mary	20.20	10	50	40	0	0	2.70
Sheffield	17.25	15	40	45	0	0	2.70
Loughborough	11.40	10	45	45	0	0	2.65
Exeter	5.00	10	45	40	5	0	2.60
Glasgow	16.32	15	40	35	10	0	2.60
Leeds	23.20	10	45	40	5	0	2.60
Leicester	10.00	10	40	50	0	0	2.60
Nottingham	15.00	15	35	45	5	0	2.60
Birmingham	18.00	15	40	35	5	5	2.55
York	12.34	10	35	50	5	0	2.50
Lancaster	10.00	10	40	35	15	0	2.45
Liverpool	15.00	10	35	45	10	0	2.45
London School of Economics	12.50	5	40	50	5	0	2.45
Queen's, Belfast	8.20	5	40	50	5	0	2.45
Southampton	15.75	5	45	40	10	0	2.45
Newcastle upon Tyne	10.00	5	30	60	5	0	2.35
Swansea	20.50	5	35	50	10	0	2.35
Aberystwyth	8.30	5	35	45	15	0	2.30
Cardiff	30.45	5	35	45	15	0	2.30
London Met	4.00	10	25	50	15	0	2.30
St Andrews	12.00	5	30	55	10	0	2.30
Kent	6.00	0	35	55	10	0	2.25
Open University	16.50	5	25	40	30	0	2.05
Royal Holloway	26.60	0	25	35	20	20	1.65

Applied mathematics

	Staff submitted (FTE)	4*	3*	2*	1*	Unclassified	Average ranking
Cambridge	80.30	30	45	25	0	0	3.05
Oxford	54.25	30	45	25	0	0	3.05
Bristol	38.00	25	45	30	0	0	2.95
Bath	19.80	20	50	30	0	0	2.90
Portsmouth	16.00	15	60	25	0	0	2.90
St Andrews	15.00	25	45	25	5	0	2.90
Durham	26.00	15	60	20	5	0	2.85
Imperial College	37.20	20	45	35	0	0	2.85

	Staff submitted (FTE)	4*	3*	2*	1*	Unclassified	Average ranking
Manchester	28.80	25	35	40	0	0	2.85
Southampton	17.00	15	55	30	0	0	2.85
Warwick	29.25	30	30	35	5	0	2.85
Nottingham	34.40	20	45	30	5	0	2.80
Surrey	17.42	15	55	25	5	0	2.80
Edinburgh	17.00	15	50	30	5	0	2.75
Heriot-Watt	18.46	15	50	30	5	0	2.75
Exeter	18.00	10	50	40	0	0	2.70
Keele	9.00	15	45	35	5	0	2.70
King's College London	18.00	15	50	25	10	0	2.70
Liverpool	23.33	15	45	35	5	0	2.70
Newcastle upon Tyne	11.00	15	45	35	5	0	2.70
Leeds	24.90	15	40	40	5	0	2.65
Brunel	19.00	5	55	30	10	0	2.55
Kent	6.00	10	35	55	0	0	2.55
Strathclyde	24.33	10	40	45	5	0	2.55
York	22.00	10	40	45	5	0	2.55
Glasgow	19.00	10	40	40	10	0	2.50
Loughborough	20.40	10	40	40	10	0	2.50
Queen Mary	15.00	10	40	40	10	0	2.50
Sheffield	17.00	10	35	50	5	0	2.50
Sussex	13.00	10	40	40	10	0	2.50
UCL	16.50	10	40	40	10	0	2.50
Dundee	10.70	10	35	45	10	0	2.45
Leicester	12.00	5	40	50	5	0	2.45
UEA	7.00	5	40	45	10	0	2.40
Birmingham	25.00	10	35	35	20	0	2.35
Reading	21.30	5	35	45	15	0	2.30
City	8.20	5	15	65	15	0	2.10
Coventry	7.00	0	20	70	10	0	2.10
Plymouth	4.00	0	25	55	20	0	2.05
Glamorgan	4.00	0	20	45	30	5	1.80
Oxford Brookes	5.71	0	10	55	35	0	1.75
Brighton	3.00	0	15	45	35	5	1.70
Chester	5.80	0	15	45	35	5	1.70
UWE Bristol	9.00	0	10	50	40	0	1.70
Glasgow Caledonian	1.00	5	5	30	60	0	1.55
Staffordshire	1.00	0	0	0	95	5	0.95

Statistics and operational research

	Staff submitted (FTE)	4*	3*	2*	1*	Unclassified	Average ranking
Oxford	24.50	40	50	10	0	0	3.30
Cambridge	16.00	30	45	25	0	0	3.05
Imperial College	13.90	25	50	25	0	0	3.00
Bristol	23.00	25	45	30	0	0	2.95
Warwick	24.00	25	45	30	0	0	2.95
Nottingham	9.00	20	50	30	0	0	2.90
Leeds	11.00	25	40	30	5	0	2.85
Kent	12.00	20	45	30	5	0	2.80
Bath	15.00	20	40	35	5	0	2.75
Southampton	28.00	15	50	30	5	0	2.75
Lancaster	21.65	15	45	35	5	0	2.70
St Andrews	7.00	10	50	35	5	0	2.65

	Staff submitted (FTE)	4*	3*	2*	1*	Unclassified	Average ranking
Manchester	10.90	20	35	30	15	0	2.60
Newcastle upon Tyne	13.00	10	45	40	5	0	2.60
Sheffield	10.70	10	50	30	10	0	2.60
Brunel	10.00	15	35	40	10	0	2.55
Glasgow	13.00	15	35	40	10	0	2.55
London School of Economics	13.00	15	40	35	5	5	2.55
Open University	7.00	10	40	45	5	0	2.55
Durham	11.60	5	45	45	5	0	2.50
UCL	13.50	10	40	40	10	0	2.50
Edinburgh	11.00	10	35	45	10	0	2.45
Heriot-Watt	19.00	10	35	45	10	0	2.45
Queen Mary	8.20	10	30	45	15	0	2.35
Strathclyde	10.33	10	30	45	15	0	2.35
Reading	7.70	5	30	55	10	0	2.30
Salford	9.80	0	35	55	10	0	2.25
Greenwich	2.00	0	40	40	20	0	2.20
Liverpool	5.00	0	35	50	15	0	2.20
Plymouth	4.00	0	30	45	25	0	2.05
London Met	4.00	5	20	40	35	0	1.95

Computer science and informatics

	Staff submitted (FTE)	4*	3*	2*	1*	Unclassified	Average ranking
Cambridge	44.83	45	45	10	0	0	3.35
Edinburgh	104.25	35	50	15	0	0	3.20
Imperial College	53.40	35	50	15	0	0	3.20
Southampton	41.40	35	50	15	0	0	3.20
Manchester	72.05	30	55	15	0	0	3.15
Oxford	55.75	35	45	20	0	0	3.15
UCL	54.40	35	45	20	0	0	3.15
Glasgow	30.00	30	50	20	0	0	3.10
Nottingham	30.50	30	50	20	0	0	3.10
Lancaster	30.25	25	55	20	0	0	3.05
Leeds	32.50	25	55	20	0	0	3.05
Liverpool	28.00	30	45	25	0	0	3.05
Birmingham	34.00	30	45	20	5	0	3.00
Plymouth	11.25	25	50	25	0	0	3.00
Queen Mary	28.00	25	50	25	0	0	3.00
Aberystwyth	15.53	25	45	30	0	0	2.95
Bath	24.33	25	50	20	5	0	2.95
Bristol	36.20	30	40	25	5	0	2.95
Open University	24.00	25	45	30	0	0	2.95
York	34.60	25	50	20	5	0	2.95
Aberdeen	14.80	20	50	30	0	0	2.90
Newcastle upon Tyne	30.60	20	50	30	0	0	2.90
Swansea	22.00	25	45	25	5	0	2.90
Cardiff	22.15	20	50	25	5	0	2.85
Sussex	33.00	20	50	25	5	0	2.85
Durham	22.00	20	45	30	5	0	2.80
Leicester	19.00	20	45	30	5	0	2.80
Royal Holloway	20.83	25	40	25	10	0	2.80
Birkbeck College	19.00	15	50	30	5	0	2.75
Dundee	15.20	15	50	30	5	0	2.75
UEA	17.50	20	45	30	0	5	2.75

	Staff submitted (FTE)	4*	3*	2*	1*	Unclassified	Average ranking
Essex	31.00	15	50	30	5	0	2.75
Kent	26.70	15	50	30	5	0	2.75
Sheffield	34.00	15	50	30	5	0	2.75
Warwick	26.50	15	50	30	5	0	2.75
Goldsmiths	21.20	20	40	30	10	0	2.70
King's College London	24.00	15	45	35	5	0	2.70
St Andrews	21.00	15	45	35	5	0	2.70
Exeter	6.00	15	50	25	5	5	2.65
Heriot-Watt	20.10	15	45	30	10	0	2.65
Queen's, Belfast	21.00	15	45	30	10	0	2.65
Brighton	9.00	15	40	35	10	0	2.60
City	23.30	15	40	35	10	0	2.60
Hertfordshire	25.00	10	45	40	5	0	2.60
Loughborough	16.20	15	40	35	10	0	2.60
Strathclyde	13.40	15	35	40	10	0	2.55
Ulster	41.00	10	45	35	10	0	2.55
Bangor	6.95	15	35	40	5	5	2.50
Lincoln	9.00	15	35	35	15	0	2.50
Liverpool John Moores	4.00	5	45	45	5	0	2.50
Oxford Brookes	10.67	15	35	35	15	0	2.50
Teesside	7.00	10	45	30	15	0	2.50
De Montfort	22.30	10	35	40	15	0	2.40
Stirling	10.00	5	40	45	10	0	2.40
UWE Bristol	15.80	10	35	40	15	0	2.40
Bradford	23.00	5	40	40	15	0	2.35
Glyndŵr	3.20	5	35	50	10	0	2.35
Robert Gordon	19.60	5	40	40	15	0	2.35
Surrey	16.20	10	40	30	15	5	2.35
Bournemouth	10.20	5	30	50	15	0	2.25
Glamorgan	22.45	5	35	40	20	0	2.25
Middlesex	22.30	10	25	45	20	0	2.25
Kingston	17.45	5	30	45	20	0	2.20
London South Bank	7.00	5	25	50	20	0	2.15
Manchester Met	13.00	5	30	40	25	0	2.15
Nottingham Trent	6.00	0	30	55	15	0	2.15
Reading	22.00	5	25	50	20	0	2.15
Bedfordshire	16.20	0	30	50	20	0	2.10
Coventry	8.50	5	20	50	25	0	2.05
Huddersfield	6.00	5	20	50	25	0	2.05
Staffordshire	7.00	0	30	45	25	0	2.05
Westminster	20.25	5	20	50	25	0	2.05
Napier	26.70	0	20	60	20	0	2.00
West of Scotland	2.00	0	30	45	20	5	2.00
Greenwich	16.80	0	20	50	30	0	1.90
Portsmouth	12.20	5	20	40	30	5	1.90
Sunderland	33.97	5	20	35	40	0	1.90
Glasgow Caledonian	8.00	0	15	55	25	5	1.80
Liverpool Hope	4.20	0	20	40	35	5	1.75
Thames Valley	5.00	0	15	40	40	5	1.65
London Met	23.00	0	10	35	50	5	1.50

● Group G

Electrical and electronic engineering

	Staff submitted (FTE)	4*	3*	2*	1*	Unclassified	Average ranking
Leeds	22.00	30	50	15	5	0	3.05
Bangor	8.00	30	40	25	5	0	2.95
Manchester	46.00	25	45	30	0	0	2.95
Surrey	65.65	30	40	25	5	0	2.95
Imperial College	44.00	20	55	20	5	0	2.90
Sheffield*	18.00	25	40	30	5	0	2.85
Southampton	65.00	25	40	30	5	0	2.85
Glasgow	37.50	20	45	30	5	0	2.80
UCL	33.00	25	35	35	5	0	2.80
Bath	15.70	25	35	30	10	0	2.75
Bristol	32.00	10	55	30	5	0	2.70
Essex	11.45	20	40	30	10	0	2.70
Liverpool John Moores	2.00	20	40	30	10	0	2.70
Loughborough	26.20	15	45	35	5	0	2.70
Nottingham	22.00	10	55	30	5	0	2.70
Queen's, Belfast	32.00	20	40	30	10	0	2.70
Newcastle upon Tyne	30.70	15	45	30	10	0	2.65
Liverpool	25.00	15	40	35	10	0	2.60
Cardiff	18.26	10	40	45	5	0	2.55
Queen Mary	22.00	15	35	40	10	0	2.55
Strathclyde	65.00	15	35	40	10	0	2.55
York	21.00	10	45	35	10	0	2.55
Birmingham	26.44	10	50	25	10	5	2.50
Lancaster	9.50	10	45	35	5	5	2.50
Kent	16.00	15	25	45	15	0	2.40
Coventry	3.20	5	45	25	25	0	2.30
King's College London	15.00	5	35	40	20	0	2.25
De Montfort	6.00	5	30	45	20	0	2.20
Reading	19.00	5	35	35	25	0	2.20
Swansea	15.00	10	20	35	30	5	2.00
Plymouth	17.50	5	15	45	30	5	1.85
Bradford	8.20	0	10	50	35	5	1.65
Westminster	5.00	0	15	40	40	5	1.65

General engineering and mineral & mining engineering

	Staff submitted (FTE)	4*	3*	2*	1*	Unclassified	Average ranking
Cambridge	150.00	45	45	10	0	0	3.35
Oxford	85.40	25	60	15	0	0	3.10
Leeds	48.00	20	60	20	0	0	3.00
Nottingham	16.00	25	50	25	0	0	3.00
Imperial College*	44.90	25	45	30	0	0	2.95
Swansea	18.00	15	65	20	0	0	2.95
Manchester	52.16	20	50	30	0	0	2.90
Surrey	44.60	15	60	25	0	0	2.90
Warwick	69.45	20	50	25	5	0	2.85
Heriot-Watt*	27.50	20	45	30	5	0	2.80
Edinburgh	87.39	15	40	45	0	0	2.70
Liverpool John Moores	5.00	20	40	30	10	0	2.70
Nottingham Trent	10.00	15	40	40	5	0	2.65

	Staff submitted (FTE)	4*	3*	2*	1*	Unclassified	Average ranking
Sussex	22.50	10	50	35	5	0	2.65
Aberdeen	31.10	20	35	30	15	0	2.60
Durham	31.20	10	50	30	10	0	2.60
Exeter*	22.33	10	45	40	5	0	2.60
Glamorgan	9.85	5	55	35	5	0	2.60
London South Bank	17.06	5	55	35	5	0	2.60
Strathclyde	11.00	15	45	25	15	0	2.60
Brunel	65.30	5	45	50	0	0	2.55
Lancaster	14.00	10	40	45	5	0	2.55
UWE Bristol	6.60	10	45	35	10	0	2.55
Keele	43.80	10	40	40	10	0	2.50
Leicester	30.20	15	30	45	10	0	2.50
City	34.95	10	35	45	10	0	2.45
Staffordshire	6.00	5	45	40	10	0	2.45
Hertfordshire	4.00	15	35	30	15	5	2.40
Northumbria	14.00	5	45	35	15	0	2.40
Hull	25.60	0	40	55	5	0	2.35
Aston	58.73	10	25	50	15	0	2.30
Dundee	30.90	5	30	55	10	0	2.30
Huddersfield	10.00	5	30	55	10	0	2.30
Queen Mary	33.00	10	35	30	25	0	2.30
Oxford Brookes	11.60	5	40	25	30	0	2.20
Cranfield	42.90	5	25	50	20	0	2.15
De Montfort	6.00	5	25	55	10	5	2.15
Manchester Met	6.00	0	35	45	20	0	2.15
Swansea Met	2.20	10	20	45	25	0	2.15
Bolton	15.20	10	15	50	25	0	2.10
Bournemouth	11.20	5	35	30	25	5	2.10
Central Lancashire	5.60	0	30	50	20	0	2.10
Robert Gordon	14.60	5	15	65	15	0	2.10
Teesside	16.40	0	25	55	20	0	2.05
Abertay Dundee	10.00	5	20	40	35	0	1.95
Kingston	16.00	5	20	40	35	0	1.95
Glasgow Caledonian	10.00	0	20	50	20	10	1.80
Greenwich	14.60	0	20	40	20	20	1.60
Southampton Solent	7.00	5	5	20	50	20	1.25

Chemical engineering

	Staff submitted (FTE)	4*	3*	2*	1*	Unclassified	Average ranking
Cambridge	30.50	30	55	15	0	0	3.15
Imperial College	38.00	30	55	15	0	0	3.15
Manchester	32.73	25	60	15	0	0	3.10
UCL	27.00	15	60	20	5	0	2.85
Birmingham	26.40	20	45	30	5	0	2.80
Newcastle upon Tyne	25.25	10	50	35	5	0	2.65
Sheffield	20.00	15	40	40	5	0	2.65
Bath	13.00	10	45	40	5	0	2.60
Heriot-Watt	11.40	10	35	40	15	0	2.40
Strathclyde	11.00	5	35	35	25	0	2.20

	Staff submitted (FTE)	4*	3*	2*	1*	Unclassified	Average ranking
Civil engineering							
Imperial College	49.40	40	55	5	0	0	3.35
Swansea	18.00	35	60	5	0	0	3.30
Cardiff	21.30	25	65	10	0	0	3.15
Newcastle upon Tyne	41.00	20	70	10	0	0	3.10
Nottingham	30.01	25	60	15	0	0	3.10
Sheffield	28.70	20	65	15	0	0	3.05
Southampton	35.67	25	55	20	0	0	3.05
Bristol	18.00	25	55	15	5	0	3.00
Dundee	16.90	15	70	15	0	0	3.00
Queen's, Belfast	24.05	20	55	25	0	0	2.95
De Montfort	1.00	25	45	25	5	0	2.90
Birmingham	22.55	10	55	30	5	0	2.70
Loughborough	27.50	15	50	25	10	0	2.70
UCL	35.60	15	40	40	5	0	2.65
Leeds	22.20	10	45	40	5	0	2.60
Bradford	8.20	5	50	35	10	0	2.50
Heriot-Watt	18.00	5	50	35	10	0	2.50
Plymouth	7.40	15	30	40	15	0	2.45
Glasgow	14.00	15	40	20	20	5	2.40
Liverpool	13.33	5	45	25	25	0	2.30
Napier	31.35	5	25	45	25	0	2.10
Strathclyde	21.00	5	35	30	25	5	2.10
Greenwich	8.00	5	30	30	30	5	2.00

	Staff submitted (FTE)	4*	3*	2*	1*	Unclassified	Average ranking
Mechanical, aeronautical and manufacturing engineering							
Imperial College	67.00	30	50	15	5	0	3.05
Bristol*	19.10	25	55	15	5	0	3.00
Sheffield	30.20	30	45	20	5	0	3.00
Greenwich	5.50	30	40	25	5	0	2.95
Nottingham	46.50	25	50	20	5	0	2.95
Leeds	40.50	20	55	20	5	0	2.90
Loughborough	143.43	20	50	25	5	0	2.85
Birmingham	18.44	20	50	20	10	0	2.80
Cardiff	25.60	20	45	30	5	0	2.80
Newcastle upon Tyne	31.80	15	50	30	5	0	2.75
Queen's, Belfast	25.00	15	50	30	5	0	2.75
Brighton	4.70	5	65	25	5	0	2.70
Cranfield	95.81	20	40	30	10	0	2.70
Liverpool	23.00	15	45	35	5	0	2.70
Southampton	132.49	15	45	35	5	0	2.70
UCL	28.00	20	35	35	10	0	2.65
Bath	43.40	10	45	40	5	0	2.60
Glasgow*	0.00	10	45	35	10	0	2.55
Strathclyde*	15.00	10	45	35	10	0	2.55
Brunel	38.46	10	40	40	10	0	2.50
Swansea	12.50	10	35	50	5	0	2.50
De Montfort	10.00	5	45	40	10	0	2.45
Bradford	28.60	10	30	50	10	0	2.40
King's College London	18.00	10	35	40	15	0	2.40
Portsmouth	11.20	5	40	40	15	0	2.35

	Staff submitted (FTE)	4*	3*	2*	1*	Unclassified	Average ranking
Plymouth	11.20	0	25	55	20	0	2.05
Wolverhampton	8.00	5	25	35	30	5	1.95
Coventry	8.00	0	25	35	30	10	1.75
Newport	1.00	10	15	20	30	25	1.55
Sunderland	9.25	5	15	20	40	20	1.45

Metallurgy and materials

	Staff submitted (FTE)	4*	3*	2*	1*	Unclassified	Average ranking
Cambridge	29.50	40	55	5	0	0	3.35
Kent	6.00	25	55	20	0	0	3.05
Liverpool	11.00	35	35	30	0	0	3.05
Oxford	37.30	25	55	15	5	0	3.00
Manchester	49.33	20	60	15	5	0	2.95
Birmingham	26.51	15	60	25	0	0	2.90
Sheffield Hallam	38.40	15	50	35	0	0	2.80
Imperial College	27.00	20	35	40	5	0	2.70
Swansea	15.00	15	45	35	5	0	2.70
Queen Mary	30.10	15	40	35	10	0	2.60
Ulster	12.00	5	45	45	5	0	2.50
Open University	6.00	5	45	40	10	0	2.45
Salford	22.00	10	40	35	15	0	2.45
West of Scotland	3.00	0	50	40	10	0	2.40
Sheffield Hallam	20.00	5	30	40	25	0	2.15
Glyndŵr	6.80	5	30	35	30	0	2.10
Manchester Met	13.80	0	30	40	30	0	2.00
Northampton	6.40	0	20	35	35	10	1.65
Coventry	10.50	0	20	35	30	15	1.60
London Met	4.00	0	0	35	45	20	1.15

● Group H

Architecture and built environment

	Staff submitted (FTE)	4*	3*	2*	1*	Unclassified	Average ranking
Cambridge	15.17	30	50	20	0	0	3.10
UCL	49.62	35	40	20	5	0	3.05
Liverpool	17.30	30	45	20	5	0	3.00
Sheffield*	19.60	35	35	25	5	0	3.00
Loughborough	27.00	25	50	20	5	0	2.95
Bath	23.30	25	45	25	5	0	2.90
Edinburgh	18.00	25	45	25	5	0	2.90
Edinburgh College of Art	13.60	25	45	25	5	0	2.90
Reading	22.00	25	45	25	5	0	2.90
Salford	75.10	25	40	25	10	0	2.80
Cardiff	23.30	20	45	25	10	0	2.75
Ulster	32.80	15	50	30	5	0	2.75
De Montfort	14.00	15	50	25	10	0	2.70
Liverpool John Moores	8.00	15	45	35	5	0	2.70
Newcastle upon Tyne	7.00	25	35	30	5	5	2.70
Westminster	9.64	20	40	30	10	0	2.70
Glasgow Caledonian	12.30	15	45	25	15	0	2.60
Heriot-Watt	25.40	10	50	30	10	0	2.60
Wolverhampton	12.50	10	40	40	10	0	2.50

	Staff submitted (FTE)	4*	3*	2*	1*	Unclassified	Average ranking
Northumbria	12.80	5	45	40	10	0	2.45
Glamorgan	6.20	10	40	35	10	5	2.40
Nottingham	36.00	10	30	45	15	0	2.35
UWE Bristol	8.20	5	40	40	10	5	2.30
Sheffield Hallam	6.00	5	40	35	15	5	2.25
Strathclyde	11.30	5	35	40	20	0	2.25
Central Lancashire	6.00	5	35	40	15	5	2.20
Greenwich	10.00	10	30	40	10	10	2.20
Napier	11.00	5	30	45	20	0	2.20
Dundee	7.70	5	35	30	25	5	2.10
London Met	15.50	15	25	25	25	10	2.10
Bolton	5.00	10	30	25	25	10	2.05
Robert Gordon	20.80	10	20	40	25	5	2.05
Lincoln	17.60	5	30	30	30	5	2.00
Nottingham Trent	19.60	0	30	40	25	5	1.95

Town and country planning

	Staff submitted (FTE)	4*	3*	2*	1*	Unclassified	Average ranking
Cambridge	19.56	30	45	25	0	0	3.05
Sheffield	17.00	35	30	30	5	0	2.95
Cardiff	42.40	30	35	25	10	0	2.85
Leeds	31.65	20	45	30	5	0	2.80
Newcastle upon Tyne	27.90	25	40	25	10	0	2.80
Aberdeen	7.90	20	40	30	10	0	2.70
Glasgow	17.39	15	45	35	5	0	2.70
Manchester	17.90	20	40	30	10	0	2.70
Reading	14.20	25	35	30	5	5	2.70
UCL	22.50	20	40	25	15	0	2.65
Sheffield Hallam	18.80	20	30	35	15	0	2.55
Heriot-Watt	13.80	20	30	35	10	5	2.50
Liverpool	9.00	10	40	35	15	0	2.45
Birmingham	11.00	10	40	30	20	0	2.40
UWE Bristol	24.50	5	45	35	10	5	2.35
Gloucestershire	5.40	5	35	45	15	0	2.30
Oxford Brookes	32.60	5	35	40	15	5	2.20
Queen's, Belfast	12.00	10	20	45	25	0	2.15
London Met	7.50	5	30	35	30	0	2.10
Westminster	15.80	5	20	45	25	5	1.95
Birmingham City	8.00	10	15	30	40	5	1.85
Liverpool John Moores	4.00	5	20	30	40	5	1.80
Coventry	6.10	0	20	30	40	10	1.60
Kingston	5.20	0	10	30	50	10	1.40
UHI Millennium Institute	7.50	0	10	35	40	15	1.40

Geography and environmental studies

	Staff submitted (FTE)	4*	3*	2*	1*	Unclassified	Average ranking
Bristol	36.00	30	40	25	5	0	2.95
Cambridge	42.67	30	40	25	5	0	2.95
Durham	56.00	30	40	25	5	0	2.95
Oxford	28.50	30	40	25	5	0	2.95
Queen Mary	32.00	25	50	20	5	0	2.95
Leeds	37.70	25	45	25	5	0	2.90
King's College London	31.20	20	50	25	5	0	2.85

	Staff submitted (FTE)	4*	3*	2*	1*	Unclassified	Average ranking
London School of Economics	23.35	20	50	25	5	0	2.85
Sheffield	32.90	20	50	25	5	0	2.85
UCL	43.35	25	40	30	5	0	2.85
Aberystwyth	31.33	20	45	30	5	0	2.80
Royal Holloway	32.10	20	45	30	5	0	2.80
Exeter	36.00	20	40	35	5	0	2.75
Manchester	22.00	15	50	30	5	0	2.75
Nottingham	37.00	20	40	35	5	0	2.75
St Andrews	29.00	20	40	35	5	0	2.75
Sussex	19.30	15	50	30	5	0	2.75
Dundee	17.70	15	45	35	5	0	2.70
Open University	18.00	20	35	40	5	0	2.70
Swansea	29.30	15	45	35	5	0	2.70
Birmingham	32.20	15	40	40	5	0	2.65
Southampton	32.50	20	35	35	10	0	2.65
Edinburgh	36.80	20	35	30	15	0	2.60
Hull	24.90	15	40	35	10	0	2.60
Glasgow	15.00	10	40	45	5	0	2.55
Liverpool	29.20	10	45	35	10	0	2.55
Newcastle upon Tyne	32.00	10	45	35	10	0	2.55
Plymouth	27.50	10	40	45	5	0	2.55
Queen's, Belfast	20.00	10	40	45	5	0	2.55
Aberdeen	25.70	10	40	40	10	0	2.50
Loughborough	24.25	10	40	40	10	0	2.50
Westminster	5.80	10	40	40	10	0	2.50
Leicester	25.20	10	30	50	10	0	2.40
Reading	18.90	10	35	40	15	0	2.40
Bournemouth	11.00	10	35	35	20	0	2.35
Middlesex	12.15	5	35	40	20	0	2.25
Kingston	17.20	5	25	55	15	0	2.20
Portsmouth	11.00	5	25	55	15	0	2.20
Brunel	7.86	5	20	60	15	0	2.15
Salford	9.10	5	25	45	25	0	2.10
Anglia Ruskin	8.40	5	15	45	30	5	1.85
UWE Bristol	22.90	0	20	50	25	5	1.85
UC Plymouth St Mark & St John	1.00	0	0	85	5	10	1.75
Gloucestershire	12.00	0	15	45	35	5	1.70
Chester	4.00	0	10	45	40	5	1.60
Bath Spa	4.00	0	15	30	50	5	1.55
Worcester	5.00	0	10	45	35	10	1.55
Edge Hill	6.00	0	5	30	45	20	1.20
Swansea Met	3.20	0	5	20	60	15	1.15

Archaeology

Durham	26.40	35	40	20	5	0	3.05
Reading	19.00	40	25	25	10	0	2.95
Cambridge	45.35	30	30	40	0	0	2.90
Oxford	35.50	35	30	25	10	0	2.90
Liverpool	21.20	25	40	30	5	0	2.85
Leicester	29.13	25	40	25	10	0	2.80
Southampton	21.45	25	35	35	5	0	2.80
UCL	61.70	30	30	30	10	0	2.80

	Staff submitted (FTE)	4*	3*	2*	1*	Unclassified	Average ranking
Exeter	15.30	15	50	30	5	0	2.75
Queen's, Belfast	15.00	25	30	40	5	0	2.75
Sheffield	27.00	25	35	30	10	0	2.75
York	21.90	25	35	30	10	0	2.75
Nottingham	16.50	20	40	30	10	0	2.70
Manchester	13.00	15	45	30	10	0	2.65
Bradford	20.00	20	30	40	10	0	2.60
Cardiff	21.33	15	40	35	10	0	2.60
Birmingham	18.20	10	40	45	5	0	2.55
Lampeter	15.00	15	35	35	15	0	2.50
Newcastle upon Tyne	8.50	15	35	35	15	0	2.50
Bristol	15.42	15	35	35	10	5	2.45
Glasgow	20.86	10	40	35	15	0	2.45
Bournemouth	7.50	10	25	40	20	5	2.15
Nottingham Trent	2.00	5	25	45	25	0	2.10
Central Lancashire	5.00	5	15	45	35	0	1.90
Winchester	4.75	0	20	55	20	5	1.90
UHI Millennium Institute	3.30	5	15	40	40	0	1.85

● Group I

Economics and econometrics							
London School of Economics	41.60	60	35	5	0	0	3.55
UCL	32.20	55	40	5	0	0	3.50
Essex	34.31	40	55	5	0	0	3.35
Oxford	78.50	40	55	5	0	0	3.35
Warwick	49.63	40	55	5	0	0	3.35
Bristol	19.45	30	55	15	0	0	3.15
Nottingham	47.25	30	55	15	0	0	3.15
Queen Mary	23.00	30	55	15	0	0	3.15
Cambridge	38.00	30	45	25	0	0	3.05
Manchester	34.80	25	55	20	0	0	3.05
Glasgow	20.80	25	50	25	0	0	3.00
Royal Holloway	22.50	20	60	20	0	0	3.00
Southampton	27.25	20	60	20	0	0	3.00
Edinburgh	18.00	25	45	30	0	0	2.95
Exeter	13.50	20	55	25	0	0	2.95
Kent	13.00	15	60	25	0	0	2.90
Leicester	26.20	20	50	30	0	0	2.90
Aberdeen	14.00	20	45	35	0	0	2.85
Birkbeck College	25.10	20	50	25	5	0	2.85
Sheffield	15.00	15	55	25	5	0	2.80
Surrey	14.60	15	50	35	0	0	2.80
Birmingham	21.38	15	50	30	5	0	2.75
UEA	13.50	15	50	30	5	0	2.75
Stirling	7.60	15	45	40	0	0	2.75
Swansea	18.20	15	45	40	0	0	2.75
York	40.60	15	45	40	0	0	2.75
St Andrews	27.15	15	40	45	0	0	2.70
Sussex	10.00	10	50	40	0	0	2.70

	Staff submitted (FTE)	4*	3*	2*	1*	Unclassified	Average ranking
Brunel	25.00	10	50	35	5	0	2.65
City	14.20	10	45	45	0	0	2.65
Dundee	14.00	5	40	50	5	0	2.45
Loughborough	21.25	5	40	50	5	0	2.45
London Met	8.00	0	35	55	10	0	2.25
Kingston	4.00	5	15	55	25	0	2.00
Manchester Met	4.75	0	10	50	40	0	1.70

Accounting and finance

	Staff submitted (FTE)	4*	3*	2*	1*	Unclassified	Average ranking
Bangor	13.75	15	50	30	5	0	2.75
Essex	30.50	10	45	40	5	0	2.60
Exeter	19.25	10	45	40	5	0	2.60
Bristol	11.00	10	45	35	10	0	2.55
Glasgow	15.00	10	35	35	20	0	2.35
Stirling	10.80	0	45	45	10	0	2.35
Dundee	19.00	5	35	40	20	0	2.25
UWE Bristol	7.00	10	30	40	15	5	2.25
Huddersfield	2.00	0	30	50	15	5	2.05
Open University	4.50	10	25	30	20	15	1.95
West of Scotland	4.00	5	25	35	30	5	1.95
Robert Gordon	7.80	5	15	50	25	5	1.90
Glasgow Caledonian	7.00	0	15	50	35	0	1.80
Liverpool John Moores	8.00	0	5	40	50	5	1.45

Business and management studies

	Staff submitted (FTE)	4*	3*	2*	1*	Unclassified	Average ranking
London Business School	89.86	55	30	10	5	0	3.35
Imperial College	47.60	35	50	15	0	0	3.20
Cambridge	45.40	35	40	20	5	0	3.05
Cardiff	114.85	35	35	25	5	0	3.00
Bath	62.70	30	40	25	5	0	2.95
King's College London	28.25	30	40	25	5	0	2.95
Lancaster	113.36	25	50	20	5	0	2.95
London School of Economics	86.41	30	40	25	5	0	2.95
Oxford	53.00	30	40	25	5	0	2.95
Warwick	130.70	25	50	20	5	0	2.95
Leeds	69.66	20	50	25	5	0	2.85
Manchester	182.22	25	40	30	5	0	2.85
Nottingham	90.40	20	50	25	5	0	2.85
Strathclyde	88.88	25	40	30	5	0	2.85
Cranfield	46.36	25	40	25	10	0	2.80
Aston	88.82	15	45	35	5	0	2.70
Loughborough	57.40	15	45	35	5	0	2.70
Sheffield	43.30	15	45	35	5	0	2.70
Birmingham	47.03	20	35	35	10	0	2.65
Durham	48.80	15	40	40	5	0	2.65
Exeter	24.00	15	45	30	10	0	2.65
Queen's, Belfast	44.00	15	40	40	5	0	2.65
Royal Holloway	43.90	15	40	40	5	0	2.65
St Andrews	22.00	10	50	35	5	0	2.65
City	94.50	15	40	35	10	0	2.60
Queen Mary	25.70	15	40	35	10	0	2.60

	Staff submitted (FTE)	4*	3*	2*	1*	Unclassified	Average ranking
Southampton	36.20	15	40	35	10	0	2.60
Leicester	36.40	15	40	30	15	0	2.55
Bradford	40.60	15	30	45	10	0	2.50
Glasgow	22.15	10	45	30	15	0	2.50
Kent	38.60	10	45	30	15	0	2.50
Newcastle upon Tyne	39.90	10	40	40	10	0	2.50
Reading	38.30	10	40	40	10	0	2.50
Surrey	46.40	10	40	40	10	0	2.50
Birkbeck College	31.90	10	40	35	15	0	2.45
UEA	21.00	10	35	45	10	0	2.45
Edinburgh	52.65	10	40	35	15	0	2.45
Kingston	21.10	10	35	45	10	0	2.45
Liverpool	39.00	10	40	35	15	0	2.45
York	17.00	10	40	35	15	0	2.45
Heriot-Watt	36.23	10	35	40	15	0	2.40
Brunel	51.10	10	35	35	20	0	2.35
Hull	60.60	5	40	40	15	0	2.35
SOAS	14.00	5	35	50	10	0	2.35
Swansea	21.75	10	30	45	15	0	2.35
Brighton	19.75	20	25	25	25	5	2.30
Keele	38.40	10	35	35	15	5	2.30
Stirling	31.90	10	30	40	20	0	2.30
Aberdeen	21.25	10	30	40	15	0	2.25
De Montfort	18.60	10	25	45	20	0	2.25
Open University	33.40	5	35	40	20	0	2.25
Ulster	30.50	5	30	50	15	0	2.25
Manchester Met	26.40	5	30	45	20	0	2.20
Hertfordshire	12.40	5	30	45	15	5	2.15
Middlesex	38.79	5	25	50	20	0	2.15
Nottingham Trent	31.40	5	25	50	20	0	2.15
UWE Bristol	33.00	0	30	55	15	0	2.15
Portsmouth	56.80	5	30	35	30	0	2.10
Robert Gordon	12.90	5	35	30	25	5	2.10
Plymouth	29.00	5	25	45	20	5	2.05
Bristol	6.20	0	30	45	20	5	2.00
Salford	16.00	5	25	35	35	0	2.00
Westminster	21.40	5	25	40	25	5	2.00
Aberystwyth	16.00	5	25	35	30	5	1.95
Bournemouth	23.80	5	25	35	30	5	1.95
Central Lancashire	26.00	5	25	35	30	5	1.95
Glasgow Caledonian	17.00	0	25	50	20	5	1.95
Oxford Brookes	18.00	5	20	45	25	5	1.95
Sheffield Hallam	23.10	5	20	40	30	5	1.90
Teesside	12.00	5	20	35	40	0	1.90
Wolverhampton	9.00	0	20	55	20	5	1.90
Glamorgan	27.10	5	10	50	35	0	1.85
West of Scotland	5.00	5	25	25	40	5	1.85
Leeds Met	16.80	0	20	45	30	5	1.80
Northumbria	19.00	0	20	45	30	5	1.80
Coventry	7.20	0	20	40	35	5	1.75
Greenwich	22.60	5	15	40	30	10	1.75
Bedfordshire	8.00	0	15	45	35	5	1.70

	Staff submitted (FTE)	4*	3*	2*	1*	Unclassified	Average ranking
Bucks New University	2.60	0	20	40	30	10	1.70
Lincoln	21.40	0	20	40	30	10	1.70
Napier	31.00	0	15	45	35	5	1.70
Birmingham City	8.00	5	20	20	45	10	1.65
London South Bank	3.69	5	15	30	40	10	1.65
Abertay Dundee	9.00	0	15	35	40	10	1.55
London Met	28.00	0	15	35	40	10	1.55
Northampton	6.90	5	10	30	45	10	1.55
Gloucestershire	13.80	0	10	35	40	15	1.40
Bolton	3.40	0	10	30	45	15	1.35
UWIC	8.25	0	10	25	55	10	1.35
Queen Margaret	19.00	0	5	25	60	10	1.25

Library and information management

Sheffield	22.20	30	35	25	10	0	2.85
City	11.30	15	50	30	5	0	2.75
King's College London	23.50	35	30	15	15	5	2.75
Robert Gordon	11.00	15	45	40	0	0	2.75
UCL	11.70	30	25	35	10	0	2.75
Wolverhampton	4.00	25	40	20	15	0	2.75
Glasgow	6.40	25	30	35	10	0	2.70
Brunel	50.00	20	30	35	15	0	2.55
Loughborough	27.70	15	40	30	10	5	2.50
Napier	5.50	10	50	25	10	5	2.50
Aberystwyth	11.20	10	40	35	15	0	2.45
Leeds Met	11.60	10	35	45	10	0	2.45
Salford	29.60	25	20	30	20	5	2.40
Coventry	5.00	5	35	45	10	5	2.25
Brighton	7.00	10	30	35	20	5	2.20
Sheffield Hallam	24.10	5	20	35	40	0	1.90
Liverpool John Moores	5.00	5	20	30	45	0	1.85
Manchester Met	16.50	0	20	45	35	0	1.85
Staffordshire	3.00	0	25	35	35	5	1.80
West of Scotland	3.00	0	20	40	25	15	1.65
London South Bank	8.00	0	15	30	45	10	1.50

● Group J

Law

London School of Economics	50.95	45	30	15	10	0	3.10
UCL	42.80	35	40	20	5	0	3.05
Oxford	103.50	35	35	25	5	0	3.00
Durham	31.00	30	35	30	5	0	2.90
Nottingham	46.43	30	35	30	5	0	2.90
Kent	36.50	30	35	25	10	0	2.85
Cambridge	83.27	25	35	35	5	0	2.80
Cardiff	24.85	25	35	35	5	0	2.80
Queen's, Belfast	35.50	25	35	35	5	0	2.80
Edinburgh	48.74	30	25	35	10	0	2.75
Queen Mary	48.83	20	40	30	10	0	2.70

	Staff submitted (FTE)	4*	3*	2*	1*	Unclassified	Average ranking
Reading	21.90	20	40	30	10	0	2.70
Birmingham	26.00	15	45	30	10	0	2.65
Strathclyde	20.50	20	40	25	15	0	2.65
Ulster	24.40	20	35	35	10	0	2.65
Bristol	43.70	15	40	35	10	0	2.60
Glasgow	37.95	15	40	35	10	0	2.60
Sussex	17.20	5	50	45	0	0	2.60
Dundee	27.00	5	45	50	0	0	2.55
King's College London	53.55	15	35	40	10	0	2.55
Leeds	35.20	15	40	30	15	0	2.55
Manchester	61.80	10	40	40	10	0	2.50
Sheffield	31.58	15	35	35	15	0	2.50
Southampton	32.45	5	45	45	5	0	2.50
Brunel	29.00	5	45	40	10	0	2.45
Essex	25.30	5	45	40	10	0	2.45
Keele	25.60	10	40	35	15	0	2.45
Liverpool	23.50	10	45	25	20	0	2.45
Swansea	25.05	5	40	50	5	0	2.45
Lancaster	22.00	5	40	45	10	0	2.40
Oxford Brookes	13.20	10	35	40	15	0	2.40
Warwick	47.33	10	35	40	15	0	2.40
Hull	23.50	5	40	40	15	0	2.35
SOAS	21.30	5	40	40	15	0	2.35
Exeter	26.00	10	35	30	25	0	2.30
UEA	20.00	5	35	40	20	0	2.25
Newcastle upon Tyne	19.00	0	40	45	15	0	2.25
Aberdeen	35.70	5	30	45	20	0	2.20
East London	9.00	5	30	45	20	0	2.20
Leicester	45.40	5	35	35	25	0	2.20
Westminster	28.60	0	35	50	15	0	2.20
Stirling	7.00	5	35	30	30	0	2.15
City	14.05	5	30	35	30	0	2.10
Aberystwyth	21.00	5	30	30	35	0	2.05
Abertay Dundee	3.00	0	20	60	20	0	2.00
Birkbeck College	20.90	5	25	35	30	5	1.95
De Montfort	15.00	0	20	45	35	0	1.85
Wolverhampton	12.60	0	25	40	30	5	1.85
UWE Bristol	15.00	5	15	40	35	5	1.80
Salford	5.00	0	20	35	45	0	1.75
Nottingham Trent	16.00	0	10	50	40	0	1.70
Middlesex	7.30	0	15	35	50	0	1.65
Central Lancashire	17.60	0	15	35	45	5	1.60
Glamorgan	6.80	0	15	30	55	0	1.60
Lincoln	3.00	0	10	40	50	0	1.60
London Met	6.50	0	10	50	25	15	1.55
Glasgow Caledonian	4.50	0	15	30	45	10	1.50
Kingston	4.75	0	10	35	50	5	1.50
Robert Gordon	9.60	0	5	50	35	10	1.50
Greenwich	7.00	0	5	40	45	10	1.40
Sheffield Hallam	9.00	0	5	35	55	5	1.40
Sunderland	11.00	0	0	35	60	5	1.30
Bournemouth	6.20	0	0	25	75	0	1.25

	Staff submitted (FTE)	4*	3*	2*	1*	Unclassified	Average ranking
Coventry	7.00	0	5	15	70	10	1.15
Napier	6.00	0	5	20	55	20	1.10
West of Scotland	2.50	0	0	15	75	10	1.05
Southampton Solent	7.20	0	0	10	65	25	0.85

Politics and international studies

	Staff submitted (FTE)	4*	3*	2*	1*	Unclassified	Average ranking
Essex	28.95	45	30	20	5	0	3.15
Sheffield	25.00	45	30	20	5	0	3.15
Aberystwyth	33.00	40	25	25	10	0	2.95
Oxford	88.85	35	25	30	10	0	2.85
London School of Economics	69.45	30	30	30	10	0	2.80
UCL	15.00	20	45	25	10	0	2.75
SOAS	18.25	15	45	30	10	0	2.65
Sussex*	15.00	15	40	40	5	0	2.65
Warwick	31.00	20	40	25	15	0	2.65
Exeter	29.50	20	35	30	15	0	2.60
Cambridge	26.00	20	30	30	20	0	2.50
Manchester	46.40	20	30	30	20	0	2.50
Nottingham	34.00	15	35	35	15	0	2.50
Edinburgh	30.00	10	45	25	20	0	2.45
Bradford	28.39	15	35	25	25	0	2.40
Durham	23.00	15	35	30	15	5	2.40
Queen's, Belfast	31.00	10	40	30	20	0	2.40
Birkbeck College	17.00	10	35	35	20	0	2.35
Birmingham	28.00	5	40	40	15	0	2.35
Queen Mary	19.00	5	40	40	15	0	2.35
St Andrews	27.00	10	35	35	20	0	2.35
Glasgow	20.00	15	30	30	20	5	2.30
King's College London	61.30	15	30	30	20	5	2.30
Newcastle upon Tyne	18.00	15	25	35	25	0	2.30
York	21.00	15	30	30	20	5	2.30
Bristol	24.00	10	30	35	20	5	2.20
Hull	21.20	10	25	40	20	5	2.15
Keele	29.75	10	20	50	15	5	2.15
Reading	15.00	10	25	35	30	0	2.15
Ulster	8.00	10	25	35	30	0	2.15
Dundee	9.00	10	20	40	30	0	2.10
UEA	9.00	10	15	50	25	0	2.10
Goldsmiths	16.40	10	20	45	20	5	2.10
Kent	21.00	0	35	40	25	0	2.10
Royal Holloway	14.00	5	25	45	25	0	2.10
Aberdeen	18.00	5	20	55	15	5	2.05
Brunel	16.00	5	20	50	25	0	2.05
Southampton	18.25	5	25	40	30	0	2.05
Swansea	13.00	5	15	60	20	0	2.05
Strathclyde	13.00	0	30	45	20	5	2.00
Oxford Brookes	10.50	0	20	55	25	0	1.95
Robert Gordon	8.20	0	25	45	30	0	1.95
Lancaster	18.00	5	15	50	25	5	1.90
De Montfort	14.00	5	15	45	30	5	1.85
Leeds	28.60	5	10	50	30	5	1.80
Leicester	11.00	5	10	50	30	5	1.80

	Staff submitted (FTE)	4*	3*	2*	1*	Unclassified	Average ranking
Liverpool	17.00	0	15	55	25	5	1.80
Westminster	14.40	5	15	40	35	5	1.80
Stirling	6.00	5	10	45	35	5	1.75
Lincoln	8.20	5	15	30	45	5	1.70
London Met	19.60	5	15	30	40	10	1.65
Coventry	12.00	5	5	45	35	10	1.60
UWE Bristol	11.00	0	15	30	50	5	1.55
Sunderland	3.70	0	5	35	50	10	1.35
Greenwich	1.00	0	0	40	45	15	1.25
Central Lancashire	10.00	0	5	20	65	10	1.20
Huddersfield	7.00	0	0	25	55	20	1.05
Liverpool Hope	9.00	0	0	25	45	30	0.95

Social work and social policy & administration

	Staff submitted (FTE)	4*	3*	2*	1*	Unclassified	Average ranking
London School of Economics	50.70	50	30	20	0	0	3.30
Bath	23.70	35	40	25	0	0	3.10
Southampton*	31.50	35	35	25	5	0	3.00
Kent	55.70	30	40	25	5	0	2.95
Leeds	31.90	35	30	30	5	0	2.95
UCL	7.00	15	60	25	0	0	2.90
City	3.00	20	45	35	0	0	2.85
Edinburgh	43.90	30	35	25	10	0	2.85
York	53.75	25	40	30	5	0	2.85
Oxford	22.83	20	50	20	10	0	2.80
Sheffield	26.60	20	45	30	5	0	2.80
Keele	39.50	15	50	30	5	0	2.75
Lancaster	42.25	20	40	35	5	0	2.75
Birmingham	26.12	15	45	35	5	0	2.70
Bristol	47.36	20	40	30	10	0	2.70
London South Bank	18.80	15	45	35	5	0	2.70
Nottingham Trent	14.70	15	45	35	5	0	2.70
Sussex	9.00	15	45	35	5	0	2.70
Durham	35.00	15	45	30	10	0	2.65
Open University	12.30	10	50	35	5	0	2.65
Queen's, Belfast	21.61	20	35	35	10	0	2.65
Ulster	15.60	10	50	35	5	0	2.65
Warwick	22.80	10	50	35	5	0	2.65
Stirling	25.80	10	45	40	5	0	2.60
Swansea	17.50	10	50	30	10	0	2.60
Bradford	16.40	10	40	45	5	0	2.55
UEA	16.00	10	45	35	10	0	2.55
Manchester	13.00	15	30	50	5	0	2.55
Plymouth	16.70	5	50	40	5	0	2.55
Bedfordshire	9.10	5	45	45	5	0	2.50
Nottingham	30.50	10	40	40	10	0	2.50
Reading	8.90	5	45	45	5	0	2.50
Glamorgan	18.10	5	40	50	5	0	2.45
Middlesex	15.20	5	45	40	10	0	2.45
Salford	33.20	5	45	40	10	0	2.45
Huddersfield	16.80	10	35	40	15	0	2.40
London Met	20.40	10	40	30	20	0	2.40
Royal Holloway	13.70	10	35	40	15	0	2.40

	Staff submitted (FTE)	4*	3*	2*	1*	Unclassified	Average ranking
Hull	30.80	10	30	45	15	0	2.35
Leicester*	10.00	5	30	60	5	0	2.35
Central Lancashire	14.14	10	30	40	20	0	2.30
Glasgow	4.00	5	35	45	15	0	2.30
Lincoln	12.50	5	30	55	10	0	2.30
Strathclyde	10.15	5	35	45	15	0	2.30
Anglia Ruskin	7.70	5	25	60	10	0	2.25
Bolton	4.00	5	40	30	25	0	2.25
Brighton	24.00	0	35	55	10	0	2.25
Dundee	5.50	5	30	50	15	0	2.25
Goldsmiths	6.80	10	25	45	20	0	2.25
Bangor	15.40	5	25	55	15	0	2.20
Newport	4.80	5	40	30	20	5	2.20
Northumbria	11.00	5	30	45	20	0	2.20
Birmingham City	6.00	5	15	70	10	0	2.15
Brunel	11.20	5	30	40	25	0	2.15
Coventry	4.80	5	20	60	15	0	2.15
De Montfort	21.20	5	25	50	20	0	2.15
East London	9.30	0	35	40	25	0	2.10
UWE Bristol	14.80	0	25	55	20	0	2.05
West of Scotland	7.00	15	15	30	40	0	2.05
Manchester Met	19.50	5	15	50	25	5	1.90
Hertfordshire	3.70	0	15	55	30	0	1.85
Glyndŵr	3.00	0	20	40	35	5	1.75
Chester	10.80	0	15	40	40	5	1.65
Edge Hill	20.50	0	15	30	50	5	1.55
Gloucestershire	4.60	0	10	35	50	5	1.50
Liverpool Hope	4.00	5	0	30	50	15	1.30

Sociology

	Staff submitted (FTE)	4*	3*	2*	1*	Unclassified	Average ranking
Essex	43.70	35	25	30	10	0	2.85
Goldsmiths	32.60	35	25	30	10	0	2.85
Manchester	49.20	40	20	25	15	0	2.85
York	21.20	30	30	35	5	0	2.85
Lancaster	29.80	35	25	25	15	0	2.80
Edinburgh	46.30	30	25	35	10	0	2.75
Surrey	21.40	30	25	35	10	0	2.75
Cardiff	61.40	25	30	35	10	0	2.70
Exeter	18.72	20	35	40	5	0	2.70
Warwick	37.80	30	25	30	15	0	2.70
Cambridge	21.00	20	35	35	10	0	2.65
Oxford	18.75	25	30	35	5	5	2.65
Aberdeen	14.00	15	40	35	10	0	2.60
Open University	42.30	20	35	30	15	0	2.60
Queen's, Belfast	23.00	20	35	30	15	0	2.60
Sussex	14.00	25	30	25	15	5	2.55
Newcastle upon Tyne	21.60	15	35	35	15	0	2.50
Brunel	11.00	10	40	35	15	0	2.45
Bristol	17.93	10	40	30	20	0	2.40
London School of Economics	37.75	20	25	35	15	5	2.40
Loughborough	47.22	25	20	30	20	5	2.40
Nottingham	8.30	15	30	35	20	0	2.40

	Staff submitted (FTE)	4*	3*	2*	1*	Unclassified	Average ranking
City	27.20	15	30	30	20	5	2.30
Glasgow	27.50	10	30	35	25	0	2.25
East London	31.90	10	30	35	20	5	2.20
Manchester Met	22.50	5	30	40	25	0	2.15
Plymouth	23.00	5	30	40	25	0	2.15
Birkbeck College	24.55	5	30	40	20	5	2.10
Leicester	12.50	10	20	45	20	5	2.10
Roehampton University	16.25	5	25	45	20	5	2.05
Birmingham	18.00	5	25	35	30	5	1.95
Liverpool	21.00	5	25	35	30	5	1.95
Strathclyde	9.00	0	20	55	25	0	1.95
Teesside	10.00	5	20	40	35	0	1.95
Huddersfield	9.00	0	25	25	45	5	1.70
UWE Bristol	12.00	0	15	40	40	5	1.65
Napier	6.80	0	10	40	45	5	1.55
Glasgow Caledonian	11.20	5	5	35	45	10	1.50
Robert Gordon	6.00	0	15	25	45	15	1.40

Anthropology

	Staff submitted (FTE)	4*	3*	2*	1*	Unclassified	Average ranking
Cambridge*	17.80	35	35	25	5	0	3.00
London School of Economics	17.00	40	25	30	0	5	2.95
SOAS	19.50	30	40	25	5	0	2.95
Roehampton	6.50	15	65	15	5	0	2.90
UCL	26.50	30	30	25	15	0	2.75
Sussex	22.35	25	30	35	10	0	2.70
Aberdeen	7.00	30	25	25	20	0	2.65
Edinburgh	18.00	25	35	25	10	5	2.65
Goldsmiths	16.70	25	30	30	15	0	2.65
Oxford	36.90	25	30	30	15	0	2.65
Queen's, Belfast	12.00	35	20	20	25	0	2.65
St Andrews	11.66	25	30	30	15	0	2.65
Manchester	24.33	20	30	40	10	0	2.60
Brunel	8.20	20	30	35	15	0	2.55
Durham	33.60	20	35	25	15	5	2.50
Kent	15.70	20	30	30	20	0	2.50
Liverpool John Moores	9.00	10	35	35	20	0	2.35
Oxford Brookes	12.20	5	30	35	25	5	2.05

Development studies

	Staff submitted (FTE)	4*	3*	2*	1*	Unclassified	Average ranking
Oxford	26.80	35	30	30	5	0	2.95
Manchester	37.45	25	40	25	10	0	2.80
UEA	32.00	25	35	25	15	0	2.70
Bath	16.50	15	30	40	15	0	2.45
Open University	22.21	15	30	40	15	0	2.45
SOAS	30.50	10	30	40	20	0	2.30
Birmingham	7.84	10	25	40	25	0	2.20
Bradford	7.70	5	25	40	30	0	2.05
Swansea	4.60	5	10	55	30	0	1.90
Greenwich	14.25	0	25	40	30	5	1.85

● Group K

Psychology

	Staff submitted (FTE)	4*	3*	2*	1*	Unclassified	Average ranking
Cambridge	24.00	35	50	15	0	0	3.20
Oxford	39.10	35	45	15	5	0	3.10
Birmingham	45.13	25	55	20	0	0	3.05
UCL	56.42	30	45	20	5	0	3.00
Birkbeck	23.70	25	45	25	5	0	2.90
Cardiff	59.35	25	45	25	5	0	2.90
Royal Holloway	28.00	15	55	30	0	0	2.85
St Andrews	33.90	20	45	35	0	0	2.85
Glasgow	26.00	20	40	40	0	0	2.80
York	29.00	20	45	30	5	0	2.80
Bangor	39.00	20	45	25	10	0	2.75
Durham	31.00	15	45	35	5	0	2.70
Edinburgh	38.51	15	45	35	5	0	2.70
Sheffield	40.45	15	45	35	5	0	2.70
Southampton	39.10	15	45	35	5	0	2.70
Sussex	45.00	15	45	35	5	0	2.70
Nottingham	35.00	10	50	35	5	0	2.65
Reading	28.80	10	50	35	5	0	2.65
Warwick	18.00	5	60	30	5	0	2.65
Bristol	31.10	10	50	30	10	0	2.60
Essex	22.00	10	45	40	5	0	2.60
Exeter	33.53	15	40	35	10	0	2.60
Leeds	37.40	10	40	45	5	0	2.55
Goldsmiths	26.85	10	40	40	10	0	2.50
Aberdeen	26.00	5	45	40	10	0	2.45
City	10.80	5	45	40	10	0	2.45
Manchester	31.20	10	35	45	10	0	2.45
Lancaster	31.00	10	30	45	15	0	2.35
Newcastle upon Tyne	21.00	10	30	45	15	0	2.35
Surrey	34.80	10	30	45	15	0	2.35
Kent	31.00	10	30	40	20	0	2.30
Anglia Ruskin	4.00	5	40	35	15	5	2.25
Brunel	25.60	5	30	50	15	0	2.25
Dundee	22.00	5	30	50	15	0	2.25
Hertfordshire	17.00	5	25	55	15	0	2.20
Hull	20.70	5	30	45	20	0	2.20
Plymouth	34.55	5	25	55	15	0	2.20
Swansea	26.00	5	30	45	20	0	2.20
Liverpool	28.00	5	25	50	20	0	2.15
Northumbria	16.00	0	25	65	10	0	2.15
Queen's, Belfast	19.50	5	25	50	20	0	2.15
East London	10.20	0	20	65	15	0	2.05
Portsmouth	16.00	0	25	55	20	0	2.05
Strathclyde	17.00	0	30	45	25	0	2.05
Lincoln	5.80	5	20	45	30	0	2.00
Oxford Brookes	13.20	0	25	50	25	0	2.00
Ulster	27.00	5	20	45	30	0	2.00
Central Lancashire	30.90	5	15	50	30	0	1.95

	Staff submitted (FTE)	4*	3*	2*	1*	Unclassified	Average ranking
Keele	14.20	0	25	45	25	5	1.90
Roehampton	20.10	0	20	50	30	0	1.90
Stirling	24.20	5	10	55	30	0	1.90
Leicester	26.00	5	10	50	35	0	1.85
London South Bank	9.50	0	20	50	20	10	1.80
UEA	12.00	0	15	45	40	0	1.75
Westminster	9.50	0	15	45	40	0	1.75
Abertay Dundee	10.00	0	15	40	45	0	1.70
Greenwich	7.00	0	15	45	35	5	1.70
Bath Spa	3.00	0	5	65	20	10	1.65
Derby	12.00	0	10	45	45	0	1.65
Kingston	8.00	0	20	35	35	10	1.65
Nottingham Trent	25.00	0	15	35	50	0	1.65
Glasgow Caledonian	18.70	0	10	40	50	0	1.60
London Met	11.00	0	10	45	40	5	1.60
Sheffield Hallam	12.00	0	10	35	55	0	1.55
Middlesex	14.50	0	10	30	60	0	1.50
Heriot-Watt	9.20	0	5	30	65	0	1.40
Leeds Trinity & All Saints	1.00	0	0	55	30	15	1.40
Sunderland	8.00	0	5	30	65	0	1.40
Glamorgan	12.70	0	10	25	55	10	1.35
Gloucestershire	7.00	0	10	30	45	15	1.35
Bolton	5.50	0	5	30	55	10	1.30
Napier	6.80	0	5	30	55	10	1.30
Liverpool Hope	8.00	0	5	20	65	10	1.20
Coventry	1.00	0	0	25	65	10	1.15
Thames Valley	8.00	0	0	30	50	20	1.10
York St John	6.00	0	0	30	45	25	1.05

Education

	Staff submitted (FTE)	4*	3*	2*	1*	Unclassified	Average ranking
Institute of Education	218.03	35	30	25	10	0	2.90
Oxford	36.00	30	35	30	5	0	2.90
Cambridge	49.60	30	35	25	10	0	2.85
King's College London	34.15	30	35	25	10	0	2.85
Bristol	42.56	25	35	30	10	0	2.75
Leeds	33.60	20	40	35	5	0	2.75
Exeter	23.83	20	40	30	10	0	2.70
Manchester Met	22.80	20	35	35	10	0	2.65
Warwick	35.43	20	40	25	15	0	2.65
York	13.49	15	45	30	10	0	2.65
Durham	30.80	20	35	30	15	0	2.60
Stirling	20.60	15	40	35	10	0	2.60
Sussex	21.50	20	35	30	15	0	2.60
UEA	14.60	15	35	40	10	0	2.55
Manchester	40.60	20	35	30	10	5	2.55
Bath	32.70	15	30	40	15	0	2.45
London Met	10.80	10	40	35	15	0	2.45
Newcastle upon Tyne	11.10	10	40	35	15	0	2.45
Lancaster	17.90	15	30	35	20	0	2.40
Nottingham	51.20	20	25	35	15	5	2.40
Open University	77.01	10	35	40	15	0	2.40
Sheffield	24.20	15	25	45	15	0	2.40

	Staff submitted (FTE)	4*	3*	2*	1*	Unclassified	Average ranking
Birmingham	46.80	10	35	35	20	0	2.35
Queen's, Belfast	19.00	10	40	30	15	5	2.35
Edinburgh	84.97	15	30	30	20	5	2.30
Southampton	24.40	10	25	45	20	0	2.25
Roehampton	27.20	5	25	50	20	0	2.15
Canterbury Christ Church	19.00	10	25	35	25	5	2.10
Ulster	13.00	10	15	50	25	0	2.10
Brighton	10.74	10	25	30	30	5	2.05
Leicester	41.30	5	25	45	20	5	2.05
Plymouth	15.40	10	20	40	25	5	2.05
Winchester	9.90	5	35	30	20	10	2.05
Glasgow	62.30	10	20	35	30	5	2.00
Glasgow Caledonian	6.90	0	25	50	25	0	2.00
Lincoln	3.40	5	30	40	10	15	2.00
Oxford Brookes	11.00	5	25	40	25	5	2.00
Reading	8.60	10	20	35	30	5	2.00
Strathclyde	54.08	5	25	40	25	5	2.00
Goldsmiths	17.70	10	20	30	35	5	1.95
Hull	18.10	5	20	45	25	5	1.95
Staffordshire	8.30	5	30	25	35	5	1.95
Aberdeen	11.23	5	20	40	30	5	1.90
Birmingham City	3.55	5	20	40	30	5	1.90
Gloucestershire	5.60	10	15	40	20	15	1.85
Sheffield Hallam	14.00	5	20	35	35	5	1.85
UWE Bristol	12.50	5	10	50	35	0	1.85
Huddersfield	7.00	5	10	50	30	5	1.80
Bangor	4.66	10	20	20	35	15	1.75
Liverpool John Moores	11.19	0	20	40	35	5	1.75
Newman UC	3.00	0	25	35	30	10	1.75
Sunderland	9.80	0	25	30	40	5	1.75
Wolverhampton	14.00	5	15	35	40	5	1.75
Coventry	12.00	0	20	40	30	10	1.70
Dundee	13.00	5	15	35	35	10	1.70
East London	7.80	5	20	30	30	15	1.70
West of Scotland	5.00	5	25	25	25	20	1.70
Glamorgan	6.75	0	20	35	35	10	1.65
Greenwich	5.30	5	5	45	40	5	1.65
Hertfordshire	5.70	0	20	35	35	10	1.65
Leeds Met	13.70	0	20	35	35	10	1.65
Northampton	17.00	5	10	40	35	10	1.65
Thames Valley	1.40	0	25	30	30	15	1.65
Brunel University	15.50	5	10	35	40	10	1.60
Kingston	4.00	0	25	25	35	15	1.60
Loughborough	7.00	5	15	30	35	15	1.60
St George's Hospital Medical School	3.20	0	25	25	35	15	1.60
Stranmillis UC	6.00	5	20	15	40	20	1.50
Swansea Met	8.89	5	10	30	40	15	1.50
Bolton	8.40	0	15	30	40	15	1.45
Liverpool Hope	8.80	0	20	30	25	25	1.45
Bath Spa	10.00	0	15	30	35	20	1.40
Central Lancashire	11.60	0	5	25	50	20	1.15
Edge Hill	15.91	0	5	25	50	20	1.15

	Staff submitted (FTE)	4*	3*	2*	1*	Unclassified	Average ranking
St Mary's UC	4.60	0	10	20	40	30	1.10
UWIC	10.00	0	0	30	50	20	1.10
Newport	1.00	0	0	25	55	20	1.05
Cumbria	9.10	0	5	25	35	35	1.00
Bishop Grosseteste UC	5.00	0	10	15	35	40	0.95
UC Plymouth St Mark & St John	8.80	0	5	15	50	30	0.95
Glyndŵr	5.70	0	5	20	35	40	0.90
York St John	3.60	0	0	15	55	30	0.85

Sports-related studies

	Staff submitted (FTE)	4*	3*	2*	1*	Unclassified	Average ranking
Birmingham	32.80	25	35	30	10	0	2.75
Loughborough	41.80	25	35	30	10	0	2.75
Bristol	8.60	20	35	35	10	0	2.65
Liverpool John Moores	22.00	25	25	35	15	0	2.60
Stirling	11.60	15	25	45	15	0	2.40
Bath	11.00	15	20	45	20	0	2.30
Leeds Met	32.90	15	25	35	25	0	2.30
Bangor	16.80	10	25	45	20	0	2.25
Brunel	21.00	15	20	40	25	0	2.25
Exeter	26.00	10	25	40	25	0	2.20
Leeds	7.30	10	20	50	20	0	2.20
Sheffield Hallam	31.40	10	25	40	20	5	2.15
Brighton	22.00	10	25	30	35	0	2.10
Ulster	7.00	5	25	45	25	0	2.10
Sunderland	4.00	5	25	40	30	0	2.05
Aberdeen	5.00	5	25	40	25	5	2.00
UWIC*	25.70	5	20	45	30	0	2.00
London South Bank	6.00	5	20	40	35	0	1.95
Chester	5.80	5	20	40	30	5	1.90
Chichester	11.80	5	15	40	40	0	1.85
Heriot-Watt	8.20	10	15	35	30	10	1.85
Aberystwyth	8.00	0	15	50	35	0	1.80
Bedfordshire	10.50	5	15	35	45	0	1.80
Northumbria	10.25	5	15	40	35	5	1.80
Canterbury Christ Church	12.00	0	20	40	35	5	1.75
Staffordshire	12.30	0	20	40	30	10	1.70
Glamorgan	9.50	5	15	30	40	10	1.65
Bucks New University	5.00	0	5	50	45	0	1.60
Coventry	4.00	0	15	40	35	10	1.60
Hull	11.00	0	10	35	55	0	1.55
Nottingham Trent	8.00	0	0	55	35	10	1.45
Gloucestershire	7.20	0	10	30	50	10	1.40
St Mary's UC	5.20	0	10	30	50	10	1.40
York St John	6.50	0	0	50	40	10	1.40
Newman UC	4.00	0	0	35	60	5	1.30
Roehampton	7.70	0	0	30	65	5	1.25
Swansea	9.28	0	0	35	55	10	1.25
UC Plymouth St Mark & St John	3.00	0	0	20	60	20	1.00

● Group L

American studies and anglophone area studies

	Staff submitted (FTE)	4*	3*	2*	1*	Unclassified	Average ranking
Sussex	9.00	30	30	35	5	0	2.85
Birmingham	8.00	20	25	45	10	0	2.55
UEA	11.00	20	30	40	5	5	2.55
Nottingham	29.00	25	20	35	15	5	2.45
King's College London	8.00	15	35	20	15	15	2.20
Liverpool	6.00	15	20	35	15	15	2.05
London Met	5.00	10	15	45	30	0	2.05
Swansea	11.00	10	20	35	25	10	1.95

Middle Eastern and African studies

	Staff submitted (FTE)	4*	3*	2*	1*	Unclassified	Average ranking
Cambridge	15.00	35	40	20	0	5	3.00
Edinburgh	8.00	25	45	30	0	0	2.95
Oxford	44.28	40	30	20	5	5	2.95
Durham	2.00	20	45	25	10	0	2.75
SOAS	25.30	25	35	30	10	0	2.75
Birmingham	7.00	20	40	30	5	5	2.65
Manchester	12.00	15	45	20	15	5	2.50
Exeter	18.00	15	25	40	15	5	2.30

Asian studies

	Staff submitted (FTE)	4*	3*	2*	1*	Unclassified	Average ranking
SOAS	28.00	30	35	20	10	5	2.75
Oxford	32.85	25	30	30	10	5	2.60
Cambridge	18.00	15	35	30	15	5	2.40
Leeds	18.00	5	40	40	15	0	2.35
Manchester	7.00	10	25	45	20	0	2.25
Nottingham	13.00	10	20	40	30	0	2.10
Westminster	2.00	10	20	40	30	0	2.10
Sheffield	22.00	5	25	40	25	5	2.00
Edinburgh	7.00	10	25	25	30	10	1.95
Northampton	2.00	0	10	40	30	20	1.40

European studies

	Staff submitted (FTE)	4*	3*	2*	1*	Unclassified	Average ranking
London School of Economics	15.10	20	45	30	5	0	2.80
Southampton	23.00	30	25	30	10	5	2.65
Sussex	13.00	15	45	30	10	0	2.65
Bath	33.00	10	35	40	15	0	2.40
Birmingham	19.46	20	25	35	15	5	2.40
Cardiff	33.40	15	30	35	20	0	2.40
Portsmouth	38.40	15	30	35	20	0	2.40
Aberystwyth	5.00	20	15	45	15	5	2.30
Liverpool	6.20	20	20	35	20	5	2.30
Glasgow	9.00	5	35	45	10	5	2.25
London Met	16.14	5	30	50	15	0	2.25
Loughborough	17.60	10	30	40	15	5	2.25
Lancaster	13.00	5	30	50	10	5	2.20
Heriot-Watt	13.20	10	20	40	30	0	2.10
Surrey	30.40	5	25	45	25	0	2.10

	Staff submitted (FTE)	4*	3*	2*	1*	Unclassified	Average ranking
Stirling	12.03	5	25	45	20	5	2.05
Salford	28.40	5	20	50	20	5	2.00
Bangor	9.00	5	20	45	25	5	1.95
Strathclyde	4.40	10	10	40	40	0	1.90
Aston	33.10	5	15	45	30	5	1.85
Manchester Met	32.40	0	20	50	20	10	1.80
Anglia Ruskin	11.10	0	20	40	35	5	1.75
Wolverhampton	9.00	0	25	30	40	5	1.75
Kingston	17.80	5	15	35	35	10	1.70
Brighton	5.00	0	10	35	55	0	1.55
West of Scotland	4.00	0	5	45	45	5	1.50
UHI Millennium Institute	4.00	0	5	15	60	20	1.05

● Group M

Russian, Slavonic and East European languages

	Staff submitted (FTE)	4*	3*	2*	1*	Unclassified	Average ranking
Manchester	6.30	35	35	25	5	0	3.00
Oxford	10.50	35	35	15	10	5	2.85
Sheffield	8.00	25	45	20	10	0	2.85
Cambridge	5.00	25	30	40	5	0	2.75
Bristol	5.33	15	45	30	10	0	2.65
Exeter	4.00	5	55	35	5	0	2.60
Nottingham	9.00	20	40	25	10	5	2.60
Queen Mary	3.00	20	20	55	0	5	2.50
UCL	43.50	10	35	40	15	0	2.40
Keele	2.00	15	20	35	30	0	2.20
Durham	4.00	5	35	30	25	5	2.10
Edinburgh	3.00	5	35	25	35	0	2.10
Leeds	4.00	5	10	40	40	5	1.70
St Andrews	4.00	0	20	40	30	10	1.70
Glasgow	6.00	0	5	25	40	30	1.05

French

	Staff submitted (FTE)	4*	3*	2*	1*	Unclassified	Average ranking
Oxford	35.00	30	35	25	10	0	2.85
King's College London	13.00	25	40	25	10	0	2.80
Warwick	13.00	20	45	30	5	0	2.80
Aberdeen	7.00	20	35	35	10	0	2.65
Cambridge	25.00	20	35	35	10	0	2.65
St Andrews	8.33	10	50	35	5	0	2.65
Kent	10.00	15	35	45	5	0	2.60
Leeds	18.30	15	40	35	10	0	2.60
Nottingham	21.00	20	35	30	15	0	2.60
Sheffield	14.00	25	25	35	15	0	2.60
Exeter	15.50	15	35	40	10	0	2.55
UCL	13.08	10	45	35	10	0	2.55
Durham	13.00	15	35	35	15	0	2.50
Edinburgh	15.00	10	45	30	15	0	2.50
Manchester	15.00	15	35	35	15	0	2.50
Newcastle upon Tyne	10.00	15	35	35	15	0	2.50
Queen Mary	11.00	10	45	30	15	0	2.50

	Staff submitted (FTE)	4*	3*	2*	1*	Unclassified	Average ranking
Reading	9.20	20	25	40	15	0	2.50
Glasgow	10.50	15	30	40	15	0	2.45
Liverpool	10.00	15	25	45	15	0	2.40
Royal Holloway	12.00	15	30	35	20	0	2.40
Queen's, Belfast	9.00	5	45	30	20	0	2.35
Birmingham	14.00	10	35	35	15	5	2.30
Swansea	8.00	5	30	50	15	0	2.25
Bristol	13.00	5	30	45	20	0	2.20
Leicester	4.00	0	25	65	10	0	2.15
Oxford Brookes	4.45	5	30	40	20	5	2.10
Nottingham Trent	5.80	0	30	45	25	0	2.05
Ulster	9.00	5	20	35	35	5	1.85
Birkbeck College	9.00	5	15	40	35	5	1.80
British Institute in Paris	4.00	0	30	20	40	10	1.70
Westminster	3.60	0	25	25	45	5	1.70
Roehampton	3.50	0	5	50	45	0	1.60

German, Dutch and Scandinavian languages

	Staff submitted (FTE)	4*	3*	2*	1*	Unclassified	Average ranking
Oxford	21.50	25	30	40	5	0	2.75
Cambridge	16.00	25	30	30	15	0	2.65
Durham	6.00	20	40	25	15	0	2.65
King's College London	9.00	25	35	20	20	0	2.65
Leeds	8.00	25	25	40	10	0	2.65
Royal Holloway	6.50	20	35	35	10	0	2.65
St Andrews	5.00	20	40	25	15	0	2.65
UCL (German)	9.00	25	30	30	15	0	2.65
Birmingham	9.00	15	45	25	15	0	2.60
Manchester	11.00	20	35	30	15	0	2.60
Edinburgh	10.00	25	25	30	20	0	2.55
Exeter	8.00	15	40	30	15	0	2.55
Newcastle upon Tyne	6.00	20	25	45	10	0	2.55
Swansea	8.00	10	40	40	10	0	2.50
Bristol	7.00	15	35	35	10	5	2.45
Liverpool	5.00	10	35	40	15	0	2.40
Warwick	8.00	15	30	35	20	0	2.40
Nottingham	12.00	10	30	45	15	0	2.35
UCL (Scandinavian)	6.42	10	45	25	10	10	2.35
Queen Mary	8.00	5	35	35	25	0	2.20
Birkbeck College	5.90	5	30	40	25	0	2.15
Sheffield	9.00	10	20	45	20	5	2.10
Ulster	3.00	10	15	50	25	0	2.10
Reading	3.20	5	35	25	30	5	2.05
Aberdeen	3.00	0	25	50	25	0	2.00
UCL (Dutch)	4.50	5	35	25	25	10	2.00
Kent	5.00	5	15	50	25	5	1.90
Queen's, Belfast	3.50	5	10	50	35	0	1.85
Glasgow	6.00	10	25	15	35	15	1.80

Italian

	Staff submitted (FTE)	4*	3*	2*	1*	Unclassified	Average ranking
Cambridge	7.00	45	35	15	5	0	3.20
Leeds	6.50	25	50	25	0	0	3.00
Warwick	7.00	30	30	35	5	0	2.85
Reading	8.25	25	40	25	10	0	2.80

	Staff submitted (FTE)	4*	3*	2*	1*	Unclassified	Average ranking
Bristol	6.33	20	35	40	5	0	2.70
Oxford	7.50	30	30	20	20	0	2.70
Manchester	7.00	20	35	40	0	5	2.65
Birmingham	6.20	15	35	40	10	0	2.55
UCL	10.00	20	25	45	5	5	2.50
Exeter	4.33	10	25	45	20	0	2.25
Durham	4.00	5	20	65	5	5	2.15
Swansea	4.00	0	40	40	15	5	2.15
St Andrews	4.00	5	25	45	25	0	2.10
Leicester	2.00	10	15	40	35	0	2.00
Strathclyde	2.00	0	20	60	20	0	2.00
Glasgow	3.00	0	40	25	25	10	1.95
Royal Holloway	6.00	5	35	25	20	15	1.95
Edinburgh	4.00	0	25	35	40	0	1.85

Iberian and Latin American languages

	Staff submitted (FTE)	4*	3*	2*	1*	Unclassified	Average ranking
Manchester	14.00	30	45	20	5	0	3.00
Nottingham	12.00	30	45	20	5	0	3.00
Cambridge	14.50	30	40	20	10	0	2.90
King's College London*	6.50	30	35	25	5	5	2.80
Birkbeck College	11.00	20	40	35	5	0	2.75
Durham	6.00	20	45	25	10	0	2.75
Queen Mary	10.00	25	35	25	15	0	2.70
Leeds	14.00	20	40	30	5	5	2.65
St Andrews	7.00	10	55	25	10	0	2.65
Newcastle upon Tyne	6.00	15	35	45	5	0	2.60
Queen's, Belfast	9.00	15	40	35	10	0	2.60
Oxford	15.75	15	45	25	10	5	2.55
Sheffield	9.00	25	30	25	15	5	2.55
Birmingham	9.00	5	45	45	5	0	2.50
Edinburgh	8.00	15	35	35	15	0	2.50
Liverpool	9.00	15	35	35	15	0	2.50
Aberdeen	5.00	10	35	45	10	0	2.45
Swansea	6.00	10	35	40	15	0	2.40
UCL	7.00	10	35	40	15	0	2.40
Leicester	3.00	5	45	30	20	0	2.35
Exeter	9.50	15	30	35	10	10	2.30
Royal Holloway	6.00	15	30	30	20	5	2.30
Bristol	10.00	10	20	45	20	5	2.10
Kent	4.00	5	20	50	25	0	2.05
Roehampton	3.00	5	25	40	30	0	2.05
Glasgow	4.00	5	25	30	40	0	1.95
Strathclyde	3.50	0	20	55	25	0	1.95
Ulster	3.00	0	10	50	40	0	1.70

Celtic studies

	Staff submitted (FTE)	4*	3*	2*	1*	Unclassified	Average ranking
Cambridge	12.50	45	30	20	5	0	3.15
Ulster	11.20	35	40	25	0	0	3.10
University of Wales Centre for Advanced Welsh and Celtic Studies	12.50	35	45	15	5	0	3.10
Aberystwyth	13.20	25	40	25	10	0	2.80
Swansea	5.00	20	45	30	5	0	2.80

	Staff submitted (FTE)	4*	3*	2*	1*	Unclassified	Average ranking
Bangor	6.75	10	45	35	10	0	2.55
Cardiff	8.00	15	40	30	15	0	2.55
Glasgow	6.00	10	50	30	5	5	2.55
Edinburgh	12.00	20	30	35	10	5	2.50
Queen's, Belfast	5.00	10	20	35	35	0	2.05
Aberdeen	5.00	0	15	45	35	5	1.70
UHI Millennium Institute	4.00	5	10	35	30	20	1.50
Lampeter	2.50	0	5	45	35	15	1.40

English language and literature

	Staff submitted (FTE)	4*	3*	2*	1*	Unclassified	Average ranking
York	40.83	45	30	20	5	0	3.15
Edinburgh	33.61	40	30	25	5	0	3.05
Manchester	33.45	30	45	25	0	0	3.05
Queen Mary	34.95	40	30	25	5	0	3.05
Exeter	44.00	45	20	25	10	0	3.00
Nottingham	35.00	35	35	25	5	0	3.00
Oxford	93.25	40	25	30	5	0	3.00
Cambridge	70.45	40	25	25	10	0	2.95
De Montfort	19.80	40	20	35	5	0	2.95
Glasgow	49.83	35	35	20	10	0	2.95
Leeds	49.40	35	30	30	5	0	2.95
St Andrews	24.99	35	35	20	10	0	2.95
Warwick	34.32	35	30	30	5	0	2.95
Aberdeen	20.50	30	35	30	5	0	2.90
Liverpool	27.45	30	35	30	5	0	2.90
Newcastle upon Tyne	30.80	25	45	25	5	0	2.90
Queen's, Belfast	36.10	35	30	25	10	0	2.90
Bristol	18.40	20	50	25	5	0	2.85
Cardiff	44.20	35	25	30	10	0	2.85
Kent	18.25	30	35	25	10	0	2.85
Royal Holloway	29.20	30	35	25	10	0	2.85
UCL	25.00	30	35	25	10	0	2.85
Birkbeck College	33.65	35	25	30	5	5	2.80
Birmingham	42.05	25	35	35	5	0	2.80
Durham	28.60	30	30	30	10	0	2.80
UEA	26.75	20	45	30	5	0	2.80
King's College London	20.50	15	55	25	5	0	2.80
Reading	31.50	25	40	25	10	0	2.80
Sheffield	42.00	30	25	40	5	0	2.80
Southampton	23.20	25	40	25	10	0	2.80
Anglia Ruskin	11.00	15	45	35	5	0	2.70
Lancaster	29.00	20	40	30	10	0	2.70
Leicester	23.25	15	45	35	5	0	2.70
Open University	14.85	15	50	25	10	0	2.70
Sussex	33.50	20	35	40	5	0	2.70
Goldsmiths	29.05	15	50	25	5	5	2.65
Essex	19.00	10	45	40	5	0	2.60
Swansea	24.28	10	50	30	10	0	2.60
Bangor	14.25	15	30	50	5	0	2.55
Hull	34.30	10	45	35	10	0	2.55
Keele	15.00	10	40	45	5	0	2.55
Stirling	17.00	10	45	35	10	0	2.55

	Staff submitted (FTE)	4*	3*	2*	1*	Unclassified	Average ranking
Brunel	16.50	15	30	45	10	0	2.50
Loughborough	20.40	10	40	40	10	0	2.50
Nottingham Trent	24.25	10	45	30	15	0	2.50
Strathclyde	14.60	15	30	45	10	0	2.50
Aberystwyth	22.00	10	30	55	5	0	2.45
Dundee	13.60	10	35	45	10	0	2.45
Glamorgan	15.00	15	25	50	5	5	2.40
Hertfordshire	6.00	10	35	45	5	5	2.40
Kingston	18.35	10	30	50	10	0	2.40
Oxford Brookes	15.00	5	35	55	5	0	2.40
Sunderland	5.00	10	30	50	10	0	2.40
Manchester Met	26.95	15	20	50	15	0	2.35
Salford	17.00	10	25	55	10	0	2.35
Roehampton	22.20	10	25	50	15	0	2.30
Middlesex	8.50	5	30	50	15	0	2.25
Ulster	17.75	5	30	50	15	0	2.25
Sheffield Hallam	18.51	5	25	55	15	0	2.20
UWE Bristol	14.00	5	25	55	15	0	2.20
Bath Spa	18.70	5	25	50	20	0	2.15
Gloucestershire	9.00	5	30	40	25	0	2.15
Bedfordshire	3.60	15	25	25	25	10	2.10
Liverpool John Moores	10.70	5	25	45	25	0	2.10
Northumbria	8.50	5	20	55	20	0	2.10
Birmingham City	13.40	5	15	60	20	0	2.05
Plymouth	10.00	10	20	35	35	0	2.05
Chichester	7.50	0	25	45	30	0	1.95
Huddersfield	10.51	5	15	50	30	0	1.95
Napier	6.50	5	15	55	20	5	1.95
Central Lancashire	9.00	0	20	50	30	0	1.90
Chester	6.00	5	15	45	35	0	1.90
Leeds Trinity & All Saints	8.00	0	35	30	25	10	1.90
Northampton	13.60	0	15	55	30	0	1.85
Worcester	5.40	5	20	35	35	5	1.85
Westminster	10.20	0	20	40	40	0	1.80
Greenwich	5.75	0	25	25	45	5	1.70
St Mary's UC	9.50	10	10	35	30	15	1.70
Edge Hill	12.00	0	20	30	45	5	1.65
Bishop Grosseteste UC	3.00	0	0	75	10	15	1.60
Canterbury Christ Church	11.00	0	20	25	50	5	1.60
Lampeter	12.90	0	15	45	25	15	1.60
Cumbria	5.00	0	10	35	45	10	1.45
Liverpool Hope	6.20	0	10	30	55	5	1.45
Bolton	6.40	0	10	30	50	10	1.40
York St John	6.00	0	10	30	40	20	1.30
UC Plymouth St Mark & St John	1.00	0	0	40	20	40	1.00

Linguistics

Queen Mary	4.45	25	55	15	0	5	2.95
Edinburgh	36.00	30	30	30	10	0	2.80
York	13.00	20	45	30	5	0	2.80
Essex	16.00	25	35	25	15	0	2.70
Sheffield	13.50	20	40	30	10	0	2.70

	Staff submitted (FTE)	4*	3*	2*	1*	Unclassified	Average ranking
Wolverhampton	5.00	15	40	45	0	0	2.70
Manchester	15.00	10	45	35	10	0	2.55
UCL	14.50	20	30	35	15	0	2.55
Central Lancashire	6.00	15	25	55	5	0	2.50
Lancaster	31.70	20	25	40	15	0	2.50
Cambridge	10.00	20	30	35	5	10	2.45
UWE Bristol	6.00	10	35	40	15	0	2.40
Leeds	7.00	5	45	30	20	0	2.35
Newcastle upon Tyne	28.43	15	25	40	15	5	2.30
Reading	14.60	10	25	50	15	0	2.30
Ulster	3.00	15	25	40	10	10	2.25
Oxford	16.50	10	30	35	20	5	2.20
Bangor	6.22	5	30	40	20	5	2.10
Queen Margaret	15.60	10	30	25	30	5	2.10
Salford	9.60	5	30	40	20	5	2.10
SOAS	19.00	10	25	35	20	10	2.05
Birkbeck College	6.40	5	15	45	30	5	1.85
Greenwich	1.00	0	20	40	35	5	1.75
Sussex	5.00	0	30	25	35	10	1.75
Westminster	3.50	5	5	40	35	15	1.50

● Group N

Classics, ancient history, Byzantine and modern Greek studies

	Staff submitted (FTE)	4*	3*	2*	1*	Unclassified	Average ranking
Cambridge	40.10	45	25	30	0	0	3.15
Oxford	71.26	40	30	25	5	0	3.05
UCL	12.50	30	35	35	0	0	2.95
Durham	17.00	25	40	30	5	0	2.85
King's College London	27.75	30	35	25	10	0	2.85
Warwick	14.00	25	40	30	5	0	2.85
Exeter	18.00	30	30	30	10	0	2.80
Bristol	20.00	20	35	40	5	0	2.70
Manchester	16.80	25	30	35	10	0	2.70
St Andrews	18.00	15	45	35	5	0	2.70
Birmingham	18.50	20	30	40	10	0	2.60
Nottingham	13.00	10	45	35	10	0	2.55
Reading	13.20	10	40	40	10	0	2.50
Edinburgh	18.00	10	35	45	10	0	2.45
Newcastle upon Tyne	10.00	10	35	45	10	0	2.45
Liverpool	11.35	10	40	35	10	5	2.40
Royal Holloway	17.00	10	25	45	20	0	2.25
Open University	10.00	5	25	55	15	0	2.20
Leeds	8.00	5	25	50	20	0	2.15
Glasgow	8.20	10	15	50	20	5	2.05
Swansea University	13.60	5	20	50	25	0	2.05
Queen's, Belfast	2.50	20	10	25	40	5	2.00
Kent	10.00	5	5	65	25	0	1.90
Lampeter	6.20	5	15	40	40	0	1.85

	Staff submitted (FTE)	4*	3*	2*	1*	Unclassified	Average ranking
Philosophy							
St Andrews	19.18	40	35	25	0	0	3.15
UCL	16.28	45	30	20	5	0	3.15
King's College London	21.03	35	40	20	5	0	3.05
Reading	12.00	30	45	25	0	0	3.05
Sheffield	19.00	35	35	30	0	0	3.05
Cambridge*	35.00	35	30	30	5	0	2.95
London School of Economics	13.55	35	30	30	5	0	2.95
Oxford	78.99	35	30	30	5	0	2.95
Stirling	11.00	25	45	30	0	0	2.95
Bristol	16.00	30	35	30	5	0	2.90
Essex	8.20	20	55	20	5	0	2.90
Birkbeck College	14.50	25	35	40	0	0	2.85
Edinburgh	17.00	20	45	30	5	0	2.80
Leeds	27.00	20	45	30	5	0	2.80
Middlesex	7.00	20	45	30	5	0	2.80
Nottingham	15.50	25	35	35	5	0	2.80
Sussex	11.50	10	50	40	0	0	2.70
Warwick	22.00	15	40	40	5	0	2.65
York	15.00	15	40	40	5	0	2.65
Durham	18.00	15	40	35	10	0	2.60
Glasgow	12.50	5	50	45	0	0	2.60
Queen's, Belfast	6.33	5	60	25	10	0	2.60
Bolton	2.00	0	55	45	0	0	2.55
Dundee	7.00	10	35	50	5	0	2.50
Manchester	13.50	10	35	50	5	0	2.50
Lancaster	9.00	10	30	55	5	0	2.45
Southampton	9.50	5	35	60	0	0	2.45
Manchester Met	5.50	5	35	55	5	0	2.40
Birmingham	12.00	5	40	40	15	0	2.35
Kent	8.00	10	25	55	10	0	2.35
Open University	8.00	0	40	55	5	0	2.35
UEA	8.00	5	30	55	10	0	2.30
Cardiff	8.00	5	25	60	10	0	2.25
Hertfordshire	7.80	0	35	55	10	0	2.25
Aberdeen	3.00	0	25	70	5	0	2.20
Hull	10.00	5	30	45	20	0	2.20
Liverpool	11.00	0	25	60	15	0	2.10
Staffordshire	2.00	0	20	60	20	0	2.00
UC Plymouth St Mark & St John	1.00	0	20	50	30	0	1.90
Oxford Brookes	4.80	0	0	75	25	0	1.75
Heythrop College	7.00	0	5	50	35	10	1.50
Theology, divinity and religious studies							
Durham	19.00	40	25	30	5	0	3.00
Aberdeen	18.00	15	65	20	0	0	2.95
Cambridge	32.00	35	25	35	5	0	2.90
Oxford	41.00	30	35	30	5	0	2.90
UCL	7.20	30	40	20	10	0	2.90
Manchester	23.85	25	40	30	5	0	2.85
Sheffield	8.00	20	45	35	0	0	2.85
Edinburgh	30.00	30	30	25	15	0	2.75

	Staff submitted (FTE)	4*	3*	2*	1*	Unclassified	Average ranking
Nottingham	11.25	20	40	35	5	0	2.75
King's College London	16.00	10	55	30	5	0	2.70
SOAS	16.90	15	50	25	10	0	2.70
Birmingham	22.90	15	45	30	10	0	2.65
St Andrews	16.00	20	30	45	5	0	2.65
Lancaster	10.00	15	40	35	10	0	2.60
Leeds	8.00	15	30	50	5	0	2.55
Bristol	10.00	15	30	40	15	0	2.45
Exeter	11.79	10	40	35	15	0	2.45
Glasgow	16.50	10	35	35	15	5	2.30
Lampeter	23.00	5	30	55	10	0	2.30
Cardiff	12.00	5	30	55	5	5	2.25
Open University	10.00	15	20	40	25	0	2.25
Gloucestershire	4.00	0	40	45	10	5	2.20
St Mary's UC	10.70	10	30	35	20	5	2.20
Chester	5.75	0	30	55	15	0	2.15
Kent	4.50	10	30	30	25	5	2.15
Bangor	7.45	5	25	45	20	5	2.05
Roehampton	6.50	5	15	55	25	0	2.00
Liverpool Hope	13.90	5	15	55	20	5	1.95
Chichester	3.40	0	15	60	20	5	1.85
Sunderland	1.00	0	5	85	0	10	1.85
Cumbria	5.40	5	10	45	35	5	1.75
Leeds Trinity & All Saints	2.00	0	40	10	25	25	1.65
Canterbury Christ Church	5.70	0	20	25	50	5	1.60
Winchester	5.60	0	10	45	40	5	1.60
Heythrop College	16.50	0	10	40	40	10	1.50
York St John	6.50	0	5	40	50	5	1.45
UHI Millennium Institute	3.60	0	10	30	50	10	1.40
Bath Spa	4.00	0	10	10	65	15	1.15

History

	Staff submitted (FTE)	4*	3*	2*	1*	Unclassified	Average ranking
Imperial College	5.00	40	40	20	0	0	3.20
Essex	13.36	35	35	25	5	0	3.00
Kent	22.00	35	35	25	5	0	3.00
Liverpool	25.00	35	35	25	5	0	3.00
Oxford	109.00	35	35	25	5	0	3.00
Warwick	36.75	30	45	20	5	0	3.00
Birkbeck College	33.50	35	35	20	10	0	2.95
Cambridge	102.00	40	25	25	10	0	2.95
Hertfordshire	9.00	25	45	30	0	0	2.95
Southampton	23.15	30	40	25	5	0	2.95
UCL	49.00	40	25	25	10	0	2.95
London School of Economics	48.35	35	30	25	10	0	2.90
Sheffield	29.00	35	30	25	10	0	2.90
Aberdeen	25.60	30	30	35	5	0	2.85
Oxford Brookes	23.05	25	40	25	10	0	2.80
Queen Mary	28.80	30	30	30	10	0	2.80
SOAS	27.40	30	30	30	10	0	2.80
Sussex	21.60	25	40	25	10	0	2.80
Exeter	39.73	20	40	35	5	0	2.75
Glasgow	41.00	25	35	30	10	0	2.75
King's College London	21.50	25	35	30	10	0	2.75

	Staff submitted (FTE)	4*	3*	2*	1*	Unclassified	Average ranking
Leeds	31.20	15	50	30	5	0	2.75
St Andrews	41.49	20	40	35	5	0	2.75
York	32.00	25	30	40	5	0	2.75
Birmingham	33.15	20	40	30	10	0	2.70
Dundee	16.00	15	50	25	10	0	2.70
Durham	29.00	20	40	30	10	0	2.70
UEA	26.00	20	40	30	10	0	2.70
Hull	29.70	15	50	25	10	0	2.70
Manchester	34.20	20	40	30	10	0	2.70
Queen's, Belfast	30.50	15	45	35	5	0	2.70
Royal Holloway	30.70	20	40	30	10	0	2.70
Anglia Ruskin	3.50	20	40	25	15	0	2.65
Edinburgh	60.98	25	35	25	10	5	2.65
Lancaster	25.63	15	40	40	5	0	2.65
Bristol	26.00	15	40	35	10	0	2.60
Keele	19.00	20	35	30	15	0	2.60
Leicester	33.00	20	30	40	10	0	2.60
Nottingham	25.20	15	35	45	5	0	2.60
Glamorgan	6.00	10	40	45	5	0	2.55
Swansea	18.00	15	35	40	10	0	2.55
Ulster	20.00	15	40	30	15	0	2.55
Winchester	7.40	15	40	35	5	5	2.55
Reading	18.50	10	40	40	10	0	2.50
Stirling	18.50	15	35	40	5	5	2.50
Bangor	17.00	15	35	35	10	5	2.45
Cardiff	29.00	10	35	40	15	0	2.40
Huddersfield	8.75	5	40	45	10	0	2.40
Newcastle upon Tyne	28.30	15	25	45	15	0	2.40
Open University	20.60	10	30	50	10	0	2.40
Teesside	10.41	10	40	30	20	0	2.40
Aberystwyth	20.80	10	35	35	20	0	2.35
Chester	3.20	15	30	35	15	5	2.35
Sunderland	7.50	15	20	50	15	0	2.35
UWE Bristol	17.50	5	35	50	10	0	2.35
Bath Spa	6.00	5	40	35	20	0	2.30
De Montfort	14.50	0	45	40	15	0	2.30
Northampton	8.50	5	35	45	15	0	2.30
Roehampton	9.70	10	25	50	15	0	2.30
Strathclyde	15.10	5	35	45	15	0	2.30
Greenwich	12.40	10	25	45	20	0	2.25
Lincoln	8.50	0	40	50	5	5	2.25
Central Lancashire	15.20	10	25	40	25	0	2.20
Glasgow Caledonian	7.00	10	25	40	20	5	2.15
Wolverhampton	16.50	5	25	50	20	0	2.15
Bradford	6.50	5	20	55	20	0	2.10
Kingston	10.65	5	25	45	25	0	2.10
Nottingham Trent	13.75	5	25	45	25	0	2.10
Plymouth	9.00	0	25	60	15	0	2.10
Goldsmiths	13.00	10	20	45	15	10	2.05
Sheffield Hallam	14.60	10	20	40	25	5	2.05
Canterbury Christ Church	11.00	0	30	45	20	5	2.00
Chichester	5.00	0	30	45	20	5	2.00
Cumbria	4.60	0	20	65	10	5	2.00

	Staff submitted (FTE)	4*	3*	2*	1*	Unclassified	Average ranking
Leeds Trinity & All Saints	4.00	5	20	50	20	5	2.00
Westminster	4.00	0	15	70	15	0	2.00
Gloucestershire	10.00	5	20	40	30	5	1.90
Liverpool John Moores	7.00	0	15	65	15	5	1.90
Edge Hill	5.00	10	15	35	30	10	1.85
Northumbria	8.11	0	20	45	35	0	1.85
Newman UC	0.80	0	0	85	5	10	1.75
Newport	3.50	0	20	40	35	5	1.75
Worcester	4.50	0	0	45	50	5	1.40

● Group O

Art and design

	Staff submitted (FTE)	4*	3*	2*	1*	Unclassified	Average ranking
Loughborough*	36.48	55	30	15	0	0	3.40
Reading*	11.10	45	35	10	10	0	3.15
Lancaster	33.70	25	55	20	0	0	3.05
Newcastle upon Tyne	15.00	25	60	10	5	0	3.05
Open University	16.80	35	45	10	10	0	3.05
Westminster	22.05	20	55	25	0	0	2.95
Royal College of Art	51.65	40	25	25	5	5	2.90
UCL	19.20	35	35	20	5	5	2.90
Bournemouth	14.50	15	55	30	0	0	2.85
Brighton	71.58	35	30	20	15	0	2.85
Oxford	9.66	30	35	20	15	0	2.80
Newport	17.20	10	60	25	5	0	2.75
UWIC	20.60	10	60	25	5	0	2.75
Birmingham City	34.50	30	30	20	20	0	2.70
Dundee	52.40	35	20	25	20	0	2.70
Goldsmiths*	25.00	35	20	30	10	5	2.70
Hertfordshire	5.10	10	50	25	15	0	2.55
Leeds	14.70	15	40	30	15	0	2.55
UWE Bristol	15.70	10	50	25	15	0	2.55
University of the Arts London*	206.19	25	25	30	15	5	2.50
City	4.60	5	40	50	5	0	2.45
Coventry	25.35	5	55	20	20	0	2.45
Oxford Brookes	4.25	15	15	70	0	0	2.45
Glasgow School of Art	76.85	25	25	20	25	5	2.40
East London	9.90	10	30	45	15	0	2.35
Plymouth	17.45	10	45	20	20	5	2.35
Sheffield Hallam	30.05	20	30	15	35	0	2.35
Manchester Met	61.75	10	35	35	15	5	2.30
Ulster	46.25	20	25	30	15	10	2.30
Wolverhampton	27.05	10	25	50	15	0	2.30
Northumbria	22.40	15	30	25	25	5	2.25
Norwich University College of the Arts	8.70	5	30	50	15	0	2.25
Heriot-Watt	10.65	15	35	20	15	15	2.20
Robert Gordon	23.00	5	40	25	30	0	2.20
UC Falmouth	17.05	5	25	55	15	0	2.20
De Montfort	17.37	5	40	25	25	5	2.15
Swansea Met	10.80	5	25	55	10	5	2.15
Bath Spa	17.88	5	15	65	15	0	2.10

	Staff submitted (FTE)	4*	3*	2*	1*	Unclassified	Average ranking
Brunel	10.50	0	35	45	15	5	2.10
Edinburgh College of Art	45.82	10	35	20	25	10	2.10
Liverpool John Moores	12.40	0	35	40	25	0	2.10
Sunderland	33.07	5	35	35	15	10	2.10
Kingston	16.15	0	30	50	15	5	2.05
Middlesex	19.00	5	20	55	15	5	2.05
Southampton	16.12	5	20	50	20	5	2.00
Anglia Ruskin	10.54	5	25	40	20	10	1.95
Bucks New University	13.05	5	25	40	20	10	1.95
Nottingham Trent	46.39	5	30	30	25	10	1.95
Salford	18.70	5	15	55	20	5	1.95
Derby	9.25	5	20	45	20	10	1.90
University for the Creative Arts	43.15	5	25	35	25	10	1.90
Southampton Solent	17.70	5	15	50	20	10	1.85
Gloucestershire	11.46	5	5	60	25	5	1.80
Leeds Met	8.80	5	10	45	40	0	1.80
Napier	10.75	0	25	35	25	15	1.70
Lincoln	20.70	5	10	45	25	15	1.65
Thames Valley	4.20	0	20	25	55	0	1.65
London Met	36.60	0	10	45	40	5	1.60
Portsmouth	20.80	0	10	45	35	10	1.55
Dartington College of Arts	7.70	0	0	50	50	0	1.50
Glyndŵr	2.30	0	5	40	55	0	1.50
Central Lancashire	13.90	0	15	25	50	10	1.45
Cumbria	9.23	0	10	25	50	15	1.30
Northampton	9.00	0	5	25	60	10	1.25
Staffordshire	10.50	0	10	15	65	10	1.25
Arts Institute at Bournemouth	7.50	0	10	10	70	10	1.20
Bolton	3.50	0	0	30	60	10	1.20
Chester	4.70	0	5	5	75	15	1.00

History of art, architecture and design

Glasgow	18.42	45	40	15	0	0	3.30
Courtauld Institute of Art	25.50	40	40	20	0	0	3.20
UEA	16.00	50	20	25	5	0	3.15
Manchester	17.00	40	40	15	5	0	3.15
Sussex	7.00	45	25	30	0	0	3.15
York	15.00	45	25	25	5	0	3.10
Birmingham	6.25	30	40	30	0	0	3.00
UCL	16.00	30	50	10	10	0	3.00
Essex	7.35	25	50	15	10	0	2.90
Nottingham	7.20	20	55	20	5	0	2.90
Open University	12.00	25	40	35	0	0	2.90
Birkbeck College	19.00	20	55	15	10	0	2.85
Warwick	9.00	15	55	30	0	0	2.85
St Andrews	14.20	15	60	15	10	0	2.80
Edinburgh	16.00	15	45	40	0	0	2.75
Reading	6.00	15	45	40	0	0	2.75
Aberdeen	8.30	20	35	40	5	0	2.70
Cambridge	12.00	10	50	40	0	0	2.70
Goldsmiths	11.50	20	30	50	0	0	2.70
SOAS	11.50	30	20	40	10	0	2.70
Middlesex	12.00	15	40	35	10	0	2.60

	Staff submitted (FTE)	4*	3*	2*	1*	Unclassified	Average ranking
Plymouth	5.20	5	50	45	0	0	2.60
Leeds	14.40	25	20	40	15	0	2.55
Oxford Brookes	4.00	15	40	30	15	0	2.55
Southampton	5.80	15	35	40	10	0	2.55
Bristol	6.00	15	30	45	10	0	2.50
Kingston	8.90	10	40	40	10	0	2.50
Leicester	6.80	10	30	50	10	0	2.40
Northumbria	7.00	15	15	55	15	0	2.30
Aberystwyth	7.75	5	20	40	35	0	1.95

Drama, dance and performing arts

	Staff submitted (FTE)	4*	3*	2*	1*	Unclassified	Average ranking
Warwick*	9.60	60	30	10	0	0	3.50
Queen Mary	12.00	50	40	5	5	0	3.35
Roehampton*	8.90	55	30	10	5	0	3.35
St Andrews	5.00	50	35	15	0	0	3.35
Manchester	10.02	45	40	15	0	0	3.30
Bristol	11.30	45	30	25	0	0	3.20
King's College London	7.00	40	45	10	5	0	3.20
Glasgow	16.50	40	45	5	10	0	3.15
Warwick	15.00	30	55	15	0	0	3.15
Exeter	16.00	35	40	20	5	0	3.05
Royal Holloway	18.63	35	40	20	5	0	3.05
Kent	24.90	35	35	20	10	0	2.95
Leeds	8.00	20	50	20	10	0	2.80
Reading	11.20	30	25	35	10	0	2.75
Aberystwyth	22.90	30	30	20	20	0	2.70
Birmingham	7.60	15	50	25	10	0	2.70
Goldsmiths	12.50	20	45	25	5	5	2.70
Dartington College of Arts	8.13	15	40	35	10	0	2.60
Central School of Speech and Drama	11.20	15	40	30	15	0	2.55
Hull	8.20	15	30	50	5	0	2.55
Middlesex	12.10	20	35	25	20	0	2.55
Surrey	7.10	20	40	15	25	0	2.55
De Montfort	6.80	20	30	30	20	0	2.50
Queen's, Belfast	14.20	15	40	30	10	5	2.50
Brunel	10.60	15	25	45	15	0	2.40
Chester	3.95	5	25	70	0	0	2.35
East London	5.20	5	30	55	10	0	2.30
Winchester	12.70	5	30	50	15	0	2.25
Chichester	5.95	0	40	45	10	5	2.20
Manchester Met	10.80	5	25	55	15	0	2.20
Glamorgan	15.40	5	25	45	25	0	2.10
Kingston	4.00	5	30	30	35	0	2.05
York St John	11.10	10	15	40	35	0	2.00
Plymouth	7.40	5	15	55	20	5	1.95
Northampton	9.50	0	25	40	35	0	1.90
Sunderland	6.66	0	25	40	30	5	1.85
Lincoln	8.00	5	15	25	50	5	1.65
London Met	6.50	0	25	15	55	5	1.60
Rose Bruford College	9.30	0	15	30	30	25	1.35
Liverpool Hope	4.50	0	0	30	50	20	1.10
Queen Margaret	5.60	0	0	20	60	20	1.00

	Staff submitted (FTE)	4*	3*	2*	1*	Unclassified	Average ranking
Communication, culture and media studies							
Leicester*	8.80	65	30	5	0	0	3.60
Westminster	16.00	60	30	10	0	0	3.50
UEA	9.00	50	40	10	0	0	3.40
Goldsmiths	21.70	45	35	15	5	0	3.20
London School of Economics	10.65	45	30	25	0	0	3.20
Cardiff	16.50	45	30	20	5	0	3.15
East London	14.90	20	60	15	5	0	2.95
Royal Holloway	17.00	20	55	20	5	0	2.90
Sussex	18.45	15	60	25	0	0	2.90
Nottingham Trent	25.05	25	45	15	15	0	2.80
Ulster	17.00	10	65	20	5	0	2.80
Lincoln	10.00	15	55	25	0	5	2.75
Stirling	14.00	10	60	25	5	0	2.75
Sunderland	13.44	15	50	30	5	0	2.75
De Montfort	12.50	25	35	30	5	5	2.70
Leeds	19.00	15	35	50	0	0	2.65
Oxford	8.83	20	35	35	10	0	2.65
UWE Bristol	22.00	15	45	35	0	5	2.65
Bedfordshire	7.90	10	40	45	5	0	2.55
Leeds Met	21.00	15	40	30	15	0	2.55
Salford	18.00	15	35	40	10	0	2.55
Bournemouth	11.90	15	35	40	5	5	2.50
Derby	12.20	25	15	45	10	5	2.45
Queen Margaret	6.00	10	30	55	5	0	2.45
Brunel	13.00	10	25	60	5	0	2.40
London South Bank	5.50	15	25	45	15	0	2.40
Sheffield Hallam	12.00	5	35	55	5	0	2.40
London Met	12.50	15	25	40	20	0	2.35
Roehampton	17.50	5	30	60	5	0	2.35
Glasgow Caledonian	5.90	10	15	70	5	0	2.30
Nottingham	7.00	5	35	45	15	0	2.30
Winchester	14.90	5	30	50	15	0	2.25
Brighton	11.00	5	30	45	20	0	2.20
Central Lancashire	11.00	15	20	35	30	0	2.20
Sheffield	7.00	5	50	10	30	5	2.20
Glamorgan	8.00	10	20	45	25	0	2.15
Middlesex	4.00	0	45	25	30	0	2.15
Swansea	7.70	10	25	25	40	0	2.05
West of Scotland	10.00	10	20	25	40	5	1.90
Staffordshire	8.50	5	20	30	45	0	1.85
Bath Spa	3.00	10	10	30	50	0	1.80
Bradford	6.60	5	15	20	60	0	1.65
Greenwich	7.00	0	10	45	45	0	1.65
Thames Valley	5.00	0	20	30	45	5	1.65
Gloucestershire	4.00	0	0	20	80	0	1.20
Huddersfield	3.75	0	0	15	70	15	1.00

	Staff submitted (FTE)	4*	3*	2*	1*	Unclassified	Average ranking
Music							
Royal Holloway	19.25	60	30	5	5	0	3.45
Birmingham	10.00	50	35	10	5	0	3.30
Manchester	14.00	50	35	10	5	0	3.30
Cambridge	14.75	45	40	10	5	0	3.25
King's College London	12.10	45	40	10	5	0	3.25
Sheffield	12.40	45	35	20	0	0	3.25
Southampton	17.50	50	30	15	5	0	3.25
Oxford	22.25	50	25	20	5	0	3.20
York	15.10	50	25	20	5	0	3.20
Newcastle upon Tyne	12.70	35	45	15	5	0	3.10
Nottingham	10.25	25	60	15	0	0	3.10
SOAS	8.20	35	45	10	10	0	3.05
Queen's, Belfast	18.50	35	35	20	10	0	2.95
Bristol	8.00	10	75	10	5	0	2.90
City	11.00	30	35	30	5	0	2.90
Glasgow	10.75	35	30	25	10	0	2.90
Goldsmiths	17.20	30	40	20	10	0	2.90
Huddersfield	12.60	20	55	20	5	0	2.90
Royal Academy of Music	12.70	25	45	25	5	0	2.90
Bangor	10.50	25	45	20	10	0	2.85
Surrey	7.00	15	60	20	5	0	2.85
Keele	8.00	20	45	30	5	0	2.80
Leeds	14.10	20	45	30	5	0	2.80
Sussex	7.00	20	45	30	5	0	2.80
Cardiff	13.20	15	55	20	10	0	2.75
Durham	11.00	30	30	25	15	0	2.75
Edinburgh	14.90	20	45	20	15	0	2.70
De Montfort	8.50	15	40	30	15	0	2.55
Liverpool	13.20	10	50	30	5	5	2.55
Open University	11.50	15	30	50	5	0	2.55
Royal College of Music	17.90	15	35	35	15	0	2.50
Aberdeen	7.60	5	45	35	15	0	2.40
Birmingham City	13.50	15	25	45	15	0	2.40
Brunel	9.60	15	30	40	10	5	2.40
Royal Scottish Academy of Music and Drama	11.80	15	25	45	10	5	2.35
Hull	9.70	5	35	40	20	0	2.25
Oxford Brookes	5.50	15	20	40	25	0	2.25
Bath Spa	5.00	10	20	50	20	0	2.20
Royal Northern College of Music	15.05	5	30	50	10	5	2.20
Canterbury Christ Church	7.40	10	20	45	25	0	2.15
UEA	5.00	0	40	40	15	5	2.15
Ulster	8.00	0	30	50	15	5	2.05
Dartington College of Arts	6.30	5	5	75	15	0	2.00
Guildhall School of Music & Drama	14.92	10	25	30	25	10	2.00
Leeds College of Music	4.83	10	15	40	35	0	2.00
Salford	9.41	0	25	50	25	0	2.00
Westminster	2.20	10	15	40	35	0	2.00
Anglia Ruskin	6.50	5	10	65	15	5	1.95
Liverpool Hope	4.00	0	30	35	30	5	1.90
Hertfordshire	3.70	5	10	40	40	5	1.70
Kingston	5.50	0	10	30	55	5	1.45
Thames Valley University	11.50	0	10	25	50	15	1.30
Napier	7.10	0	5	25	40	30	1.05

International
students

International students

Robert Hudson

More than 350,000 students from overseas took up places at universities in the UK in 2006-07, of which nearly 185,000 were postgraduates. They made up 66 per cent of students on full-time taught postgraduate courses, 41 per cent on all taught postgraduate courses, they held 49 per cent of full-time research postgraduate places and 42 per cent of all research places.

What accounts for the UK's incredible popularity among international postgraduates?

The UK offers extremely high quality education at a competitive rate. The fact that a master's degree in the UK typically takes one year rather than the two it requires elsewhere makes it attractive financially and also if you are considering taking a break from employment.

Studying here gives international students the opportunity to develop their English, which is an increasingly attractive skill in the global environment. Moreover, the British education system offers a vast range of subjects, and approaches them in very flexible ways, which means that almost any post-graduate will be able to find an appropriate course. British qualifications are also well regulated – the Quality Assurance Agency for Higher Education ensures that academic standards and quality are maintained in UK higher education – and are internationally recognised.

In independent global university rankings, UK institutions are represented better than any nation's outside the USA. Cambridge and Oxford are behind only Harvard, with London's Imperial College and UCL also both in the top 10. A further 13 UK institutions feature among the top 100: King's College London, Edinburgh, Manchester, Bristol, London School of Economics, Warwick, Glasgow, Birmingham, Sheffield, York, St Andrew's, Nottingham and Southampton. The impressive Open University, which runs a dizzying array of distance learning courses that you can study in your own time, also makes it into the top 500. Fees for international students at the Open are typically nearly double what UK-based students pay, but they are still much cheaper than physically attending a university. So if it is the course or qualification that attracts you rather than the opportunity to study in the UK, or if you are having difficulty raising the money to travel, The Open University website may well be worth a look (www.open.ac.uk).

Specific rankings for particular subjects are available from various sources, especially for the globally competitive MBA. The business school rankings at www.ft.com put the London Business School joint first in the world, Cambridge and Oxford universities in the top 20, and five other British business schools in the top 40. (See page 40 for more details on the MBA.)

Other institutions have internationally recognised specialisms – the profiles from page 213 of this guide will tell you what the institutions themselves consider their strengths to be. All this makes qualifications from UK universities appealing to potential employers, and postgraduate qualifications especially so. The British Council estimates, that men with a postgraduate degree typically earn 20 per cent more than men with only a first degree, while for women the figure is 34 per cent.

The UK is also an attractive destination for historical and cultural reasons, and many international students are drawn to the idea of immersing themselves in its society and traditions. The success of British institutions in attracting international students has also become self-fulfilling. In coming to the UK, students know they will be treading a well-trodden path. This is especially true in major multicultural cities such as Manchester and London.

Having said all this, serious thought and planning needs to go into your decision. Do you know for instance what Hull is like, and how it differs from Brighton, if it does? (It does.) And then there are issues such as immigration, the status of international qualifications, and costs and culture to consider, some of which are obvious, some less so.

● Where to do it?

Your first port of call should be HERO (www.hero.ac.uk), the official gateway to UK colleges, universities and research organisations. It introduces the institutions, lets you click through to their websites, browse course types and structures and should generally help you decide where would be the best place to research, for example, killer squid.

This process will mirror that of any UK student looking for a place to study, but coming from another country makes some extra demands, and the best source of information on these is the British Council. This is a UK public body, supported by the government but operationally independent, whose purpose is to 'build mutually beneficial cultural and educational relationships between the United Kingdom and other countries, and increase appreciation of the United Kingdom's creative ideas and achievements.' It has 233 offices in 107 territories – find one where you live by going to www.britishcouncil. org Even if there isn't an office near you, the website itself is packed with vital information.

The British Council organises a series of regular exhibitions that promote UK education around the world. In 2005 it held 60 exhibitions in 30 countries, attracting 250,000 visitors. These help UK institutions recruit, and give potential students first-hand information. A calendar giving the dates of exhibitions can also be found on the website.

A useful source of information on courses is Prospects, which lists nearly 60,000 research and taught-course options on its website at www.prospects. ac.uk These range from ecotourism to brewing science, and from neonatal nursing to creative writing to water resource management. To negotiate all the choices on offer, you'll need to have a clear idea of what you are interested in and then find somewhere to study that suits your needs.

There's no denying that this multitude of choices can be bewildering. From historic universities like York and St Andrews to established seats of learning in major towns such as Warwick and Bristol, to modern institutions of more specialised education in major metropolitan centres like London, Birmingham and Glasgow, almost anyone can find their niche. But, conversely, anyone who fails to do his or her research before applying could be in for a nasty shock. If for example you apply to Royal Holloway, part of the University of London, dreaming of big city lights, you'll be really disappointed when you find yourself studying in leafy Egham, outside the M25 ring road and a world away from central London.

If you want general information about the UK try www.visitbritain.com and then, when looking at specific institutions and areas, move on to www. upmystreet.com or www.uklocalarea.com – both give overviews of council services, education and hospital information, crime figures and more. These are particularly useful if you want to find out more about the ethnic mix of an area, or whether it has mosques, synagogues or Sikh temples. Another useful guide is the broadcaster Channel 4's annual survey of the best and worst places to live in the UK. This tends to give 'best' scores to prosperous suburban areas, and the sorts of locations where you're likely to find affordable student housing are often some of the 'worst'. But don't be put off – in a city such as London a hundred yards can make a huge difference and can take you from an unappealing estate to a millionaires' playground (see www.channel4 .com/4homes/on-tv/best-and-worst).

● How to apply

The general applications advice given in the other chapters of this guide applies to international students. There are however, a few other things that you'll need to keep in mind.

Before you start, do you know if your English is up to the required standard? IELTS – the International English Testing System – is a good marker of where you stand, and the British Council gives the following as a rough guide to the level of English you will need along with the level of degree you will be expected to have obtained (equivalent to what any UK student would require):

Pre-master's	Undergraduate degree plus IELTS 5.0-5.5
Pg Cert/Pg Dip	Undergraduate degree plus IELTS 6.5-7.0 or a pre-master's course
Master's degree	First or upper second class undergraduate degree plus IELTS 7.0, or a pre-master's course
MBA	First degree, 2-3 year's business experience, IELTS 6.5-7.0
PhD	Master's degree, IELTS 6.5-7.0

As an international student you are more likely than UK students to need a pre-master's course. These are tailored towards candidates who, while academically able, need to top up their qualifications or language skills. They might also cover cultural awareness and general instruction, and courses can last anything from a term to a year.

As a way of attracting international students, UK universities have been rapidly improving their pre-master's courses. They often come with full student status, flexible entry dates, a full programme of care and support and, sometimes, a conditional place on an appropriate master's programme at the same institution. Courses can be tailored to each student's specific needs: for example, the duration of the course may vary according to the amount of English tuition needed.

When it comes to traditional master's and PhD degrees, your reasons for choosing a particular path or course of study will be similar to those of any UK student. Do you want to be taught intensively for a year in a vocational area like public relations or do you want to spend three years studying a new and interesting type of squid? It should be pretty clear to you already which you are most interested in.

Once you know what you want to study, start investigating institutions. You will need to apply direct to the institutions, and while you can apply to as many as you want, it is probably sensible to focus on no more than 10 because the application process is quite time-intensive, with plenty of forms to complete. You can find more details in the other sections of this guide, but this is an area where, if you are less confident in your English, you would be well advised to get things checked over by someone more fluent.

When you are making your choice of institution, there are plenty of factors to take into account. First of all, is it the best place for your course? Teaching quality varies, as does the prestige attached to different institutions. This is where local knowledge can be important. If you've grown up in a country, you'll most likely have a sense of which of its institutions are considered to be the best, and perhaps even what they excel at. If you're from half way around the world, it won't be so easy. This is where a good look at league tables (like those published by the *Guardian*) will come in handy.

If you are doing a research degree it is important to know who will be supervising you. There is no point trying to research squid at a landlocked university where the biology department specialises in conifers and beetles. Enquire about the specific department and also check out the Teaching Quality Information website (www.tqi.ac.uk) and the Quality Assurance Agency (www.qaa.ac.uk). The former gives results of student surveys and charts some of the careers students have gone on to following their postgraduate studies, while the latter ensures that standards are maintained across the UK's academic institutions.

Next, where is it? If you can't stand the heat, you've come to the right place. If you can't stand the cold, you'll also be fine, but you'll probably want to focus on the south of England. If you like the bright lights of the metropolis, you might want to avoid studying in Bangor. If you like open country, then central Birmingham is not for you. Think carefully about these things, especially if you are signing up for three years. Like any other country, the UK is a very varied place and there are huge differences in atmosphere between, say, Falmouth and Glasgow.

And finally, what will it cost? The next section will focus on how to find funding, but be aware that the cost of studying at UK institutions varies widely. Arts and humanities courses tend to cost between £7,000 and £9,000 a year, science courses between £7,500 and £12,000 a year, clinical courses between £10,000 and £21,000 a year, while MBA courses range crazily from £4,000 to such astronomical-sounding amounts as £45,000 for the 15-21 months of tuition at the London Business School. (However, as the LBS points out, its hugely desirable MBA often sets high-flying students on paths to the kind of mega-money that make it well worth the investment. Tables on its website explain that the mean salary for those leaving its course in 2007 was around £60,000.)

The important thing to remember is that you'll need to plan ahead for whichever course you apply for. Popular courses fill up early, and are highly competitive. You may well have to begin the process, especially for a taught course, in October or November of the year before you want to start studying. Some courses will accept much later applications, but you should aim to get started a year in advance.

Forms, forms, and more forms! Sorry, but you will have to fill these in, and, as the rest of this book makes abundantly clear, your research proposal (if you are required to submit one) will play a vital role in whether you are accepted. Also, if you are being interviewed, do at least do some cursory research into UK culture and attitudes. A recent international applicant to Birkbeck in London informed his stunned interviewer that he would fund his degree – and the rest of his life – from the profits of lucrative off-shore money-juggling. He was not accepted.

● Academic costs and funding

Studying in the UK is cheaper than the USA but it is still an expensive business. Most international students are privately funded, usually via some combination of personal savings, loans and family support. Scholarships are available from a variety of sources but, even if you are lucky (or good) enough to win one of them, most will not cover all your costs and you will have to make up the shortfall. Don't assume other sources of funding and scholarships will be available in the UK.

To find out whether your home country offers scholarships, your best bet, as usual, is to enquire at your local British Council office – or, if this is not possible, to email the organisation's UK headquarters. Check whether you are eligible, because of your national or ethnic background, or because of what you are studying, for awards from the UK government, from your own government or from the institution to which you are applying.

The British Council's site also has an award-finding tool: you fill in your proposed subject area and country of residence and up comes a list of awards for which you might be eligible. For instance, selecting 'architecture' and 'Australia', will produce 23 results, which include a £2,500 scholarship at Sussex University and a 10 per cent bursary for the University of Salford. What you are studying matters – if for example you come from Chad, and want to study performing arts, there are 132 awards available. If however you are a Chadian who wants to study agriculture, there are only 28 awards open to you, which might seem odd given the importance of agriculture to Chad.

You would be crazy not to follow up every possibility and, as well as institutional awards, there are several highly competitive schemes admin- istered by the British government. Some of the prominent ones are listed below:

- British Chevening Scholarship. Administered by the British Council on behalf of the Foreign and Commonwealth Office (FCO), approximately 2,400 Chevening scholarships are offered each year in more than 150 countries to enable talented graduates and young professionals to study in the UK and to gain skills that will benefit their home countries. Most awards are for one-year courses – postgraduate diplomas and master's – and candidates are selected by British Embassies and High Commissions overseas. Some Chevening scholars are full-funded, some part-funded. You can find out more at www.chevening.com

- British Marshall Scholarships and the Commonwealth Scholarship and Fellowship Plan. Operated through the British consular organisation in eight regional areas, these finance young US students of high ability (with first degrees and a minimum 3.7 GPA) to study in the UK. The scholarships cover two years at any UK university, in any discipline, at either undergraduate or postgraduate level. The scholarships cover university fees, living expenses, annual book grant, research and daily travel, air fares and, where applicable, a contribution towards the support of a dependent spouse. Up to 40 Scholarships are awarded annually. Information can be found online at www.marshallscholarship.org

- Commonwealth Scholarships and Fellowship Plan. A system of awards aimed at potentially high-achieving Commonwealth students, which intends to promote international understanding and cooperation. Up to 200 full scholarships are awarded each year. These require recommendation by the Scholarship Agency in the country in which the candidate permanently resides. Enquire at www.csfp-online.org

- Commonwealth Shared Scholarship Scheme. The Department for International Development, together with participating institutions, supports this scheme designed for students from Commonwealth countries who are not covered by other British government schemes. Around 150 awards are made annually to those taking taught postgraduate courses only. While there is no formal list of eligible subjects, the course must be demonstrably relevant to the economic, social or technological development of the candidate's home country. Enquire at www.cscuk.org.uk

- Overseas Research Students Awards Scheme (ORSAS). These awards are made according to a complex formula whose basic aim is to fund the difference between UK tuition and the tuition fee in the candidate's home country. Awards are made through institutions and via the England, Scotland, Wales and Northern Ireland regional higher education bodies. England's body is now phasing out ORSAS. For further information on which institutions can make ORSAS awards, visit www.orsas.ac.uk

Then there are those national awards that are similar in operation to the above, but not organised by the UK government. For example the Fulbright Programme – one of the most prominent – is designed to promote mutual understanding between the US and other countries. It awards a number of postgraduate scholarships that allow US citizens to study in the UK and covers maintenance and tuition for a first postgraduate year. Find out more about it at www.iie.org and about other awards through the British Council.

● Living costs and work

As well as finding a way to pay for your fees you will also have to cover the high cost of living in the UK. It is extremely difficult to know what any individual will consider essential, but www.prospects.ac.uk estimates that you'll need £7,200 a year or £9,200 if you are living in London or the south east. It is probably sensible to regard this as enough for a frugal student lifestyle.

A number of sites have budget planners for international students. These cover most of your likely areas of expenditure, and allow you to fill in figures based on your specific circumstances – the cost of rent where you want to live, how much you think you'll need for socialising, your sources of funding and so on. Examples can be found at www.educationuk.org which is useful if you have a clear idea of what things are likely to cost, and at www.studentcalculator.org.uk/international which is much more thorough and links to fact sheets on subjects such as work and rent as it takes you through the various options.

One problem international students often have when using these calculators is that they don't know how much things like socialising and transport are likely to cost. A neat single-page guide that will give you a good idea of day-to-day expenses like a bottle of wine, a train trip or movie is available at www.workgateways.com/working-cost-of-living.html.

University accommodation, if it is offered, might not always seem like the cheapest option at first, but it will usually come with bills and internet access included. Private rent is likely to be anything from £200-£500 a month, depending on where you are living. When budgeting, you need to be very clear about exactly which bills you are expected to pay. Fuel, electricity, telephone line, internet access and water can all be significant costs, and you should check the average prices for wherever you are planning to live. Either ask the student union at your chosen institution, which should have this sort of information to hand, or look online at websites such as www.upmystreet.com

The greatest choice of accommodation is probably available in June/July, before the summer holiday, when landlords are looking to fill houses for the coming year. You might not need the house over the summer, and you might be able to negotiate a cheaper deal over this period. The closer you wait to the start of term, the less availability there will be in desirable areas.

For price reasons, students often live in areas where crime rates, even though low by global standards, are higher than average for the UK. Insurance is sensible, and many insurers offer special deals to students. Try a comparison website – www.moneysupermarket.com is a good example – to get an idea of prices.

Another budgeting tip is to think of what you eat in an average week, and then visit a major UK supermarket website, such as www.tesco.com and see how much it costs. Some supermarkets are cheaper than others – Waitrose is quite expensive, for instance, while Lidl and Aldi are cheaper. You may well be able to save money by shopping at outdoor markets, but the Tesco site will give a fair impression of likely prices.

The UNIAID calculator (www.studentcalculator.org.uk) is full of brilliant information. The electricity section tells you that a dishwasher costs 10p a load, an electric cooker costs £55-65 a year for a family of four and a fridge costs £20-30 a year. It also explains that the average annual household water bill in 2006-07 was somewhere around £300 and, in areas where prices vary widely depending on the required service, such as internet or mobile phone, links to places where you can find more information.

Also, if you have a television, you need a licence, which costs £139.50 regardless of whether you are a student.

One obvious way of making up a shortfall in your budget is to work. EU students can work as much as any UK resident, but your university may have rules about the number of hours you are allowed to work during term-time. Some institutions – Oxford and Cambridge for instance – will not allow you to do any work at all during term-time if you are on a taught course.

Non-EU students who have student immigration permission allowing them to take jobs (which will usually be the case for anyone whose course lasts longer than six months) may work for up to 20 hours a week during term-time and full-time during the holidays. This does not mean an average of 20 hours a week over time, but a maximum of 20 hours in any single week. You can do most kinds of work but there are some restrictions, for example you mustn't provide services as a professional sportsperson or entertainer. For full details go to www.ukcisa.org.uk/student/working_during.php

Furthermore, you must not lose focus on your primary objective. Many taught courses are intense and there is no point coming to the UK to study if other commitments mean you don't focus on your course. Similarly, the final year of any research degree will be more intensive as you write up your results, and so it will be harder to find time for employment.

But if you do decide to work there will often be a job shop somewhere at your university, which will advertise jobs suitable for students. If the job shop isn't actually at the student union, they should be able to tell you where it is.

The obvious financial benefits are not the only reason to work. For many international students part of the reason for coming to the UK is the opportunity to learn English and immerse yourself in British culture. Working will help with both of these things, as it is an easy way to interact with people outside your course.

As a student on an MBA or similar qualification, you are likely to do some reasonably well-paid work as part of your study. At the London Business School, students are expected to do various internships during their two-year course. MBA students graduating in 2008 received an average of £1,003 a week over the summer internships, which lasted up to 12 weeks. For their second year projects, which lasted 25-30 days, they tended to earn anywhere between £100 and £300 a day.

Obviously, this is unusual even for MBA students. The London Business School is extremely prestigious, and London wages are high. A much more realistic gauge of potential earnings for students would be the UK's minimum wage which (as of 2009) is £4.77 an hour if you are aged 18-21, and £5.73 thereafter.

The UNIAID student calculator mentioned above gives some sample jobs and likely rates of pay. Bar work is sociable and flexible at around £6 an hour (£84 for 14 hours over a reasonably typical week), and while UNIAID focuses on working in your student union, bar work can of course be found elsewhere. Working as a retail assistant or as an assistant in your university's library is likely to be closer to the minimum wage at around £5.60 an hour.

If you are working you will have to pay national insurance. Everyone working in the UK needs a national insurance (NI) number. Money from your wage packet is deducted automatically by your employer via this number. You will also need to pay income tax on your earnings if they exceed the minimum annual allowance (£6,035 in 2008-09). Further information on tax and students is available from the UK government at www.hmrc.gov.uk/students and information on applying for an NI number can be found at www.hmrc.gov.uk/faqs/ynino.htm You may feel that all this tax is a bit of a swindle, since – unless you end up becoming a permanent resident of this country – you are not going to be around to benefit from the British pension system, to which you are nevertheless required to contribute. On the other hand think how grateful you will be when, if you catch some hideous disease from the venomous squid you came here to study, the National Health Service saves your life.

● Immigration and the law

The UK government intends to make big changes to the immigration system for students in 2009 and these changes are happening rapidly. The advice given here is intended only as a starting point and you should check the UKCISA website at www.ukcisa.org.uk for the latest information.

Permission to stay in the UK as a student will be dependent on you having a confirmed and unconditional place to study at a recognised institution – a list of these institutions is available at www.dcsf.gov.uk/providersregister

If you are from outside Europe and need to come to the UK before you get a place on a course (for example, for an interview or an exam), you can apply for permission to enter the UK as a 'prospective student' for up to six months. This isn't however always a great idea. You will not be allowed to work during this period, you will have to show you have a plan for finding a place to study, and getting a permit to extend this permission if you don't manage to find a place within the six months can cost up to £500. You will also have to show you can afford to spend the six months in the UK without working.

For those who have a place, immigration rules vary depending on where you come from.

European Economic Area and Switzerland

If you hail from the European Economic Area (Austria, Belgium, Bulgaria, Republic of Cyprus, Czech Republic, Denmark, Estonia, Finland, France, Germany, Greece, Hungary, Iceland, Ireland, Italy, Latvia, Liechtenstein, Lithuania, Luxembourg, Malta, Netherlands, Norway, Poland, Portugal, Romania, Slovakia, Slovenia, Spain, Sweden and the United Kingdom) or are from Switzerland then it's easy.

You already have an automatic right of residence for three months, and once you have been accepted as a student, you can stay until your course finishes. You don't have to fill in any forms, but you can choose to register for a certificate confirming your status. Details of how to do this can be found at www.ukcisa. org.uk/student/eea.php The form you fill in is very slightly different if you are Bulgarian or Romanian.

You can bring your family with you as long as they are also EEA citizens or Swiss. If they are from elsewhere, they can come with you if they are your legally recognised partner or a dependent child (either yours or your partner's). Details about applying for permission for other family members are also available at www.ukcisa.org.uk/student/eea.php

If you are not from the EEA or Switzerland

You will be given permission to reside in the UK if you have been accepted by a recognised institution and can prove that you can pay for your course and your living expenses without relying on money from part-time or holiday work in the UK. There are two exceptions to this: the first is if you are doing a sandwich course and your institution provides you with a letter that guarantees a work placement is available for you and states how much you will earn; the second is if you are studying at a publicly-funded institution of further or higher education and the institution can confirm in writing that it will offer you work and specify your hours and wages.

The evidence you will need to enter the UK as a student is as follows:

- A letter confirming that you have accepted the offer of a place.

- Documentation giving the title of the course, the qualification it leads to, whether or not it is full-time and when it starts and finishes.

- Proof that you have the necessary qualifications for entry, including English language tests.

- Confirmation, if the course is not full-time, that it involves 15 hours of organised daytime study a week.

- Details of the course's cost and how you expect to pay. Thus, if you are being funded privately, you will need to provide evidence. For instance, if you are being supported by a family member they will need to give you a letter explaining their relationship to you and providing proof that they will be able to pay. If you are funding yourself, you will need to give bank or employment details confirming your ability to do so.

As we have said above, changes are being made to the immigration system and for the latest on these you should go to www.ukcisa.org.uk

Driving in the UK

If you are going to study in a major city such as London, Leeds or Cardiff, where public transport services are good, a car is likely to be an expensive and unnecessary hassle. Smaller towns and cities, such as Stoke-on-Trent (Staffordshire University) and Leicester (De Montfort University) are still navigable by public transport and by foot. But, as a general rule, the smaller your destination town, the more appealing a car will be for day-to-day things like shopping and trips to the cinema.

If you don't need a car on a daily basis, but are interested in travelling around the UK during vacations, you may be interested in hiring one. This is not a particularly cheap option but it is the most convenient way to get to some of the UK's more picturesque and distant outposts – north Wales or the Scottish Highlands for instance.

Again things are simpler if you are from the EEA. Your licence is valid here for as long as it is valid in your home country. The next tier is a list of designated countries – Australia, Barbados, the British Virgin Islands, Canada, the Falkland Islands, Hong Kong, Japan, Monaco, New Zealand, Republic of Korea, Singapore, South Africa, Switzerland and Zimbabwe (Northern Ireland's list is slightly stricter than the rest of Great Britain's and excludes Canada, the Falkland Islands, Monaco, the Republic of Korea and South Africa, but does include Malta and the Republic of Cyprus) – whose residents can drive freely for a year in the UK before they must apply to exchange their licence for a GB or Northern Ireland one. The list of countries is available on the information sheet at www.ukcisa.org.uk (click on 'A-Z Index' on the top right corner of the screen and then select the 'Driving in the UK' information sheet from the list). This sheet also explains that any other international licence holders can drive for 12 months, but to carry on they will need to obtain a provisional GB or Northern Ireland licence and pass a driving test.

Anyone wanting to drive a moped or motorcycle in the UK will need to take the Compulsory Basic Training course. Mopeds, if you can afford them, are a quick way around cities but do be careful.

Health

If you are being treated for an ongoing condition, you will need to bring documentation and current prescriptions with you. You may also need to show various medical certificates when you arrive at a UK airport. Possibilities include vaccinations for diphtheria, tetanus, polio, meningitis, measles, mumps and rubella or, if you are coming from a tuberculosis (TB) high-risk area, a chest X-ray report. Check with your local UK Embassy or High Commission to confirm what you will need.

If you are registered on a course lasting longer than six months, you and your family are eligible for free treatment by the National Health Service. The first step is to register with a general practitioner (GP), so it is sensible to do this as soon as you can. You will need proof of student status, your passport and proof of address to register. Consultations are free, but prescriptions cost £7.20.

Day-to-day remedies, such as pain relievers and medicines for colds, can be bought at supermarkets and pharmacies, which will offer good advice on their use. If you are unsure how serious your illness is, it is also sensible to contact the excellent NHS Direct phone line, which offers advice for the cost of a local telephone call on 0845 4647.

If you are registered with the NHS you also qualify for reduced-rate dental treatment. You may need to hunt around for a practice that accepts NHS patients – some are for private patients only.

If you have a disability, contact your institution and make them aware of this. They will be able to provide advice and details relating to where you will be living, studying and so on.

Preparing to travel

Once you have accepted a place, your institution will almost certainly send you an information pack. Read this carefully. Also learn as much as you can about the area you'll be moving to. Think in terms of practical information such as accommodation, transport issues, shop opening times and bank accounts.

Arriving in the UK, especially if you are flying to London, can be overwhelming. Again, there are some very simple steps you can take to ease this process. The first thing to think about is transferring from the airport (or railway station, if you are coming by train from Europe) to your new home. Try to arrive during the week – railways can be disrupted at weekends for engineering work – and if at all possible in the morning. Apart from the fact that everything seems less stressful in daylight, trains, buses and taxis are all more likely to be available.

Your educational institution's information pack will almost certainly recommend various transport options, but these will often start with something like, 'When you arrive at Bath Railway Station'.

Therefore, consider making arrangements for connecting travel between your arrival airport and your destination town or city before you leave home. Most airports have dedicated railway stations and bus routes serving local cities, and if you know you have that next stage sorted out before landing, it can provide peace of mind. If you are landing at London Heathrow and need to travel to Bath for example, map out a route in advance. The train, tube and bus are all likely to be options, depending on how much stress you are prepared to endure and how much you are willing to spend. Compare likely prices at www.thetrainline.com (train), www.nationalexpress.com (bus) and www.easybus.co.uk (cheap London airport buses).

● UK culture

There are a squillion guides to living in the UK. Moving to any new country is likely to be stressful, and will involve coming to terms with a society unlike yours in ways that will be small and large, obvious and unexpected. It is impossible to predict precisely which aspects will affect any individual student, because these will be based on the country you are coming from, the research you have done, where in the UK you are going to and who you meet when you get there. Here, however, are some of the most obvious things to plan for.

Climate

Thanks to the Gulf Stream, the UK is a temperate place. It doesn't get very cold (sub-zero temperatures are rare, except in the north of Scotland, and if it snows all the trains stop in bemused shock), and it doesn't get very hot either (there can be a few days of over 30C(86F) in the south of England during summer when everyone goes barmy and starts jumping in fountains, and all the trains stop in bemused shock – again). It rains quite a lot, and it is quite grey, but probably slightly less of both of these things than you might have been led to expect. It rains more in the west and in Northern Ireland. If you really want to know, check out the Met Office's reports and averages for different parts of the UK (www.metoffice.gov.uk/climate/uk/). As for London fog – well London was a foggy place prior to the passing of the clean air act of 1956 but hasn't been so much since.

Food

The cliche of bland, inedible English food is one to take with a pinch of salt (or any other seasoning you choose). Institutional cooking can be a bit unadventurous, but British high streets, especially in large towns, are a multicultural mix of curry houses, Chinese takeaways, Italian restaurants and anything else you can think of. In big cities you will find food from all around the world, and at supermarkets and grocers in large towns you will find an enormous range of basic ingredients.

Accents

You might think you speak fluent English, then turn up in Liverpool or Glasgow and struggle to understand a word the locals are saying. Regional accents in the UK can be extremely broad, especially given how physically small the country is. You can try to prepare by visiting www.bl.uk/learning/langlit/sounds which has examples from around the UK, but it will mainly be a matter of tuning in.

Dress

You'll find that pretty much anything goes – particularly in larger towns and cities. To get a good idea of current trends and what people are likely to be wearing, take a look online at the latest ranges from popular clothes shops (rather than fashion sites, which can be misleading). Top Shop and Top Man are for a slightly younger and more 'studenty' and budget-conscious clientele (www.topshop.com). Urban Outfitters are a bit more cool, but pricier (www.urbanoutfitters.co.uk). French Connection (www.frenchconnection .com) offers more in the way of glamour.

If you are coming from somewhere hot, you'll also need to buy some warm, waterproof clothes. You may find them bulky and uncomfortable to begin with but you'll soon appreciate the fact that they keep you warm and dry.

Social behaviour

Wherever you travel to in the world, you are likely to encounter small differences in accepted behaviour. The key thing is not to worry too much. We all make mistakes. If you are generally considerate and cheerful and ask when unsure, it's unlikely that you'll go far wrong.

A number of websites provide tips on etiquette – take www.ukstudentlife. com/Personal/Manners.htm for example – but none of them would be agreed on by all English, let alone all British, people. *Debrett's* (www.debretts.co.uk) is a traditional guide (by which we mean very traditional), while www.cyborlink. com is aimed at business travellers and has tips and links that will give you a safe grounding. If you really want to get to grips with your new host culture, then books such as *Watching the English* by Kate Fox or *The Xenophobe's Guide to the English*, are probably better options. In the end, you'll find that good manners count for a lot. Britain is a fundamentally open, tolerant and permissive society. In general, people get along by not imposing on others. This might seem unfriendly, but it is better described as a style that allows a heterogeneous population, in which many people hold very differing values about such subjects as religion and sexuality, to rub along together.

Having said that, there are certain areas where international visitors often come unstuck. First up is queuing. There is a stereotype that the British are a nation of queue lovers. You might come from somewhere with a less formal attitude to waiting in line, but in the UK you'll be expected to wait your turn like everybody else. The British queue in an orderly way. It's first-come-first-served, and you wont be very popular if you attempt to jump the queue. You'll get away with it three times and then a little old lady will crack and stab you with an umbrella.

Next, when you go to a pub or bar, it is perfectly acceptable not to drink alcohol, and pubs are legally obliged to serve you free tap water (though some might give you a funny look when you ask for this). If you are drinking anything that costs money, though, there is a culture of buying drinks in 'rounds' where one person buys for all, and then the next person takes his or her turn. Do not shirk your turn – you must at least offer to buy a round if others have included you in theirs.

Knowing when to turn up at social events is not always straightforward. Pre-arranged, formal events, such as meetings, almost invariably start on time – a 4.00pm meeting will start at 4.00pm sharp. Social events are more flexible. If you are invited to a dinner party with 10 other people, and asked to arrive at 8.00pm, you should aim to arrive on time and no more than 10 or 15 minutes later otherwise you could upset dining plans. On the other hand, if you are invited to a large drinks party at someone's house, and again told 8.00pm, it is unlikely that anyone will arrive much before 8.30pm, and you should probably turn up around 9.00pm. The conventions are complicated and until you are used to them don't be afraid to ask when you are really expected.

Away from study

The UK is one of the world's top tourist destinations, and if you are over here and can afford it you should try to make the most of the chance to take in its various natural and historic sights. Guide books are plentiful – the *Rough Guide* and *Lonely Planet* are both perennially popular options.

The UK has museums and galleries to rival anywhere in the world, and they are not just in London. Find them and keep tabs on upcoming exhibitions at www.24hourmuseum.org.uk Theatre and music are similarly well represented. UK Theatre Web lets you search thousands of shows from around the country (www.uktw.co.uk), Gig Guide lists gigs by professional, amateur and semi-professional bands (www.gig-guide.co.uk) and www.classicalmusic.org.uk does the same for classical music. Anyone interested in classical music should make a pilgrimage to the BBC's promenade concerts ('The Proms' – www.bbc.co.uk/proms) which form an eight week summer season of events at London's Albert Hall. These are cheap, incredibly good and are attended by fans with a genuine passion for the music.

The UK's many historic buildings are a fantastically rich resource. The National Trust maintains a network from Lyme Park on the edge of the Peak District, where Colin Firth leapt in the pool in the BBC's classic adaptation of *Pride and Prejudice*, to Springhill in Northern Ireland's County Londonderry, with its important collection of costumes dating from the 18th century to the 1930s (www.nationaltrust.org.uk). English Heritage (www.english-heritage.org.uk), a similar organisation, has its own collection of treasures to visit, including the must-see Stonehenge.

The National Trust is not simply concerned with the protection of historic buildings – it also maintains many natural sites and gardens. Many visitors are surprised by the amount of green space, and many areas of great natural beauty, they discover in the UK. Cornwall, the South Downs, the Welsh Coast, the Lake District and the Scottish Highlands are just some of the great places to visit for scenery and walking, as well as more vigorous pursuits such as cycling, running and climbing.

Sports facilities are also widely available. Many universities have excellent facilities, and all will be able to tell you about local gyms, swimming pools and the like. Also, almost all institutions will run various sports teams. If you are a keen footballer or cricketer, tennis player, hockey player or athlete, you will find teams willing to have you, either within your institution or nearby.

In addition, you will be able to participate in almost any kind of cultural activity you can think of, be it drama, music, dance or whatever. Again the best place to start looking will probably be your student union.

Culture shock

While accepting that every individual's experience will be unique, the UK Council for International Student Affairs (UKISA) describes culture shock in various stages.

The first stage is the honeymoon, where excitement and stimulation, combined with the fact that home is still fresh in the memory, makes things seem easy, or at least interesting.

This is followed by a degree of distress as differences and problems that are not easily solved become apparent. This can be followed by a time of rejecting UK culture and comparing it unfavourably with your own.

Following this is autonomy, as you settle into the UK and begin to feel comfortable, and finally a confident independence, where you feel you are in control of your environment, and you are making decisions based on your own preferences and needs, and your understanding of how to do so within a British context.

This is all perfectly normal, and the Council suggests you keep in touch with family as much as possible, as well as contacting your student union and asking what support services or organisations might help to ease the transition.

CASE STUDY 1

The international students' officer

Ayushman Sen, international students' officer, LSE students' union

When I was at high school and college, I noticed that most people going to study abroad chose the UK and the USA because their institutions tended to rank highly in international tables, although there was an increasing share in East and South Asia, Canada and Europe. The fact that studying in the UK is appreciably cheaper than the USA is a deciding factor for many students — you get a comparable education at a fraction of the cost.

My personal experience — and it has been a very happy one — is of London. The capital is one of the world's most culturally diverse cities, which is a major selling point, and the general consensus of people of all ethnic and cultural backgrounds is that they can stay here without discrimination. Its colourful and vibrant communities exude a sense of harmonious co-existence.

Even so, moving away from home, family and friends can be daunting. I would say that all international students go through some degree of 'culture shock' and, naturally, this can be a barrier to settling in comfortably. The best remedies are mixing with British people and, of course, time. It's not a matter of warning new arrivals, but rather of making sure that anyone intending to study in the UK is properly informed about the place they're choosing to make their home. Some students arrive from societies with very similar values and views to those prevalent in the UK — Australia or New Zealand, for instance — but for some their new society will have hugely different attitudes, standards of public behaviour and cultural ideals.

I would say that some crucial things for anyone preparing to come to the UK are: make sure you speak enough English to get by comfortably day to day, inside and outside your studies; if you have brought original documents and certificates with you, make sure you have good photocopies of them back home as loss/theft can happen to anyone; read up on the specific area you are moving to, both in terms of geography and culture; and if you've done your research, you won't be shocked when you find out how cold it is in Inverness.

As far as teaching is concerned, many students come from an A-level background, which makes the transition easy, and many other academic systems worldwide are based on the British one. On the whole, the British system is based more on a steady pace of learning with more intense exam sessions, rather than regular, assessed pieces of work. There are obviously exceptions to this.

Every country and university has its own characteristics and charms. I would encourage anyone with an enquiring mind and looking for an outstanding education at an affordable price to come to the UK. Quite apart from anything else, it's an international transport centre, acting as a hub between Asia and Europe on the one hand and the Americas and East Asia on the other. That might even help you with travel costs!

CASE STUDY 2
The international student

Andrew Gaczol, from Australia, is doing an MPhil in international studies at Cambridge University.

I chose Cambridge for a variety reasons, not the least of which is my fascination with the history of one of the world's great universities. It is, from a personal standpoint, a once-in-a-lifetime opportunity. The academic study is part of that, but so is the 'Cambridge experience'. Professionally, of course, I hope it will open doors. I am currently on unpaid leave from the Australian Public Service and I will try to use the qualification — having done a relevant dissertation — to get a job at one of Australia's foreign policy think tanks or, if not there, at an international institution such as Chatham House or the United Nations.

The application process was straightforward enough. I applied for all the various scholarships from Australia. The Cambridge Commonwealth Trust, the Gates Trust Awards, are associated with Cambridge and I applied for them through the university's website. The Chevening Scholarships are government-run and I applied through the British High Commission. I was delighted to get a bursary from the Cambridge Commonwealth Trust. I am self-funded but it has really helped out.

I found the process of moving to Cambridge very easy. I had no language issue to worry about, and while moving always has its annoyances, such as organising visas and shipping clothes and other possessions, they're just part of the experience of living overseas. Australian and British cultures are very similar and the people in Cambridge, students and university staff, have been friendly and welcoming.

The academic workload is certainly a step up from what I had experienced before, and I'm having to stay disciplined to stay on top of it but, having said that, I am also taking part in as many extra-curricular seminars as I can and also in the many and varied social activities that are organised through my college and at other colleges, such as film societies' evenings.

I can't think of anything that should put off prospective international students — it's occasionally a bit cold but my day-to-day experience has been very pleasant, and I will be taking the chance to see other parts of the UK. The social life is good too — there are lots of quaint and interesting pubs in which to catch up with friends. My advice to anyone is take your opportunities when they come. If you want to come to the UK to study, then take the chance. There is a reason why the phrase carpe diem has become cliche. All the very best of luck to you!

University profiles

Reading the profiles

What follows are short introductions to more than 160 universities and higher education institutions to help you with the all-important decision about where to study. We don't have room in this book to include exhaustive information on every place, so these profiles are merely tasters, with lots of links to help you find more detailed information. If somewhere appeals do follow the links to that university's website or drop them an email (contact details are included). Here are a few notes on the profiles to keep things clear ...

Courses and qualifications
This section will give you an idea of the range of postgraduate qualifications on offer at each institution. A full list of the abbreviations used in this section is included on page 383.

Fees
Fees for postgraduate courses vary widely and the figures given here should be used only as general guidelines. Where the fees vary so widely that we have been unable to give a useful indication of prices, we have tried to include a link to the fees area of the institution's website.

Fees information is also available on the postgraduate tables from page 81. Please check the price of particular courses with the institutions concerned before making your application.

Funding
This section covers scholarships and bursaries available to postgraduate students, as well as discounts for continuing students. Links to the postgraduate funding area of the institution's website may be provided.

Accommodation
We don't assume that all postgraduate students have a partner/family they wish to accommodate, but as this is likely to be an important consideration for

those who do, we have asked institutions to tell us whether this is something they offer.

Facilities
Facilities that institutions are pleased to be able to offer postgraduate students – including everything from sports centres and Wi-Fi access, to dedicated postgraduate resources and research facilities – are described here.

Specialism
Independent rankings for particular subjects are, as we have mentioned elsewhere in this guide, available from various sources including the RAE (see page 140). This section tells you what the institutions themselves regard as their specialist areas.

Student view
The profiles also include a quote from a current student or recent graduate, to give you a tiny flavour of a 'real' experience. So they'll be subjective, biased and unreliable. They might just be right though! And there's only one way for you to find out ...

Useful websites
Department for Employment and Learning in Northern Ireland
  www.delni.gov.uk

Department for Innovation, Universities & Skills   **www.dius.gov.uk**

Directgov **www.direct.gov.uk**

European Social Fund **www.esf.gov.uk**

Higher Education Statistics Agency **www.hesa.ac.uk**

Higher Education Careers Service Unit **www.hecsu.ac.uk**

Higher Education Funding Council for Wales **www.hefcw.ac.uk**

National Postgraduate Commitee **www.npc.org.uk**

National Union of Students **www.nus.org.uk**

Prospects **www.prospects.ac.uk**

Research Councils UK **www.rcuk.ac.uk**

Student Awards Agency for Scotland **www.student-support-saas.gov.uk**

Training and Development Agency for Schools **www.tda.gov.uk**

UK Council for International Student Affairs **www.ukcisa.org.uk**

Note on the University of London

The colleges and institutes of this federal university are bound together by the prestigious London degree. As far as central facilities go, students have access to the University of London Union (ULU), some student accommodation in intercollegiate halls and some central sporting facilities. Teaching and social events are collegiate.

The following colleges and schools have individual profiles: Birkbeck, Central School of Speech and Drama, Courtauld Institute of Art, Goldsmiths, Heythrop College, Institute of Education, King's, London Business School, London School of Economics and Political Science, London School of Hygiene and Tropical Medicine, Queen Mary, Royal Academy of Music, Royal Holloway, Royal Veterinary College, St George's, School of Pharmacy, Soas, University College London. The Institute of Cancer Research also belongs to the University of London but does not have a profile here.

Note on the University of Wales/Prifysgol Cymru

The University of Wales/Prifysgol Cymru is a large federal university. It was founded by Royal Charter in 1893, bringing together the aims and aspirations of three existing colleges in Aberystwyth, South Wales and Monmouthshire, and Bangor.

The following institutions award University of Wales degrees: Aberystwyth; Bangor; Lampeter; University of Wales, Newport; Glyndŵr University; Swansea Metropolitan University; Trinity College Carmarthen; and University of Wales Institute Cardiff (UWIC). These institutions all have separate profiles in the guide.

Degrees of the University of Wales are also offered in certain subjects at Cardiff University and the Royal Welsh College of Music and Drama (also profiled separately), as well as other HE institutions in the rest of the UK and overseas.

Key to symbols

 Total number of students (undergraduates and postgraduates).

PG   The percentage of students who are postgraduates.

(UK)   The percentage of postgraduates who are home (UK) students.

London institutions

1 University of the Arts London
2 Birkbeck, University of London
3 Brunel University
4 Central School of Speech and Drama
5 City University London
6 Conservatoire for Dance and Drama
7 Courtauld Institute of Art
8 University of East London
9 Goldsmiths, University of London
10 University of Greenwich
11 Heythrop College
12 Imperial College London
13 Institute of Education
14 King's College London
15 Kingston University
16 London Business School
17 London Metropolitan University
18 London School of Economics

19 London School of Hygiene & Tropical Medicine
20 London South Bank University
21 Middlesex University
22 Queen Mary, University of London
23 Roehampton University
24 Rose Bruford College
25 Royal Academy of Music
26 Royal College of Music, London
27 Royal Holloway, University of London
28 Royal Veterinary College, University of London
29 St George's, University of London
30 St Mary's University College, Twickenham
31 School of Oriental and African Studies (Soas)
32 School of Pharmacy
33 Thames Valley University
34 Trinity Laban
35 University College London
36 University of Westminster

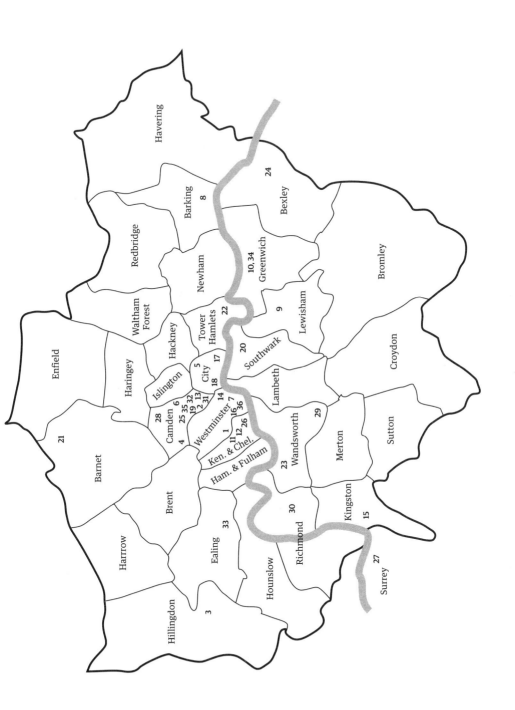

Havering

Barking 8

Bexley

Redbridge

Newham

Greenwich 10, 34

Bromley

Enfield

Waltham Forest

Haringey

Hackney

Tower Hamlets 22

Southwark 20

Lewisham 9

Croydon

Islington

City 5

18 17

Lambeth

Camden 28 6 25 35 19 32 13 2 31 14

Westminster 4 12 26 36 1 II 16 7

Wandsworth 29

Sutton

Merton

Barnet 21

Ken. & Chel.

Ham. & Fulham 23

Kingston 15

Brent

Ealing 33

Hounslow

Richmond 30

Surrey 27

Harrow

Hillingdon 3

University of Aberdeen

University Office,
King's College,
Aberdeen AB24 3FX

t 01224 272090/91
e sras@abdn.ac.uk
↗ www.abdn.ac.uk/sras

» www.abdn.ac.uk/prospectus/pgrad

 14,000   **PG** 25%   (UK) 20%

Aberdeen

Aberdeen is an ancient university with a strong academic reputation. Four Nobel prizes have been awarded for work carried out or begun at Aberdeen. Its picturesque 15th-century King's College campus lies just outside the city centre. The university is investing heavily in new facilities – a new library, student centre and an Olympic sports facility for starters. Aberdeen (or the Granite City, after the rock it's built of) is a charming, student-friendly city with plenty of good pubs.

Courses and qualifications Over 140 courses leading to DLP, DPS, EngD, LLM, MBA, MEd, MLitt, MMus, MPhil, MRes, MSc, MTh, Pg Dip, Pg Cert, PGDE and PhD.

Fees
UK/EU students: fees for most degrees are £3,315. The MBA is £11,500.
International students: £9,000 for arts based programmes; £11,250 for science based programmes and £11,500 for the MBA.

Funding A 20 per cent discount is available for anyone with a first degree from the university. Details can be found at www.abdn.ac.uk/funding

Accommodation There are no specific halls of residence for postgraduates, but most halls have a designated postgraduate area. No family accommodation on campus but the accommodation office can help you find private accommodation close to the university which is suitable for couples or families.

Facilities Aberdeen has one of the largest and best equipped libraries in Scotland. Its computing facilities are state of the art and it is especially proud of its museum collections. A £23m sports centre is due to open in 2009 and there is wireless network access across the campus. The university has a large postgraduate society, postgraduate common rooms and postgraduate research students are provided with their own office space where possible.

Transport Aberdeen is up on the north east coast of Scotland. There's an airport, a station that connects directly to Edinburgh and London and good road links. It's an easy stroll or quick bus ride from the university into town.

Specialism The university is renowned for its strong links with the energy industries. New programmes that have launched recently include the MSc energy futures, MSc subsea engineering, LLM oil and gas law and the MSc international business, energy and petroleum.

❝ STUDENT VIEW ❞
'The University of Aberdeen has an international reputation, which was a top priority for me, but also, Aberdeen as a city caters for all tastes. The beach is perfect, the people friendly and the landscape beautiful.'
Vidushi Guila, MBA.

University of Abertay Dundee

40 Bell Street,
Dundee DD1 1HG

t 01382 308080
e sro@abertay.ac.uk
↗ www.abertay.ac.uk

》 www.abertay.ac.uk/Courses/UPCourses.cfm?Type=2&Key=004.003

 4,500   **PG** 13%   (UK) 36%

Abertay Dundee has some of the best IT facilities in the UK, and an £8m library. Dundee itself is a bustling, hard-working city. It's the fourth largest city in Scotland and also the warmest, thanks to its south-facing aspect. In 2005, a £6m student centre opened with a cinema, coffee shop, nightclub and exhibition space.

Courses and qualifications There are 33 courses leading to MA, MBA, MSc, Mtech, MPhil, Pg Dip, Pg Cert and PhD.

Fees
UK/EU students: fees range from £1,658 for a part-time MPhil or PhD, to £7,850 for the full-time MBA.
International students: the full-time MBA is £10,000.

Funding A 10 per cent discount on tuition fees is offered for continuing students who enrol on specific graduate courses.

Accommodation The university has very limited accommodation set aside for married students or students with families. The accommodation officers at the university will advise on finding suitable accommodation in the private sector or in local authority housing.

Facilities Abertay has a higher rate of PCs to students that almost any other university. There are new teaching facilities and a student centre too. Postgraduates also benefit from laboratory facilities and study space.

Transport The campus is right in the city centre, so short walks will take you most places you want to be. Dundee is 90 minutes by train from Glasgow and an hour from Edinburgh. There's an airport with direct links to London.

Specialism Abertay Dundee has a strong reputation for computer games technology and computer arts and is Scotland's highest rated university for environmental science research.

66 STUDENT VIEW **99**
'The staff at Abertay University are extremely helpful and motivated and this in turn influences how the students interact with each other. This is something I have really benefited from and appreciate very much.' Artur Banaszkiewicz, Pg Dip in enterprise creation.

Aberystwyth, University of Wales

Old College, King Street,
Aberystwyth,
Ceredigion SY23 2AX

t 01970 622021
e pg-admissions@aber.ac.uk
↗ www.aber.ac.uk

 www.aber.ac.uk/en/postgrad

 9,468   **PG** 17%   (UK) 59%

The university is central to life in 'Aber': in a town of 12,000 people, the addition of 9,500 students is going to make an impact. It is frequently rated highly in student satisfaction surveys. The town itself, while small, has a lovely, breezy position on the west coast of Wales, and is known for a thriving local music scene. Good transport links, too, should you need to get away.

Courses and qualifications There are 118 taught postgraduate courses on offer, with research options available in all 18 departments. You can study for an LLM, MA, MBA, MPhil, MSc, MScEcon, MRes, PGCE, Pg Cert, PGDE, Pg Dip, PhD or a PhDFA.

Fees
UK/EU students: £3,300 for arts subjects and both classroom and laboratory based science; £11,250 for the MBA.
International students: £8,475 for arts subjects and classroom based science; £10,750 for laboratory based science and £11,250 for the MBA.

Funding There are various departmental bursaries and scholarships available. The university funds 12 new full-time EU PhD students each year under the Aberystwyth Postgraduate Research Studentships. See www.aber.ac.uk/pga for details of this and other funding opportunities.

Accommodation In university accommodation postgraduates are allocated rooms together when possible. Family accommodation within the university is limited. It is better to apply early or investigate options in the private sector.

Facilities The university library is very well equipped but should it fall short you can always pay a visit to the National Library of Wales which is based in Aberystwyth. It's a copyright library, which means it is entitled to a copy of every book published in Britain. Many departments have dedicated workspaces for their postgraduates.

Transport Trains will whisk you to Birmingham and beyond. Road links will take you to north or south-west Wales with ease.

Specialism The Department of International Politics, established in 1919, was the first academic department of this kind in the world, and it is highly rated for both its teaching and research.

Anglia Ruskin University

Bishop Hall Lane,
Chelmsford CM1 1SQ

t   0845 271 3333
e   answers@anglia.ac.uk
↗   www.anglia.ac.uk

» www.anglia.ac.uk/ruskin/en/home/study/ukstudents/postgraduate_students.html

 23,970   **PG** 16%   (**UK**) 74%

Based at two main campuses in Cambridge and Chelmsford, Anglia Ruskin is fiercely committed to widening access to higher education. The university has nearly 24,000 students, 97 per cent of whom are from state schools. Cambridge-based students will have access to a lovely and deeply student-centric historic city. Chelmsford, while not so much of a tourist centre, has plenty to keep you occupied.

Courses and qualifications There are 182 programmes leading to ACCA, CIM, CIPD, CIPFA, DBA, Grad Dip, EdD, LLD, LLM, MA, MBA, MFA, MPhil, MSc, Pg Cert, PGCE, Pg Dip, PhD, Professional Doctorate, Professional Masters, Postgraduate Diploma in Professional Research or Univ Dip.

Fees Fees vary. Check the website for details: www.anglia.ac.uk/ruskin/en/home/prospectus/course_fee_calc.html

Funding There are no bursaries or scholarships specific to UK postgraduates. The university offers a range of financial support to international postgraduates. This includes the International Merit Scholarship scheme, which provides awards of either £500 or £1,000 to well qualified students applying for any full-time bachelor's or master's degree. The Transfer Scholarship Scheme offers all students transferring from partner institutions, which have a specific cooperation agreement with Anglia Ruskin, a £1,000 reduction on their tuition fees. The university also offers a 3 per cent discount on tuition fees if paid early.

Accommodation The university does not offer accommodation for postgraduates unless they are from overseas. However, the university accommodation service can help you find private sector housing either on your own or in shared accommodation.

Facilities There are good sports facilities, particularly at Chelmsford. Postgraduates have access to the same facilities and resources as undergraduate students. This includes extensive university libraries on both campuses; open access computing and IT areas; e-vision, the online communication system; a careers advisory service and employment bureau; personal tutors; student advisers; childcare facilities and an international student support service.

Transport Both Cambridge and Chelmsford have easy access to motorways, main roads, rails links and Stansted airport.

Specialism The university is proud of its allied health professions, nursing and midwifery.

❝ STUDENT VIEW ❞

'Anglia Ruskin is a good environment to study in. The layout is compact and friendly with a great international feel to the campus.' Del White, MA in arts management.

Arts Institute at Bournemouth

Wallisdown, Poole,
Dorset BH12 5HH

t 01202 533 011
e general@aib.ac.uk
↗ www.aib.ac.uk

» www.aib.ac.uk/courses/postgraduatestudy.aspx

 2,000 **PG** 2% (UK) 70%

Bournemouth

The Arts Institute at Bournemouth is a specialist institution offering undergraduate, foundation degree, postgraduate and further education courses in contemporary arts, design and media. The campus is situated two miles from the centre of Bournemouth, on the border between Bournemouth and Poole, in Dorset, and consists of a series of purpose-built studios accommodating approximately 2,000 students on full-time courses.

Courses and qualifications There are five courses on offer, leading to an MA or PGCE.

Fees
UK/EU students: £3,450 (full-time).
International students: £9,500.

Funding There are four bursaries available for UK and EU students. These are provided in the form of a fees waiver which covers the equivalent of two terms' fees. For international students two bursaries will be available from 2009 onwards.

Accommodation There are no halls of residence for postgraduates nor does the institute offer family accommodation. The student advice team is available to help you find suitable accommodation in the local area. The student pad website has details of all the accommodation registered by landlords with the Arts Institute; flats, houses, bedsits and lodgings, either catered or self-catered. It also has a message board where students can post notices of available rooms. For details see: www.aibstudentpad.co.uk

Facilities A purpose-built library provides material to support all the taught courses. The postgraduate centre is within the library and has both a reading and a seminar room. It has a number of facilities including multi-media audio-visual equipment and Wi-Fi access. Postgraduates may also access the equipment and facilities available to institute students across all areas of study. This includes film and photographic equipment, multi-media technology and workshops supervised by skilled technicians. The institute also boasts a contemporary arts gallery which has received national recognition.

Transport London is two hours away, with regular train and coach services and good road networks. A sponsored bus service runs in term time which links students to the places they are likely to want to go.

Specialism The institute has been providing specialist education within arts, design and media for over a century and enjoys a strong reputation both nationally and internationally.

❝ STUDENT VIEW ❞

'You have to be very self-driven, which is good practice for working in the industry. The master's is challenging in many ways, which has led to greater self-development and confidence. I have already noticed an improvement in my business and people skills.' Kat Connelly, MA in costume pathway.

University of the Arts London

65 Davies Street, London W1K 5DA	**t** 020 7514 6000 **e** info@arts.ac.uk ↗ www.arts.ac.uk

》 **www.arts.ac.uk/pg-fees.htm**

 20,930   **PG** 11%   (UK) 49%

University of the Arts is Europe's largest university for art, design, fashion, communication and the performing arts. It is a federation of six internationally renowned colleges: Camberwell College of Arts, Central St Martins College of Art and Design, Chelsea College of Art and Design, London College of Communication, London College of Fashion and Wimbledon College of Art. In 2006, the student hub opened in the West End as a point of contact for students from across the university.

London

Courses and qualifications There are 172 postgraduate courses, leading to Grad Cert, Grad Dip, MA, MPhil, MSc, Pg Dip, Pg Cert and PhD.

Fees Check with the individual colleges.

Funding Check with the individual colleges for details.

Accommodation The Coopers Court halls of residence are dedicated to postgraduate and mature students. They provide accommodation for 55 students in five self-catering flats.

The university housing service has entered into a partnership with Goodenough College in London to provide family accommodation. Goodenough College is home to 47 families in flats with two or three bedrooms, 75 couples in flats with one bedroom and 420 single study bedrooms.

Facilities There is a broad range of specialist resources and facilities. This includes the fashion technology resource centre at London College of Fashion, broadcast studios and newsrooms at London College of Communication, and unique collections including the Stanley Kubrick Archive. Postgraduates also benefit from dedicated study rooms and studio space.

The university's research student network (RNUAL) brings students together via seminars, workshops, annual symposiums and a regular newsletter. The network provides postgraduates with the opportunity to interact and learn from staff and research students from other colleges within the university.

Transport All the colleges are close to tube or bus links.

Specialism The university is Europe's largest specialist university for art, design, fashion, communication and the performing arts.

 STUDENT VIEW 》

'At Chelsea, I was able to put my ideas into a visual arts context, and formulise them. The tutors were really encouraging, and they helped me evolve it, and then let me get on with it. As soon as I started at Chelsea, my network increased tenfold. Suddenly, the right people were seeing my work. The best thing about studying there is the support that the university offers as a whole.' Haroon Mirza, MA in fine art, Chelsea College of Art and Design.

Aston University, Birmingham

Aston Triangle,
Birmingham B4 7ET

t 0121 204 3000
e pgenquiries@aston.ac.uk
↗ www.aston.ac.uk

 www.aston.ac.uk/prospective-students/graduateschool/index.jsp

 9,500   **PG** 20%   (UK) 20-25%

Birmingham

Aston is located on a green, self-contained campus right in the centre of Birmingham. It is five minutes from the Bullring and 15 from the station, so you're perfectly placed to take full advantage of the shops, clubbing and all other ways to divest yourself of whatever money you might have. Recent developments include a £22m extension to the business school and a £4m IT network upgrade.

Courses and qualifications There's around 60 different courses at taught level on offer, plus over 40 different research groups. You can study for a DBA, MA, MBA, MRes, MSc, Pg Dip, Pg Cert or PhD.

Fees Fees range from £3,500 to over £20,000 depending on the programme: www.aston.ac.uk/pg

Funding A range of scholarships, bursaries and research studentships are available. Check the website for further details: www.aston.ac.uk/fees

Accommodation Accommodation on campus is guaranteed for first year postgraduates and they are normally placed together. Although there is no family accommodation on campus at present, new accommodation, which will include some family apartments, is being developed. The university will help find accommodation for families. For more information go to: www.astonstudentpad.com

Facilities The campus boasts two sports centres and a 25-metre pool. Recent developments include The Loft, a state of the art social space. There's a postgraduate common room and bar and an active postgraduate society. Most postgraduate programmes have dedicated IT and study suites, with swipe card access. The campus is completely Wi-Fi enabled.

Transport There's no need to worry about getting into town: you're there already. There's excellent road and train links to virtually anywhere, especially Manchester, London and going west. Can be busy though.

Specialism Aston is proud of a wide range of subjects and courses, including business and management; MBA; TESOL/English language; life and health sciences; pharmacy; biology and other subjects allied to medicine; European studies and social sciences; psychology; engineering and applied sciences; photonics and bio-energy.

❝ STUDENT VIEW ❞

'The Aston experience is so worth it! I now have a great job, working and living abroad, and I have adapted very easily because while at Aston I learnt how to work with, and understand, international students' work ethic and way of life. Plus the quality of teaching was very high, as all the lecturers have worked in business and finance, so they were always up to date with their notes and anecdotes.' Ella, MSc in accounting and finance.

Bangor, University of Wales

Bangor,
Gwynedd LL57 2DG

t 01248 382018
e admissions@bangor.ac.uk
↗ www.bangor.ac.uk

》 www.bangor.ac.uk/courses/postgrad/index.php.en?menu=1

 12,453 **PG** 19% (UK) 39%

It's close to the sea and the mountains, so perfectly placed for healthy, fresh-air activities of all kinds. The cost of living is low and part-time work is fairly easy to come by. The town – actually one of the UK's smallest cities – has a significant proportion of Welsh speakers. As for the university itself, major investment is taking place to provide more student accommodation and it is expanding academically, too – funding for 50 new academic posts has been announced and new courses are being introduced every year.

Courses and qualifications There are over 150 programmes leading to DClinPsy, LLM, MA, MBA, MMus, MPhil, MRes, MSc, MTh, PGCE, Pg Cert, Pg Dip or PhD.

Fees
UK/EU students: fees vary depending on course and type of study. Check the website for a detailed breakdown: www.bangor.ac.uk/ar/main/fees/euhome0809.php.en
International students: check the website for details: www.bangor.ac.uk/ar/main/fees/int0809.php.en

Funding For details view: www.bangor.ac.uk/studentfinance/postgrad/index.php.en?menu=11&catid=1841&subid=0

Accommodation There are postgraduate halls of residence on the main accommodation site. Family accommodation is very limited. The student services centre offers assistance for families looking in the private sector.

Facilities There is one main library each for arts and sciences, and numerous satellite libraries. Nine computer rooms are open 24 hours a day.

Transport Bangor is on the main rail line between London and Holyhead and has good road links to the motorway network along the A55.

Specialism The university specialises in programmes of study for bilingualism; business and finance; computer science; conservation; evolutionary ecology; electronics (including organic electronics); forestry; marine biology; music; psychology (theoretical and applied); sport and exercise sciences; Welsh and Celtic studies (medieval and modern).

❝ STUDENT VIEW ❞

'Bangor University is predominant within the sports science industry, and is consistently ranked in the top three in the country for teaching and research. The course is great, it's very hands-on and we as students get to do a lot of work. It's more about developing yourself and having tutors there to help and support you, than tutors telling you what to do all the time. The tutors are widely renowned in my school, and their expertise is evident in lectures and workshops – it really is great to be working under these individuals. The school itself is in a great location, and the facilities are fantastic, on a par with the industry if not better.' Mark Adamoulas, MSc in applied sport and exercise psychology.

University of Bath

Bath BA2 7AY

t 01225 388388
e admissions@bath.ac.uk
↗ www.bath.ac.uk

 www.bath.ac.uk/prospectus/postgrad

 13,023 **PG** 29% (UK) 48%

Bath could hardly be more visually charming, and the location of the campus on a hill overlooking the city means you're perfectly placed to soak in the view. The droves of tourists ensure there's plenty of shopping and leisure activity to join in with, and you can always dash off to neighbouring Bristol for some urban grit. Sport is a big deal at the university, with excellent facilities and teams that will vanquish all comers. But sporty or not, everyone seems to have a good time: the university boasts impressive student satisfaction results.

Courses and qualifications There are over 100 programmes leading to DBA, EngD, EdD, MA, MBA, MD, MPhil, MS, MSc, MRes, PGCE or PhD.

Fees
UK/EU students: full-time study is £4,000 per year. *International students:* £10,000 for arts research; £10,300 for arts taught programmes; £12,750 for science based research and £13,150 for science taught programmes. For full information check the website: www.bath.ac.uk/grad-office/finance/pgfeeschedule.pdf

Funding Some bursaries are available, although predominantly for research students. For more information check the website: www.bath.ac.uk/prospectus/postgrad/finance/

Accommodation There is postgraduate accommodation available at seven locations throughout the university. Accommodation is guaranteed for international students.
   There are a limited number of flats available for couples in university accommodation. They are mainly situated off-campus.

Facilities The library is one of the few in the country to stay open 24 hours a day, seven days a week. Sports facilities were already some of the best in the country, even without the addition of a £30m training village. The university is currently building a brand new graduate centre, scheduled for completion in 2010. The centre will be the social, training and academic centre for postgraduate life at the university, and will include postgraduate-specific seminar rooms, postgraduate association offices and a postgraduate social area.

Transport A frequent bus runs into town and takes about 10 minutes. The train to Bristol takes 15 minutes and it's an hour and a half to London.

Specialism Management, interpreting and translating, politics, engineering, pharmacy and pharmacology, biology and the euromasters programme (www.bath.ac.uk/esml/em/students.html).

❝ STUDENT VIEW ❞

'I chose to study the MSc in advanced management practice at Bath because it is packed full of interesting modules, a work placement that would give me the experience I needed to enter a graduate scheme, and ultimately the chance to prove my potential in a 'top five' business school. It has allowed me to really get to grips with my future and put in place a solid platform from which to enter my professional career. Providing an opportunity to stretch both my theoretical and practical knowledge of business, it has broadened my horizons as a graduate and brought me into contact with a unique bunch of people, both culturally and intellectually.'
Ben Piercy-Hughes, MSc in advanced management practice.

Bath Spa University

Bath Spa University,
Newton Park, Newton St Loe,
Bath BA2 9BN

t   01225 875875
e   enquiries@bathspa.ac.uk
↗ www.bathspa.ac.uk

» www.bathspa.ac.uk/courses/postgraduate

 5,500   **PG** 22%

Bath Spa is a relatively new university and prides itself on its teaching focus and emphasis on employability. Applications are on the increase and the university is expanding its range of courses. The university is split over four sites. Newton Park may be a few miles from town, but it's so lovely-looking you couldn't possibly mind. Bath city itself is equally dreamy and nearby Bristol is the place to party.

Bath

Courses and qualifications There are approximately 60 taught courses on offer. You can study for an MA, MFA, MRes, MSc, MTeach, PGCE, Pg Cert or Pg Dip.

Fees
UK/EU students: £4,090 for an MA. £3,390 per year for an MPhil or PhD.
International students: £9,000 to £10,950 for an MA. £9,000 to £9,950 per year for MPhil/PhD.

Funding There is an international postgraduate scholarship scheme. Once admitted to a master's course the student is automatically considered for one of these academic merit-based scholarships.

Accommodation There's no accommodation on campus for postgraduates. The accommodation office will supply a list of properties available in the private sector. Contact the office for further details or to be included on the share list: accommodation@bathspa.ac.uk

Facilities The students' union is a well established music venue. The university offers support and advice on a range of issues including student welfare, money advice, counselling, health services and pastoral care. There is a nursery on campus that offers a discount for Bath Spa students. There is also a postgraduate study room comprising open access computing, research workshop, seminar space and an informal social area.

Transport About 90 minutes to London by train. Bristol is virtually on the doorstep.

Specialism The MA in creative writing is the flagship taught postgraduate course and has become established as one of the leading courses of its kind. The MA in songwriting is the only master's degree in songwriting in the world.

University of Bedfordshire

Park Square,
Luton,
Bedfordshire LU1 3JU

t 01234 400 400
e admission@beds.ac.uk
↗ www.beds.ac.uk

 www.beds.ac.uk/postgraduate

 16,000   **PG** 14%   (UK) 52%

Bedfordshire was born from the merging of the University of Luton with the Bedford campus of De Montfort University. Luton has a busy social scene and Bedford boasts a nice riverside position. It is a forward-thinking university with an excellent graduate employment record and a diverse student population. It is also investing over £70m over the next three years into redeveloping the Luton campus.

Courses and qualifications There are over 100 courses leading to a Cert Ed, DBA, LLM, MA, MBA, MSc, PGCE, MPhil, Pg Dip or PhD. To view all courses check: www.beds.ac.uk/courses

Fees
UK/EU students: £4,500 for classroom/laboratory based study.
International students: £8,950 for classroom/laboratory based study and £10,950 for the MBA.
View: www.beds.ac.uk/fees

Funding There is a social work bursary for full-time postgraduate courses. This bursary is available to students ordinarily resident in England, studying on an approved full-time postgraduate course. The bursary consists of a non-income assessed basic grant and income-assessed maintenance grant and allowances for certain living costs. There is an alumni discount for continuing students. View: www.beds.ac.uk/Funding

Accommodation The university has dedicated postgraduate accommodation at both its Luton and Bedford campuses. At the Luton campus £1m has recently been invested in accommodation, and two halls of residence are allocated to postgraduate and mature students. The Liberty Park hall of residence, located in Bedford, also offers accommodation to postgraduate and mature students.

The university does not provide family accommodation, but the towns of Luton and Bedford offer a variety of affordable private accommodation within easy reach of the campuses and town facilities. Contact: accommodation@beds.ac.uk

Facilities There are good sports facilities on both campuses, as well as libraries, computers and bars. There is a range of facilities that are exclusive to the postgraduates, including an MSc laboratory for computing students.

Transport The airport is close by, the bus station is a short walk from Park Square and there are regular trains to London.

Specialism At postgraduate level it is business and health.

❝ STUDENT VIEW ❞

'The lecturers teach us the necessary skills and then put us to the test by letting us apply such skills or theories to a chosen piece of work of our own interest. They help us develop confidence in ourselves by understanding the topics we are discussing and they also encourage teamwork.' Oloruntoyin Keshinro, MA mass communication.

Birkbeck College, University of London

Malet Street,
Bloomsbury,
London WC1E 7HX

t 0845 601 0174 (Bloomsbury);
0845 602 4169 (Stratford)
e info@bbk.ac.uk
or info@birkbeckstratford.ac.uk

» **www.bbk.ac.uk/study/pg**

 19,350   **PG** 41%   (UK) 66%

The institution was founded in 1823 by George Birkbeck to extend educational opportunities to Londoners who might otherwise miss out. Almost 200 years on and it's still fulfilling the same role. As well as being a respected teaching and research institution, Birkbeck is unique among the colleges of the University of London for its emphasis on part-time, non-residential teaching. Fees are competitive and the ability to work while studying makes Birkbeck a good choice for those concerned about debt. Birkbeck has a central London location, and since September 2007 a range of courses has also been available in Stratford, east London. Applications are direct to the college.

London

Courses and qualifications There are 160 courses on offer. You can study for a Grad Dip, LLM, MA, MFA, MPhil, MRes, MSc, Pg Cert, Pg Dip or PhD.

Fees
UK/EU students: most courses £3,330.
International students: range from £10,290 to £15,534.
    For full details of fees for taught courses check the website: www.bbk.ac.uk/prospective/pgtaught/full-time/money/pgttuition

Funding There is postgraduate funding and college awards on offer. Check the website for details: www.bbk.ac.uk/studentfinance/pgt_finance/pgt_academic

Accommodation There is no student accommodation at Birkbeck College but some is available through the University of London's International Hall and also through Goodenough College, which provides residential accommodation for postgraduates from all over the world. Go to www.goodenough.ac.uk

Facilities There is a new library and access to computing facilities. You have access to the University of London's students' union, with great facilities for sport and socialising.

Transport All campuses are easily accessible by public transport.

Specialism Crystallography, earth sciences, economics, English, German, history, history of art, law, philosophy, politics, psychology and Spanish. The college won a 2006 Queen's Anniversary Prize for higher education for its neuropsychological research.

❝ STUDENT VIEW ❞

'I was intimidated by the time and cost of postgraduate study, but I realised that at Birkbeck I could fit studying round my full-time job. I knew about the good reputation of the college, and the course in European cultures offered me the chance to expand what I had learnt in my undergraduate degree. The lectures were really enjoyable and never felt like a chore. The course put me in touch with a huge range of subjects and literature that I would not have had the time or opportunity to study otherwise.' Graham Fallowes, MA European cultures.

University of Birmingham

Edgbaston,
Birmingham B15 2TT

t 0121 414 3344
e admissions@bham.ac.uk
↗ www.bham.ac.uk

» **www.ucb.ac.uk/asp/postgraduateDegrees.asp**

 25,328   **PG** 30%

Large, prestigious and rather grand – you wouldn't expect anything less from Birmingham's university. Established in 1900, it was the first 'redbrick' university to receive its royal charter. Striking examples of Victorian architecture remain on the large, leafy campus in Edgbaston, which also comes equipped with all mod cons: bars, cafes, shops, a hair salon, a concert hall, banks, an art gallery, a medical practice, a nursery – even its own train station (only one stop to the city centre).

Courses and qualifications There are over 350 taught programmes leading to DBA, EdD, EngD, Grad Dip, LLM, MA, MBA, MEd, MJur, MLitt, MMus, MPhil, MPH, MRes, MSc, PGCE, Pg Cert, Pg Dip, PhD, ThD and professional doctorates eg AppEd, ChildPsyD, ClinPsyD, EdPsychD, ForenPsyD and SocScD.

Fees

UK/EU students: £4,350 for a full-time taught master's degree and £3,390 for a full-time research programme.
International students: £9,880 to £23,350.
For a further breakdown of fees check: www.postgraduate.bham.ac.uk/finance/fees

Funding The university has a number of scholarships available to postgraduates. These cover both research and taught programmes, and assist with the cost of tuition fees. For full details of all funding and scholarships check: www.postgraduate.bham.ac.uk/finance/scholarships.shtml

Accommodation The accommodation for postgraduates is located in two student villages, both within walking distance of the main

campus. The university has a limited number of properties for students with families and also has a partnership with a local housing association, which owns and manages accommodation for students with families. See: www.postgraduate.bham.ac.uk/life/Accommodation

Facilities The university library is the largest research support facility in the West Midlands and there's even an art gallery housing Monets, Turners and Picassos on campus. Wireless technology is being rolled out across the university, creating access to the campus network in social spaces, lecture theatres and libraries. There is dedicated postgraduate study space and postgraduates also have access to the-performance research computing facility BlueBEAR which, together with the Visualisation Centre, forms part of the Birmingham Environment for Academic Research.

Transport Good for rail, road and air.

Specialism For further information see: www.postgraduate.bham.ac.uk/research/partnerships.shtml

❝ STUDENT VIEW ❞

'The Executive MBA at Birmingham was ideal for me as it offered a flexible modular structure that included intensive blocks and various assessment methods. Although study modules were run at pre-determined times throughout the year, we did have the opportunity to skip modules and take them at a later date; this potential flexibility was very reassuring to me as I already held a senior position and have an unpredictable diary.' Tony Leach, Executive MBA.

Birmingham City University

Perry Barr,
Birmingham B42 2SU

t 0121 331 5000
e choices@bcu.ac.uk
↗ www.bcu.ac.uk

» **www.bcu.ac.uk/courses/postgrad.html**

 25,000 **PG** 16% (UK) 75%

Birmingham City University, formerly the University of Central England, is a forward-looking university. It has around 25,000 students, spread across seven campuses around the city. The largest campus is situated at the modern Perry Barr site, three miles north of the city centre. Courses have a strong focus on relevance for the job market and there's an excellent careers service. The university prides itself on its reputation for widening participation and you'll find a broad spectrum of cultures, nationalities and ages here. The city itself is similarly diverse, with plenty to see and do around town, and excellent transport links, should you feel the need to escape for any reason.

Birmingham

Courses and qualifications There are approximately 270 courses leading to DBA, Grad Dip, MA, MPhil, MSc, Pg Dip, Pg Cert, PGCE or PhD.

Fees
UK/EU students: fees vary, students should check with the faculties for individual courses. PGCE fees are set at £3,145 and the MBA is £10,600.
International students: the fees for most postgraduate programmes are £9,550. The MBA is £10, 900.

Funding For full information on funding opportunities including scholarships check: www.bcu.ac.uk/students/international/scholarships.html

Accommodation With the exception of the studio flats at Hamstead, which can accommodate couples and one child under the age of three, all other study bedrooms are designed for single occupancy. Larger family units are advised to contact property owners on the private sector list to enquire whether they have anything suitable in their portfolio.

Facilities Specialist facilities support the different faculties, with the libraries, computers and bars you'd also expect.

Transport Birmingham is easy to get to by road or rail.

Specialism The university has a wide range of specialisms, from teacher training to acting at the Birmingham School of Acting to jewellery at the Birmingham School of Jewellery.

ᏬᏬ STUDENT VIEW ᎓᎓

'I chose to do a postgraduate course at Birmingham City University because I wanted to go to a university where creativity and culture were top of the agenda. By doing this course I have pushed my boundaries and challenged myself in lots of different ways. As a result of the amount of time I've spent in the city I have decided to live in Birmingham, as I have established a home and family here. I'm proud to be an honorary Brummie and I'm proud to have studied at the university.' Richard Anderson-Baguley MA English literary studies (specialising in film).

Bishop Grosseteste
University College Lincoln

Lincoln LN1 3DY

t 01522 527347
e info@bishopg.ac.uk
↗ www.bishopg.ac.uk

» **www.bishopg.ac.uk/?_id=10159**

 1,805   **PG** 40%   (**UK**) 95%

Robert Grosseteste was a 13th-century bishop of Lincoln. The college bearing his name was established in 1862 and has a long-standing reputation as an independent Anglican higher education institution; its mission statement recognises faith as part of human experience and provides for its practice and nurture. As well as that, it offers courses in arts and education (it was until recently a teacher training college) and is firmly committed to diversity and opening access to higher education. Lincoln itself is a charming historical city, perhaps a touch on the quiet side, but who's complaining about that?

Lincoln

Courses and qualifications There are five courses at the university, leading to an MA or PCGE.

Fees
UK/EU students: the MA is £2,310, the full-time PGCE is £3,225.
International students: £7,775 for one year's study.

Funding There is no financial support for international students.

Accommodation There is no postgraduate specific accommodation.

Facilities A new sports and fitness centre opened in 2006, and there's good library and IT facilities too. The students' union has enjoyed some recent revamping.

Transport One to two hours to London by train. It's a 20-30 minute (uphill!) walk from the station to campus.

Specialism Teaching.

 STUDENT VIEW »
'I believe that my experience of MA research was partially responsible for my promotion to assistant headteacher.' University College graduate.

University of Bolton

Deane Road,
Bolton BL3 5AB

t 01204 900800
e enquiries@bolton.ac.uk
↗ www.bolton.ac.uk

» www.bolton.ac.uk/ProspectiveStudents/Postgraduate/Home.aspx

 10,126   **PG** 18%   (UK) 80%

Bolton is still a relatively new university, with £8m being spent to move all subjects to the main Deane campus in the centre of town. Of the 10,000-odd students, around three-quarters are north-west natives. Bolton itself may not be massive, but there's a rich cultural heritage and plenty to do. Manchester is just a short hop away for some real big-city life.

Courses and qualifications There are around 84 courses leading to DBA, MA, MSc, MPhil, Pg Cert, Pg Dip or PhD.

Fees Vary depending on the level and duration of the course.

Funding The university does not offer any scholarships or funding.

Accommodation Family accommodation is only available through private rented accommodation.

Facilities There's a range of sports teams to join or classes to take part in at the sports centre. The library is open until late and there is 24 hour access to computing facilities. Postgraduates have access to all the facilities available to undergraduates; a student learning zone, with bars, cafes and shops.

Transport Bolton station is half a mile away with frequent connections to Manchester. The motorway network is on the doorstep.

Specialism The university focuses on material science, teacher education, health and social care. There are two dedicated research centres each multi-disciplined and designed to promote and develop research and innovation in their fields of expertise.

The Centre for Materials Research and Innovation (CMRI) is the focus of the advanced work in smart materials, auxetic fibres, medical and bio textiles.

The Institute for Educational Cybernetics is the research centre for e-learning and technology enhanced learning.

❝ STUDENT VIEW ❞

'I would recommend the University of Bolton as a place of study. All the lecturers I have had contact with operate an open door policy and always have, or find time to help with personal or academic issues. The class sizes are small, meaning you get a greater interaction in lectures rather than just the opportunity of note taking. In terms of resources the university offers a significant range of software packages, PCs and resources in terms of books and journals. Overall I would have no issues in recommending the University of Bolton to friends and family.' Lee Swallow, PhD student studying smart materials in CMRI.

Bournemouth University

Fern Barrow,
Poole,
Dorset BH12 5BB

t 08456 501501
e askBUenquiries@bournemouth.ac.uk
↗ www.bournemouth.ac.uk

» **www.bournemouth.ac.uk/futurestudents/postgraduate/index.html**

 16,226   **PG** 10%

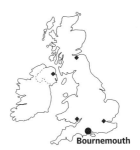

There's nothing head-in-the-clouds about Bournemouth — and that's not only because the lovely weather on the south coast means there are rarely any clouds. The university is firmly rooted in the professional application of education. It works closely with key employers and courses are designed with future career success in mind. The students enjoy all the benefits of living in a tourist town, with some of the best beaches in the UK.

Bournemouth

Courses and qualifications There are approximately 75 courses leading to DBA, LPC, MA, MBA, MSc, MPhil, Pg Dip, Pg Cert and PhD.

Fees
UK/EU students: taught master's range from £3,800 to £12,000, the MBA is £14,000 and research degrees are £4,000 to £8,000 per academic year.
International students: taught master's range from £8,500 to £12,000, the MBA is £14,000 and research degrees are £7,500 to £11,000 per academic year.

Funding Bournemouth offers some scholarships, discounts and other awards to support postgraduates. Further information is available at: www.bournemouth.ac.uk/scholarships

Accommodation The accommodation office at Bournemouth can offer a range of options including shared houses, studio flats, modern halls and home stay accommodation. Postgraduates have priority access to university allocated accommodation provided applications are received by the middle of August.

Facilities There are award-winning learning facilities. There's a Sony HD TV studio (the only one in the UK) and the National Centre for Computer Animation. There's a great cricket ground and unrivalled sailing and watersports facilities. Postgraduates have a designated area of the main library for study, open access facilities for 24/7 learning and extensive e-learning support via the virtual learning.

Transport There's an inter-campus bus, extensive cycle routes in town and there are ferry services and rail and road links.

Specialism The university prides itself on its postgraduate courses in forensic sciences. It was the first in the UK to offer a master's-level qualification in forensic archaeology. Other specialisms include IT computer animation and digital media, creative media, tourism and hospitality management, sustainable development and computing.

‹‹ STUDENT VIEW ››

'The BU experience has enabled me to go on and have a successful career in an area which excites me every day. I got a job within months of graduating which demonstrates how highly employers regard the skills BU students can offer.' Kevan Shorey, MA computer animation — has worked in computer animation on major films including Shrek and Madagascar.

University of Bradford

Bradford,
West Yorkshire BD7 1DP

t 0800 073 1225
e course-enquiries@bradford.ac.uk
↗ www.bradford.ac.uk

》 **www.brad.ac.uk/university/pgpros**

 11,483   **PG** 22.8%   (**UK**) 59%

Bradford is a bustling, diverse, friendly and energetic city
— and the university follows suit. It continues to attract
large numbers of applicants, drawn by the promise of good
employment prospects, a low cost of living and arguably the
best curry in the country. The city-centre campus fosters
a close-knit student community and is undergoing a huge
refurbishment. The university is committed to sustainable
development: campus cafes sell Fairtrade products and new
student accommodation will aim for low environmental
impact.

Courses and qualifications There are 190
courses leading to DBA, DPharm, EURMSc, GDL,
IntMasters, MA, MBA, MEd, MSc, MPhil, PhD,
Pg Cert or Pg Dip.

Fees
UK/EU students: £3,960 for a full-time taught
master's degree; £17,950 for an MBA.
International students: £8,500 to £11,000 (the
cost varies according to subject), £18,950 for
the MBA.

Funding There's a £500 bursary for UK and
EU students although conditions apply. There
are studentships offered by research councils
depending on the subject studied. Some
departments offer specialised scholarships, such
as the Anna Radcliffe Funding available through
the languages and European studies department.
There are up to 10 scholarships for self-funded
international master's students. For more
information on the financial support offered by
the university check: www.brad.ac.uk/external/
prospectus/pg/fees.php

Accommodation There are 250 self-
catering places in halls of residence reserved
for postgraduates. There is no family
accommodation available.

Facilities The students' union boasts no fewer
than three nightclubs and the university has
one of the highest PC-to-student ratios in
the country. There is an art gallery, theatre
and music centre on the campus. While there
are no designated facilities exclusively for
postgraduates, most departments do provide
quiet rooms for postgraduate study.

Transport Walking to the town centre takes
about 15 minutes. Leeds is approximately 20
minutes away by train and Bradford is within
reach of Leeds/Bradford International Airport
and the M62 motorway.

Specialism Bradford prides itself on its
department of peace studies, institute of cancer
therapeutics, institute of pigmentary disorders
and institute of pharmaceutical innovation.

 STUDENT VIEW 》

*'The course has been amazing so far; it's definitely the most rewarding academic experience I've ever had,
more so because of the vast amount of experience accumulated by the staff, who are always willing to further
your understanding of the coursework.'* Michelle Carvalho, MSc in scientific methods in archaeology.

University of Brighton

Mithras House,
Lewes Road,
Brighton BN2 4AT

t 01273 600900
e admissions@brighton.ac.uk
↗ www.brighton.ac.uk

》 www.brighton.ac.uk/prospective/postgrad/index.php?PageId=250

 21,135   **PG** 17%   (**UK**) 76%

Despite its size Brighton is a laid-back university. Its varied degrees have a strong professional focus with good graduate employment rates. The student body is diverse, with many part-time and mature students. The university is split over campuses in Brighton and Eastbourne. The appeal of the former is legendary and the steady spread of smart bars and boutiques by Brighton's pebble beach shows no sign of slowing. It does make the cost of living a bit pricey, though. Eastbourne is a more sedate seaside resort, but it's not too hard to get to Brighton for some ritzy fun.

Brighton

Courses and qualifications There are 247 courses leading to CPE, CMI Diploma, CMI Executive Diploma, Grad Cert, Grad Dip, MA, MBA, MComp, MDes, MEng, MFA, MPA, MPharm, MSc, Pg Cert, Pg Dip, PGCE/ProfGCE.

Fees
UK/EU students: £3,780 is the standard full-time, taught and research tuition fee. Some courses have non-standard fees and may be higher. Rates for these courses can be found on the website: www.brighton.ac.uk/studentlife/money/index.php?PageId=500
International students: £9,500 to £11,000.

Funding International students can apply for a scholarship of £2,000 off the cost of the fees. These scholarships are merit-based and limited in number.
   View: www.brighton.ac.uk/studentlife/money/scholarships/international.php?PageId=533

Accommodation UK and EU postgraduates are eligible to apply for halls of residence, but an offer of accommodation is not guaranteed.

International postgraduates are guaranteed a place in halls of residence for the first year of study if an offer is firmly accepted and the accommodation application form is returned by July 15. There's no family accommodation.

Facilities There are extensive sporting facilities, the students' union hosts its own club nights and there are good computing resources. The university has a number of graduate centres for postgraduate researchers, including the centre for research and development, based within the faculty of arts and architecture. This has dedicated IT facilities, seminar and research spaces and virtual conferencing. These are principally for postgraduate research students and offer quiet space for working and meeting.

Transport London is less than an hour by train. Gatwick and Newhaven ferry ports are both nearby. Eastbourne is about 40 minutes away from Brighton by car.

Specialism The university has many strong departments.

❝ STUDENT VIEW 》

'The course has surpassed my expectations — the structure is very flexible enabling students to specialise in their area of interest. Mine is geography of sport/sociology of football which fits in really well with the academic expertise here. Eastbourne is a friendly, close-knit town, and the campus reflects that. I like living here. I have thoroughly enjoyed coming back to studying. It has really opened my eyes to new opportunities. Brighton is an excellent university, a wonderful place to study.' Simon Penny, MA in sport, culture and society.

University of Bristol

Senate House,
Tyndall Avenue,
Bristol BS8 1TH

t 0117 928 9000
e pg-admissions@bristol.ac.uk
↗ www.bristol.ac.uk

» **www.bristol.ac.uk/prospectus/postgraduate/2009**

 17,132   **PG** 28%

Bristol is a diverse, international university, with over 100 nationalities represented on campus among the staff and students. The university is one of the most popular in the UK, partly because of its excellent research and teaching and partly because Bristol is an attractive city with a great social scene. Most of the university's main buildings are located within a few minutes' walk of each other in a lively part of the city centre, which is itself only a 30-minute walk from the student residences in leafy Stoke Bishop.

Bristol

Courses and qualifications There are 150 courses on offer leading to AdvCert, ChM, DSocSci, DEdPsy, DDS, EdD, EngD, LLM, MA, MD, MPhil, MSc, MEd, MLitt, MMus, MClinDent, MRes PGCE, PGCert, PGDip or PhD.

Fees There is a wide range of fees across programmes and student funding categories. See www.bristol.ac.uk/academicregistry/fees/ for a full breakdown of the details.

Funding Extensive support is available, though eligibility will depend on programme of study and funding category, as well as on competition. The university offers 10 postgraduate scholarships of £2,000 for taught postgraduate programmes – this would be deducted from the tuition fees.

Accommodation International students are guaranteed a place in halls provided that they meet certain criteria. There is some family accommodation available. See: www.bristol. ac.uk/accommodation/unires/coupfam.html

Facilities The library has the largest academic collection in south-west England – 1.4m volumes. The university has invested over £8m in facilities for sport and exercise in recent years. These include a £5m indoor sports centre, tennis centre, 33-metre swimming pool and rowing facility. Drama and music are also well catered for. Extensive facilities are available, normally provided through the department or the faculty. The normal entitlement is specified at www. bristol.ac.uk/tsu/policy/cop-research-degrees. html but further information is available via the faculties' and departments' own websites.

Transport Good road and rail links including the M4 and M5. Convenient for Bristol airport.

Specialism The university has a broad research base across the arts, humanities, social sciences, education, law, engineering, science, medical science, medicine, dentistry and veterinary science.

❝ STUDENT VIEW ❞

'What an excellent grounding the master's BPS (British Psychological Society) conversion degree at Bristol gave me. Not only was I able to apply what I was learning at the time to my teaching practice, but it is also really helping me now as I train in educational psychology.'

Brunel University

Uxbridge,
Middlesex UB8 3PH

t 01895 274000
e admissions@brunel.ac.uk
↗ www.brunel.ac.uk

》 www.brunel.ac.uk/pgstudy

 13,883   **PG** 26%

Since becoming a university in 1966, Brunel's mission has been to combine academic rigour with the practical, entrepreneurial and imaginative approach pioneered by its namesake, Isambard Kingdom Brunel. It's proving successful. All students are now on a single campus at Uxbridge, west London, which has enjoyed £250m of investment in recent years. Brunel enjoys the rare distinction of being a campus university in London, with all the bars, cafes and facilities you'd expect. Uxbridge itself might not be all big city lights but it is compact and less frenetic than central London — which is, after all, very easy to get to.

London

Courses and qualifications There are over 200 courses leading to DrPH, LLM, MRes, EdD, EngD, MMus, MTech or Pg Dip.

Fees
UK/EU students: £3,315 is the average fee.
International students: £10,500 is the average fee.
    Check the website for more details: www.brunel.ac.uk/courses/pg/pgfees

Funding Check the website at www.brunel. ac.uk/courses/pg/funding for details.

Accommodation Accommodation is guaranteed for all new, full-time postgraduates who have confirmed their acceptance and met the conditions for a course by September each year. There is some availability for couples in studio flats within the university halls of residence, but children cannot be accommodated.

Facilities The library has enjoyed recent investment, and there is good access to computing facilities. There is 24-hour swipe card access 365 days a year. There is a postgraduate common room, postgraduate study centre and postgraduate society. The university also carries out a laptop loan scheme.

Transport Uxbridge is at the end of the Metropolitan underground line, so it's easy to get to London. Heathrow and the motorways are also handy.

Specialism The university specialises in environmental sciences, in particular the EngD in environmental technology. Brunel offers a unique DrPH in public health; world-class research in cancer genetics and pharmacogenomics; and support MScs in molecular medicine. There is also a range of innovative performing arts degrees covering contemporary music, cult film, digital games and Shakespeare authorship.

❝ STUDENT VIEW ❞

'As an international student, being reasonably close to London and Heathrow was important to me. I also wanted a university that was rated highly for its teaching. On all counts, Brunel fitted perfectly. It's a great place and, with some 4,000 students living on campus, there's a real sense of being part of a community.'
Zaneb, MSc student.

University of Buckingham

Hunter Street,
Buckingham MK18 1EG

t 01280 814080
e info@buckingham.ac.uk
↗ www.buckingham.ac.uk

》 **www.buckingham.ac.uk/study/postgrad**

 845   **PG** 24%   (UK) 20%

Buckingham is a unique institution: Britain's only private university. It consequently does things a little differently and organises its academic year with four 10-week terms a year. It has an impressive staff-student ratio and Buckingham students are among the most satisfied with their university experience. The pretty campus is compact, but big enough to boast its own cinema. It has a rural feel, but is between Milton Keynes and Oxford, should you need a shot of urban adrenaline.

Buckingham

Courses and qualifications There are 19 taught postgraduate programmes. You can study for an MA, MBA, MD, MPhil, MSc, PGCE or PhD.

Fees There are a range of fees depending on the subject, from £1,525 a term to £3,050 term for an MBA. UK, EU and international students all pay the same fees except in computing where there are differential rates.

Check the website for full costs: www.buckingham.ac.uk/study/fees/postgrad.html

Funding There are a limited number of academic scholarships available.

For further details see: www.buckingham.ac.uk/study/fees/scholarship/open-scholarships.html

Accommodation Sunley House is the accommodation block for postgraduates and mature students, although it is now also a designated quiet area, so younger students who want to live in a quiet place may also stay there.

The university does have some accommodation suitable for married couples although children are not permitted on campus. The accommodation office will assist families in finding accommodation in the town or outlying villages.

Facilities The students' union is based at the hub of student entertainment in Tanlaw Mill at the Hunter Street campus. Facilities include a bar, refectory, gym, studio and common room. The local cinema is housed in one of the university lecture halls.

Transport Good public transport service with regular buses linking the town to Oxford, Milton Keynes and Cambridge. Milton Keynes railway station is 20 minutes away from the university and there are regular trains to London, a journey that takes 30 minutes. The university has a minibus that runs five times a day between the two campuses.

Specialism Service management.

◀◀ **STUDENT VIEW** ▶▶

'The MSc service management is unique to Buckingham and enabled me to develop my business skills in the area of customer service. The work placement was invaluable as it gave me the opportunity to put theories into practice. Knowing I would have easy access to my tutors, all experts in this field, and working in small groups, were deciding factors in my decision to study at Buckingham.'

Buckinghamshire New University

Queen Alexandra Road,
High Wycombe HP11 2JZ

t 0800 0565 660
e advice@bucks.ac.uk
↗ www.bucks.ac.uk

» **www.bucks.ac.uk/courses/postgraduate.aspx**

 9,295   **PG** 6.8%   (**UK**) 73%

Buckinghamshire New University, or Bucks, nestles in
the beautiful countryside of the Chiltern Hills. Formerly
Buckinghamshire Chilterns University College, Bucks was
awarded full university status in 2007. From September 2009,
all of its courses, with the exception of nursing, will be based
at its campus in High Wycombe. The university offers a varied
range of vocationally-targeted degrees and studying options not
widely available in the sector, from commercial pilot training
to music management, textiles and furniture. Its faculties are
aligned to employment markets: creative and cultural industries;
the management and information management sectors; and the
public sector. There is a large proportion of mature students,
and many students come from the Buckinghamshire region. The
town centre, with a new shopping centre opened in 2008, is in
easy walking distance, and London is a short train ride away

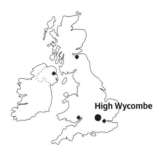

High Wycombe

Courses and qualifications There are over 40
postgraduate programmes. You can study for a
DipHE, MA, MBA, MEng MPhil, MSc, Pg Cert or
PhD.

Fees
UK/EU students: £3,720 for full-time study.
International students: fees range from around
£7,000 to £9,400.
   See the website for more details: www.bucks.
ac.uk/courses/postgraduate/fees_bursaries.aspx

Funding There is competitive funding for some
PhD study. This would be a bursary of £7,500
over three years, plus a fee waiver.

Accommodation There is no designated
postgraduate accommodation on campus nor is
there family accommodation. There are a large
number of suitable properties in the private
sector. The accommodation service will provide
details of these and offer assistance to married
students or students with children in finding
accommodation in the private sector.

Facilities The campus boasts a brand new
learning resources centre, including music,
drama and sports facilities, and newly
refurbished workshops and seminar rooms. There
are no facilities exclusively for postgraduates.

Transport The local main line station connects
to the London underground in 40 minutes.

‹‹ STUDENT VIEW ››

*'I am studying a furniture design MA. It is a very well respected course and I heard about it from trusted
sources. Since starting the course I have realised how qualified the tutors are. A number of them hold PhDs
and all are very well connected, offering great opportunities for work placements within industry. Through
tutors we have access to and involvement in a number of industry design shows. This is all subsidised by the
university.'* Benjamin Baker, MA furniture design & technology.

University of Cambridge

Cambridge CB2 1TN

t 01223 333308
e admissions@gradstudies.cam.ac.uk
↗ www.cam.ac.uk

» **www.admin.cam.ac.uk/univ/gsprospectus/**

 18,129   **PG** 35%   (**UK**) 50%

With a history stretching back 800 years (making it the second oldest university in Britain), a solid-gold academic reputation, a wealth of lore and tradition and some truly glorious architecture, Cambridge has plenty of justification for its boast of being one of the best universities in the world. It's also slightly tainted by the accusation that only posh types need apply, but the university is vigorous in its attempts to encourage people from all backgrounds to have a go: if you fancy a Cambridge education for yourself, there's no reason to be dissuaded. It's made up of 31 colleges and the college you belong to will be the focus of your university life. Academic pressure is intense, though most students find time to throw themselves into extra-curricular activities on the side.

Courses and qualifications There are over 700 courses leading to EngD, MBA, MEd, MLitt, MSc, MPhil, MSt, LLM, Pg Dip, Pg Cert or PhD.

Fees Postgraduates are charged a university composition fee and a college fee for each year of the course. Postgraduates from outside the UK are also required to pay a one-off settling in fee of £325 for the first year of the course. Students must show evidence that they can maintain themselves whilst at Cambridge. *UK/EU:* £3,390 university composition fee, £2,175 college fee, £9,847 maintenance. *International students:* £9,747 to £12,768 university composition fee (depending on course), £2,175 college fee, £9,847 maintenance.

Funding For details: www.admin.cam.ac.uk/offices/gradstud/funding/aid

Accommodation See individual colleges for details.

Facilities Cambridge has extensive resources and students enjoy access to 149 libraries, eight specialist museums and collections, and the University Botanic Garden. Most student rooms are connected to the university network and wireless hotspots are available throughout the university.

Transport Almost all the colleges and departments are fairly central — most students walk or cycle everywhere. In addition the Uni4 bus service connects many departments and colleges. London is about an hour away by train. Stansted Airport is nearby.

Specialism Cambridge is a world leading research and academic institution; it is more known for excellence in general.

❝ STUDENT VIEW ❞

'I chose Cambridge for my MPhil for the same reason that I chose it for my first degree: fantastic one-to-one teaching from the best academics in my field in Europe, and all in a beautiful and vibrant city.' Neil Myler, MPhil student in linguistics at Corpus Christi College.

Canterbury Christ Church University

University Centre Folkestone,
Mill Bay,
Folkestone CT20 1JP

t 01227 782900
e admissions@canterbury.ac.uk
↗ www.canterbury.ac.uk

» **www.canterbury.ac.uk/courses/prospectus/postgraduate/index.asp**

  15,000   **PG** 23%

Canterbury, yes, but not only there – the university has campuses all over Kent, in Broadstairs, Folkestone, the Medway and Salomons, near Tunbridge Wells. 15,000 students study a broad range of courses with often innovative approaches to learning. It's the largest centre in the region for training people for careers in the public services such as education, policing, health and social care. Whichever campus you end up on, you'll always be handily placed for London, but also perfectly poised to enjoy life in the 'garden of England'. The university fosters a friendly, cooperative atmosphere and getting involved in all aspects of student life is actively encouraged.

Canterbury

Courses and qualifications 168 courses on offer. You can study for a Doctorate, MA, MPhil, MSc, PGCE, Pg Dip, Pg Cert or PhD.

Fees
UK/EU students: £3,700 to £6,400.
International students: £8,500.

Funding None available.

Accommodation The university may be able to offer you accommodation but there is not a postgraduate designated halls of residence. There in no accommodation for families. For further information see: accommodation@canterbury.ac.uk

Facilities The students' union boasts CTV, its own TV production facility, the Unified student newspaper and CSR Radio – a full FM community radio licence shared with the University of Kent. The library at the Medway campus is reputed to be the longest library in Europe. There are separate computing services for research associates and assistants.

Transport London by train or car is one and a half hours away.

Specialism Education and health.

 STUDENT VIEW »

'I feel I now have an understanding of what it is to be critical. Class discussion and the extracts from the tutor have helped enormously.' MA in school development.

Cardiff University

Cardiff CF10 3XQ	t 029 2087 4455
	e enquiry@cardiff.ac.uk
	↗ www.cardiff.ac.uk

» **www.cardiff.ac.uk/for/prospective/pg/index.html**

 26,000   **PG** 20%   (UK) 62%

Cardiff seems to have it all: grand civic architecture in a breezy waterside location; super-smart city bars and venues just a short hop from lovely countryside. The university is as confident and forward-looking as the city it's located in. It has 26,000 students and an excellent reputation for the quality of its teaching and research. It is ranked among the top 100 universities in the world. 2008 saw the 125th anniversary of the university and it continues to invest heavily in its teaching and learning facilities in order to see the next 125 out in similar style.

Courses and qualifications Over 320 courses leading to BVC, DClinPsy, EngD, LLM, LPC, MA, MBA, MSc, MScEcon, MTh, MMus, MPhil, MScD, Pg Dip, Pg Cert, Professional Doctorate or PhD.

Fees
UK/EU students: £3,300 per year.
International students: £9,100 to £11,700.
    The tuition fees are variable and many are higher than the standard postgraduate fees above.

Funding The university offers a range of studentships to support postgraduate study. For more information on postgraduate funding opportunities check the website: www.cardiff. ac.uk/for/prospective/pg/funding/index.html

Accommodation The university has postgraduate accommodation and a small number of family flats are available for EU and international first year students.

Facilities 18 libraries contain 1m books and journals. Computer rooms with 24/7 access and wireless connections across the campus. The students' union has a cafe, a bookshop, a computer shop, a general shop, nightclub, bar and 1,500-capacity concert hall. There are nearly 60 athletic clubs for students. There's a modern multipurpose sports centre, a fitness centre with gym and six squash courts, 33 acres of grass pitches and four county-standard cricket wickets. There is a graduate centre at the university, which acts as an additional academic and social focus for postgraduates.

Transport Good for road and rail; London is two hours by train, Manchester three. Closer cities: Swansea takes 40 minutes and Bristol 45 minutes.

Specialism Cardiff's school of journalism, media and cultural studies has an excellent reputation.

⟨⟨ STUDENT VIEW ⟩⟩
'Cardiff University is an experience of a lifetime, academically and socially. I have felt supported and encouraged by the resources and opportunities provided by the university. The academic staff are committed, invigorating and provide me with expert advice to guide my research. Complemented by the exclusive postgraduate use of a graduate centre, a student development unit and 5* quality teaching, these facilities have made me proud to be a postgraduate at Cardiff.' Sam Paul, MSc occupational psychology.

University of Central Lancashire

Preston,
Lancashire PR1 2HE

t 01772 892400
e cenquiries@uclan.ac.uk
↗ www.uclan.ac.uk

» www.uclan.ac.uk/information/prospective_students/postgraduate_study/postgraduate_study.php

 32,000 **PG** 14%

UCLan is one of the country's largest universities, with 32,000 students, and it aims to provide an excellent experience for every single one of them. £60m is currently being invested in new facilities for learning, leisure and living. The recently opened £15.3m 'media factory' will support work in art, design and performing arts as well as providing business facilities for entrepreneurial graduates.

Courses and qualifications There are over 200 courses leading to MA, MD, MPhil, MSc and PhD.

Fees
UK/EU students: £3,300; £11,000 per year for the MBA.
International students: £7,950 to £8,200 for classroom based courses.
    Further information can be obtained from 01772 892440 or see: www.uclan.ac.uk/other/registry/finance

Funding The Gilbertson scholarship is offered to any student achieving a first class honours degree from UCLan, from June 2008 onwards. This will cover the full cost of a standard, full-time postgraduate course at the university. The scheme, available to all UK and EU students, is worth £3,300 and can be used as payment for a UCLan full-time master's or postgraduate programme. Other UCLan graduates may be entitled to 20 per cent discount on most postgraduate course fees.

Accommodation There is no postgraduate accommodation available on campus but there is plenty of private accommodation registered with the university.

Facilities Libraries are open 24 hours a day and there are extensive indoor and outdoor sports facilities, including the Preston Sports Arena. Research students have their own special facilities for study and office space where appropriate.

Transport The campus is on the edge of the city centre — it's a 10 minute walk into town. Under three hours on the train to London or Glasgow, and an hour from Manchester.

Specialism Dentistry.

❝ STUDENT VIEW ❞

'I have found the PhD programme to be very challenging and rewarding. Some aspects of my work were presented within the university in the weekly postgraduate forum and I have also delivered my work to an international audience at a workshop on comparative genomics in the USA.' Kultum Karama Mohammed, MPhil/PhD molecular biology.

Central School of Speech and Drama

Embassy Theatre,
Eton Avenue,
London NW3 3HY

t   020 7722 8183
e   enquiries@cssd.ac.uk
↗   www.cssd.ac.uk

» **www.cssd.ac.uk/postgrad.php**

 462   **PG** 57%   (UK) 56%

Founded in 1906, Central is a highly regarded drama and theatre school, near Swiss Cottage in north London. Courses range from acting to costume, design, lighting, sound, prop making, voice studies and stage management – plus a course in drama, applied theatre and education. Famous alumni include Peggy Ashcroft, Harold Pinter and Vanessa Redgrave, so to say you've got the chance to follow in some big footsteps at Central would be something of an understatement...

London

Courses and qualifications There are more than 14 courses leading to MA, Pg Cert, Pg Dip, PhD.

Fees
UK/EU students: the full-time taught MA ranges from £3,435 to £7,345.
International students: £12,565 to £13, 510 for the full-time MA.

Funding None available.

Accommodation There is very limited provision for Central students at the University of London's intercollegiate halls. Renting in the private sector will cost anywhere from £90 a week. There is no accommodation for families or specifically for postgraduates.

Facilities Facilities include the £5m 224-seat Embassy Theatre, plus the Embassy Studio and New Studio, each of which can accommodate 100 people.

Transport Access to good tube, bus and rail services.

Specialism Training for the theatre.

 STUDENT VIEW »
'PGCE allows you to be truly effective in your practice. At Central there is no formula for what is right in teaching, but an emphasis on your own understanding of effective teaching and what you can do to develop the skills and techniques which will benefit your professional practice.' Michael Cloherty.

University of Chester

Parkgate Road,
Chester CH1 4BJ

t 01244 511000
e enquiries@chester.ac.uk
↗ www.chester.ac.uk

» **www.chester.ac.uk/postgraduate/index.html**

 15,000   **PG** 23%   (UK) 90%

Chester

Chester is a handsome, historical town in the north-west of England. The appeal of the place might be revealed in the fact that around a third of the students at the university come from the area. They might also be attracted by the wide array of subjects – how about natural hazard management or youth work? There are two campuses – one in Chester and one in Warrington. A new £2m students' union building has recently opened on the Chester campus. Both centres are student friendly, manageable and close to Liverpool for some big nights out.

Courses and qualifications Several leading to PhD, MPhil, MA, MBA, MEd, MSc, MTh, PGCE, GTP, Pg Dip, Pg Cert, Grad Dip, Grad Cert.

Fees
UK/EU students: range from £3,510 to £9,000. Research programmes are £3,300 a year.
International students: £7,182 to £9,540. Research programmes are £9,400 to £11,900 a year.

Funding Up to eight Gladstone Fellowship scholarships are awarded annually. In 2008-09: stipend of £12,940 per year, plus all fees at the UK/EU rate.
   Tuition fee bursaries are awarded by faculties giving between a 50 per cent and 66 per cent remission on tuition fees.

Accommodation There is no university accommodation available for postgraduates. The accommodation office will help you find something suitable in the private sector: accommodation@chester.ac.uk

Facilities A new library and learning resources centre has recently opened in Warrington, to complement the rather larger one at Chester. Specialist degrees in sports science are run at both campuses, so facilities are good. They include playing fields, all-weather pitches, a swimming pool and squash courts. They are all available for recreational use by university members.

Transport There is a shuttle bus service between campuses and the city centre is within walking distance from the Chester campus. Good connections to Manchester and Liverpool.

Specialism Biological sciences, theology and religious studies.

❝ STUDENT VIEW ❞

'It has been three challenging but wonderful years. Whilst the PhD research can be daunting at times, the diligent support of my supervisor, the department and the graduate school has made my time at the university worthwhile and fulfilling. I would not hesitate to recommend the University of Chester to anyone. The close-knit university community, with its beautiful grounds and excellent research facilities, combine to create an optimum atmosphere for learning.' Servel A Miller.

University of Chichester

College Lane,
Chichester,
West Sussex PO19 6PE

t 01243 816000
e admissions@chi.ac.uk
↗ www.chiuni.ac.uk

 www.chiuni.ac.uk/research/index.cfm

 5,081   **PG** 20%   (UK) 95%

Chichester gained full university status in 2005 and prides itself on its friendly, close-knit feel. It's based on two historic campuses in Chichester and Bognor Regis. They're both relatively small places, so the university feels accessible and integrated. West Sussex boasts some genuinely gorgeous scenery and the coast is within easy reach. Chichester has an excellent student satisfaction rating and some of the best student retention rates in the country.

Chichester

Courses and qualifications Several leading to PGCE, MSc, MA, PG Dip, MA, MSc, PGCE, PhD, MPhil.

Fees
UK/EU students: £3,500 to £4,000.
International students: £8,200 for most courses.

Funding There are a number of bursaries for research programmes.

Accommodation
For details email: accommodation@chi.ac.uk

Facilities Chichester will be an Olympic training camp for international athletes, leading up to the 2012 London Olympic games, so there are some pretty nifty sports facilities.
     Students have access to Learning Resources Centres on both the Bishop Otter and Bognor Regis Campus. The BOC Centre houses a large number of open access computers, and the whole LRC building has wireless access for students. The BOC students' union and staff club also provide wireless access. Online resources include access to online journals and eBooks and they also have access to University of Southampton's library facilities. Within the LRC are media facilities and teaching support for preparation of conference posters and audiovisual material.

Transport Free bus service between Chichester and Bognor Regis campuses. Both campuses are within 10 minutes' walk of the town centre. London is 90 minutes away.

Specialism Education, sports science, arts and humanities.

Christie's Education London

153 Great Titchfield Street,
London W1W 5BD

t 020 7665 4350
e education@christies.com
↗ www.christies.com/services/education

» www.christieseducation.com/london_gradprogrammes.html

 150   **PG** 90%

Christie's is the only major auction house in the world that directly runs educational programmes at master's, graduate diploma, and undergraduate degree levels — it is validated by the University of Glasgow to run these courses. An international team of dedicated art-world experts, academics and practitioners have been brought together and are committed to educating and inspiring the next generation of art-world professionals.

London

Courses and qualifications There are four courses leading to master's degrees and three courses leading to graduate diplomas. The MLitt and Graduate Diploma are both accredited by the University of Glasgow.

Fees UK/EU and international students all pay the same. Graduate Diploma prices range from £14,000 to £15,000. Master's fees range from £16,000 to £17,000.

Accommodation Students are offered help finding suitable places to live via the accommodation lists. Many share flats or take up residence with landlords who have offered accommodation to our students over many years. Information about finding accommodation is given immediately after an offer has been made and accepted.

Facilities Common room, library, slide room, IT room and reading room.

Specialism Christie's Education is owned by Christie's auction house and offers university qualifications specifically aimed at professionals training for careers in the art world. It is renowned for object-based study and transferable skills for art world careers, from the auction house, museums and galleries, dealers, publishing, and other art related businesses.

◄◄ STUDENT VIEW ►►

'The Christie's programme is in my opinion probably the best. You're handling objects that are museum quality and you spend a lot of time in the auction rooms actually working with the objects and spending time with the experts to gain that practical knowledge that is so necessary when one leaves the academic setting for employment. I am very, very happy to have undertaken this course at Christie's. I can't recommend it enough. Albert Zecher, diploma, fine and decorative arts.

City University London

Northampton Square,
London EC1V 0HB

t 020 7040 5060
e enquiries@city.ac.uk
↗ www.city.ac.uk

 24,000   **PG** 39%   (UK) 47%

London

As the name suggests, City is located in the heart of London, but its outlook is truly international. Students are drawn from 157 countries around the world, while staff come from over 40 different countries. There are commendable graduate employment rates, state-of-the-art facilities and an extensive public lecture and events programme. The West End and the City of London are virtually on your doorstep.

Courses and qualifications There are 67 courses leading to MA, MSc, MPhil, PhD, MBA, MEng, MMus, PGDip, PGCert, LLM, DPsych, MRes.

Fees A range of fees depending on the subject.

Funding There are a wide range of scholarship opportunities available for postgraduate students in the School of Arts, Cass Business School and School of Informatics.

Accommodation There are three halls for postgraduates; they are all single rooms, not for families. For information on private accommodation view: www.city.ac.uk/studentcentre/housing/index.html

Facilities There is a brand new students' union, cutting edge classroom technology including touch screen control, video conferencing software and high quality audio to increase the focus of student generated input.

The university offers postgraduate libraries including at The City Law School's Professional Studies Centre in Gray's Inn Place and laboratories such as The School of Social Sciences' Testing Laboratories in the Department of Psychology. All Cass postgraduates study in Cass Business School's state-of-the art £50m building on the doorstep of the City.

Transport City's central London location ensures that it benefits from excellent transport links – there are several bus routes, tube and the mainline stations of Farringdon and Barbican.

Conservatoire for Dance and Drama

1-7 Woburn Walk,
London WC1H 0JJ

t 020 7387 5101
e info@cdd.ac.uk
↗ www.cdd.ac.uk

 1,184   **PG** 7%

London

The CDD was founded in 2001 and is a higher education institution with a unique structure. It's made up of eight schools around the country – all of them small and all of them specialist providers of education and training in different areas of performance. The CDD doesn't have its own degree-awarding powers so degrees are validated by different universities.

Courses and qualifications Seven courses leading to MA, MPhil, PhD.

Fees Information on postgraduate fees is available from the individual schools that deliver the courses. There are three schools offering postgraduate courses: RADA, Bristol Old Vic Theatre School and London Contemporary Dance School.

Funding There is none available for postgraduates, although the affiliate schools may offer certain support schemes.

Facilities Each school has different facilities.

Accommodation There is no postgraduate specific or family accommodation.

Specialism The individual schools are known for their expertise in dramatic art and stage management, technical theatre (RADA and Bristol Old Vic) and in contemporary dance (LCDS).

❛❛ STUDENT VIEW ❜❜

'As a postgraduate student at London Contemporary Dance School, I will be working with some of the country's leading artists and choreographers, and gain lots of performance experience. You're part of a dance company, but the focus is on your individual research and development. I will also gain teaching experience on tour, working in schools and colleges.' Myrto Gkouzelou, Pg Dip/MA student.

Courtauld Institute of Art

Somerset House, Strand, London WC2R 0RN	**t** 020 7848 2645 **e** pgadmissions@courtauld.ac.uk ↗ www.courtauld.ac.uk

» **www.courtauld.ac.uk/research/index.shtml**

 400   **PG** 60%   (**UK**) 50%

The Courtauld is one of Britain's most famous galleries and art institutes and the 400-or-so students (of whom undergraduates make up about a third) have unrivalled access to it. As well as that, the spectacular location at Somerset House means that all of London's resources are on your doorstep. The emphasis is on small-group teaching and the institute prides itself on its friendly feel and academic excellence. Degrees are awarded by the University of London, so you have access to the main university library at Senate House.

Courses and qualifications There are five courses leading to MA history of art, MA curating the art museum, Pg Dip conservation of easel paintings, MA conservation of wall paintings, MPhil/PhD.

Fees
UK/EU students: £3,400 to £4,745.
International students: £11,804 to £14,437.

Funding There is a wide range of financial support available in the form of scholarships.

Accommodation The institute aims to house as many first year students as possible in intercollegiate halls in Bloomsbury or its own residence near Somerset House. About half of first years (and all subsequent years) find private accommodation. A small number of rooms available are reserved for married couples. For further information see: www.lon.ac.uk

Facilities Outstanding libraries and the gallery collection of paintings, drawings and prints, and sculpture and decorative arts. Separate study room and some dedicated postgraduate accommodation.

Transport Located in central London and therefore connected to most underground, rail and bus networks.

Specialism The Courtauld is a world leader in the teaching and research of the history of art, and in the conservation of easel and wall paintings.

Coventry University

Priory Street,
Coventry CV1 5FB

t 02476 887688
e studentenquiries@coventry.ac.uk
↗ www.coventry.ac.uk

» **wwwp.coventry.ac.uk/postgraduate**

Perhaps you won't mind being sent to Coventry when you realise it means life on an impressive 33-acre campus in the heart of one of the largest cities in England. A pleasant Cathedral Quarter and city centre showcase 1,000 years of history, and the city has all the facilities you'd expect. The university thinks of itself as modern and forward-looking. Courses have close vocational links with major global corporations and employability is a key concern at the university.

● Coventry

Courses and qualifications There are approximately 200 courses on offer. You can study for an LLM, MA, MBA, MRes, MPhil, Pg Dip or PhD.

Fees
UK/EU: full-time research degrees are £3,420. *International:* £9,000 for research postgraduate programmes.

Funding An alumni discount of £500 is available to all the university's UK and EU graduates who progress directly from an undergraduate course to a full-time postgraduate course. Students who receive this discount will not be eligible for additional university scholarships or bursaries offered by the university or by schools and faculties. There are 50 university merit scholarships of £1,000 available to UK and EU students on postgraduate programmes.

Accommodation The university has two dedicated postgraduate properties. Accommodation is offered to postgraduate students in Priory Hall on a 40-week contract or Singer Hall on a 50-week postgraduate contract. Both properties offer easy access to campus.

Facilities Students benefit from an award-winning library, a new sports centre and a £5m student centre.

Transport Close to the M1/M6 intersection and half an hour from Birmingham by train; an hour and a quarter to London.

University College for the Creative Arts

New Dover Road, Canterbury, Kent CT1 3AN	**t** 01227 817302 **e** info@ucreative.ac.uk ↗ www.ucreative.ac.uk

University for the Creative Arts at Epsom Ashley Road, Epsom, Surrey KT18 5BE	01372 728811
University for the Creative Arts at Farnham Falkner Road, Farnham, Surrey GU9 7DS	01252 722441
University for the Creative Arts at Maidstone Oakwood Park, Maidstone, Kent ME16 8AG	01622 620000
University for the Creative Arts at Rochester Fort Pitt, Rochester, Kent ME1 1DZ	01634 888702

» **www.ucreative.ac.uk/index.cfm?articleid=15822**

 7,287   **PG** 4%   (UK) 52%

Or... the University College for the Creative Arts at Canterbury, Epsom, Farnham, Maidstone and Rochester, to give it its full title. Existing in its present form since 2005, it's one of the UK's leading providers of specialist education and research in art, design, architecture, media and communication. A diverse community of students, staff and researchers is spread across the south-east in the five constituent colleges. Students come from all over the world to study here, win industry awards and showcase their work at national and international festivals. Courses aim to equip students for successful careers and the college has ambitions to win full university status soon.

Canterbury

Courses and qualifications There are 35 courses leading to Grad Cert, Grad Dip, MA, MBA, Pg Cert.

Fees Fees vary. See website for details.

Funding Funding is available. For details see: www.ucreative.ac.uk/mascholarships

Accommodation Postgraduate accommodation is available. No family accommodation. For further details contact: accommodation@ucreative.ac.uk

Facilities Good specialist libraries and active student support networks in place. The university is home to several public galleries. Research centres include the Centre for Sustainable Design, The Animation Research Centre, The Hasselblad Centre for High Resolution Digital Imaging, and The Anglo-Japanese Textile Centre.

Transport All campuses are close to motorways, rail networks and international airports.

Specialism Creative arts subjects.

❝ STUDENT VIEW ❞

'Studying at UCA in Canterbury was a great experience. I had chosen UCA because of the way the courses were structured, which gave me great freedom to explore ideas through my work. There is also a good range of workshops and technical help available throughout the year.' Jessica Miller, MA in fine art.

Cranfield University

Cranfield Campus,
Cranfield,
Bedfordshire MK43 0AL

t 01234 750111
e info@cranfield.ac.uk
↗ www.cranfield.ac.uk

 23,300   **PG** 100%   (UK) 45%

Cranfield

Cranfield is a postgraduate institution and its focus is squarely on the application of its research. Cranfield has three campuses, two in Bedfordshire (Cranfield and Silsoe) and one in Wiltshire (Shrivenham). Cranfield campus is home to the School of Applied Sciences, School of Engineering, School of Management and Cranfield Health. Cranfield is located between the historic town of Bedford and the new city of Milton Keynes, both of which offer a variety of entertainment and shopping facilities.

Shrivenham campus in Wiltshire is home to the defence college of management and technology. The village is six miles from the town of Swindon, which has shopping, sport and leisure facilities, and 22 miles from Oxford.

Courses and qualifications Over 150 courses leading to MSc, MBA, MTech, MDes, MRes, FMM, Pg Dip, Pg Cert, PhD, PhD with integrated studies, DBA, DM, EngD, MPhil, MSc, pre-master's course in engineering.

Fees Fees vary depending on subject, fee status and qualifications.
UK/EU: £3,300 for master's and research degrees, £28,000 for the MBA.
International: £16,000 for a full-time master's and research degrees, £28,000 for the MBA.

Funding Cranfield Health, the School of Applied Sciences, the School of Management and the School of Engineering all offer bursaries for UK MSc students with good first degrees if the students are unable to obtain funding from other sources. These funds are limited and students are expected to have explored all other suitable sources of funding before applying to this scheme. It should be noted that recipients may be required to specialise in areas dictated by the source of funding.

Occasionally, Cranfield is able to offer junior research posts to UK and EU nationals accepted for PhD study. A salary is attached to such posts and is usually at a comparable level to that paid to fresh graduates.

Accommodation There is a wide range of accommodation available, for individuals, couples and families.

Facilities Cranfield campus includes a general store, post office, bank and a petrol station. Shrivenham campus includes an outdoor heated swimming pool, golf course, riding stables and many other sporting opportunities. The campus also has a computer centre, an e-learning centre and a newly refurbished library.

Transport Cranfield campus lies about 10 minutes from the M1 motorway, the UK's main north/south artery, and has rail and road access to most major airports.

Specialism Aerospace, automotive, bioscience, environment, energy, manufacturing and security and defence.

 STUDENT VIEW ▶▶

'I chose to study at Cranfield because it was a world-renowned postgraduate centre that offers fantastic learning facilities as well as an inviting atmosphere. All the expert knowledge and the very good library services were of great benefit to me. I especially enjoyed the close and straightforward teamwork. The MSc programme gave me the best opportunities as well as challenges which I was able to overcome due to the excellent support of the people I worked with at Cranfield.' Medical diagnostic MSc student.

University of Cumbria

Fusehill Street,
Carlisle,
Cumbria CA1 2HH

t 01228 616234
e admissions@cumbria.ac.uk
↗ www.cumbria.ac.uk

» **www.cumbria.ac.uk/FutureStudents/Howtoapply/Postgraduate
/Postgraduatecourses.aspx**

The University of Cumbria was formed on August 1 2007, from an amalgamation of St Martin's College, Cumbria Institute of the Arts, and the Cumbrian campuses of the University of Central Lancashire. The university has campuses in Carlisle, Newton Rigg, Penrith, Ambleside and Lancaster, and a specialist teacher education centre in London. It is committed to learning that is innovative, flexible and student-centred and which utilises the latest technology. It prides itself on preparing its students for employment and on its links with local schools, colleges, businesses and the community that it serves.

Courses and qualifications 200 courses leading to an MA, MSc, MPhil, Pg Cert, PGCE, Pg Dip and PhD.

Fees
UK/EU: £3,145 for a PGCE, MA, MBA or MSc.
International: £8,250 for an MA, MSc, MBA or MPhil.

Funding None offered by the university.

Accommodation There's a wide variety of accommodation on offer and prices vary, though rents in the area are fairly reasonable. For further details see: www.cumbria.ac.uk/Accommodation

Facilities Sport plays a significant part in the life of the university and facilities for it are extensive and of a high standard. Integrated services for library, media and IT support.

Transport Good links by motorway and rail, and international airports and big cities, including Manchester and Glasgow, are accessible.

Specialism Education.

❝ STUDENT VIEW ❞

'I was fortunate to have an enthusiastic and inspiring PhD supervisor, Professor Hilary Cooper, based at the Ambleside Campus, who encouraged me tremendously over the course of my research.'
Dr Lindsey Winterton, PhD

De Montfort University

The Gateway,
Leicester LE1 9BH

t 08459 454647
e enquiry@dmu.ac.uk
↗ www.dmu.ac.uk

 www.dmu.ac.uk/Subjects/Db/index.php?index=pro&list=3

 20,300 **PG** 16% (UK) 78%

The De Montfort of today has emerged from the unification of a wide range of specialist institutions and has shown an impressive ability to re-invent itself. Most recently this has meant allowing the Bedford campus to merge with the University of Luton to create the new University of Bedfordshire, and there's a constant programme of investment and development. The main campus is in Leicester's city centre, with a second – the Charles Frear campus – on the outskirts. Leicester is England's 10th largest city, with good transport links and all the facilities you'd expect. It's also brilliantly multicultural – the Diwali celebrations are something to be seen.

Courses and qualifications There are over 100 courses leading to PG Cert, PG Dip, MSc, MBA, LLM, LPC, MPhil, PhD.

Fees
UK/EU students: standard postgraduate fees from £3,400.
International students: standard postgraduate fee range is £8,500 to £9,500.
    Plus a range of non-standard fees for other postgraduate courses.

Funding See website for details.

Accommodation Students with families can be helped to find private accommodation. Contact: housing@dmu.ac.uk

Facilities £1.7m has been spent on revamping the library to enable students to study in the way that best suits them. Good sports and social facilities too. Faculties have dedicated graduate centres and host special events for postgraduates throughout the year, including staff-student seminars and an annual multi-disciplinary postgraduate conference. It also has dedicated halls of residence on campus near the library for postgraduates.

Transport Both campuses are within walking distance of the city centre. Road and rail links to the rest of the UK are excellent.

Specialism Visit: dmu.ac.uk/research for an overview of the many areas of internationally recognised research.

❝ STUDENT VIEW ❞

'I'd recommend the DMU MA in television scriptwriting to anyone serious about trying to work in the industry as a scriptwriter. The academic qualification is nice but the real benefits are the excellent range of guest speakers, the practical instruction on writing and especially re-writing and the inspiration you get from working with other writers who also want to make a career out of screenwriting. It sent me out into the competitive world of TV with a better understanding of the needs of the industry and a realistic view of the best way to get paid work. I loved every minute.' Phil Nodding, MA TV scriptwriting graduate (*Shameless* writer).

Derby University

Kedleston Road,
Derby DE22 1GB

t 01332 591167
e askadmissions@derby.ac.uk
↗ www.derby.ac.uk

》 **www.derby.ac.uk/postgraduate**

Flexibility is something of a watchword at Derby. It invites you to create your own degree, study part-time or choose a fast-track degree. It also emphasises its vocational slant – links with employers and other partners are carefully maintained – and 2008 saw the launch of a £12m division dedicated to engaging with employers and businesses, as well as developing enterprise and entrepreneurship at this university. Derby is a pleasant, historical city and Buxton, location of the University's Grade II listed Devonshire Campus, is an equally charming spa town. Both are handy for some lovely countryside and easygoing enough to make you feel right at home.

Courses and qualifications Approximately 150 courses on offer. You can study for a LLM, MA, MBA, MPhil, MSc, Pg Cert, Pg Dip, PGCE or PhD.

Fees
UK/EU students: £5,400 for an MA, £6,600 for the MBA.
International students: £8,200 for the MA, £9,200 for the MBA.

Funding Continuing students may receive a 10 per cent discount on fees. The university also has a limited number of excellence bursaries that are allocated on a competitive basis.

Accommodation
Visit: www.derby.ac.uk/Accommodation

Facilities Sir Richard Branson opened the university's new £21m bespoke arts, design and technology site in November 2007. Other specialised facilities enable vocational and academic education to be combined.

Transport The university has an excellent sustainable transport plan throughout Derby, also servicing the Buxton Campus during term time. Derby is 10 minutes from the M1 and on the main line from London St Pancras.

Specialism Business, computing and law.

⟨⟨ STUDENT VIEW ⟩⟩
'Would I recommend Derby? Most certainly. To people of all ages and all walks of life I would say come and learn what I did: that Derby is a great place to grow but be aware that it does take some hard work to achieve all that you can be. Believe me, it's worth the effort.'

University of Dundee

Nethergate,
Dundee DD1 4HN

t 01382 384000
e university@dundee.ac.uk
↗ www.dundee.ac.uk

 18,000   **PG** 27%   (UK) 50%

Thanks to its south-facing position, Dundee has claims to be the sunniest city in Scotland. It's also large enough to be interesting but compact enough to be friendly and manageable. And it's close to Edinburgh if you have a surplus of cultural requirements, and also nice countryside and coast if you have a surplus of physical energy to expend by doing outdoorsy things. The university has recently invested £200m in campus improvements, including £39m for new student accommodation. Expect your digs to be pretty fancy, then.

Courses and qualifications Around 210 courses leading to MA, MSc, MLitt, LLM, MBA, PGDE, MRes, PG Cert, PG Dip, PhD, MPhil.

Fees Cost varies depending on course.
UK/EU students: approx £3,300.
International students: £8,500 to £10,500.
   Some courses (typically medicine) are higher. Check with individual course pages on www.dundee.ac.uk/postgraduate/courses

Funding See individual course pages: www.dundee.ac.uk/postgraduate/courses

Accommodation One hall of residence is for postgraduates only. There is some family accommodation. For further information contact: residences@dundee.ac.uk

Facilities The main library has been extended at a cost of £5.5m and has excellent modern facilities for silent and group study. £4m has also been spent on extending indoor sports facilities. The union has bars and clubs over five floors and students in the College of Arts and Social Sciences have their own study centre.

Transport The main campus is in the city centre. Transport links to the rest of the country are excellent.

Specialism Energy, petroleum and mineral law and policy, orthopaedic surgery, accounting, computing, remote sensing, humanities, design.

Durham University

University Office,
Old Elvet,
Durham DH1 3HP

t 0191 334 6128
e admissions@durham.ac.uk
↗ www.durham.ac.uk

» www.dur.ac.uk/postgraduate

 15,000   **PG** 23%   (UK) 49%

Durham is home to one of the country's top universities. The city is picturesque, wooded, hilly and aching with heritage. The brooding Norman cathedral dominates the skyline – and it tells you something about the prestige of the university that one of its colleges is housed in the castle right next door. Durham is a collegiate university, meaning that student life has a real sense of focus and community to it. There's also more than a whiff of Oxbridge to proceedings – fun, if you like that sort of thing. If you don't, you'll probably be relieved to know that Durham has put its money where its mouth is when it comes to widening participation. Its Queen's campus in nearby Stockton-on-Tees boasts plenty of local and mature students. Durham students are well placed for glorious countryside and coastline and there are good transport links.

Durham

Courses and qualifications There are 493 separate programmes leading to DBA, DIP, DMin, EDD, GDip, LLM, MA, MAR, MBA, MEd, MJur, ML, MLitt, MM, MPH, MProf, MRes, MSc, MSCR, MSW, MTh, Pg Cert, Pg Dip, PGCE, PhD.

Fees Fees vary depending on the course. See the website for details.

Funding A range of funding sources are available. For details see: www.durham.ac.uk/postgraduate/finance/search

Accommodation Dryburn Court contains one, two and three bedroom flats for couples and families with children. Car parking is available, and there is a small playground for children. See: www.dur.ac.uk/colleges

Facilities Excellent, well-stocked library in an award-winning building – it is one of only six libraries in the UK with National Archive Status. Durham has good IT facilities and 64 acres of sports fields. Each college provides its own range of services too.

Transport Good road and rail links to the rest of the east coast and country, with two regional airports around half an hour away. A free shuttle bus operates between campuses in term time.

Specialism Arts and humanities, social science and health, science and the business school.

** STUDENT VIEW »**

'I'm currently studying a PGCE here at Durham. I'm in my second placement at Framwellgate School in Durham, which I've really enjoyed. The staff at the university have been excellent all the way through the course, and when you are on your placement you still get a lot of support from them. They come out and visit you and are always contactable if you need to speak to them.' Rosalind McFadden, PGCE secondary.

University of East Anglia

Norwich NR4 7TJ

t 01603 591515
e admissions@uea.ac.uk
↗ www.uea.ac.uk

» **www.uea.ac.uk/home/courses/postgraduate**

 19,585   **PG** 22%

The UEA campus is just a couple of miles from the centre of Norwich. The campus has excellent sports facilities, bars and cafes, a centre for visual arts, not to mention some striking 1960s architecture. It came joint top in the 2006 National Student Survey and performed well last year too. UEA also prides itself on being at the forefront of green awareness and aims to have its energy needs met by an on-campus biomass generating plant.

Courses and qualifications There are 270 different courses leading to MA, MSc, MPhil, MRes, PhD, MBA, PGCE, LLM, DipSW, MMus, ClinPsyD, DipHE, Grad Dip, PG Dip, PGCE.

Fees
UK/EU students: £3,300 for most courses.
International students: range from £9,500 to £14,500.

Funding
UK students on taught programmes:
www1.uea.ac.uk/cm/home/services/units/mac/aao/courses/PG/fees/pg_taught
UK students on research programmes:
www1.uea.ac.uk/cm/home/services/units/mac/aao/courses/PG/fees/res_student (which includes the UEA Research Studentships).

Accommodation International students are guaranteed accommodation as a single student in university residences, provided they meet certain criteria. The university owns and maintains 46 houses, to let to students with children.

Facilities The library is open seven days a week. There's a £17.5m Sportspark with facilities including a 50-metre pool, athletics track, indoor arena, a climbing wall, fitness centre, dance studios and 40 acres of playing fields. The union hosts top-name bands and regular club nights. The Graduate Students' Association is run by and for postgraduates. The Graduate Students' Club provides a social space with a more mature atmosphere and puts on regular entertainment events including live music and a weekly quiz night. A designated reading room and individual study carrels in the library, a number of which are equipped with networked workstations.

Transport You can walk to Norwich city centre, but there is a 24-hour bus service connecting the two. Two hours by road or rail to London. Norwich airport is nearby and Stansted 90 minutes away.

Specialism Creative writing and English literature, environmental sciences, biological sciences, film studies, history, MBAs, social work, teacher training.

❝ STUDENT VIEW ❯❯

'I chose to pursue a PhD dealing with global climate change at the School of Environmental Sciences. It was one of the longest established, largest and most fully developed schools with the highest 5** research ranking and awarded an "excellent" rating in the recent Teaching Quality Assessment. The multicultural, international environment has enriched my learning, giving me loads of friends from across the globe.' Michelle Fernandes, PhD in oceanography.

University of East London

Docklands Campus, 4-6 University Way, London E16 2RD	**t** 020 8223 3000 **e** admiss@uel.ac.uk ↗ www.uel.ac.uk

» **www.uel.ac.uk/courses/postgraduate/index.htm**

 20,742   **PG** 25%   (UK) 70%

UEL is centred on the ultra-modern Docklands campus by the Thames, with another base at Stratford in east London, the hub of one of Europe's largest urban regeneration programmes, thanks to the 2012 Olympics. The university prides itself on developing new ways of teaching and learning that make the university as accessible and as flexible as possible. Almost all students come from state schools and many students are from ethnic minorities. Courses are innovative and responsive to the needs of students and industry.

London

Courses and qualifications Around 130 courses leading to MA, MSc, MPhil, PhD, MBA, PGCE plus professional doctorates, Master of Research, PG Diploma.

Fees
UK/EU students: range from £3,675 to £4,350.
International students: range from £8,500 to £9,000.

Funding UEL provides and advises on a number of funding opportunities available to postgraduates. These include:
part-time postgraduate fee waivers for UK/EU students: UEL has a range of 25 per cent and 50 per cent (up to £500) fee waivers available for part-time MPhil or PhD students from low-income households and rebates worth up to 35 per cent of final-year fees on completion.
Sir John Cass Foundation scholarships: if you are a full-time UK postgraduate student applying for an MA/MSc programme in science, information and computer technology, a health related subject or financial management, are under

24 years of age at enrolment and a permanent resident from selected London boroughs, you may be eligible for one of 10 £3,000 scholarships.

Accommodation There is no family or postgraduate specific accomodation available through the university. See: www.uel.ac.uk/residential

Facilities Modern and inspiring buildings at the Docklands campus, with purpose-built teaching and learning facilities. Good libraries and learning resources plus an on-site manufacturing facility and two industry-standard television studios.

Transport Easy access to rail, tube, buses and the Docklands Light Railway. And the rest of the UK links to the capital quite nicely.

Specialism Architecture and visual arts, PGCE, psychology, health and bioscience, computing, technology and engineering, law.

❝ STUDENT VIEW ❞

'I'm extremely grateful to my tutors for their constant support and motivation. With all the skills and expertise I'm developing, I'm very confident of becoming a highly proficient and sought-after specialist in the expanding field of environmental control.' Eric Loh, MSc in civil engineering, PhD.

'The best day of my life was the day I graduated, because of the sense of achievement and confidence it gave me.' Stevie Firminger, MSc in occupational and organisational psychology.

Edge Hill University

Ormskirk,
Lancashire L39 4QP

t 01695 575171
e enquiries@edgehill.ac.uk
↗ www.edgehill.ac.uk

 www.edgehill.ac.uk/study/courses/masters

👥 22,700   **PG** 36%   (UK) 95%

Edge Hill only became a university in 2006 but is growing rapidly. It has over 20,000 students and has experienced a consistent increase in UCAS applications in recent years, outstripping the national average. Edge Hill is expanding physically, too, and is due to double in size by 2020. A new building that houses the e-learning centre and the faculty of health opened in 2008 and the £8m business school opened in 2009. The main campus is a 75-acre site on the outskirts of Ormskirk, Lancashire. It's a small market town, but is close to Liverpool and Manchester. Also worth a mention is Edge Hill's award-winning student finance package.

Ormskirk

Courses and qualifications 160 courses leading to MA, MSc, MPhil, PhD, PGCE, Early Years Professional Status, Postgraduate Professional Development (for serving teachers).

Fees
UK/EU students: most courses are £3,600.
The MBA is £7,500.
International students: most courses are £7,900.
The MBA is £9,250

Funding A discount of 50 per cent on tuition fees is available on a range of postgraduate programmes to students graduating in 2007 and 2008. An attainment scholarship of £500 is available to all international students who have paid their fees and successfully complete their first semester of study.

Accommodation None for families, see:
accomodationteam@edgehill.ac.uk

Facilities The campus boasts a lake, piazza area and plenty of green space. The on-campus sports centre provides high-quality facilities that recently received top recognition by being included in the Olympic pre-games training guide for London 2012. The Woodlands Centre is specifically for Postgraduate Professional Development students. MPhil and PhD students have a dedicated workroom and IT facilities.

Transport The motorway connections to the rest of the UK are easy enough but the train journey means a change at Liverpool or Preston.

Specialism Education — OFSTED has just rated Primary Education (including the PGCE programmes) at the highest level of 'outstanding'.

❝ STUDENT VIEW ❞

'I'd always thought about teaching as a career but as a graduate in textiles I tried to get into commercial buying. That didn't work out and I ended up in a couple of jobs that weren't really for me. I'm so glad that I decided to take up the PGCE at Edge Hill — the facilities, teaching and support were amazing. The placements and taught sessions really did help prepare you for work.' Jennifer Hewitt, PGCE in applied art and design.

University of Edinburgh

Old College,
South Bridge,
Edinburgh EH8 9YL

t 0131 650 1000
e sra.enquiries@ed.ac.uk
↗ www.ed.ac.uk

» www.ed.ac.uk/studying/postgraduate

 25,753   **PG** 29%   (UK) 58%

Edinburgh was founded in the 1580s and has forged a special position in academia. Its national and international reputation is excellent, and it has a large, diverse and multinational student body. Edinburgh itself is vibrant and cosmopolitan, with stately architecture and green spaces. University buildings are spread throughout the city. Many of them are historic, but the university continues to develop.

Courses and qualifications There are over 200 programmes leading to MSc, MPhil, PhD, MBA, PGCE, PGDE, MInf, MSW, PG Dip, MEd, LLM.

Fees Full details regarding tuition fees can be found on the Registry website at: www.registry.ed.ac.uk/fees

Funding Full details regarding funding opportunities, including a searchable database, can be found at: www.scholarships.ed.ac.uk

Accommodation Postgraduates from outside of the EU are guaranteed accommodation providing an application is made by July 31 of the year of study and the place of study is confirmed as unconditional. The university will try to offer to accommodation to new, single, postgraduates from within the EU (other than the UK) but cannot guarantee that an offer of university accommodation will be made. Accommodation services have over 80 flats for students with families.

Facilities There is a range of first-class facilities, including one of the largest and most important academic libraries in the world as well as national centres of excellence such as the National eScience Centre, the Centre for the Advanced Study of the Arab World, and the Confucius Institute (which promotes the study of Chinese language and culture). More recently, the university's Edinburgh Parallel Computing Centre has been chosen to house, manage and direct a £113m computing facility, known as HECToR (High End Computing Terascale Resource), the largest supercomputer in the UK and one of the top 12 fastest in the world. Another new resource, to be opened in 2010, is the new £59m home of the Scottish Centre for Regenerative Medicine.

The Centre for Sport and Exercise has several state-of-the-art gyms, swimming pool, sports halls and a climbing wall.

The Postgraduate Transferable Skills Unit delivers a programme of generic and bespoke training to all postgraduate research students and a large number of students on master's programmes.

Transport Excellent transport links you'd expect from a capital city. Edinburgh airport is eight miles away.

Specialism Humanities, science and engineering and medicine and veterinary science.

‹‹ STUDENT VIEW ››

'In my field, Edinburgh enjoys the highest research rating among UK Middle Eastern Studies departments, so it was a natural first choice. The programme really lived up to my expectations. I really believe that my Edinburgh MSc has laid the foundations for my intellectual and professional credentials.'
Samy A Ayoub, MSc in Islamic and Middle Eastern studies (Egypt).

Edinburgh College of Art

Lauriston Place,
Edinburgh EH3 9DF

t 0131 221 6027
e registry@eca.ac.uk
↗ www.eca.ac.uk

 » **www.eca.ac.uk/study**

 1,850 **PG** 20% (**UK**) 43%

Based in the old town of Edinburgh near the famous Grassmarket, the Edinburgh College of Art offers courses in all disciplines of art and design, architecture, and visual and cultural studies. The college traces its origins back to 1760 but today there are just under 2,000 students from all over the world.

Courses and qualifications There are 60 courses leading to MA, MFA, MSc, MPhil, Phd, PG Dip.

Fees The tuition fees for postgraduate study vary across subjects and qualifications.
UK/EU students: range from £2,400 to £4,975.
International students: range from £9,630 to £12,840.

Funding A number of scholarships and bursaries are awarded to students, based on merit and/or financial need, following nominations made by heads of school.

Accommodation No postgraduate specific accommodation but it can forward requests for family accommodation to the University of Edinburgh. (ECA is an accredited institution of University of Edinburgh).

Facilities The college library lies at the heart of the newly-developed Evolution House Learning Zone, providing an innovative environment for learning, teaching and research resources. All aspects of the college's teaching and research are covered, with an emphasis on contemporary issues and practice. It has wireless internet, and laptops may be borrowed for use anywhere within the Learning Zone.

Depending on the area of study, studio, exhibition, and office space is available; 24 hour access (for research students only).

Transport Regular trains from London King's Cross, and the airport is about 10 miles away.

Specialism ECA is also the only art college in Scotland to offer postgraduate programmes in glass, contemporary art theory and 'art, space and nature' — a degree configured to consider the interrelationships between various art and architecture disciplines.

❝ STUDENT VIEW ❞

'I got the freedom to pursue my own projects, with the right advice and guidance from my tutors when I needed it. I would highly recommend it to people who are focused on what they want to do.'
Emily Hogarth, MA in textiles.

University of Essex

Wivenhoe Park,
Colchester CO4 3SQ

t 01206 873666
e admit@essex.ac.uk
⌐ www.essex.ac.uk

 www.essex.ac.uk/pg

8,500   **PG** 22%

Essex is a 1960s university, but it has remained smaller than many of its contemporaries. It has 200 acres of landscaped campus on the outskirts of Colchester. The students' union has invested more than £3m at the Colchester campus over the past five years and recently opened a nightclub, following a £1.25m redevelopment. Essex boasts a consistently strong academic performance, which it hopes to extend to students on the recently opened Southend campus, which boasts state-of-the art facilities. There's also a base in Loughton where the East 15 Acting School is based.

Courses and qualifications Several courses leading to MA, MSc, MPhil and PhD. There are also a number of Professional Doctorate opportunities, as well as some Postgraduate Certificates and Diplomas. The university offers hundreds of taught postgraduate courses, while numerous research opportunities exist across the university's schools, departments and research centres.

Fees
UK/EU students: range from £3,640 to £10,250.
International students: range from £9,990 to £11,990.

Funding The university offers some postgraduate student scholarships to support talented postgraduates from the UK, EU and international (particularly PhD) students.

Accommodation There is some family accommodation available at the Colchester Campus. Contact: accom@essex.ac.uk

Facilities The union nightclub has been named the best student venue in the UK and there are three further bars to tempt you. 40 acres of the Colchester campus is devoted to sport.

There is a postgraduate common room and accommodation specifically allocated to postgraduates. The students' union has an elected postgraduate officer and, as postgraduates make up a significant proportion of the student population at Essex, it runs a postgraduate students' assembly to offer support.

Transport Colchester campus is two miles away on major bus routes. Three stations in Colchester; London takes an hour. Excellent road links. Convenient for Stansted.

Specialism Social sciences: government and sociology.

❝ STUDENT VIEW ❞

'I chose to study my MA theory and practice of human rights at the University of Essex because the Human Rights Centre has an excellent reputation worldwide. Settling into Essex socially was easy. The Colchester campus is self-contained, with all the facilities you could ask for within walking distance of each other, making it easy to make lots of new friends. What I like most about my course is its interdisciplinary nature. The broad knowledge I have gained in this field will be of considerable help when it comes to finding a job related to my studies. I now have a clearer idea of the areas that I am most interested in.' Sarah Slator MA theory and practice of human rights.

University of Exeter

The Queen's Drive,
Exeter,
Devon EX4 4QJ

t 01392 263855
e pg-ad@exeter.ac.uk
↗ www.exeter.ac.uk

》 www.exeter.ac.uk/postgraduate

 14,252 **PG** 26% (UK) 80%

One of the lesser-known recipes for happiness is to live somewhere that other people pay to go to on holiday. Students at Exeter are likely to have permanent smiles on their faces: it has campuses in the cathedral city and also near Falmouth, in Cornwall, as well as plenty of coastline, countryside and glorious weather. Add to that the fact that the Streatham campus is widely regarded as one of the most beautiful in the country. Of course, you'll have to do some work, too – Exeter has an excellent academic reputation. Looking to the future, the university is near to completing a £140m investment programme in new buildings and facilities ranging from new research centres and teaching facilities to the students' guild building and nightclub.

Exeter

Courses and qualifications There are 15 courses leading to Pg Dip, Pg Cert, MEd, DEdPsyc, EdD, MPA, MRes, DClinPsy and it is starting to offer master's by research.

Fees
UK/EU students: £3,500 to £4,000.
International students: £9,600 to £11,655.
Some courses command different fees, such as the MBA.

Funding Contact the university for further information.

Accommodation At the Streatham campus there are self-contained flats for students with children under 16. In Exeter there is postgraduate only accommodation. View: www.exeter.ac.uk/Accommodation

Facilities Library facilities are currently undergoing a £9m investment and users benefit from 24/7 access, self-service machines, state-of-the-art multimedia facilities, enhanced group and silent study areas and an extended Wi-Fi network. Excellent sports facilities too.

There are dedicated postgraduate facilities at all three campuses, including a postgraduate centre on the Streatham Campus (food/bar area, common room, Wi-Fi enabled quiet study room, laundrette, seminar rooms), a postgraduate common room at St Luke's Campus and a postgraduate IT suite at the Cornwall Campus. Transport Short walks into town from either campus in Exeter. The Cornwall campus is a 15 minutes bus ride into Falmouth. The M5 is handy for Exeter and London is two hours by train. Two hours or more in the other direction to Falmouth from Exeter.

Specialism Exeter teaches and researches across a range of subjects in the arts, humanities, sciences and social sciences.

❝ STUDENT VIEW ❞

'I was so impressed with the prestige of the university and the master's degree I applied for, that I did not apply to any other universities in the UK. Most of the lecturers here have worked in the City and I thought that it would be a great opportunity to learn from them too. The School of Business and Economics has first class facilities. I now understand that learning is not only by reading books but by knowing what is happening in the real world and how to practically implement things that we have learnt.' Vanisha Bumma, MSc finance and investment.

Glamorgan University

Pontypridd CF37 1DL	**t** 0800 716925
	e enquiries@glam.ac.uk
	↗ www.glam.ac.uk

 www.postgrad.glam.ac.uk

👥 21,496   **PG** 15%

The University of Glamorgan boasts three modern campuses, two in Treforest near the town of Pontypridd and a brand new state-of-the-art facility in the heart of Cardiff city centre. The Cardiff campus is a £35m development which opened in September 2007 and is home to the Cardiff School of Creative and Cultural Industries. Glamorgan is committed to innovation in teaching and learning and to equipping students with the skills they will need for their chosen careers. The university attracts more than 21,000 students across its campuses and is known for its friendly community atmosphere.

Courses and qualifications Several courses leading to MA, MSc, MA by Research, MSc by Research, MBA, DBA, MPhil, PhD, Pg Cert, Pg Dip, BSc (mainly courses for post-registration nurses), DHealth, DSocial Care, LLM, LPC, GDL, CIPD, CIPS, ACCA.

Fees
UK/EU: full-time £3,254 to £3,300.
International students: £7,450 to £13,000.

Funding For UK/EU students on full-time taught courses there are bursaries up to £2,000.

Accommodation No accommodation for families. Contact: accom@glam.ac.uk

Facilities The campus boasts good IT facilities and sports facilities that are some of the best in the country. A new postgraduate centre is opening in autumn 2009.

Transport On the M4 corridor and 20 minutes by train or car to Cardiff.

Specialism Computer forensics and hydrogen research.

🎓 STUDENT VIEW 🎓

'The lecturers were excellent and, without exception, brought considerable experience of industry with them to the lecture room. Also, the skills I developed during the course, particularly critical thinking, have certainly helped with two promotions obtained during and after the course.' David Browne, MSc human resource management.

University of Glasgow

1 The Square,
University Avenue,
Glasgow G12 8QQ

t 0141 330 2000
e pgadmissions@admin.gla.ac.uk
↗ www.gla.ac.uk

 » www.gla.ac.uk/postgraduate

 20,018   **PG** 23%   (UK) 20%

Glasgow, established more than 550 years ago, is Scotland's second oldest university, the UK's fourth oldest, and an important pillar of Scotland's biggest city. As well as excellent teaching and a worldwide reputation, students enjoy a compact campus at the heart of the city's stylish west end that boasts more listed buildings than any other campus in the country. There are many local students: almost half come from west Scotland. Among the rest are representatives of 124 other countries. Glasgow is a confident and dynamic city that has reinvented itself in recent years. Facilities for shopping, entertainment and cultural pursuits are excellent, and there is dramatic countryside nearby.

Courses and qualifications There are over 170 courses leading to MA, MSc, MPhil, PhD, MBA, PGCE.

Fees For the range of fees see: www.gla.ac.uk/media/media_85671_en.pdf

Funding For information see: www.gla.ac.uk/studying/scholarships

Accommodation For accommodation contact: accom@gla.ac.uk

Facilities The university library is one of the best academic libraries in Europe, with more than 2m items on 12 floors. Glasgow has invested in the multimillion pound HUB building project to create a one-stop-shop for a wide range of student services placed at the centre of the main campus. Excellent sports facilities too, common room, library and halls of residence. All of these plus newly developed postgraduate offices and workspace.

Transport Travel within Glasgow is made easy by an underground system that connects the university to the city centre in around ten minutes. There are bus and train services too. Two train stations, good road links and an airport nearby too.

Specialism Medicine.

Glasgow Caledonian University

Cowcaddens Road,
Glasgow G4 0BA

t 0141 331 3000
e admissions@gcal.ac.uk
↗ www.gcal.ac.uk

» www.gcal.ac.uk/study/postgraduate/index.html

 16,000   **PG** 15%   (**UK**) 67%

With more than 15,000 students, Glasgow Caledonian University is Scotland's fourth largest university in terms of recruitment. Its campus is in the Cowcaddens area, close to the city centre. Key academic strengths are health, the environment, creative culture, business and social justice. Widening access is central to Glasgow Caledonian's philosophy, as is being known for social entrepreneurship and actively engaging in social and economic regeneration in Glasgow. Like the city it is in, its confidence is high.

Courses and qualifications There are 85 distinct programmes plus research, leading to MSc, Pg Cert, Pg Dip, MA, MAcc, MFin, MLitt, MBA, LLM, MRes, DPsych, MPhil, PhD, ProfDoc.

Fees Fee levels for each programme are listed throughout the postgraduate prospectus.

Funding Full-time Scottish and EU applicants may receive their fees paid by SAAS for certain programmes. Some scholarships are available from endowments and from private sector companies. A number of research studentships are available from the university. In addition, a limited number of grants may be available from the Research Councils and for international students through the International Research Students Awards Scheme (ORSAS).

Accommodation No family accommodation, but it does help you to find private accommodation. Contact: accommodation@gcal.ac.uk

Facilities The Saltire Centre, the hub of the campus, is the first university building of its kind to integrate all learning and student services: library, study spaces, a student services mall and a learning cafe, across four floors. Innovative teaching facilities, like the virtual hospital.

The city centre campus is one of the most modern and innovative in the UK. Combining state-of-the-art facilities with a welcoming, friendly atmosphere, it offers a unique learning environment to students.

The Caledonian Graduate Centre lies at the heart of the university's vibrant research community. Its recently opened GRADspace offers a dedicated area where postgraduates, supervisors and researchers can meet and work.

The Continuing Professional Development (CPD) Centre offers a flexible space for seminars, conferences, consultancy and training services.

Transport Extensive public transport and good links. The airport is seven miles away.

Specialism GCU's excellence in postgraduate education is underpinned by its reputation for applied research, in areas as diverse as waste and environmental management, professions allied to medicine, social justice and creative businesses and technologies.

New programmes include Caledonian Business School's ground-breaking MA television fiction writing.

《 STUDENT VIEW 》

'I enjoyed studying the MSc enterprise systems development course at Glasgow Caledonian University: it was a very challenging course which provided up-to-date material and technology which is all very relevant in the IT jobs market today. I am sure this course will help me achieve my future career goals.' Mike Deng, MSc enterprise systems development.

Glasgow School of Art

167 Renfrew Street,
Glasgow G3 6RQ

t 0141 353 4500
e registry@gsa.ac.uk
↗ www.gsa.ac.uk

» **www.gsa.ac.uk/researchandpostgraduate/content/**

 1,800 **PG** 10% (UK) 50%

Glasgow

The Glasgow School of Art (GSA) is an internationally recognised independent school or art, design and architecture, based in the heart of Glasgow and occupying premises designed in 1896 by the famous Scottish architect Charles Rennie Mackintosh. Founded in 1845, the school is proud of it heritage and of the creative, stimulating environment that continues to inspire its students. Courses are offered within the schools of architecture, design or fine art.

Courses and qualifications Several programmes leading to Pg Cert, Pg Dip, MRes, MFA, MDes, MArch, MLitt, MPhil, PhD.

Fees As a rough guide, fees for UK/EU students are around £4,000 for a year; international student fees are closer to £10,000 per year.

Funding Full information can be found online at: www.gsa.ac.uk/gsa.cfm?pid=2456

Accommodation There are a range of accommodation options for students in Glasgow, with most postgraduates choosing to stay in private-rented accommodation.
Contact: welfare@gsa.ac.uk

Facilities Include a digital design studio, a centre for advanced textiles and several galleries and exhibition spaces. The school also boasts a nightclub and venue, The Arts School.

It has specific events and resources that are only for postgraduates – such as the Postgraduate Forum, which takes place twice a term, but postgraduates can take advantage of the broad range of resources also available to undergraduates. These include: the specialist art, design and architecture library; the Mackintosh archive and library; four exhibition spaces; specialist research centres. In addition, as the degrees are validated by the University of Glasgow, students have access to many of that institution's facilities.

Transport Five hours by train to London. Short walk to the city centre from campus.

Specialism At postgraduate level, the best known programmes are arguably the two-year MFA, and the one-year MDes in animation.

University of Gloucestershire

The Park,
Cheltenham GL50 2RH

t 08707 210210
e admissions@glos.ac.uk
↗ www.glos.ac.uk

» www.glos.ac.uk/prospective/Pages/postgraduate.aspx

 8,699   **PG** 20%   (UK) 60%

Students are spread over four campuses – three in Cheltenham and one in Gloucester. Cheltenham, in particular, is attractive, but both can support a decent social life and have good links to bigger cities, as well as some appealing rural surroundings. The university is proud of its green credentials and sustainable policies – they've used green electricity since the early 1990s and have recycling points on all the campuses. Learning is flexible – there are large groups of mature and part-time students – and courses are innovative. There is emphasis on industry links and work placements, with an eye to preparing you for a future career.

Courses and qualifications There are 61 courses leading to MA, MSc, MPhil, PhD, MBA, PGCE, LLM, PG Dip, PG Cert, MRes.

Fees
UK/EU students: range from £1,270 to £15,000.
International students: range from £3,285 to £10,000.

Funding CSSS Scholarship (one per annum), discounts for continuing graduates, a range of full-time research studentships advertised annually.

Accommodation For assistance finding suitable accommodation, contact:
accommodation@glos.ac.uk

Facilities There are learning centres on each campus with differing provision. Designated library facilities for postgraduates.

Transport Good (free) bus links are provided between campuses. Road and rail links are generally pretty good, depending on which of the campuses you are on.

Specialism Landscape architecture, teacher training/education.

 STUDENT VIEW »

'So far it has been really interesting, the lectures have been engaging and very relevant to what is currently happening in the global financial system. The class has a good mix of nationalities too which is great in terms of understanding differing perspectives on international issues' Ger Purcell, MBA student.

Glyndŵr University (formerly NEWI)

Plas Coch Campus,
Mold Road,
Wrexham LL11 2AW

t 01978 290666
e sid@glyndwr.ac.uk
↗ www.glyndwr.ac.uk

» **www.glyndwr.ac.uk/en/Coursesandfees/Postgraduate**

 6,346 **PG** 10% (UK) 15%

Based in Wrexham, north Wales, Glyndŵr (or NEWI to give it its easier-to-say name) is based at two campuses: Plas Coch, which has the students' union, the 'student village' and a new sports centre; and the school of art and design, on the other side of the station, nearer the town centre. A full member of the University of Wales since 2004, Glyndŵr attracts getting on for 6,500 full- and part-time students. There's a good rate of postgraduate employment.

Courses and qualifications There are over 40 programmes leading to MA, MSc, MPhil, PhD, MBA, PGCE, PG Dip or PhD.

Fees Fees range from £793 to £3,300 depending on the programme, study mode and route chosen.

Funding Postgraduate scholarships which provide fee reductions are available to Glyndŵr university graduates. Subject to meeting criteria, fee waiver scholarships are available to MPhil/PhD students. International students are also eligible to apply for the university's international scholarships.

Accommodation University-owned family accommodation is not available at present.

Facilities There is a postgraduate common room.

Transport The nearest stations are in Wrexham, five to 15 minutes' walk from the campus. Manchester International and Liverpool airports are both a 45 minute drive away.

Specialism Science areas including water soluble polymers, nanotechnology, and hologram technology.

❝ STUDENT VIEW ❞

'After spending over two years at Glyndŵr I can proudly say I made the right decision to come here. It's not only met my expectations, it's actually gone over them quite a way. My time at the university has been like a dream come true for me and I'm so grateful for that. The experiences I've had have broadened my horizon and I can now pursue my career in any part of the world. All of this would not have been possible without the personalised attention I've received while I've been here.' Arijit Dey, MBA.

Goldsmiths, University of London

Lewisham Way,
New Cross,
London SE14 6NW

t 020 7919 7766
e admissions@gold.ac.uk
↗ www.goldsmiths.ac.uk

 www.gold.ac.uk/pg

 7,979 **PG** 35% (UK) 59%

Goldsmiths is best known for creativity and culture, and has a reputation for producing visual artists. The university is almost entirely based on one site in New Cross, south-east London, an area regularly described as 'up and coming'. It is vibrant, with excellent links to the centre of London, and the cost of living is more reasonable than in many areas. You are, however, deep in the urban sprawl, with everything that brings with it. There is plenty of creative energy flowing among the students; a high proportion are mature students and a third are international, which makes for a diverse student body.

Courses and qualifications There are 133 programmes at postgraduate level leading to MA, MEng, MFA, MMus, MSc, MRes, MPhil, PGCE, Pg Dip, Pg Cert and PhD.

Fees
UK/EU students: £3,145 to £6,320.
International students: £9,580 to £13,290.

Funding See the website for details.

Accommodation None for families.
Contact: accommodation@gold.ac.uk

Facilities Facilities include an award-winning students' union, including a new state-of-the-art gym and fitness centre on campus, a well-equipped library (including excellent IT facilities), wireless hotspots throughout the campus, a Virtual Learning Environment where lecturers can provide students with course materials, practice assessments and learner support, and media facilities.

In addition to excellent general facilities — both college-wide and department-specific (see www.goldsmiths.ac.uk/facilities) — postgraduates

at Goldsmiths can benefit from the resources and training of the new Graduate School. The Graduate School has been created in response to increasing numbers of postgraduates, changing needs for research training, and Goldsmiths' growing research profile. The Graduate Centre is open 24 hours a day, and offers facilities that include open access computer facilities, a seminar room for training purposes, and a social area with refreshment facilities. The Graduate School Office is located nearby, enabling students to get help in an informal setting.

For further details see: www.goldsmiths.ac.uk/graduate-school

Transport Goldsmiths is in New Cross, south-east London, in travelcard zone 2. It has great travel connections to central London. The campus is also well-placed in terms of bus routes and Deptford Bridge DLR (which links to the tube network) station is a short walk away.

Specialism Media and communications, sociology, anthropology, art, design, English, music.

❝ STUDENT VIEW ❞

'I feel extraordinarily privileged to study at Goldsmiths with such an array of distinguished academics. The research culture is very strong, and there is a robust sense of purpose and scholarship.' Sian Weston, MPhil/PhD in sociology.

University of Greenwich

Old Royal Naval College,
Park Row, Greenwich,
London SE10 9LS

t 0800 005006
e courseinfo@gre.ac.uk
⌤ www.gre.ac.uk

» www.gre.ac.uk/about/pg_apply

 23,184   **PG** 25%   (UK) 58%

There aren't many universities that can boast a World Heritage Site, but this is one of them. The main campus is on the banks of the Thames in three baroque buildings designed by Sir Christopher Wren at the end of the 17th century. Other sites are Avery Hill, in an 86-acre park in Eltham, south-east London, and Medway, another charming campus full of Edwardian redbrick and ivy, near Chatham's historic dockyard. As a result, students are spread between city and more rural locations, though all are part of an institution that is proud of its diversity and committed to widening participation.

Courses and qualifications Several courses including MA, MSc, MPhil, PhD, MBA, PGCE.

Fees
UK/EU students: most fees are £3,720.
International students: most fees are £8,900.

Funding There are bursaries available for research students. Apply directly to the Research Office or the director of research within the relevant school in writing.

Accommodation Devonport Halls at the Greenwich campus is for postgraduate and mature students only.

Facilities Major libraries, computing facilities, students' union facilities, catering facilities and bars at all campuses. Avery Hill has a gym and sports fields. Medway has a sports centre. Greenwich is near a council run sports centre.

Transport The Greenwich campus can be reached by Docklands Light Railway, rail and boat. You can be at London Bridge in 20 minutes. Avery Hill to London Bridge involves a 10-15 minute walk to the station and 25 minute rail journey. Greenwich provides an inter-campus bus service linking Avery Hill to Greenwich and Medway.

❝ STUDENT VIEW ❞
'Greenwich is a beautiful part of London and you have access to all London has to offer.'

Harper Adams University College

Newport,
Shropshire TF10 8NB

t 01952 820280
e admissions@harper-adams.ac.uk
↗ www.harper-adams.ac.uk

》 **www.harper-adams.ac.uk/postgraduate**

 1,800   **PG** 6%   (**UK**) 60%

This former agricultural college is small, so you experience living in a close-knit community. The location can only add to that sense – set in the lovely Shropshire countryside, there's little around but peace and quiet and the small town of Newport (though nearby Telford might fill some of the gaps). Despite this, or perhaps because of it, the on-campus entertainments will easily satisfy the bits of you that thirst for noise, raucous fun and beer. It will come as little surprise that most of the courses focus on rural and land-based subjects. Its course list is ever-expanding, though, as it aims to educate the future innovators and guardians of a sustainable rural economy.

Courses and qualifications There are 15 (includes all MBA options) leading to Pg Cert, Pg Dip, MSc, MBA, MPhil, PhD.

Fees
UK/EU students: £4,315 (MSc).
International students: £8,730 (MSc).

Funding See the website for details.

Accommodation See the website for details.

Facilities The modern library and IT suite are situated at the heart of the campus, which also contains a working farm. There are also specialist facilities for students studying engineering, animal health and veterinary nursing programmes.

The students' union building houses bars, a shop and cafeteria. There are also some sports facilities.

The university college is planning a dedicated modern postgraduate centre with social facilities, computer room, support staff offices and teaching rooms. Dedicated postgraduate housing is also located in the university grounds.

Transport A bus services is available to take students into the nearby market town of Newport, about three miles away from the campus. The larger towns of Shrewsbury and Telford (for the nearest station) are also conveniently located.

Specialism Rural and land-based subjects.

◀◀ STUDENT VIEW ▶▶

'What attracted me to Harper Adams was the excellent facilities, and the way the MSc course is designed which allowed me to undertake it part-time over three years, whilst remaining in full-time work. There are few colleges offering such distance learning MSc courses and that's why I chose Harper Adams – it has the facilities to do it. The Aspire Centre (Advancing Skills for Professionals in the Rural Economy) and the comprehensive library is a credit to the college which aids this distance learning. Whilst hard work, the course has given me greater knowledge and confidence to change career. I would definitely recommend it.'
Adrian Cannon, MSc in rural environment and land management.

Heriot-Watt University

Edinburgh EH14 4AS

t 0131 451 3451
e enquiries@hw.ac.uk
↗ www.hw.ac.uk

 www.hw.ac.uk/home/dir/15/postgraduate-students

 7,430   **PG** 23%   (UK) 30%

Uniquely among Scottish universities, Heriot-Watt can boast near-constant sunshine, a glamorous beachside locale and sky-scrapers as far as the eye can see. Though, admittedly, only if you are studying on the Dubai campus. Other students don't do too badly, however. The Edinburgh campus occupies 380 acres of meadow and woodland and the Scottish borders campus in Galashiels, south of Edinburgh, is right in the very heart of the borders. Heriot-Watt emphasises career progression and flexible learning. Strengths include subjects related to the petroleum industry, brewing and distilling. Well, it is Scottish, even if it does have a Middle Eastern outpost.

Courses and qualifications Several leading to PhD, EngD, DBA, MBA, MSc, MPhil, MDes, MURP, MSc by research.

Fees Details available at: www.hw.ac.uk/registry

Funding See website for details.

Accommodation Some apartments are available, see: www.hw.ac.uk/welfare/Accommodation

Facilities The Heriot-Watt University Archive and Museum contains many unique records relating to the history of science, engineering, technology and business going back to 1821. The Textile Collection at the Scottish borders campus houses one of the finest collections of textile records and artefacts to be found anywhere in the world.

With a 1,750 strong community of postgraduates from 100 countries at Heriot-Watt, the opportunities for interdisciplinary and cross-cultural interaction are huge. Recent growth in research pooling at Scottish universities is leading the demand for multi-site lectures, tutorials and research meetings, and the new postgraduate centre opened in spring 2009 at Heriot-Watt's Edinburgh Campus will fulfil these needs. The landmark building, dedicated to postgraduate taught courses, researcher training and professional research interactions will include a lecture theatre, seminar and meeting rooms, study and social space, a café and an exhibition area.

Transport Edinburgh's the capital, so all the links by road, rail and air are what you would expect.

Specialism Specialisms include engineering (including petroleum engineering), MBA, brewing and distilling, photonics, actuarial mathematics, design.

❝ STUDENT VIEW ❞

'Heriot Watt University has given me much, both socially and academically, as I am developing every day. By studying here I have obtained great expectations for the future and hopefully a solid base for job prospects.' Hanne M Gabriel, MSc logistics and supply chain management.

University of Hertfordshire

Collge Lane,
Hatfield AL10 9AB

t 01707 284000
e ask@herts.ac.uk
↗ www.herts.ac.uk

》 **www.herts.ac.uk/courses/postgraduate-courses.cfm**

 23,000   **PG** 17%   (UK) 61%

The university is located on two sites in Hatfield, within easy reach of each other, and a third in St Albans. The purpose-built De Havilland campus has excellent facilities for sport and 24/7 learning. It's all fairly close to London, too. Hertfordshire takes a flexible approach to learning, with possibilities for e-learning and part-time study. A new focus on creative and cultural industries has given rise to a host of new courses. The new £10m building based at the university in Hatfield houses the latest technology for the teaching of music, animation, film, television and multimedia.

Courses and qualifications There are 123 courses leading to MA, MSc, MPhil, PhD, MBA, PGCE, Pg Dip, Pg Cert, MRes, DClinPsy, DMan, DBA, CIM, Pg Dip, EngD, MEng, MPharm, MD, Professional Doctorate, Graduate Diploma, MEd, EdD, LLM, LPC.

Fees
UK/EU students: approx £4,500.
International students: approx £9,500.
MBA fees are higher.

Funding Most UH graduates returning to the university for a master's degree will benefit from the UH Graduate Scholarship. See: www.herts.ac.uk/international-students/fees/scholarships/uh-graduate-scholarship.cfm

Accommodation Couples who are both full-time students are eligible for university accommodation.
Contact: accommodation@herts.ac.uk

Facilities A pool and climbing wall are among the sports facilities. There's also the Weston Auditorium for arts events, two art galleries and one of the best teaching observatories

in the UK. There are separate resource rooms for undergraduates, postgraduates and staff. Postgraduate computing: a set of Macs and PCs are set aside to support postgraduate studies in a variety of art and design practice. The postgraduate laboratory and group interaction lab are supported by IBM compatible pc systems and AV facilities. Projects laboratory: this laboratory is dedicated to the support of final year and taught postgraduate students' individual projects. The facilities include computing platforms, test and measurement equipment and PDA development environment. Additionally, the school hosts four postgraduate research laboratories that have a direct impact on the design and delivery and support of the school's taught provision. These include the System-on-Chip and Mobil-Communications.

Transport Good transport links to the rest of the UK. Only 25 minutes by train to London King's Cross tube and rail station.

Specialism Education, health, business, creative and cultural industries.

◀◀ STUDENT VIEW ▶▶

'I strongly recommend the university for its excellence academically and the dynamic social platforms it provides that embrace people from all the different cultures and backgrounds.' Isra Zaater, MA in literature.

Heythrop College

University of London,
Kensington Square,
London W8 5HQ

t 020 7795 6600
e enquiries@heythrop.ac.uk
↗ www.heythrop.ac.uk

» **www.heythrop.ac.uk/index.php/content/view/100/108**

 955   **PG** 53%   (UK) 93%

Heythrop is one of the constituent colleges of the University of London and teaches philosophy, theology and psychology. Its teaching is highly specialised and it offers just eight undergraduate degrees. It prides itself on its one-to-one teaching: a privilege enjoyed by students at Oxbridge and few other places. Its home is Kensington, London – a central and attractive location.

Courses and qualifications 11 MAs, one Graduate Diploma in Theology, MPhilStud, MPhil and PhD.

Fees
UK/EU students: £3,453 full-time, £1,792 part-time.
International students: £8,680 full-time, £4,340 part-time.

Funding Bursaries are available on some courses.
MA in Philosophy of Religion: There is a 50 per cent bursary offer for anyone who has taken their PGCE in the last three years.

Accommodation No postgraduate specific or family accommodation is available. You will be able to apply for accommodation through the University of London: www.housing.lon.ac.uk

Facilities Excellent libraries with specialist collections. You have access to the University of London's students' union facilities too.

Transport In central London, the college has ready access to all forms of transport.

Specialism Philosophy, theology, psychology of religion.

 STUDENT VIEW »
'Heythrop is a small, friendly and a great place to study.' Gemma, MA psychology of religion.

University of Huddersfield

Queensgate,
Huddersfield HD1 3DH

t 01484 422288
e admissions@hud.ac.uk
↗ www.hud.ac.uk

» www2.hud.ac.uk/studying_here/postgrad/index.php

 22,195   **PG** 15%   (**UK**) 75%

'To boldly go where no student has gone before.' Declaim that on the Huddersfield city centre campus and you'll soon be pulled up on your split infinitives by a fellow student, or perhaps by the actor Patrick Stewart – the bald one off *Star Trek* – who is actively involved in the life of the university of which he is chancellor. Huddersfield is a pleasant town close to both Manchester and Leeds with an expanding social scene – thanks, in large part, to the 22,000 or so students who make up the university. The campus straddles the old canal and there's a new £4m students' union building. Courses are modular with a strong vocational emphasis and many offer the option of a year abroad or working in industry. The university rates highly for student satisfaction.

Courses and qualifications There are approximately 90 courses leading to MA, MSc, MPhil, EdD, PhD, PGCE, MBA, PG Dip, PG Cert.

Fees
UK/EU students: £3,900.
International students: fees range from £8,500 to £9,500.
£10,480 for all MBA students. Fees for research programmes vary, check with the university.

Funding There is a progression bursary for continuing students at the university who progress directly onto a postgraduate programme. Fee waivers available to some research students.

Accommodation No family accommodation. Contact: accommodation@hud.ac.uk

Facilities The students' union is active, with great facilities including a stylish bar and a restaurant providing 'home style' cooking, whatever that means. The five floor library and computing centre is at the heart of the campus. No facilities specifically for postgraduates.

Transport Transport from the campus to the town is good, with the M62 and the M1 within striking distance. Good rail links too.

University of Hull

Hull HU6 7RX

t 0870 126 2000
e admissions@hull.ac.uk
↗ www.hull.ac.uk

 www.hull.ac.uk/postgraduate/index.html

 14,708   **PG** 15%   (UK) 73%

There's an excellent Blackadder joke about the 'great' universities: 'Oxford … Cambridge … Hull.' And, you know, it's not too far off the mark. Anyone who goes there will tell you it's friendly and down to earth, with a diverse population and a very low cost of living. It has a strong research reputation and its teaching is very well regarded. The Hull campus is 15 minutes' walk from the city centre and there are plenty of student-friendly bars and venues to investigate. The smaller campus in Scarborough is close to the faded seaside glamour of the resort. The coastline hereabouts is marvellous and a lunchtime surf is a real possibility.

Courses and qualifications There are around 200 leading to Adv Diploma, ClinPsyD, EdD, LLM, MA, MBA, MD, MEd, MJur, MMus, MPhil, MRes, MSc, MSc(Econ), Pg Cert, Pg Dip, PGCE, PhD, PsyD.

Fees
UK/EU students: £3,300 full-time, £1,650 part-time.
International students: £8,500 to 310,500 full-time, £4,250 to £5,250 part-time.
MBA, all students: £13,500 full-time, £6,750 part-time.
Some variation for non-standard courses.

Funding University scholarships are available. Some bursaries are also available for international students.

Accommodation The private sector meets the need. Accommodation: www.hull.ac.uk/accom

Facilities There's an award winning students' union nightclub with good sports provision too. The Enterprise Centre provides vital support for start-up businesses run by graduates and students at the university. There is a graduate school with common room, study space, PCs; postgraduate society; postgraduate accommodation; specialist teacher training facilities.

Transport Road links are good, but rail links can be slightly cumbersome.

Specialism Politics, law, geography, history, music and English.

Imperial College London

South Kensington Campus,
London SW7 2AZ

t 020 7589 5111
e info@imperial.ac.uk
↗ www.imperial.ac.uk

》 **www3.imperial.ac.uk/pgprospectus**

 13,355   **PG** 37%   (**UK**) 43%

Imperial's founding charter was signed over 100 years ago and it's been leading the way pretty much ever since in the teaching and study of all things 'sciencey'. It's not exclusively science any more, though – there's a business school and even a humanities programme these days. Given Imperial's reputation as one of the best academic institutions in the world it's unsurprising that competition for places is stiff. There's a certain grandeur about the institution that is only reinforced by its main location among the pomp and circumstance of London's swankiest boroughs. Hyde Park, the V&A (or the Science Museum, which is probably more your thing if you're at Imperial) and the Albert Hall are all on your doorstep.

London

Courses and qualifications There are over 120 programmes leading to MSc, MBA, MRes, MPhil/PhD, MD(Res), MEd, MPH, EngD. Additional or alternative college qualifications are the Diploma of the Imperial College (DIC) and the Certificate of Advanced Study (CAS).

Fees For details see: www3.imperial.ac.uk/pgprospectus/whatcanyoustudy#top

Funding For details see web pages: www3.imperial.ac.uk/pgprospectus/money/howcanipay and www3.imperial.ac.uk/registry/finance/scholarships/pg_schol

Accommodation There is a limited amount of accommodation for postgraduate students, all of which is offered on a self-catered basis. For details contact: accommodation@imperial.ac.uk

Facilities Excellent sporting facilities, underpinning the university's strong reputation in the (playing) field. Pools, gyms, climbing walls ... you name it. Predictably good libraries and labs too.

Transport You're in the centre of London with all the ease of transport that that does – or doesn't – imply. Closest tube is South Kensington.

Specialism Imperial specialises in science, technology and medicine.

《 STUDENT VIEW 》

'I have currently just started work on a PhD aiming to visualise interactions between host protein and nucleic acid, which could lead to the development of drugs against foot and mouth disease. One thing that I really enjoy about Imperial is the academic freedom to study independently under the guidance of some of the best scientists in the world in a world class research setting. The award-winning Graduate School [for Life Sciences and Medicine] provides ample opportunities for me to develop in a variety of ways, helping me further my early career in science.' Amar Joshi, PhD student, molecular biosciences.

Institute of Education, University of London

20 Bedford Way,
London WC1H 0AL

t 020 7612 6000
e info@ioe.ac.uk
↗ www.ioe.ac.uk

 www.ioe.ac.uk/course

 4,557 **PG** 97% (UK) 84%

More than a century on from its foundation as a teacher training college for London, the Institute of Education (IOE) is a world class centre of excellence in education and social research. It topped the 2008 Research Assessment Exercise in education research and is among the UK's top 10 university institutions in terms of research quality.

London

Courses and qualifications PGCEs at primary, secondary and post-compulsory (post-16) level, as well as employment-based routes into teaching.

More than 50 master's programmes in areas such as health, international development, media, psychology and sociology, as well as education.

You can also undertake research study including MPhil/PhD, research-based master's, professional doctorates (EdD, DEdPsy) and post-doctoral opportunities.

Fees For up-to-date information see: www.ioe.ac.uk/fees .

Funding For details of bursaries and scholarships, visit: www.ioe.ac.uk/courses/funding

Accommodation The student welfare and accommodation office provides advice on finding a place to live in the IOE's own halls of residence, other halls of residence and private accommodation.

The Institute's own halls provide over 260 self-catering places including some flats that can accommodate students with one child.

Facilities The Institute's Newsam Library is the largest in its field in Europe, containing over 300,000 volumes and a unique archive used by 12,000 visitors each year. Supplementing these is a full range of electronic materials, which students can access remotely.

Students also benefit from excellent web-based and ICT support, including virtual learning environments, audiovisual, multimedia and reprographic facilities.

Transport Located in central London, it is well-placed for public transport. The nearest underground station is Russell Square and several other tube and train stations are within walking distance.

Specialism A world-renowned centre for education studies and educational research, with a larger concentration of educational researchers of international quality and reputation than anywhere else in the UK.

Keele University

Keele,
Staffordshire ST5 5BG

t 01782 584005
e gradschool@keele.ac.uk
↗ www.keele.ac.uk

» **www.keele.ac.uk/depts/aa/postgraduate**

 7,000   **PG** 17%

Keele was the first university created in the 20th century and has pioneered the dual honours degree in Britain; many courses include an option for study abroad. Not that that would be the first thing current students would mention. They'd probably tell you about the friendly atmosphere created by the relatively low student numbers and the lovely, semi-rural campus. Around 70 per cent of full-time students live on campus – that's the highest level in the country – and plenty of staff call it home, too. With good facilities to hand, and a buzzing social scene, it's a wonder anyone ever leaves (though if you want to, Birmingham is an hour one way, and Manchester an hour the other).

Courses and qualifications Approximately 75 courses on offer. You can study for an MA, MBA, MSc, MRes, Pg Cert, PGCE, Pg Dip or PhD.

Fees
UK/EU students: £15,450 for the MBA.
International students: £16,500 for the MBA.

Funding Students can apply for Keele scholarships, worth up to £3,000 towards the cost of one year's tuition fees.

Accommodation International postgraduate students are guaranteed accommodation on campus, provided they apply by 30 June. All the rooms for postgraduate students are single occupancy and on a fixed, 51-week letting period. The university does not provide any family accommodation.

Facilities Good for sport, with two sports halls, squash courts, a sprung-floor dance studio, a gym (that converts into a lecture theatre!) and pitches

outside for cricket, rugby and lacrosse – and two recently refurbished FA-level football pitches.

The Keele Postgraduate Association (KPA) is the centre of the postgraduate community at Keele. With its own social and meeting area – the Clubhouse – KPA provides a place to relax and to make friends. The KPA Clubhouse has recently been extended and refurbished, with a bar and restaurant, widescreen digital TV and a heated patio area. On the first floor there is a large common room with satellite TV and a separate pool table room. The KPA is open throughout the year, including vacation time, and there are regular social events, including quiz nights, live music events, and parties.

Transport Being between Manchester and Birmingham, Keele has good links to both. It's a 20-minute car journey to the M6. The nearest stations are Stoke-on-Trent and Crewe – both can be reached by bus.

❝ STUDENT VIEW ❞

'Keele is a self-sufficient campus university with a serene atmosphere conveniently situated close to M6. The woodlands, lakes and nature walks in and around the immense campus are apt for nature lovers. Keele campus is a safe, secure and child friendly environment with excellent nursery and schooling facilities nearby.' Sheeba Rosewillia, research student.

University of Kent

Canterbury,
Kent CT2 7NZ

t 01227 764000
e information@kent.ac.uk
↗ www.kent.ac.uk

 www.kent.ac.uk/studying/postgrad

 17,000   **PG** 20%   (**UK**) 48%

Kent describes itself as 'the UK's top European university'. It's part of the Franco-British University of the Transmanche and there's even a campus in Brussels. But no matter how much it gazes continent-wards, it also takes its regional role seriously. The leafy main campus (there are also centres at Medway, Tonbridge and Wye) is about two miles from Canterbury centre. The university rates highly for student satisfaction in the National Student Survey.

Canterbury

Courses and qualifications There are several programmes leading to Pg Cert, Pg Dip, MA, MSc, LLM, MBA, MRes, MArch, MPhil, PhD. Kent is one of a consortium of 30 universities in the UK offering New Route PhDs.

Fees
UK/EU students: the postgraduate standard fee is £3,500, the MBA is £15,600.
International students: £9,870 for non laboratory courses, £11,990 for laboratory.

Funding The university offers a range of financial support for postgraduate students. This includes a number of research student scholarships, location-specific funding, sport and music scholarships, and funding specifically for international fee-paying students.

Accommodation Postgraduate students are offered self-catering accommodation at Woolf College, a new development offering en suite bedrooms in flats or studios. There is no family accommodation.

Facilities The university has three main campuses. It also has the University of Kent at Brussels — a specialist postgraduate school of international studies located in Brussels, which has attracted students from over 50 countries around the world, with 60 per cent coming from outside the European Union. Kent has a growing relationship with a number of French universities and postgraduate students have the opportunity to spend a term or a year studying in France.

A combined library provides students with access to over 1.3m books, periodicals, journals and collections of electronic material. The IT systems are second to none. Kent is one of the safest places to study, with Canterbury having the lowest crime rate of any university city in the UK.

Excellent sports facilities include a climbing wall.

Transport The Canterbury campus is a half hour walk from the city centre. Kent has good transport links to London.

Specialism Science, technology, medical studies, statistics and operational research, conservation, ecology, sociology, languages, philosophy, theology, classics, archaeology.

◄◄ STUDENT VIEW ►►

'The University of Kent always felt like a very friendly place from staff to students. Plus, the reputation of both the university and the computing laboratory is quite good.' Miguel Mendao.

King's College London

Strand,
London WC2R 2LS

t 020 7848 2929
e studentenq@kcl.ac.uk
↗ www.kcl.ac.uk

 » **www.kcl.ac.uk/graduate**

 19,713 **PG** 34% (UK) 66%

London is quite literally on your doorstep. Four of the five campuses are clustered together on a landmark-packed stretch of the Thames. Waterloo Bridge? The London Eye? The Houses of Parliament? People fly across the world to see these things; you'll pass them on the way to your lectures. The fifth campus is its own hospital in Denmark Hill, a quick trip on the overland train. King's also boasts an impeccable reputation for its teaching and research.

London

Courses and qualifications There are approximately 250 programmes leading to MSc, MPhil, PhD, MBA, Pg Dip, Pg Cert, Grad Dip, Grad Cert, EdD, DrPS, DMin, DHC, MMus, DClinPsy, MRes, PGCE.

Fees Fees vary depending on the course. See: www.kcl.ac.uk/gsp

Funding Visit the website for details: www.kcl.ac.uk/gradfunding

Accommodation Although King's does not provide accommodation for families, it does offer accommodation for graduates and mature students only and some halls offer rooms which are suitable for couples. See: accomm@kcl.ac.uk

Facilities The main Maughan Library used to be the Public Record Office and is now the largest new university library in Britain since WWII. Lots of computers, and Wi-Fi access. The college is

investing millions in its IT to achieve a state-of-the-art virtual campus that connects people, information, services and knowledge.

King's has invested over half a billion pounds in the last six years into improving the learning and teaching environment to ensure that students have access to world-class academic and social facilities. New graduate lounges and social spaces reserved for use by graduate students only are available at the Strand and Waterloo campuses.

There is a Postgraduate Student Network providing students with the opportunity to meet in both social and academic environments, and have a say in the development of the graduate school.

Transport It's close to many forms of transport.

Specialism Art and culture, medical and professional healthcare education.

Kingston University

River House, 53-57 High Street,
Kingston upon Thames,
Surrey KT1 1LQ

t 08700 841 347
e admissions-info@kingston.ac.uk
↗ www.kingston.ac.uk

 www.kingston.ac.uk/postgraduate

 21,619   **PG** 17%   (UK) 71%

Kingston is based on four campuses scattered around the rather swanky town of Kingston upon Thames. It's close to London, though you might have to go through the even swankier areas of Richmond and Twickenham to get there. The university has invested in cutting-edge e-learning systems, too, with students now able to access at least 80 per cent of course modules online. A new £20m six-storey building for teaching and studying has recently opened, as part of an £100m investment programme.

Kingston

Courses and qualifications There are over 220 postgraduate courses leading to MBA, MEng, MChem, MComp, MEnv, MPharm, MA, MArch, MBA, EdM, MFA, LLM, MMus, MSc, MSW, MPhil, PhD.

Fees
UK/EU students: £3,450 for most full-time research degrees.
International students: There are a range of fees across subjects and qualifications — from the MSc at £3,300 through to the MBA at £15,500.

Funding Bursaries, scholarships and additional financial support are currently available to international postgraduate students only.

Accommodation For details contact: accommodation@kingston.ac.uk Kingston University does not offer family accommodation for postgraduate students.

Facilities There are specialist Learning Resources Centres (LRCs) at each campus with 24-hour opening at the two larger campuses during term time. The fitness centre includes a 65-station gym boasting the latest cardiovascular equipment.

There is a dedicated postgraduate centre on each of Kingston's four campuses. These centres offer IT, social and seminar facilities tailored to the needs of postgraduate students.

Transport Two campuses are based within the town centre, with the other two a 10-minute bus ride away. Central London is less than half an hour away by train.

Specialism Kingston has an excellent reputation for all its postgraduate courses but is particularly well known for its MBA.

❝ STUDENT VIEW ❞

'Kingston is a great place to study as it has a relaxed, suburban feel about it, while still being close to London and all its facilities. The tutors on my MA in creative economy course allow me the freedom and creativity to take business ideas in my own direction but at the same time are on hand to offer support and guidance when I need it. The university has students drawn from all over the world who contribute a diversity of creative and business backgrounds, unlike anything available elsewhere.' Mohammed Alaeddin, MA in creative economy programme.

Lampeter, University of Wales

Lampeter
Ceredigion SA48 7ED

t 01570 422351
e recruit@lamp.ac.uk
↗ www.lamp.ac.uk

» **www.lamp.ac.uk/postgrads/index.html**

 6,046   **PG** 40%

Lampeter is the oldest degree-awarding institution in
Wales, founded in 1822. It's also the smallest. As a result,
the university has a close-knit atmosphere, and staff pride
themselves on being approachable. Lampeter is a small
town in rural Wales, and the campus has a beautiful setting
in the Ceredigion hills, on the banks of the River Teifi. The
campus also boasts some handsome old buildings. Town/
gown relations are excellent and if you're in search of some
peace and quiet and lots of lovely green you could do a lot
worse, though both Swansea and Cardiff are reachable and
the students' union's entertainment officers work tirelessly to
ensure campus life has its fair share of fun. Around a third of
students are over 21 when they start their course.

Courses and qualifications There are around
80 courses leading to Pg Cert, Pg Dip, MA,
MSc, MBA, MTh, MMin, DMin, MPhil, PhD, DPT
(Professional Doctorate in Practical Theology),
LicDD (Licence in Divinity (Doctoral).

Fees
UK/EU students: approx £3,300, MBA £6,600.
International students: approx £8,988, MBA
£9,500.

Funding For details see website.

Accommodation Family accommodation
available. Contact: p.thomas@lamp.ac.uk

Facilities Significant investment in online library
resources in the past year means Lampeter now
holds one of the largest collections of e-books in
Wales. A new research centre opened in January
2008 to house the priceless special collections
in a climate-controlled environment. It includes
a hand-illuminated Bible from 1279 amongst
other treasures. Most postgraduates are offered
office space and a computer (usually shared but
this does vary by department).

Transport Everything is within walking distance.
There is a bus to Carmarthen or Aberystwth to
connect to the trains.

Specialism Academically, the university rates
highly in theology and religious studies, and
English language and literature.

‹‹ STUDENT VIEW ››

*'Throughout my time as, first, a master's and then a PhD student in Lampeter, I have had a huge amount
of support and encouragement from both my department and the university. I have been encouraged to
expand my research and to get involved in the activities of my department. Lampeter is an excellent place
for postgraduate study because of the individual support from across the university, which has helped my
research, academic and personal development. As a postgraduate I have been fully involved in the social side
of the university as Lampeter provides an environment where undergraduates, postgraduates and academic
staff mix freely.'* Laura Jarvis, PhD student.

Lancaster University

Lancaster LA1 4YW

t 01524 65201
e pgadmissions@lancaster.ac.uk
↗ www.lancaster.ac.uk

» **www.lancaster.ac.uk/admissions/postgrad.htm**

 17,322   **PG** 33%

Lancaster is a collegiate university with eight undergraduate colleges and one for graduates. All students are members of one or other of the colleges which, as well as providing accommodation, also have their own bars and common rooms and an instant sense of community and belonging. Staff are also affiliated with a college and often have an active role. The campus is located outside Lancaster and students make up about a fifth of the town's population, so they are well catered for. Here, you're within easy reach of the north-west coast, the Lake District, Manchester and Liverpool. Academic standards at the university are high.

Courses and qualifications There are several courses leading to a DClinPsy, LLM, MA, MBA, MRes, MSc, Pg Dip or Pg Cert.

Fees
UK/EU students: approx £3,530 per year.
International students: approx £9,200 to £11,100 per year.

Funding Funding is available. See the website for details.

Accommodation There are around 800 study bedrooms, many with en suite facilities, including a number of studio flats on campus for postgraduates. Each room has network connections to the university central computers, and access to the internet
There are over a 100 self-contained flats on campus that are suitable for couples and families.

Facilities Includes the Ruskin Library, the Peter Scott art gallery and the Nuffield theatre. There is also a good sports centre and computing facilities.
There is a graduate college which has a bar, common room, games room, PC lab, TV room, off-campus students' showers and lockers and bike stores.

Transport There are direct trains to the major cities and good bus and coach networks, with the M6 within spitting distance.

Specialism Lancaster specialises in statistics and applied statistics, ICT, art, design, music, music technology and theatre studies, sociology, physics.

❝ STUDENT VIEW ❞
'I love this university, not only because of the academic atmosphere, but also because of the facilities and people on the campus.' Ke Wang, MSc advanced computer science.

University of Leeds

Woodhouse Lane,
Leeds LS2 9JT

t   0113 343 2336
e   ask@.leeds.ac.uk
↗   www.leeds.ac.uk

» **www.leeds.ac.uk/students/postgraduates.htm**

 30,357   **PG** 21%   (UK) 56%

Leeds is a top redbrick university — and one of the giants of the higher education system. It remains perennially popular with applicants drawn by the excellent standards for teaching and research and the chance to live in Leeds itself. A large, friendly and dynamic city, Leeds is a great place to study. It's student-friendly and opportunities for going out and having fun abound. There's also some impressive civic architecture and it's the regional centre for enjoying the arts. Leeds students have the benefit of a friendly campus between the city centre and Headingley, where many students also live. There's an active students' union, and the student newspaper and radio station are both award-winning.

Courses and qualifications There are currently 1,100 courses leading to MA, MSc, MPhil, PhD, MBA, PGCE, Pg Cert, PG Dip.

Fees
UK/EU students: www.leeds.ac.uk/students/postgraduate_finance.htm
International students: www.leeds.ac.uk/students/international_students_finance.htm

Funding See the website at: www.leeds.ac.uk/rds/postgraduate_scholarships/postgraduate_scholarships.html

Accommodation Guaranteed accommodation for international postgraduate students subject to certain criteria. UK/EU postgraduates can fill any remaining spaces. Family accommodation is available although there is a waiting list. View: www.leeds.ac.uk/accommodation

Facilities There are some of the best computing resources in the country and a renowned library with over 2.5m books. The students' union provides clubs, a theatre, bars and live music.

Transport London is two and a half hours away by train, with good links (by road and rail) to the rest of the country. Leeds Bradford airport takes you further afield.

Specialism The University of Leeds offers a broad portfolio. All areas offer postgraduate taught programmes including business, arts, sciences, medicine, engineering, environment, performing arts, social sciences, languages.

❝ STUDENT VIEW ❞

'I chose the University of Leeds because it is ranked among the top one hundred universities. The city itself is bright and vibrant, and boasts a large and diverse student atmosphere. The facilities in terms of sport, libraries and just having a good time on campus are phenomenal. My course is intense and well-structured to help me get ahead in my future career. You learn through group work, presentations and self study. The case studies provide valuable insight and the lecturers are experts in their fields.' Varun Sanam MSc international finance.

Leeds College of Music

3 Quarry Hill,
Leeds LS2 7PD

t 0113 222 3400
e enquiries@lcm.ac.uk
↗ www.lcm.ac.uk

 2,500   **PG** 4%   (UK) 72%

Leeds College of Music is the UK's largest music college, with more than 1,000 full-time and 1,500 part-time students. Courses include music (classical music), jazz, music production, sound design and pop music studies. LCM is situated on Quarry Hill, at the very heart of the city's emerging arts and cultural quarter, where its neighbours include the West Yorkshire Playhouse, live music venue The Wardrobe, South Asian Arts UK, Yorkshire Dance and BBC Yorkshire.

Courses and qualifications There are eight courses leading to MA and Pg Dip.

Fees
UK/EU students: approx £3,900.
International students: approx £9,800.

Funding Check website for details.

Accommodation For details go to:
www.lcm.ac.uk/about-lcm/student-support/accommodation.htm

Facilities The Venue, a 350-seat performance space, hosts an annual concert season. The Centre for Jazz Studies was established in 2005. The 13 studios are designed to meet a variety of needs ranging from the live recording of bands and ensembles, multi-track recording, through to sound design, sampling, production of sound for moving image, digital editing and mastering. There is a specialist library and postgraduate-only library study rooms.

Transport The central bus and coach station is opposite LCM. Leeds train station is a 10-minute walk from the college. A bus from the college to the main student areas of Hyde Park and Headingley takes about 20 minutes.

Specialism Leeds College of Music is particularly well known for the standard of its jazz courses.

 STUDENT VIEW ▸▸

'Leeds is a vibrant, energetic city and offers musicians many contrasting opportunities. From classical orchestra, to FuseLeeds contemporary music festival and the rising rock scene, Leeds has something for everyone.' Nicholas Bentley, MA in music.

Leeds Metropolitan University

Civic Quarter,
Leeds LS1 3HE

t 0113 812 3113
e course-enquiries@leedsmet.ac.uk
↗ www.leedsmet.ac.uk

 » www.leedsmet.ac.uk/gradschool

50,000+   **PG** 14%

Leeds Metropolitan is a university with a lot of clout. It has
over 50,000 students and is lauded for its contribution to
the local area — the majority of its students are from the
region. The university has a charming parkland campus in the
pleasant Leeds suburb of Headingley and a cluster of buildings
(including many recently acquired) in the city centre.

Courses and qualifications There are 190
courses leading to MA, MSc, PhD, MBA, PGCE,
Pg Dip, PG Cert.

Fees
UK/EU students: approx £3,400 to £5,000.
International students: approx £8,000 to
£12,000.

Funding If you are a recent graduate of the
university, you could qualify for a 10 per cent
discount on your tuition fees for postgraduate
study.

Accommodation For details contact:
accommodation@leedsmet.ac.uk

Facilities Excellent sports facilities, good
access to IT resources (including some specialist
software) and libraries with 24-hour access
during term-time weekdays. All facilities
are shared between undergraduate and
postgraduate students.

Transport Handy for just about anywhere, Leeds
is well served by road and rail links.

Specialism Health.

Leeds Trinity and All Saints

Brownberrie Lane,
Horsforth,
Leeds LS18 5HD

t 0113 283 7150
e enquiries@leedstrinity.ac.uk
↗ www.leedstrinity.ac.uk

» **www.leedstrinity.ac.uk/study/Postgraduate/Pages/default.aspx**

 2,703 **PG** 17% (UK) 93%

Leeds Trinity and All Saints has offered degrees validated by the University of Leeds since 1974 — mainly in vocational or humanities courses, with business, media, health and education featuring prominently. There is a focus on employment. All courses include a professional work placement and graduate employment rates are good. The college is six miles from Leeds city centre, on the edge of the Yorkshire Dales, and attracts around 2,700 students. Leeds Trinity is investing heavily in new accommodation and facilities on campus.

Courses and qualifications There are around 25 courses leading to MA, Pg Dip, Pg Cert, MPhil, PhD, PGCE, MBS.

Fees
UK/EU students: £3,225 for PGCE, other courses range from £1,545 to £5,725.
International students: £7,985 for PGCE, other courses range from £6,925 to £10,300.

Funding See the website for details of available funding.

Accommodation There is a wide choice of private accommodation in the local area, which is a popular residential location for families. Contact: accommodation@leedstrinity.ac.uk

Facilities A state-of-the-art sports and fitness centre opened in 2007. The modern purpose-built learning centre has the study resources you'll need, plus you can use the University of Leeds' libraries.

Transport Leeds is around two hours from London by train and there is a local station at Horsforth. There's ready access to the A1, M1 and M62.

Specialism Teacher training.

University of Leicester

University Road,
Leicester LE1 7RH

t 0116 252 2522
e admissions@le.ac.uk
↗ www.le.ac.uk

» **www.le.ac.uk/pgprospectus**

 18,886   **PG** 47%   (UK) 39%

Leicester was joint top for teaching quality and overall satisfaction in the National Student Survey two years in a row and the drop-out rate is notably low. The appeal might lie in the friendly and compact campus — a 10-minute walk from one end to the other, providing you don't get sidetracked by any of the on-campus facilities. Leicester puts up a consistently strong academic performance across all its subject areas. It's understandably proud of its most famous research achievement: the development of DNA genetic fingerprinting. Add on Leicester, a lively, multicultural city with great facilities and transport links, and it's no wonder everyone is so pleased to be there.

Courses and qualifications There are around 100 courses leading to MA, MSc, MPhil, PhD, MBA, PGCE, LLM, MClinSci, Pg Cert, Pg Dip, Pre-Masters Diploma.

Fees
UK/EU students: approx £3,850.
International students: approx £6,995 to £15,150.

Funding UK/EU students can apply for help with funding through the Research Councils. For international students the university offers up to 25 scholarships worth up to £3,000 for taught master's students and five scholarships worth up to £5,000 for PhD students. The university also normally has two Commonwealth Shared Scholarship Scheme awards for eligible students and a loyalty discount scheme of 10 per cent for siblings, partners or children of international students.

Accommodation Approximately 1,000 rooms in university-owned accommodation are reserved for senior, international and postgraduate students. A limited amount of university accommodation is available for couples and small families. Contact: accommodation@le.ac.uk

Facilities A new library has just opened, with access to computer facilities, a bookshop and cafe. Special postgraduate study spaces are available in most departments. The university's David Wilson Library contains a dedicated postgraduate area accommodating 200–250 people and comprising a computer suite with 50 networked PCs, a quiet study area with desks for individual and group study, and a relaxed seating area.

Transport There are direct rail services to all parts of the country and the city is well served by the M1 and M69 motorways.

Specialism Physics, astronomy and genetics.

 STUDENT VIEW »

'I had studied management before but studying the MBA at Leicester has taught me new approaches to deal with the various management problems I encounter on a day-to-day basis.' Usman Khan, distance learning MBA student.

University of Lincoln

Brayford Pool,
Lincoln LN6 7TS

t 01522 882000
e enquiries@lincoln.ac.uk
↗ www.lincoln.ac.uk

» www.lincoln.ac.uk/home/postgraduate/index.htm

 12,664   **PG** 11%

Lincoln is a cathedral city that attracts a million tourists a year. The university's main campus offers great views up to the cathedral, though you might be too busy looking around you: the waterfront developments at Brayford Pool include a multiscreen cinema, restaurants, night clubs, accommodation, and the new students' union building with great concert space and bars. The university's city-centre buildings are known as the Cathedral Quarter and there's a lovely rural campus, Riseholme Park. The university opened a new arts centre in 2007, with excellent facilities for students and the general public.

Courses and qualifications There are 80 courses leading to Pg Cert, Pg Dip, PGCE, PGDE, BArch, CIMA, CMS, DMS, MA, MSc, Integrated Masters (MComp, MChem), MBA, LLM, MRes, MArch, MFA, MPhil, MA by Research, MSc by Research, EdD, DBA, DClinPsy, DJourn, PhD.

Fees Fees vary depending on the course, but as a guide:
UK/EU students: approx £3,350 for most courses, £6,200 for the MBA.
International students: approx £8,900 to £9,900 for most courses, £9,400 for the MBA.

Funding For more information visit www.lincoln.ac.uk

Accommodation Campus accommodation is designed for first year students. The university operates an accredited landlord scheme in partnership with other agencies, such as the city council, to accredit landlord accommodation as being suitable and safe for students, including those with families.

Facilities The media, humanities and computing building is fully equipped to industry standards with media suites providing the latest broadcast television, radio and sound equipment. The award-wining library is located in the impressive Great Central Warehouse building. The Engine Shed is the region's largest live music venue and is home to the students' union. The conversion from railway engine shed to award winning arts venue was completed at a cost of £6m.

The university's graduate school works with faculties to support graduate students and provides a centralised facility with computer equipment for part-time researchers.

Transport Lincoln has train services to London, Birmingham, Newcastle and more and the A1 isn't too far away.

Specialism Architecture, art and design, business and management, computing, education, health, life and social sciences, law, media and humanities.

« STUDENT VIEW »
'The course at Lincoln was absolutely first class. It really gave me the tools I needed to take that next step.'
Dave Cressey, Master in Business Administration (MBA).

University of Liverpool

Liverpool L69 3BX

t 0151 794 2000
e pgrecruitment@liv.ac.uk
↗ www.liv.ac.uk

» **www.liv.ac.uk/study/postgraduate**

 18,309 **PG** 15% (**UK**) 56%

Liverpool has everything you'd expect from a classic redbrick university: excellent ratings in teaching and research, a large and diverse student body, a strong sense of self and a location in a top city. In 2006, the university opened the first independent Anglo-Asian university in China in partnership with Xi'an Jiaotong University in Suzhou. Students can opt to take work placements in Suzhou. £200m of investment is also taking place on the university's campus near the centre of Liverpool. Facilities for fun and relaxation are great (the students' union building is the largest in the country), the cost of living is low and there is a real commitment to opening access and the local community.

Courses and qualifications There are many programmes leading to Pg Cert, Pg Dip, MA, MSc, MBA, LLM, PhD, MPhil, MRes.

Fees
UK/EU students: approx £3,300.
International students: range from £9,100 to £11,650.
MBAs are £14,000.

Funding A number of bursaries and scholarships including the PGT Award (criteria varies each year); International Advancement Award; University of Liverpool Alumni Scholarships, Duncan Norman Scholarships and the John Lennon Memorial Scholarship.

Accommodation There are specific halls of residence for postgraduate students and some self-contained family accommodation. Contact: accommodation@liv.ac.uk

Facilities Two main libraries — one of which underwent a major refurbishment in 2008. Extensive sports grounds, and the students' union offers a choice of three bars.

Transport Good for trains and coaches and there are motorways almost on the doorstep.

Specialism Research expertise in medicine, veterinary science, bioscience, and tropical medicine.

❝ STUDENT VIEW ❞

'I had always wanted to study for a PhD, as I enjoy research and all of the challenges it brings. The University of Liverpool has a strong reputation as a research university, and when I visited the Department of Civic Design the staff were so friendly and helpful. Doing a PhD here gives lots of opportunities to mix with other research students and I have made some great friends. The university as a whole is very supportive of postgraduate study, with a graduate school that organises training and other events such as conferences.' Jessica Barker, PhD in civic design.

Liverpool Hope University

Hope Park,
Liverpool L16 9JD

t 0151 291 3000
e course-enquiry@hope.ac.uk
↗ www.hope.ac.uk

» **www.hope.ac.uk/postgraduate-study**

 7,090   **PG** 10%   (UK) 55%

True to the history of its founding institutions — religious colleges training women to be teachers — Hope is the only ecumenical university in Europe, with a significant female population, and is strong in teacher training. The number of applications to Hope continues to rise — perhaps as a reaction to it gaining full university status in 2005. It has two campuses in the thriving and confident city of Liverpool. Hope has a high-quality careers service and opportunities for part-time work and work experience are plentiful, including the chance to work on an international project with the university's award-winning charity, Hope One World. Campus developments of some £15m are planned.

Liverpool

Courses and qualifications A range of programmes leading to MA, MSc, MBA, PGCE, MPhil, PhD.

Fees There is a range depending on the programme.
UK/EU students: range from £3,360 to £6,600.
International students: range from £6,600 to £9,420.

Funding Funding is available. See website for details.

Accommodation No family accommodation. For details contact: accommodation@hope.ac.uk

Facilities Moodle is the fastest growing and most used virtual learning environment in the UK. The library has extended opening hours designed to fit around student needs and claims to be the most flexible of any university. Hope aims to provide the most up-to-date computer facilities, with access to your email and virtual learning environment from anywhere in the world.

The Alexander Jones Research and Postgraduate Centre was the focus of substantial redevelopment in 2007 and now forms the physical focal point of research and postgraduate activity in the university. It is equipped with a number of state-of-the-art lecture and seminar rooms, computer access points, a kitchen and a common room. The Sheppard-Worlock Library has a number of special collections that will be of interest to postgraduate students.

Transport Excellent transport links — even an international airport.

Specialism Computer science, education, humanities, music, social and political science, theology, religious studies.

❝ STUDENT VIEW ❞

'I thoroughly enjoyed my time as a postgraduate student at Liverpool Hope University and I want to impress upon all students, both international and domestic, that with hard work you can achieve anything that you set your mind to. I would highly recommend Hope to international students considering studying abroad; it has opened up a whole world of opportunities for me.' Bassey I Ekanem, MBA.

Liverpool John Moores University

Roscoe Court,
4 Rodney Street,
Liverpool L1 2TZ

t 0151 231 5090
e recruitment@ljmu.ac.uk
↗ www.ljmu.ac.uk

» www.ljmu.ac.uk/courses/postgraduate

 25,500   **PG** 18%   (UK) 76%

At Liverpool John Moores University (LJMU), graduate skills development and work-related learning are now integral to all undergraduate degrees. Backed by an advisory panel of leading employers, students are encouraged to develop higher world-of-work skills. Plus the university's graduate development centre offers an extensive range of 'ready for work' training courses. As part of LJMU's £100m investment in campus developments, the university opened its new £23.5m Art and Design Academy in September 2008. It has unveiled plans to develop a new £20m life sciences building.

Liverpool

Courses and qualifications There are 210 courses leading to MA, MSc, MBA, MEnt, LLM, PGCE, CPD, Pg Dip, Pg Cert, MRes, MPhil, PhD.

Fees Start from £3,980.

Funding Some funding available. For more information contact Student Welfare Services: welfare@ljmu.ac.uk

Accommodation There is designated accommodation for postgraduate students. If you would like to live in a flat with other postgraduate students, indicate this when requesting accommodation. Every effort will be made to accommodate your request.

Facilities LJMU's new Graduate Development Centre (GDC) offers a range of services to help you gain the skills, experiences and confidence you will need to succeed as a professional after you graduate. As a postgraduate student the aim is to bring you closer to the world of work.

LJMU's Learning Resource Centres (LRC), located on each of the three campuses, offer exceptional learning facilities.

Research Support Areas, which are separate from the main library floor, offer a real work environment with an open plan layout, office style desks, phones and PCs. In addition, there is a seminar room and IT suite for practising presentations and discussion groups and a 'Quiet Professional Study Area'. A new Laptop Loan Scheme means that computers may be used by postgraduate students anywhere within the LRCs thanks to a wireless network.

Transport Two campuses are in the middle of town; a third is a 15-minute bus ride away.

Specialism Health and health related research is the largest area of research within LJMU with significant activity spanning two thirds of all academic schools.

❝ STUDENT VIEW ❞

'To put it simply the standard of education delivered here is the best in Liverpool and LJMU graduates gain employment easier than other institutes in Liverpool due to the practical skills taught here.' Michael Evans, MSc in biotechnology.

London Business School

Regent's Park,
London NW1 4SA

t 020 7000 7000
e webenquiries@london.edu
↗ www.london.edu

 1,700   **PG** 100%   (UK) 13%

Located in the heart of London next to one of its finest parks, London Business School boasts some amazing views. But it is not its views that the school is most famous for - it is ranked joint first in the world for both full-time and executive MBA programmes and holds the highest average research score of any university in the UK in the business and management sector. With a presence in four international cities - London, New York, Hong Kong and Dubai - it equips students from more than 130 countries with the skills they need for business.

London

Courses and qualifications Awards 1,000 degrees every year across EMBA, MFin, MBA, MM, MSc, PhD.

Fees Fees vary for master's programmes, executive education and PhD — for further details visit: www.london.edu/programmes/index.html

Funding A range of scholarships and grants are available. For further details visit: www.london.edu/programmes/scholarshipsandgrantfunding.html

Accommodation The school's recently updated campus accommodation is available to people on some of its executive education programmes. Delegates on many of the school's short courses use rooms in its hotel suite.

Facilities Facilities include an extensive library, fitness centre with fully equipped gym and swimming pool, as well as wireless internet access across campus and well-equipped lecture theatres.

Transport London Business School overlooks Regent's Park and is within easy reach of the City of London and the West End. It is minutes from Baker Street and Marylebone stations offering tube, national rail service and London airport connections.

Specialism The school's faculty represent over 30 countries and are grouped into seven subject areas — accounting; economics; finance; management science and operations; marketing; organisational behaviour; and strategic and international management.

 STUDENT VIEW ❯❯

'I was initially attracted to London Business School because of its ranking among the top five worldwide business schools (of course it's now number one!). Being right in the heart of London has offered amazing exposure to the heart of the world economy, ideal for a student looking to apply classroom skills immediately out in the business world. With over 80 per cent of the students here coming from outside the UK, I've really come away feeling like I've studied with the best in the world.' Robin Carswell, MBA student (Canada).

London Metropolitan University

31 Jewry Street,
London EC3N 2EY

t 020 7133 4200
e admissions@londonmet.ac.uk
↗ www.londonmet.ac.uk

» www.londonmet.ac.uk/courses/postgraduate-study

 34,000

London Met is London's largest single university, with two impeccably-placed campuses. One is in the heart of the City, close to Liverpool Street. Another is in trendy north London, near the smart shops and bars of Highbury and Islington. Of the 34,000 students, almost a third are international. Courses have a firm professional and vocational bent. New buildings include a striking graduate centre and the most advanced science centre in the world, all £30m of it, featuring the 'super lab', and excellent sports facilities. In 2007, London Met's four business departments merged, creating Europe's largest business school. London offers everything a student could want. The great students' union facilities at both campuses are good places to start.

London

Courses and qualifications There are approximately 150 courses. Study for an MA, MSc, Mphil, MRes, Pg Dip, Pg Cert or Phd.

Fees
UK/EU students: master's at London Metropolitan start at around £4,000.
International students: master's degree is £9,000 to £14,000.

Funding A small number of bursaries towards fees may be available each year to students on the university's Master of Research scheme.

Accommodation For details contact: accommodation@londonmet.ac.uk

Facilities Extensive libraries, including the specialist Women's Library and the TUC collections. There's an ultra-modern science centre, sound and recording studios, a mock courtroom, a lightning laboratory and seven floors of IT facilities at the Technology Tower. The graduate centre, at the north campus is designed by world-renowned 'Ground Zero' architect Daniel Libeskind, and offers a contemporary environment for postgraduate students and researchers.

Transport London's usual embarrassment of transport riches is on offer.

Specialism Sport.

❝ STUDENT VIEW ❞
'I joined the MSc international banking and finance in February 2006. The first thing that impressed me about the university was the quality of the tutors on the course. Cutting-edge technology like the Bloomberg facility helps give students a taste of how things would be done in a live environment. The overall attitude of the university has been positive and helpful and I am very pleased that I made the decision to study at London Met.'
Amit Banerjee, international banking and finance MSc.

London School of Economics and Political Science

Houghton Street,
London WC2A 2AE

t 020 7405 7686
e pg-admissions@lse.ac.uk
↗ www.lse.ac.uk

» www.lse.ac.uk/collections/graduateAdmissions

 9,030   **PG** 58%   (UK) 19%

The LSE is the only university in the UK specialising in the study of social sciences and has a worldwide reputation in the field. The world's largest social sciences library is housed here. Students here have a reputation for being academic and determined – the fact that the university library has a borrowing rate four times the national average speaks volumes. The school is located in the heart of London, just over the road from King's College London, with which it enjoys a traditional rivalry.

Courses and qualifications 195 programmes leading to MPhil/PhD, Pg Cert, Pg Dip, MSc, MA, MPA, EMBA, LLM, PhD.

Fees There are three main fee bands: £9,504, £13,992, £18,048.

Funding LSE Graduate Support Scheme, LSE External Study Scholarships, LSE PhD Scholarships, LSE Research Studentship Scheme, International Research Student Awards and many others awarded on the basis of academic merit, financial need, country of domicile and subjects studied.

Accommodation There are self-contained flats for families solely for the use of full-time postgraduate students of the LSE and their partners.

Facilities Excellent. Great libraries and other learning resources. The students' union is so well-regarded it attracts plenty of non-students. British Library of Political and Economic Science (world's largest social science library), halls of residence, medical centre, dental service, counselling service, chaplaincy, students' union, language centre, careers service, athletics Union including gym and facilities for football, rugby, hockey and many others.

Transport Tube, bus and rail once you've breached the city limits. LSE is central: walk or cycle most places you need to be.

Specialism Economics, social sciences, law.

❝ STUDENT VIEW ❞

'After graduating with a bachelor's degree in foreign affairs from the University of Virginia in 2005, I remained committed to the study of international relations. That devotion has led me to The London School of Economics and Political Science, a leading institution for the study of IR. The opportunity to study under leading academics/experts in the field of IR was not one that I could pass up. My decision to attend LSE was further solidified by the recommendations of friends who had previously attended, coupled with its location in an international city. The LSE student and academic community has made me feel both welcomed and appreciated, making my choice to study here the right one.' Sanjay Rajpal, MSc (United States)

London School of Hygiene & Tropical Medicine

Keppel Street, London WC1E 7HT	t 020 7299 4646
	e registry@lshtm.ac.uk
	↗ www.lshtm.ac.uk

 985   **PG** 100%   (UK) 40%

The London School of Hygiene & Tropical Medicine is Britain's national school of public health and is known worldwide as a leading postgraduate institution. The school is particularly noted for the excellence of its postgraduate medical training, providing one third of the UK's postgraduate medical education and research. It is recognised by national and international employers – many graduates go on to play prominent roles in their chosen careers of research or practice.

London

Courses and qualifications There are 22 courses leading to MSc. Courses leading to MPhil/PhD and DrPH are also available.

Fees
UK/EU students: £3,810 to £5,900 for full-time study.
International students: £11,525 to £16,995 for full-time study.

Funding A range of scholarships are available for master's or research degree studies at the school.

Accommodation Students have access to the University of London Housing Service, which offers a wide range of accommodation.

Facilities The school's library has one of the most comprehensive collections of books and journals in the field of international public health and tropical medicine in the world. Students have 24-hour access to the school's computing facilities or through a remote dial-in link. Students can also benefit from the facilities and events at the University of London Union and the Student Representative Council.

Transport The school is located in the heart of London, in Bloomsbury, and immediately adjacent to the University of London's central precinct and the British Museum.

Specialism The school is a major national and international focus of collaboration in teaching and research, where clinical, population, laboratory and social sciences are integrated to address the broad issues of health. Academic staff are leading experts in their fields giving students unparalleled access to their knowledge and experience.

❝ STUDENT VIEW ❞

'Good lecturers, quality teaching, provision of in-depth course notes and a lot of support make this a really excellent course. Studying here has really been a valuable experience for me.' Robyn Drake, MSc in medical statistics.

London South Bank University

90 London Road,
London SE1 6LN

t 020 7815 7815
e enquiry@lsbu.ac.uk
↗ www.lsbu.ac.uk

 23,000 **PG** 25% (**UK**) 59%

LSBU is based at the Elephant and Castle in south London. It's an area that is always described as up and coming – though it actually might fulfil its promise soon, as major investment in the area is planned. LSBU is doing its bit, too, with £47m being put into its campus. In any case, the area has its own rough'n'tumble charm and buckets of history and it's hard to beat the location – within easy reach of London Bridge, Southwark, the South Bank, Waterloo and Westminster. Transport links to central London are good. The 23,000-strong student body is diverse and culturally rich. Half are from ethnic minorities, 3,000 come from outside the UK. Of the 'home' students, a third are from Southwark and another third from further afield in London. A large proportion are mature students. Courses are built with future careers in mind – a tactic that's paying off, since graduate salaries are very good.

London

Courses and qualifications There are around 90 courses, as well as research opportunities leading to MA, MSc, MPhil, PhD, MBA, Pg Dip.

Fees For full range see: www.lsbu.ac.uk/fees/postGrad.html

Funding Some may be eligible for charitable fund, access to learning fund or sports scholarships.

Accommodation No accommodation but there is a reduced rate nursery for those requiring childcare facilities.

Facilities Good on-site sports facilities and access to libraries and computing resources. All facilities located on all three LSBU campuses can be accessed by all students.

Transport Easy access to the tube, plentiful bus routes and overland rail services.

❝ STUDENT VIEW ❞

'I'm currently a detective inspector with the Metropolitan Police. My passion is investigation. Police management has changed over the past decade and I believe that without a firm academic background managers are limited in their skills. I had been looking at different courses and when I read about this course, it immediately struck me as relevant to the role of major crime investigator. This was the first time I had seen a course like this being offered.' Karl Amos, MSc forensic investigative psychology.

Loughborough University

Loughborough,
Leicestershire LE11 3TU

t 01509 263171
e admissions@lboro.ac.uk
↗ www.lboro.ac.uk

» **www.lboro.ac.uk/prospectus/pg/index.htm**

 15,357   **PG** 26%

Academically strong across the board it may be – and it is – but Loughborough is still famous for its strength in sport. Art and culture are taken seriously here, too. The Midlands market town is about a mile away from campus. The university is the town's biggest employer and students are a major part of the population here. The students' union is unique as it's the only one in the country that is physically owned by the students.

Loughborough

Courses and qualifications The courses available include MA, MSc, MBA, MDes, MRes, PG Dip, PG Cert, PGCE, PhD, MPhil, EngD.

Fees Fees vary by department and subject, view: www.lboro.ac.uk/admin/ar/funding/pg/fees/2008/index.htm
Research fees also vary by subject. The minimum fee in 2007-08 for UK/EU students was £3,300. Fees for international students started at £9,850.

Funding There is a wide range of support. Visit the webpage for details: www.lboro.ac.uk/admin/ar/funding/index.htm

Accommodation The supply of houses and flats for couples and families is limited on campus but the student accommodation service is able to meet all needs within walking distance of the campus by working with local landlords. Contact: sac@lboro.ac.uk

Facilities The university has the country's largest concentration of world-class training facilities across a wide range of sports, available for the enthusiastic amateur as well as elite performers. Campus facilities include: new purpose-built

teaching facilities for postgraduate students; a well-resourced library and information technology network; cafes, bars and restaurants; banks and shops; health centre, optician and dentist; nursery; an arts centre and theatres; Loughborough students' union, uniquely owned and run; new postgraduate accommodation opened in September 2008.

The university recently invested more than £5m in purpose-built teaching facilities for postgraduate students, including lecture theatres, flexible seminar space, additional, dedicated 24/7 computer facilities and private study space on central campus. It is currently investing an extra £6m in further new buildings to provide state-of-the-art research labs for students and more learning and teaching spaces.

Transport A 20-minute walk from the town centre, or take the shuttle bus. Train to Nottingham, Derby or Leicester in 30 minutes.

Specialism Sustainability, materials, systems engineering, health and life sciences, sport science, informatics, sports technology, business and economics.

❝ STUDENT VIEW ❞

'The atmosphere at Loughborough is pleasant and friendly. I find that the student to lecturer relationship is very good – they are all very approachable. The master's course is very intense but the lecturers are always there to help and support you in your studies.' Ting Diu, MSc analytical and pharmaceutical science.

The University of Manchester

Oxford Road,
Manchester M13 9PL

t 0161 306 6000
e pg-admissions@manchester.ac.uk
↗ www.manchester.ac.uk

» **www.manchester.ac.uk/postgraduate**

  34,728 **PG** 26%

Manchester is massive: it is the biggest university in the UK (bar the Open University). It's frequently the most popular in the country, too, according to UCAS applications, and one of the most targeted by the UK's top graduate employers. Given the size, it's easy to find like-minded friends to spend your time with; Manchester's continuing success is due in part to the positive experience that graduates report. The city is also a big draw — down-to-earth and friendly, but ever-increasingly hip and happening.

Courses and qualifications There are many courses leading to PG Dip, PG Cert, PGCE, DipSW, MA, MBA, MEd, MSc, LLM, MMus, MRes, MPhil, PhD, EngD.

Fees The fees vary according to the course. *UK/EU students:* £3,400 full-time, £1,700 for per annum for the part-time taught master's. *International students:* £10,800 per annum for full-time taught master's.

Funding The university offers significant funding for postgraduate taught courses and research degrees for home and international students.

Accommodation The range of halls and room-types is extensive, from modern self-catering flats through to traditional collegiate-style catered halls of residence. Both single- and mixed-sex accommodation is available, and there is the option of en suite or standard facilities. The university also offers some specially adapted rooms for students with disabilities, and possesses a limited supply of family and partner accommodation (from double rooms to two- and three-bedroom self-contained flats). All rooms are internet connected.

International students will be guaranteed a place in one of the university's halls of residence for the full duration of their course subject to certain criteria. Contact: accommodation@manchester.ac.uk

Facilities Access to one of the UK's largest academic libraries, more than 10,000 PCs across campus, e-learning facilities and excellent teaching resources for both arts and sciences.

Transport There are two mainline stations, an international airport and good motorway connections.

Specialism Fields of excellence throughout the university.

◄◄ STUDENT VIEW ►►

'The MSc management of science, technology and innovation course polished my skills in research, project management, interviewing, analysis, and report writing which are key to my work. The course covered a broad range of topics but also allowed me to focus in depth on specific areas of interest. Most importantly, I think the teaching team was outstanding. Staff were very approachable and helpful, and I'm especially grateful for their role in helping me gain an internship at the United Nations Industrial Development Organisation in Vienna, which was an important stepping stone to my current position.' Jing Liu, MSc management of science, technology and innovation.

Manchester Metropolitan University

All Saints Building,
All Saints,
Manchester M15 6BH

t 0161 247 2000
e enquiries@mmu.ac.uk
↗ www.mmu.ac.uk

» www.mmu.ac.uk/study/postgraduate

 40,000   **PG** 13%   (UK) 90%

MMU is one of the largest universities in Britain, offering around 700 courses and giving students the opportunity to undertake a range of industry placements and exchange programmes with international universities. It's investing £250m in brand new facilities at Manchester, Didsbury and Crewe and has a great social scene, having been voted best place to be a gay student by *Diva* magazine. The students' union has recently undergone a massive transformation and its bars are always heaving. Manchester boasts a rich cultural life, with a huge range of museums and live music venues.

Courses and qualifications There are 182 courses leading to MA, MSc, MPhil, PhD, MBA, PGCE, PGDip, Pg Cert, BArch, BLandArch, DBA, MRes, PDP, EdD.

Fees
UK/EU students: range from £3,420 to £14,500.
International students: range from 8,675 to £14,500.

Funding There are several bursaries. See the website for details.

Accommodation Accommodation can be arranged through the Leased House Scheme with Manchester Student Homes.
Contact: accommodation@mmu.ac.uk

Facilities Great for sport: the Manchester Aquatics Centre is a £30m purpose-built swimming pool complex located on the Manchester campus, boasting two Olympic standard main pools. There are high-spec engineering and science labs and good arts facilities.

For postgraduate students there are learning and research facilities, libraries, computer suites, drop-in centres, support services and accommodation.

Transport There are great links out to the rest of the country and (via the international airport) the world. The university operates a free bus between Cheshire campuses.

Specialism Teacher training, exercise and sport science, environmental sciences, metallurgy and materials, English language and literature, history of art, architecture and design, library and information management, art and design and education.

❝ STUDENT VIEW »
'I chose to study at MMU because it has a reputation as being one of the best for my subject area in the country and the course supervisors are well known in their field. It has been hard work but I have much broader knowledge and experience of a range of techniques that will be very useful for my career.'
Ross Atkinson, PhD psychology.

Marjon (University College Plymouth St Mark and St John)

Derriford Road,
Plymouth,
Devon PL6 8BH

t 01752 636700
e admissions@marjon.ac.uk
↗ www.marjon.ac.uk

 3,500   **PG** 43%

The University College Plymouth St Mark and St John (and... breathe) unsurprisingly shortens its name to Marjon, and is a small single-campus higher education institution, based on the south coast. It prides itself on its warm, welcoming and inclusive atmosphere. Courses are mostly humanities based, and include media, PR, community work, applied sports science and coaching. The campus itself is on the outskirts of Plymouth – but that just means you're closer to the moors.

Plymouth

Courses and qualifications Several courses leading to PhD, MPhil, MA, MEd, PGCE, Pg Dip, Pg Cert. All postgraduate qualifications are accredited by Exeter University.

Fees Fees depend on the course. As a guide:
UK/EU students: approx £3,320.
International students: approx £8,350.

Accommodation For families (not on campus) call 01752 636711.

Facilities The sports centre has a 25-metre pool, gym, squash courts, two sports halls, a fitness suite and outdoor pitches. The library is at the heart of the campus and there is 24-hour access to computing facilities. All campus facilities are available to postgraduate students as well as undergraduate.

Transport Rail and road links to most big cities, plus ferry services. Plymouth airport is very close by.

❝ STUDENT VIEW ❞

'I choose UCP Marjon because of its excellent reputation. I am passionate about ICT and like the fact that it is being integrated across the curriculum.' Stephen-Lee Farmer, PGCE secondary ICT.

Middlesex University

The Burroughs,
Hendon,
London NW4 4BT

t 020 8411 5000
e enquiries@mdx.ac.uk
↗ www.mdx.ac.uk

» **www.mdx.ac.uk/study/postgrad/index.asp**

 25,872   **PG** 24%   (UK) 54%

Middlesex is located in the further reaches of north London and spread over four campuses. All of them are less than an hour from central London, meaning all the perks of the big city are there on your doorstep, but there is some peace and quiet, should you need it. Middlesex is one of the most multinational universities in the country, with a fifth of its students coming from outside the UK and well over a hundred different countries represented.

London

Courses and qualifications Several courses leading to GDip Law, Pg Cert, Pg Dip, PGCE, MA, MSc, MProf, MPhil, DProf, PhD, EngD, ArtsD, EdD.

Fees
UK/EU students: from £4,800 (2009 entry).
International students: from £9,600 (2009 entry).

Funding Chancellor's scholarships (four categories: academic, culture, community and sport), alumni bursaries, academic alumni scholarships. Middlesex University's scholarships officer provides guidance on the availability of external scholarships.

Accommodation There is an accommodation service to assist students.
Contact: accomm@mdx.ac.uk

Facilities The Sheppard library, opened in 2004, offers fantastic views of London from its five floors. The university's Museum of Domestic Design and Architecture houses an important collection of decorative art and design. Each campus has its own separate learning resources and there are impressive facilities for the study of (and participation in) sport. Postgraduate common rooms, postgraduate quiet areas (library).

Transport It's virtually in London, with all the transport benefits (and problems) that implies.

Specialism Health and social marketing, law and minorities, mental health, secondary teacher training, modern European philosophy, choreography.

 STUDENT VIEW »

'The master's at Middlesex has been excellent. It's a chance to combine work experience and learning, theory and practical experience, and pull all that together. The best thing is learning with others who are working in industry. You can see what you do affects the rest of the organisation.' Jamie Lyons, MA in human resource management.

Napier University

Craiglockhart Campus,
Edinburgh EH14 1DJ

t 08452 606040
e info@napier.ac.uk
↗ www.napier.ac.uk

》 **www.napier.ac.uk/prospectivestudents/postgraduate/Pages/default.aspx**

 14,500 **PG** 16% (UK) 47%

Napier is a modern university of over 14,000 students spread across seven campuses in Edinburgh. Napier is committed to providing students with the skills and qualifications that employers are looking for. Student work placements, which are often paid, ensure students hit the ground running once they graduate. Modular courses allow students to customise their own courses to suit their interests. Edinburgh is home to around 100,000 students in total so you'll be exceptionally well catered for here. There's no shortage of things to do — in fact, when the festival is on in the summer there's simply too much to do — and the city is so nice that a simple stroll into town feels like a treat.

Courses and qualifications Napier offers over 75 different programmes leading to MA, MSc, MPhil, PhD, DBA, MFA, MDes, Pg Cert, Pg Dip, MRes. Napier also offers professional qualifications including ACCA, IDM, CIBS and CIMA.

Fees See website for details.

Funding Napier has a dedicated student funding team specifically to provide information and support about funding to current and prospective students. They also provide guidance on extra sources of funding for students and administer various funds and scholarships.

Accommodation Napier offers accommodation for postgraduate students in self catering flats but does not offer family accommodation.

Facilities 2007 saw the opening of a brand new fitness suite on the Craiglockhart campus.

Napier offers a number of facilities to all of its students, such as access to over 1,250 PCs and 150 Apple Macs on seven campuses, including 24/7 access to computing resources at the award-winning Jack Kilby Computer Centre and Wi-Fi network connections. All seven libraries are networked and open seven days a week. There is 24-hour access to the electronic library catalogue. Group study rooms and silent study areas are also available.

Transport Good train links from Edinburgh to London via Newcastle and York. Access to motorways and a nearby airport.

Specialism Business studies.

Newcastle University

Newcastle upon Tyne NE1 7RU	**t** 0191 222 5594
	e enquiries@ncl.ac.uk
	↗ www.ncl.ac.uk

》 www.ncl.ac.uk/postgraduate

 18,363   **PG** 24%

Newcastle has an impressive academic track record and is located in a city that inspires immense affection. The city is famous for its nightlife, but is also a regional centre for the arts, theatre and live music. It's close to great countryside and dramatic coastline. The university has a modern outlook and is embarking on a period of extensive redevelopment. There's a commitment to ethical standards here too — all the electricity used by the university comes from environmentally friendly resources.

Courses and qualifications There are over 250 programmes leading to MA, MBA, MClinEd, MEd, MFA, MGPrac, MHPrac, MMPrac, LLM, MMus, MSc, Pg Cert, Pg Dip, PGCE, DAppEdPsy, DBA, DClinPsyc, DEdPsy, EdD, EngD, MLitt, MPhil, MRes, PhD, MD, DDS, IPhD.

Fees See online postgraduate prospectus for 2009-10 tuition fees: www.ncl.ac.uk/ postgraduate

Funding Details of funding can be found at: www.ncl.ac.uk/postgraduate/funding

Accommodation The university has places in halls specifically designated for postgraduates. It also has a limited number of two and three bedroom properties suitable for students with children: www.ncl.ac.uk/accommodation/ postgrad/family Contact: accommodation-enquiries@ncl.ac.uk

Facilities The Postgraduate and Mature Students' Society provides an extensive programme of social and cultural events for postgraduates and mature students. Dedicated graduate schools administer the academic side of student life from admission to graduation. Each faculty at the university has a postgraduate research training programme, which enables postgraduates to develop their academic skills and ensure that they can be applied in academic and work-related contexts.

Transport The station is on the east coast main line for quick links to London and Edinburgh and there's an airport.

Specialism The university has 14 designated research institutes to facilitate multi-disiplinary projects.

◄◄ STUDENT VIEW ►►

'Newcastle University has a very impressive reputation and a track record to match. Newcastle is a culturally diverse, vibrant and friendly area to live in and the atmosphere on campus is warm and welcoming. Its close proximity to most of the region's attractions and ease of access via public transport (Metro, bus, train etc) mean that there is always something to do, whether it be a day at the coast, an afternoon's shopping in town or a trip to the beautiful Northumberland countryside.' Helen Lowther, MA regional development (Research), PhD geography.

Newman University College

Genners Lane,
Bartley Green,
Birmingham B32 3NT

t 0121 476 1181
e registry@newman.ac.uk
↗ www.newman.ac.uk

 www.newman.ac.uk/Courses/Postgraduate/?pg=586

 2,900   **PG** 20%   (UK) 97%

Founded in 1968 by the Catholic Education Council,
Newman is located in a purpose-built campus south-west of
Birmingham, about eight miles from the city centre. Once
exclusively a teacher-training college, it now has a small
portfolio of degrees awarded by the University of Leicester.
There are also European placement opportunities. All
students take a work placement module as part of their course
and Newman is particularly proud of its graduate employment
record — one of the best in the country.

Birmingham

Courses and qualifications There are 35
postgraduate courses leading to GTP, OTT, PGCE,
Pg Dip, GDip, MA, MEd, MSc, MPhil, PhD.

Fees
UK/EU students: approx £3,145.
International students: approx £7,500.

Funding A small number of studentships
are available for research degrees funded by
Newman which provides funding towards living
expenses.

Accommodation There is accommodation on
campus for priority students. There's no family
accommodation.

Facilities There's a big sports centre with plenty
of facilities, a library with access to computing
resources, and the students' union is pretty
active in making sure there's plenty to do in
your time off. No specific areas for postgraduate
students.

Transport Birmingham is well served by just
about every kind of transport.

Specialism Education.

❝ STUDENT VIEW ❞

*'I was impressed with the staff at Newman, they were helpful, friendly and excellent in their area of
specialism. The PhD students have a well-equipped office which provides an appropriate environment for
scholarly activity.'* Tom Michael, PhD in neuropsychology.

University of Wales, Newport

Caerleon Campus,
Lodge Road,
Newport NP20 5DA

t 01633 432432
e uic@newport.ac.uk
↗ www.newport.ac.uk

» **www3.newport.ac.uk/courses/courses.aspx?type=pg&school=0**

 9,780   **PG** 20%   (UK) 88%

The university is based on two campuses, one a short walk from the city centre and another in the pleasant village of Caerleon. Student accommodation and the students' union is on the latter. It's a small and friendly campus in a small and friendly village. The university is building a new multi-million pound campus in the centre of Newport which should open in 2010. Newport offers plenty to do and it's the focus of regeneration investment. The university has been highly rated in the national student survey. It is also growing fast, enjoying big increases in student applications. Widening access is a big deal here, too.

Courses and qualifications Approximately 100 courses leading to MA, MBA, MFA, MSc, MRes, Pg Cert, PGCE, Pg Dip and PhD.

Fees
UK/EU students: full-time MBA is £5,985.
International students: full-time MBA is £8,950.

Funding There may be bursaries available depending on your course and situation. Contact the access funds coordinator for more details on 01633 432065.

Accommodation There is no specific postgraduate hall of residence but the university will assist you in finding accommodation in the private sector.

Facilities There's a good sports centre and an elite school of golf for talented student golfers. The university is also embracing new ways of learning and teaching. Through the online learning environment, tutors can contact students by text and students can access essential resources.

Transport There's a bus between campuses. It is a two-hour drive to London on the M4 with direct train links too.

 STUDENT VIEW »
'I've really enjoyed my time here at Newport and particularly enjoyed studying alongside professionals from a diverse range of fields which provided me with a very different perspective and enabled me to broaden my networking opportunities.' Diane Powles, MA in education.

University of Northampton

Avenue Campus,
St George's Avenue,
Northampton NN2 6JD

t 0800 358 2232
e study@northampton.ac.uk
↗ www.northampton.ac.uk

» **www.northampton.ac.uk/courses/postgraduate**

 10,394   **PG** 14%   (**UK**) 69%

Northampton

Ten thousand students attend courses on two city campuses, many of them locals. The university has seen a substantial investment in campus facilities during the past few years, with a further £80m planned. The students' union regularly has live entertainment at both its campuses. Northampton is a large market town with some pleasant green spaces and architecture.

Courses and qualifications There are over 150 programmes leading to MA, MSc, MBA, Pg Dip, Pg Cert, PhD, MPhil, ACCA, CIMA, CIPD, CIM, PGCE, GTP, EYPS.

Fees
UK/EU students: approx £3,600 to £6,950.
International students: £7,950 to £8,950.

Funding The university offers a number of bursaries and scholarships. For further information contact: studentcentre@ northampton.ac.uk

Accommodation The accommodation team can advise on local off-campus accommodation. Contact: accommodation@northampton.ac.uk

Facilities Park campus has its own nightclub and Avenue campus also has a students' union bar, as well as dance and drama studios and computer-aided design suites. There is 24-hour access to IT resources. For researchers there are two dedicated research spaces with common areas, office space, computer room, meeting and conference rooms.

Transport There is a free inter-campus bus service. Northampton is close by and easily accessible. Northampton is one hour by train to Birmingham and London and is accessible by three junctions on the M1.

Specialism The university has a designated network of 10 centres of excellence including the world renowned Centre for Wastes Management and the British School of Leather Technology.

◀◀ STUDENT VIEW ▶▶

'The University of Northampton's Graduate School has a number of ways of involving postgraduate students so we have an identity and feel we belong. It's good to have the opportunity to meet up with other students who are going through the same things. Students in the same schools and divisions of the university support each other, and we have the opportunity to meet students from other schools at committee meetings, induction week, workshops and Saturday schools. I feel part of a wider research student community.'
Judy Sayers, PhD in education.

Northumbria University

Newcastle City Campus,
Ellison Place,
Newcastle upon Tyne NE1 8ST

t 0191 232 6002
e er.admissions@northumbria.ac.uk
↗ www.northumbria.ac.uk

 26,500   **PG** 17%   (UK) 66%

Northumbria is an increasingly popular choice for students
– maybe no surprise when you consider it's based in a
city renowned for its culture, friendliness and nightlife.
Northumbria has two campuses, one in the centre of
Newcastle, and the other a few miles away. Northumbria's
teaching has a good reputation, and courses allow for
flexibility. It's also mindful of providing support for students
who need it.

Newcastle
upon Tyne

Courses and qualifications Over 200
programmes leading to MA, MSc , MPhil, PhD,
MBA, PG Dip, PG Cert, MRes, LLM, BVC, DBMS,
DBA, MPA, GDL, LPC.

Fees
UK/EU students: range from £1,500 to £14,475.
International students: range from £8,300 to
£14,150.

Funding Some scholarships are available. Some
schools also offer returning alumni a discount
on fees. In addition, there is a Research Student
Conference Bursary Scheme.

Accommodation Limited availability for
married couples but no availability for those
with children. Contact: rc.accommodation@
northumbria.ac.uk

Facilities The state-of-the-art City Campus
East has won numerous awards. Sports facilities
keep the university as one of the top 10 sporting

institutions in the UK. IT initiatives include a
service that enables students to access their files
from potentially anywhere in the world.

A dedicated graduate school offers
opportunities for informal networking, a
meeting/examination room and a resource
centre. Newcastle Business School has a
postgraduate student society which provides
a social outlet for all postgraduates. The
residential weekend (a part of all NBS master's
programmes) is very highly regarded by
students.

Transport The train station is a short walk away
and there's a reliable underground (metro)
system and an international airport.

Specialism Business studies, conservation
of fine art, logistics, design, engineering and
information sciences, law, construction project
management, sustainable development.

❝ STUDENT VIEW ❞

*'I had nine great years in the army with tours of duty in Northern Ireland, Iraq and Kosovo, as well as other
international exercises and after a successful army career, I was ready for a fresh challenge which would draw
on the skills and expertise army life had afforded me. Studying at Northumbria has really equipped me for my
new role and it is a great way for anyone leaving the army to prepare themselves for a second career.'*
Dan Spencer, MSc at Northumbria's School of the Built Environment.

Norwich University College of the Arts

Francis House,
3-7 Redwell Street,
Norwich NR2 4SN

t 01603 610561
e info@nuca.ac.uk
↗ www.nuca.ac.uk

 1,125   **PG** 10%

Norwich University College of the Arts, formerly the Norwich School of Art and Design, is a specialist higher education institution focusing on — you guessed it — art and design. It's located in the centre of the charming city of Norwich. Based at the school is the Norwich Gallery, which attracts around 40,000 visitors a year and the Aurora Festival.

Courses and qualifications There are 11 taught courses plus research leading to MA, MPhil, PhD.

Fees For the range of fees, see the website.

Funding Students are eligible to apply for postgraduate student awards from the AHRC, subject to the support of the University College.

Accommodation No accommodation for families. Contact: accommodation@nsad.ac.uk

Facilities The library has good specialist resources and there's plenty of scope to access digital media as well.

Transport The train station is a short walk away and it's less than two hours to London.

Specialism Fine art, textiles and animation.

University of Nottingham

University Park,
Nottingham NG7 2RD

t 0115 951 5151
e postgraduate-enquiries@nottingham.ac.uk
↗ www.nottingham.ac.uk

 pgstudy.nottingham.ac.uk

30,444   **PG** 20%

People from 141 different nations come to Nottingham; there are also campuses in Malaysia and China. The attractive campus has great facilities for sports and the arts and the students' union is one of the largest and most active in the UK, with over 200 societies, sports clubs, student-run services, associations and a variety of social events on offer. There's also an award-winning student radio station.

Nottingham

Courses and qualifications Over 300 taught master's, diploma and certificate courses, including AMusD, MLitt, AMusM, MMath, DAppEdPsy, MMedSci, MMus, DAppPsych, DArch, DASS, MNursSci, DBA, MNutr, DClinPsy, MPA, DHSci, MPH, DLitt, MPharm, DM, MPhil, DSc, MPhys, EdD, MRes, EngD, MSc, LLM, MA, MBA, MSW, MBiol, March, NurseD, PGCE, MChem, MDiv, MEng, PhD.

Fees For the full range of fees, see the website.

Funding A funding database is available to students at: www.nottingham.ac.uk/prospectuses/postgrad/introduction/funding/postscholarship.php

Accommodation There is dedicated postgraduate accommodation. For details contact: ugaccommodation@nottingham.ac.uk

Facilities Library facilities include the new Hallward Library Learning Hub — a learning and information centre that uses state-of-the-art multimedia technology to provide a wide range of services and resources. There are extensive sports facilities and a new £1m bar, too. The central graduate school offers a research training programme, funding advice for UK postgraduate students, and a comprehensive academic and careers-focussed events programme. All academic schools have members of staff with responsibility for postgraduate academic affairs.

Transport The university provides an efficient free bus service. Good rail and road links and an international airport nearby.

Specialism A research-intensive university that offers high quality taught and research programmes across all its faculties and schools: over 60 per cent of the university's scores in the most recent Research Assessment Exercise identified the university's research as being of a level of international excellence.

❝ STUDENT VIEW ❞

'Studying pharmacy at the University of Nottingham was a great ambition as the university has a great reputation all round and high-class teaching facilities. It is challenging and demanding as the course is very extensive but at the end it is rewarding and gratifying. The timetable is almost always full with lectures as well as the laboratory classes but the support is always there from the tutors and older students. Rabab Kassam, MPharm.

Nottingham Trent University

Burton Street,
Nottingham NG1 4BU

t 0115 941 8418
e admissions@ntu.ac.uk
↗ www.ntu.ac.uk

» www.ntu.ac.uk/postgraduate_professional/index.html

 25,000   **PG** 20%

NTU is one of the largest 'new' universities in the country, with around 25,000 students. They are spread over three campuses – one in the city centre, another about five miles away and a third in the country about 12 miles out of town. NTU has close links with more than 6,000 employers across the world. The student community is diverse, with a wide range of nationalities and backgrounds represented. Nottingham is a vibrant city with a proud history. The city centre has the full range of leisure options, from sleek cocktail bars to grungy clubs.

Nottingham

Courses and qualifications There are over 130 postgraduate programmes leading to BVC, Cert Ed, DArt, DBA, DDes, DMedSci, GDL, GTP, LLM, LPC, MA, MBA, MPhil, MRes, MSc, PAQ, PGCE, PGCHE, Prof GCE, PG Cert, PG Dip, PhD, Prof Cert, Prof Dip.

Fees Costs vary depending on course studied. Different fees apply to UK/EU students and international students.

Funding The university offers competitive Graduate School Master's bursaries covering fees for master's courses. The Vice-Chancellor's PhD Bursary scheme supports research students, covering fees and providing a maintenance stipend for up to three years.

Accommodation There is no family accommodation in university residences. The student accommodation service can help find suitable private accommodation. Contact: sas.general.enquiries@ntu.ac.uk

Facilities The university offers wide-ranging facilities – including a £1m sports hall – and support to assist high-calibre athletes with their performance, training and personal development. 24-hour access to some computing facilities. Research students have use of dedicated workspaces.

Transport The city centre is easily accessible by foot or public transport, depending on which site you're on. Nottingham itself has great transport links.

Specialism Nottingham Law School is one of only eight educational establishments to be validated to offer the BVC, and Nottingham Business School runs one of the largest DBA courses in the UK.

❝ STUDENT VIEW ❞

'I have enjoyed the innovative style of learning which combines intensive workshop learning with individual study time. This has been very useful because it has given me the opportunity to learn and understand at my own pace.' Mark Chukwudum, MSc economics and finance.

Open University

PO Box 197,
Milton Keynes MK7 6BJ

t 0845 300 60 90
e general-enquiries@open.ac.uk
↗ www.open.ac.uk

》 www3.open.ac.uk/study/postgraduate/index.htm

 224,276   **PG** 8%   (UK) 80%

It might not be a typical university, but that doesn't stop
the Open from being at the forefront of academic life
in this country. It's the UK's largest university, a world
leader in distance learning, achieves high standards in
teaching and research, and has been rated top for student
satisfaction in the National Student Survey for three years
in a row. Undergraduate degrees have no prerequisite entry
requirements, and distance learning is a boon to anyone
unable to reach or commit to a campus-based education. New
ways of teaching have expanded so much that the famed OU
television broadcasts ceased at the end of 2006 and are now
through online resources and interactive DVDs. Students
work in their own time, but are supported by staff at regional
centres.

Courses and qualifications There are 155
courses leading to MA, MSc, MPhil, PhD, MBA,
PGCE, Pg Dip, Pg Cert, MPA, EdD, MRes, MEd.

Fees Fees vary. See the website for more details.

Funding There are bursaries, contact The Open
University for details.

Specialism Research school.

❝ STUDENT VIEW ❞

'I'm grateful to the OU, without which I wouldn't have been able to develop my career in this way.'
Pippa Smith, MSc in psychology.

University of Oxford

University Offices,
Wellington Square,
Oxford OX1 2JD

t 01865 288000
e graduate.admissions@admin.ox.ac.uk
↗ www.ox.ac.uk

 www.ox.ac.uk/admissions/postgraduate_courses/index.html

 20,014   **PG** 38%   (**UK**) 38%

There's no doubt that Oxford's history is very present. You'll probably live in at least one beautiful, centuries-old building, sit at the same desk as your favourite prime minister or take part in one of the ridiculous traditions that have been ridiculous since the 17th century. But Oxford is also a modern university: at, or near, the top of national and global rankings, year after year, at the forefront of research and teaching, and with tip-top facilities.

Courses and qualifications There are over 430 programmes leading to DPhil, EngD, MLitt, MSc, MSt, BCL, BPhil, MBA, EMBA, MJur, MPhil, MSc, MSt, MTh, Certificate in Diplomatic Studies, Pg Dip, PGCE.

Fees There is a range of fees across subjects and qualifications. Figures below are for entry in 2009.
UK/EU students: most courses are £3,390 (taught and research).
International students: most courses range between £11,750 (most humanities and social sciences courses), £13,450 (most mathematical, physical and life sciences courses) and £24,500 (most medical sciences courses).

Funding 45 per cent of all postgraduates are fully funded by scholarships/awards For details see: www.ox.ac.uk/admissions/postgraduate_courses/finance/index.html

Accommodation The accommodation office lets and manages 475 residential units for postgraduates and their families.

Facilities Oxford has the largest university library system in the UK, four major museums, botanic gardens and a number of significant collections in departments and colleges. There are six postgraduate-only colleges alongside 30 colleges, which take both undergraduates and postgraduates. The Middle Common Room (MCR) — a physical space within college and an active graduate community — is the hub of postgraduate life.

Transport Within Oxford, you can walk/cycle everywhere. Frequent trains and coaches to London.

Specialism Noted for excellence in general.

❝ STUDENT VIEW ❞

'Obviously there's the draw of the university's reputation but a big part of why I chose Oxford was knowing I would get to meet people from around the world who are passionate about their subject. There's a huge amount of energy here, not just academically, but as far as college life, societies and socialising are concerned. I only intended to spend a year here on an MSc course, but three years in I'm working on my doctorate.' Sarah Hutchinson, DPhil social policy.

Oxford Brookes University

Headington Campus,
Gipsy Lane, Headington,
Oxford OX3 0BH

t 01865 484848
e query@brookes.ac.uk
↗ www.brookes.ac.uk

》 www.brookes.ac.uk/studying/courses/postgraduate

 18,768   **PG** 27%   (**UK**) 75%

Oxford

Brookes is consistently rated as one of the best of the newer universities. Its students are spread over three campuses: Headington and Harcourt Hill are each a little distance from the city centre; Wheatley is about seven miles away, in the Oxfordshire countryside. Oxford is naturally a student-friendly city. The Venue at Brookes is the largest, erm, venue in Oxford, with regular club nights and concerts.

Courses and qualifications There are 152 programmes leading to PhD, MPhil, PhD by Published Work, MA, MSc, MRes, ProfDoc, MBA, Pg Dip, Pg Cert, PGCE.

Fees There is a range of fees.
UK/EU students: range from £3,990 to £8,220. MBA is £17,000.
International students: range from £9,950 to £12,500. MBA up to £17,680.
International tuition fees for individual courses can be found at: www.brookes.ac.uk/studying/finance/tuition/international_pg

Funding Funding is available. For details, see: www.brookes.ac.uk/studying/finance/support/pg_international
   Abbey Grupo Santander Scholarships: www.brookes.ac.uk/studying/finance/support/abbey-grupo

Accommodation Six of the halls of residence offer a small amount of accommodation exclusively for postgraduates. There are 12 self-contained flats available to any student with dependant children and can be used by couples or single parents with one child (or two if they are same sex). Contact: accomm@brookes.ac.uk

Facilities There is a taught postgraduate common room and a taught postgraduate computer room on the Headington Campus. The Postgraduate Centre in the Business School at the Wheatley Campus includes a state-of-the-art lecture theatre and comprehensively equipped seminar rooms for discussion and workshop activities. The postgraduate lounge, a dedicated area for private and group study, completes this excellent facility.

Transport A bus connects campuses. Well connected to London and the rest of the south. You're not bang in the city centre, so a bike or a bus pass will come in handy.

Specialism International studies, the Oxford Institute for Sustainable Development, life sciences, the built environment, nutrition and food research, primate conservation, publishing and business.

❝ STUDENT VIEW ❞

'The postgraduate courses at Oxford Brookes are really focused on boosting your career and widening your horizons. The staff are really passionate about their subjects and supportive, plus the libraries and computing services are a great resource to draw on.' Lucy Tennyson, MSc in historic conservation.

University of Plymouth

Drake Circus,
Plymouth PL4 8AA

t 01752 585858
e prospectus@plymouth.ac.uk
↗ www.plymouth.ac.uk

 www.plymouth.ac.uk/pages/view.asp?page=19930

 32,351   **PG** 14%   (UK) 82%

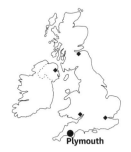

Plymouth

Plymouth is one of the largest universities in the country. A £35m complex housing the arts faculty has opened recently. The main campus is within easy walking distance of the city centre, and is a great seaside spot. Given its proximity to some of the country's loveliest beaches, watersports are popular with students. Courses relating to marine life and the oceans are particularly well-regarded. And where else could you find a degree in surf science?

Courses and qualifications There are several courses leading to DipArch, DSc, PhD, IMP, IMS, LLM, MBA, MA, MRes, MSc, NRPhD, PCET, Pg Cert, Pg Dip, DBA, DPA, EdD, MD, DClinPsy.

Fees There is a range of fees, visit: www.plymouth.ac.uk/money

Funding The university offers a number of scholarships. The taught programmes scholarship covers EU/UK tuition fees only and the research programmes scholarship covers EU/UK tuition fees, plus a stipend at least equal to the minimum given by the research councils.

Accommodation Some double rooms are available in halls of residence. A buoyant private sector, where rent is very competitively priced. Contact: accommodation@plymouth.ac.uk

Facilities The library provides 24/7 access to computing and media areas. There's a state-of-the-art sports centre and a diving and marine centre, where students can gain an internationally recognised diving qualification.

A graduate school provides a range of support including facilities for learning with open access computing and study zones within the library; access to the postgraduate portal; links to other electronic databases; opportunities for research students to develop research/professional skills; social space in which to meet staff and other postgraduates and a postgraduate society.

Transport The campus is in the city centre. About three hours by train to London.

Specialism Health and biomedicine; creative arts, design and technology; economic, social and environmental sustainability, marine sciences.

University of Portsmouth

University House,
Winston Churchill Avenue,
Portsmouth PO1 2UP

t 02392 848484
e info-centre@port.ac.uk
↗ www.port.ac.uk

» www.port.ac.uk/courses/postgraduate

 16,633 **PG** 12%

Portsmouth is based on two sites: the Langstone campus is on the eastern edge of Portsea Island, and the University Quarter is the name given to the grouping of university buildings in the city centre, which include impressive modern buildings and green park space. Portsmouth is compact and easy to navigate, and the seaside location is a real plus. There are good opportunities for part-time and vacation work, not to mention an active careers service.

Portsmouth

Courses and qualifications There are 140 programmes leading to MA, MSc, MPhil, PhD, MBA, PGCE.

Fees Fees vary and can be checked online at: www.port.ac.uk/departments/services/academicregistry/studentadministrationdivision/registrationandinvoicing/tuitionfees/feecheck

Funding There is a 20 per cent discount for Portsmouth alumni and subject-specific bursaries.

Accommodation For details of accommodation contact: student.housing@port.ac.uk

Facilities Include a state-of-the-art newsroom for the journalism course and the new Expert Centre, equipped with computerised mannequins that breathe, bleed and react to drugs (for people on health courses, not just for fun). The students' union is award-winning. There are halls of residence and specialist study facilities.

Transport London is just over an hour away. The station is near the university, so there's easy access to much of the rest of the south too.

Specialism Criminal justice studies is regarded as a national centre of excellence. The MBA is AMBA accredited.

ᴄᴄ STUDENT VIEW ᴅᴅ

'I decided to do a degree at Portsmouth after it was recommended by a friend. The lecturers here are world-class engineers in their field so deciding to stay on and do my MSc here was the best decision I ever made. When I chose to do the MSc I was lucky enough to get some funding through the Engineering and Physical Sciences Research Council (EPSRC) for my tuition fees and a maintenance grant which has helped enormously.' David Hume, MSc in mechanical engineering.

Queen Margaret University

Queen Margaret University Drive,
Musselburgh EH21 6UU

t 0131 474 0000
e admissions@qmu.ac.uk
↗ www.qmu.ac.uk

 5,655   **PG** 22%   (UK) 70%

Edinburgh's fourth university, granted full status in January 2007, is on a new, purpose-built campus in Musselburgh, just to the east of the city. Students can enjoy all the facilities of Scotland's terrific capital city but also escape the bustle. Almost 80 per cent of students are women. There's an emphasis on vocational education, which accounts for the good graduate employment rates. The university prides itself on a supportive and relaxed atmosphere and its engagement with the local community.

Courses and qualifications There are 53 different courses leading to Pg Cert, Pg Dip, MSc, MA, MBA, MPhil, PhD.

Fees For the 2008/9 academic year the fees ranged from:
UK/EU students: £3,315 to £7,350.
International students: £9,700 to £12,550.

Funding There are a number of SAAS awards available for a selection of courses. The university also offers up to 10 competitive scholarships of £1,000 each for new international students undertaking their first year of study on a postgraduate degree. The scholarship is granted as a reduction of the tuition fee and is available to students who are self-funding with an international tuition fee of more than £8,000 for a single year of study only.

Accommodation None specifically for postgraduates. There are nearly 300 rooms which can be used for postgraduate and mature students on campus.
Contact: accommodation@qmu.ac.uk

Facilities The new campus includes a purpose built students' union, an innovative learning resource centre and indoor and outdoor sports facilities. There is a designated study room for postgraduates within the Learning Resource Centre.

Transport It's the Scottish capital with all the links that that implies. The airport is eight miles away.

Specialism Research expertise in a wide range of health professions, including speech and language sciences, physiotherapy, dietetics etc which do not have a long research tradition.

❝ STUDENT VIEW ❞

'QMU has provided sponsorship for my PhD, gave me lecturing experience, allowed me to present my research findings at conferences throughout the UK and has helped me develop international career contacts. With my PhD now firmly under my belt, I'm well-equipped to pursue my dream job working as a university lecturer.' Majella Sweeney, BA (Hons) tourism management and PhD in hospitality and small business.

Queen Mary, University of London

327 Mile End Road,
Poplar,
London E1 4NS

t 020 7882 5555
e admissions@qmul.ac.uk
↗ www.qmul.ac.uk

» www.qmul.ac.uk/postgraduate/index.html?

 15,000   **PG** 13%

Queen Mary gives you the best of both worlds – life on a contained campus, but in the middle of a huge city. Queen Mary's main campus is located in the Mile End area of east London: not the most salubrious part, but handy for town and with a certain charm all of its own. It's a multicultural area, so the university fits right in: about a fifth of its students are from international backgrounds. As well as having a good standard of teaching and research, its one of the best universities for student employability – and graduate starting salaries.

London

Courses and qualifications There are 300 courses leading to LLM, MA, MSc, MPhil, PhD, MRes, MClin, DClin, MD, MS, PG Dip, PG Cert.

Fees
UK/EU students: £3,964 (taught), £3,300 (research).
International students: Arts £9,000, lab £11,000 (taught). Arts £8,800, lab £9,900 (research). Plus exceptions, medical and dentistry school prices vary.

Funding Scholarships, studentships, bursaries and prizes amounted to £17m in 2007-08.

Accommodation There is accommodation for families. Contact: residences@qmul.ac.uk

Facilities A budget of £682,000 has been allocated for upgrading the library. Over the last four years, £46m has been spent on the student village. £5.3m has been spent on the students' union Drapers Bar and Fitness Centre. £5.7m has been invested in teaching facilities and research income increased from £51.4m (2006-07) to £60.7m in 2008.

Transport Easy access to the London transport system for travel between campuses, around the city and beyond.

Specialism Law, sports medicine, English, history, drama, economics, statistics, film, Iberian languages.

❝ STUDENT VIEW ❞

'I decided to come to Queen Mary as I wanted to gain a master's degree from a world-renowned institute. When I first joined the university, the academic staff were very supportive and helpful, and I instantly felt comfortable. I am very pleased to have worked with such a great research team and remarkable academic staff. As well as such a friendly department.' Amanmammet Bugreyev, MSc in biological and chemical sciences.

Queen's University Belfast

University Road,
Belfast BT7 1NN

t 028 9024 5133
e comms.office@qub.ac.uk
↗ www.qub.ac.uk

» www.qub.ac.uk/home/ProspectiveStudents/PostgraduateStudents

 20,500   **PG** 23%

Queen's has a good academic reputation. The campus is a 15-minute walk from the city centre, by the lovely botanic gardens and the Ulster Museum. Queen's takes its role in the community seriously: there's the annual Belfast festival at Queen's, a film festival, an art gallery and Northern Ireland's only arthouse cinema. It all puts Queen's at the heart of what is rapidly becoming one of Europe's most exciting and trendy cities.

Belfast

Courses and qualifications Approximately 200 programmes of study, leading to MA, MBA, MSc, MRes, Pg Cert, PGCE, Pg Dip or PhD.

Fees
UK/EU students: full-time taught and research fees are £3,300.
International students: £8,970 for a classroom-based course, £10,990 for the laboratory-based courses.

Funding There may be funding from the university depending on your course and situation.

Accommodation There is accommodation for postgraduates. International students take precedence when allocating rooms within halls. The university has a limited amount of accommodation for married students.

Facilities The students' union features a brand new Wi-Fi-enabled social space and a recently refurbished bar (one of three on offer). It also hosts popular concerts and club nights. Good sports facilities.

Transport Easy to get out into Northern Ireland. Most major British cities are within an hour's flying time from one of Belfast's two airports. These airports offer flights to many locations in Ireland and mainland Europe, as well as several direct services to North America. Dublin is a two-hour train journey from Belfast and there are regular ferry services to Scotland and England.

Specialism The research strengths are reflected in the award of four Queen's Anniversary Prizes for further and higher education – for world-class achievement in green chemistry, environmental research, palaeoecology and law.

❝ STUDENT VIEW ❞

'I decided to come to Queen's so that I could develop professional skills under the mentorship of internationally-renowned faculty members, who are also involved in policy-making, capacity-building and international development. The focus here is on skills-development and promoting critical and independent thinking. Queen's focuses heavily on investing in knowledge for social advancement. Also, Belfast is a great city. People here are warm-hearted and friendly.' Ajith Kaliyat, PhD in urban sustainability issues in Chennai.

Ravensbourne College of Design and Communication

Walden Road,
Chislehurst,
Kent BR7 5SN

t 020 8289 4900
e info@rave.ac.uk
↗ www.rave.ac.uk

 ma.rave.ac.uk

 1,500   **PG** 35%   (UK) 60%

Apart from being the higher education institution with the most memorable web address, Ravensbourne is a single-campus college of design and communication, based in 18 acres of parkland to the south-east of London, near Chislehurst in Kent. Courses are offered within two faculties — design, where courses include fashion, interior design and product design, and communications media where courses include broadcasting, graphic and sound design and animation.

London

Courses and qualifications There are seven courses leading to MA, MSc, MArch and MInnov (Master of Innovation). More courses are planned.

Fees
UK/EU students: £3,500.
International students: £9,600.

Funding There are several based on talent and circumstances, details on website. There is a 10 per cent discount for early payment (June).

Accommodation None specifically for postgraduates, but campus accommodation is prioritised for international students. For further information contact: info@rave.ac.uk

Facilities Students enjoy large and airy open-plan studios and high-standard individual workspaces.
  There is a common room, studio, experimental lab, VR-Set (virtual studio), CAVE system.

Transport Central London is just 20 minutes away by train, and there is easy access to Europe via the Channel Tunnel.

Specialism Interactive digital media.

◀◀ STUDENT VIEW ▶▶

'Ravensbourne offered me the best opportunity to develop the advanced expertise and specialist skills needed for today's creative industries. I enjoy being in the centre of a genuinely innovative community that nurtures original thinking and produces some phenomenal award winners in every creative discipline.' JeeHyun Oh, MA in networked media environments.

University of Reading

Whiteknights, PO Box 217,
Reading,
Berkshire RG6 6AH

t 0118 987 5123
e student.recruitment@reading.ac.uk
↗ www.reading.ac.uk

 www.reading.ac.uk/Study/study-pg.asp

17,500   **PG** 27%

Reading is a redbrick university that celebrated its 80th birthday in 2006. It's a popular choice and claims to receive eight applications for every place. It's academically sound with an innovative slant to its course portfolio – as well as all the old favourites, there are courses in subjects like cybernetics. The sports centre has just been refurbished to the tune of £2.2m and there's a new student services centre, too. Reading is an easy-going, lively town with excellent facilities for shopping and leisure. It's about 45 miles west of London and transport links to the surrounding area are really good. The main Whiteknights campus is one of the most charming in the UK, with a lake, woodland and even meadows to stroll through on your way to lectures.

Courses and qualifications There are over 200 taught courses (a wide range of short courses and CPD), and more than 700 research areas leading to MPhil, MA, MARes, MFA, LLM, MRes, MSc, Pg Dip, Pg Cert, PhD, MBA, Diplomas etc.

Fees
UK/EU students: £3,575.
International students: £9,350 (average).
Some courses have different fee structures – see website for details.

Funding Available funding includes University of Reading Postgraduate Research Studentships, faculty studentships, and school and department scholarships.

Accommodation For details contact: accommodation@reading.ac.uk

Facilities The library contains more than a million volumes, there's advanced electronic media available and online study resources. Other facilities include 24-hour computer rooms, research centres and specific study facilities in graduate schools.

Transport Located within the M25, there's easy access to central London by train as well.

Specialism Climate systems science, food chain and health, biomedical and pharmaceutical science, neuroscience, ageing, ecosystems science, nanoscience, sustainable environments and technologies, computational science, modern European histories, poverty exclusion, international capital markets.

❝ STUDENT VIEW ❞

'I chose to study as a postgraduate at the University of Reading because of the quality and the expertise of the academic staff here in my field (horticulture). They have a very good reputation both nationally and internationally and I relocated from Greece just to study here.' Eleftherios K Karapatzak, postgraduate student in horticulture.

Robert Gordon University

Schoolhill,
Aberdeen AB10 1FR

t 01224 262000
e admissions@rgu.ac.uk
↗ www.rgu.ac.uk

» **www.rgu.ac.uk/prospectus/disp_ProspSearch.cfm**

 13,851   **PG** 35%

RGU is a modern university. The city-centre campus at Schoolhill is the hub of student social life; a second campus is just under three miles away at Garthdee. The emphasis at RGU is firmly on vocational and professional courses, and a wide range of placement options is on offer, both here and abroad. As a result, RGU has one of the best graduate recruitment records in the UK. Aberdeen is a smart and pleasant city with a cosmopolitan and rather wealthy feel to it, thanks to the impact of North Sea oil. It's affectionately called the Granite City after the primary building material, and it really does sparkle in the sun.

Aberdeen

Courses and qualifications There are 11 programmes leading to MSc, MPhil, PhD, MBA, MPA, Pg Cert, Pg Dip, DBA, Graduate Certificate, MFA, MDes.

Fees
UK/EU students: range from £4,420 to £14,400.
International students: range from £9,350 to £14,400.

Funding There is a wide range of scholarship opportunities, for details view: www.rgu.ac.uk/ scholarships

Accommodation There are postgraduate halls of residence but no family accommodation. Contact: accommodation@rgu.ac.uk

Facilities RGU has invested over £10m in a state-of-the-art sports facility, which sees a dramatic improvement in sporting infrastructure available for the region and also acts as a social hub for the Garthdee campus. The facility features a 25-metre swimming pool, three gyms, climbing wall and bouldering room, cafe bar, three exercise studios and a vast sports hall.

Transport Transport between campuses is easy. Aberdeen is two and a half hours' drive from Edinburgh or Glasgow or take one of the regular trains. Seven hours by train from London. Hour-long flights from London.

Specialism RGU is known worldwide for its postgraduate energy courses. It is also the only university outside of North America to have a CAPTE accredited MSc physiotherapy (pre-registration).

Roehampton University

Erasmus House,
Roehampton Lane,
London SW15 5PU

t 020 8392 3232
e enquiries@roehampton.ac.uk
↗ www.roehampton.ac.uk

》 www.roehampton.ac.uk/postgraduate-courses/index.html

 8,078 **PG** 23% (**UK**) 55%

Roehampton is a campus university based in a scenic parkland location, complete with lakes and woodland walks, overlooking Richmond Park. The campus contains a mixture of architectural styles ranging from 18th-century Grade 1 listed buildings to brand new modern structures. It's close to the chi-chi London districts of Richmond and Putney, and central London is only a few minutes away by train. Significant proportions of Roehampton's 8,000 students are mature or from an ethnic minority, and women outnumber men by three to one.

London

Courses and qualifications There are several courses leading to MA, MSc, MRes, Pg Dip, Pg Cert, MBA, MPhil, PhD, PGCE, PsychD.

Fees
UK/EU students: range from £3,700 to £6,500.
International students: £9,000.

Funding The university offers a scholarship of £1,000 to PGCE students with a first class honours degree. There are scholarships available for international students. See: www.roehampton.ac.uk/admissions/international/finance/scholarships/index

Accommodation For details contact: accommodation@roehampton.ac.uk

Facilities The library contains a cyber cafe, there are innovative teaching facilities, and sports resources are enjoying multi-million pound development work. The state-of-the-art campus facilities are central to the postgraduate student experience. The well-stocked library is staffed by helpful and knowledgeable librarians. The campus also features a range of amenities for specific subjects, such as dance studios and sport and bioscience laboratories. The university has recently refurbished all teaching rooms and is progressing with an ambitious programme of estate development. There are some specific quiet study areas and some postgraduate specific accommodation.

Transport Only 20 minutes to London by train. From there, the world's your oyster.

Specialism Arts and play therapies, children's literature, audiovisual translation, education, non-profit management, primatology, counselling psychology.

❝ STUDENT VIEW ❞

'Each week the course puts on a seminar where professionals in the field come to give a talk on their current research. It's a great way to meet contacts and it's really exciting to meet influential people in the field, people whose work I've been reading for years.' Lisa Reamer, MRes in primatology.

Rose Bruford College

Burnt Oak Lane,
Sidcup,
Kent DA15 9DF

t 020 8308 2600
e enquiries@bruford.ac.uk
↗ www.bruford.ac.uk

》 **www.bruford.ac.uk/courses.aspx**

 900   **PG** 3%   (UK) 60%

Rose Bruford College is a drama school based in attractive grounds near Sidcup, Kent, on the outskirts of south-east London. Founded in 1950, the college pioneered the first acting degree in 1976. It offers a range of honours degree courses in theatre and performance, validated by the University of Manchester. Facilities include two theatres – the 330-seat Rose, a theatre in the round, and the end-stage Barn Theatre – plus studios for rehearsals, design, lectures, teachings and recording, plus lighting-design labs and a workshop complex.

London

Courses and qualifications There are six courses leading to MA, MPhil or PhD.

Fees Contact the college for further information.

Funding No funding is available.

Accommodation None available for families.

Facilities There's an extensive library, including impressive specialist collections. Unsurprisingly, facilities for performance are good.

Transport 25 minutes journey into London.

Specialism Theatre and performance.

Royal Academy of Music

Marylebone Road,
London NW1 5HT

t 020 7873 7373
e registry@ram.ac.uk
↗ www.ram.ac.uk

» **www.ram.ac.uk/study/programmesofstudy/postgraduate+programmes**

 650   **PG** 55%

Founded in 1822, the Royal Academy of Music is one of the oldest and most prestigious conservatoires (schools of music) in the UK. It is based in upmarket Marylebone, central London – and musicians study for University of London degrees, in varying programmes including instrumental performance, composition, jazz, musical theatre and opera. There is a range of orchestras and ensembles which give public performances, in spaces such as the 400-seat Dukes Hall. The student community is international, with more than 50 countries represented; there is even an 'English for musicians' course. Musicians who have studied at the academy include Lesley Garrett, Sir Elton John and Myleene Klass.

London

Courses and qualifications MA, MMus, MPhil, PhD.

Fees
UK/EU students: range from £4,500 to £10,800.
International students: range from £10,800 to £18,500.

Funding Contact the academy for details of available funding.

Accommodation None for families. For further information contact: www.lon.ac.uk/halls

Facilities Impressive facilities for performance and rehearsal. There are no specific postgraduate facilities; all students have access to all facilities.

Transport The academy is in the heart of London, providing easy access to and from all parts of the city and beyond.

Specialism Any specialisms in music, including opera, composition, instrumental performance, musical theatre.

❝ STUDENT VIEW ❞
'Being at the academy really is a total preparation for a successful professional life.'
Milos Karadaglic, guitarist.

Royal Agricultural College

Stroud Road,
Cirencester GL7 6JS

t 01285 652531
e admissions@rac.ac.uk
↗ www.rac.ac.uk

 800   **PG** 18%   (UK) 75%

The Royal Agricultural College is a single-campus university college in Cirencester, Gloucestershire. Situated in an Oxbridge-style quadrangle in attractive parkland, the college is a charming place to live and study – though it has a reputation for being a refuge of the Land Rover-driving classes.

Courses and qualifications There are 14 programmes leading to MA, MSc, MBA, PhD, MPhil, Pg Dip plus MPhil and PhD based on individual proposals.

Fees
UK/EU students: range from £5,125 to £8,150.
International students: range from £7,650 to £9,350.

Funding Some available, contact the college for details.

Accommodation For information contact: lettings@rac.ac.uk

Facilities Facilities include three working commercial farms, with a 250-cow dairy herd, a 1,650-ewe breeding flock, and 250 hectares of crops including organic produce. Other facilities include a common room and halls of residence.

Transport Your four-wheel drive will come in handy for the journey into Cirencester. From there access to public transport is easy.

Specialism Agri-business and land and property management.

Royal College of Art

Kensington Gore,
London SW7 2EU

t 020 7590 4444
e admissions@rca.ac.uk
↗ www.rca.ac.uk

 850   **PG** 100%   (UK) 62%

The Royal College of Art is the only wholly postgraduate university of art and design in the world. It started life as the government school of design in 1836, only becoming the Royal College of Art in 1896. In 1967 the college was granted a Royal Charter, endowing it with university status and the power to grant its own degrees.

Courses and qualifications There are 19 programmes leading to MA, MPhil, PhD.

Fees 2007/08 fees:
UK/EU students: £4,780.
Channel Islands and Isle of Man students: £11,425.
International students: £28,850.

Funding To ensure that everyone offered a place is able to enrol, the college administers a bursary scheme and annually allocates £2.8m in direct student funding.

Accommodation None available through the college.

Facilities As an exclusively postgraduate college all facilities are available to postgraduate students.

Transport The college's central London location means that tubes and buses are all around.

Specialism The RCA is one of the world's top art and design universities.

Royal College of Music

Prince Consort Road,
London SW7 2BS

t 020 7859 3643
e info@rcm.ac.uk
↗ www.rcm.ac.uk

>> www.rcm.ac.uk/?pg=351

 600   **PG** 40%   (UK) 50%

Students at London's Royal College of Music have no
excuse not to feel inspired: not only are they at one of the
top conservatoires in the country, attracting more than
600 students from 49 countries; they also practice directly
opposite the Royal Albert Hall. Facilities are top-notch and the
RCM is aware that they have a duty to prepare their students
for viable careers in a difficult industry, not just teach them
how to make beautiful music.

London

Courses and qualifications Seven programmes
leading to Pg Dip, MMus or DMus.

Fees
UK/EU students: £6,552 for the master's
programmes.
International students: £15,280 for the master's
programmes.

Funding RCM scholarships and study awards
are available to home/EU and international
applicants at postgraduate level. The
scholarships and study awards provide support
for tuition fees (up to full fees). At the time
of your audition, you will automatically be
considered for an RCM scholarship provided
you audition in person and are applying for
an eligible course. They are awarded on merit
as part of the audition process. No separate
application is needed.

Accommodation The RCM's hall of residence
accommodates up to 170 full-time male and
female undergraduate and postgraduate
students. College Hall is situated in West
London, within easy travelling distance of the
college via underground train from Ravenscourt
Park to South Kensington (approximately
40 minutes door to door). Places in halls are
allocated on a priority basis with international
and new students taking precedence.

Facilities Facilities include the 400-seat Britten
Theatre and the RCM's digital studios.

Transport Easy, you're in the middle of London.

Specialism Music.

Royal Holloway, University of London

Egham,
Surrey TW20 0EX

t 01784 434455
e admissions@rhul.ac.uk
↗ www.rhul.ac.uk

>> **www.rhul.ac.uk/prospective-students/postgraduates/**

 7,680   **PG** 25%

Though part of the University of London and certainly within easy reach of the capital, Royal Holloway is actually based in Egham, Surrey. The campus is 135 acres of parkland, within walking distance of Windsor Great Park. New programmes are continually being developed, some through collaborative links such as the exciting new dual award master's degree programme in petroluem geoscience.

Courses and qualifications There are several courses leading to MA, MMus, MSc, MBA, Pg Cert, Pg Dip, MPhil, PhD.

Fees
UK/EU students: range from £3,300 to £6,368. MBA, £15,832.
International students: range from £11,555 to £15,832.

Funding There are scholarships, bursaries and assistantships.

Accommodation There are halls of residence and accommodation for families. Contact: accommodation@rhul.ac.uk

Facilities Postgraduates are supported by the graduate school and a research skills programme to develop a wide range of transferable and career-oriented skills. The support and advisory services, educational support office and careers service have staff devoted to supporting postgraduates. There is also specialist help from the postgraduate officer in the students' union. The college also offers inSTIL, a programme in teaching skills to inspire learning. The recently formed South West London Academic Network (SWAN) is a unique alliance between Royal Holloway, Kingston University and St George's University of London. SWAN is active in enhancing postgraduate provision through the pooling of expertise and resources in departments across the three institutions. An Institute of Biomedical and Life Sciences (IBLS) has already been established.

Transport Pretty well-serviced by road and rail. London is only 20 miles away.

Specialism Information security technology.

❝ STUDENT VIEW ❞

'The teaching expertise at Royal Holloway, University of London was the main reason I chose to complete my MA in history at the college, as well as its outstanding reputation in research. Following completion of my MA at Royal Holloway I hope that a variety of additional career options will be available to me.'
Daniel Hampton, history MA.

Royal Northern College of Music

124 Oxford Road,
Manchester M13 9RD

t 0161 907 5200
e info@rncm.ac.uk
↗ www.rncm.ac.uk

» **www.rncm.ac.uk/content/view/159/64/**

 663   **PG** 25%

The Royal Northern College of Music is based in a single
building in the south of central Manchester. September
2009 sees the launch of the RNCM's new graduate school,
which draws the college's exciting range of postgraduate
programmes together to create a new and vibrant community
of postgraduates. The ethos behind the school is one of
optimum flexibility at all levels. Whether students want to
pursue professional training or research at the highest level,
or are only able to study on a part-time independent basis,
graduate school programmes can be tailor-made to meet those
needs. Flexible modes of study enable students to follow
a range of specialist pathways – as a chamber musician, an
orchestral musician, or a high-flying soloist – or to create a
bespoke programme of study to suit their own needs.

Courses and qualifications There are several
programmes leading to MMus, MMus, Pg Dip,
Pg Dip, PGCE, Pg Cert PAE, MPhil, PhD.

Fees
UK/EU students: range from £3,145 to £7,150.
International students: range from £13,150 to
£14,300.

Funding Postgraduate applicants may apply
for bursaries towards the cost of fees and
maintenance.
  Each year the RNCM nominates one
outstanding postgraduate applicant for an
Associated Board Scholarship.

Accommodation None for families.

Facilities The 616-capacity Bruntwood Theatre
is one of the largest performance spaces in
Manchester.

Transport Pretty well-serviced by road and rail
in the Greater Manchester area. Oxford Road
station is an eight-minute walk from campus
and London is two and a half hours by train.
Manchester airport is 15 minutes away.

Specialism Music.

 STUDENT VIEW »
*'As part of the college ensembles you get unique opportunities to work with some of the world's best
musicians. It's always an exiting experience to hear the views of and make music with visiting artists.'*

Royal Scottish Academy of Music and Drama

100 Renfrew Street,
Glasgow G2 3DB

t 0141 332 4101
e musicadmissions@rsamd.ac.uk
or dramaadmissions@rsamd.ac.uk
↗ www.rsamd.ac.uk

》 www.rsamd.ac.uk/postgraduate

 800   **PG** 20%   (**UK**) 52%

The Royal Scottish Academy of Music and Drama (RSAMD) is a music and drama school in Glasgow, whose history can be traced back to 1847; it now attracts students from more than 20 countries. The alumni list is very impressive: Alan Cumming, James McAvoy and David Tennant, just for starters. Glasgow is a fun place to be a student, and opportunities for performance are ample.

Glasgow

Courses and qualifications There are several leading to MA, MMus, PhD, MPhil, MOpera, Pg Dip.

Fees
UK/EU students: range from £4,047 to £9,000.
International students: range from £11,499 to £13,824.

Funding Bursaries, scholarships and financial support are on offer. Contact the academy for details.

Accommodation Family accommodation is not offered.

Facilities Facilities and venues include the Sir Alexander Gibson Opera School and the 344-seat New Athenaeum Theatre, plus a studio theatre and concert hall. Students have access to the academy facilities which include practice rooms, library and IT suite.

Transport Easily accessible from major approach roads. The airport is handy, as are the stations.

Specialism The academy specializes in music and drama.

Royal Veterinary College, University of London

Royal College Street,
London NW1 0TU

t 020 7468 5149
e registry@rvc.ac.uk
↗ www.rvc.ac.uk

>> www.rvc.ac.uk/Education/Postgraduate/Index.cfm

 1,863   **PG** 22%   (UK) 66%

Founded in 1791, the Royal Veterinary College (RVC) was the UK's first veterinary school, and remains its largest. A college of the University of London, RVC is based at two campuses: Camden, north London, and Hawkshead in Hertfordshire.

Courses and qualifications There are five taught MSc courses on campus, two MSc/Pg Dip courses via distance learning, various PhDs and Clinical Training Scholarships Postgraduate Diploma, MSc, MRes, MPhil, and PhD.

Fees
UK/EU students: range from £4,640 to £7,820.
International students: range from £14,600 to £18,240.

Funding Four BBSRC scholarships a year are offered for the MSc in veterinary epidemiology. The college also offers small bursaries for the MSc in control of infectious diseases in animals. See: www.rvc.ac.uk/postgrad

Accommodation No family accommodation (although students can apply independently to some of the University of London halls). For information contact: www.lon.ac.uk/halls

Facilities Research and treatment facilities are used by the profession, meaning students have access to top-class resources. The RVC is a small veterinary college and all student facilities are shared between all students.

Transport Located in and around London, there is easy access to and from all campuses and other parts of the city — and beyond.

Specialism RVC is the only university in the world to offer the MSc in wild animal health and an MSc in wild animal biology. The MSc in veterinary epidemiology is taught jointly with the London School of Hygiene and Tropical Medicine (LSHTM), and also with teaching contributions from the UK government agencies, the VLA and Defra. Other MSc VE courses concentrate only on the veterinary aspect, RVC students share lectures with LSHTM where human epidemiology is also covered.

 STUDENT VIEW >>

'The MSc in veterinary epidemiology is a well balanced, comprehensive and compact course that has great application to my job as a veterinary officer in the Caribbean. Modules covering surveillance, farm economics, risk analysis, geographic information systems are valuable in my work in disease control and policy recommendations. Aspects of the course are conducted by both the Royal Veterinary College and the London School of Hygiene and Tropical Medicine which have the added benefit of interaction with other MSc students who most of which are professionals with medical, statistical, public health and policy focus.'
Gillian, MSc in veterinary epidemiology (Jamaica).

Royal Welsh College of Music & Drama

Castle Grounds,
Cathays Park,
Cardiff CF10 3ER

t 029 2034 2854
e music.admissions@rwcmd.ac.uk or
drama.admissions@rwcmd.ac.uk
↗ www.rwcmd.ac.uk

» **www.rwcmd.ac.uk/postgraduate_courses.aspx**

 640 **PG** 20% (UK) 82%

The Royal Welsh College of Music & Drama is based in Cardiff,
a thriving centre for the creative industries. Its campus is in
the centre of the city, in the grounds of Cardiff Castle. The
College has 640 students and therefore is able to provide a
friendly and supportive community. The events calendar
includes over 300 public performances every year.

Cardiff

Courses and qualifications 12 programmes of
study leading to MA, MMus, MPhil, Pg Dip or
PhD.

Fees
UK/EU students: fees vary depending on the
course.
International students: £11,045 for all full-time
courses, £5,685 for part-time courses.

Funding International students are
automatically considered for a scholarship when
you submit your application. Partial tuition
scholarships are available and are awarded by
the RWCMD based on merit following auditions.

Accommodation There is a separate block
in the halls of residence for international and
postgraduate students. Halls is a 10 minute walk
from the college.

Facilities Facilities include the Anthony Hopkins
Centre, two recital galleries, studio theatres, a
recording studio, courtyard performance space,
Bute Theatre, workshops and 50 music practice
rooms.

Transport Cardiff international airport is close at
hand, there is a frequent coach service to London
as well as frequent trains.

Specialism Acting, arts management, music,
music therapy, stage management and theatre
design.

 STUDENT VIEW »

'*My tutor here is world-class and someone I feel I will always be able to turn to for support and advice.
I've also been exposed to many academics, musicologists and performers of the highest level.*'
Benjamin Kaminski, MMus music.

University of St Andrews

St Andrews,
Fife KY16 9AJ

t 01334 476161
e student.recruitment@st-andrews.ac.uk
↗ www.st-andrews.ac.uk

》 www.st-andrews.ac.uk/admissions/pg

 7,500 **PG** 17%

St Andrews is a prestigious academic centre renowned for the quality of its teaching and research, and with a reputation for being a bit posh. There's a high independent-school intake and a raft of arcane traditions. But St Andrews does have an active commitment to widening access to the university. It's certainly popular with applicants and has one of the lowest drop-out rates in the UK. The location is special — a small, historical town tucked up on the coast of north-east Scotland. The university is a major part of life here and is fully integrated into the town.

Courses and qualifications There are 75 subject areas leading to Pg Dip, GDip, MLitt, MSc, MRes, PhD, MPhil, DLang, EngD, MD.

Fees
UK/EU students: from £3,300.
International students: range from £11,000 to £13,500.
Research: UK/EU and international students: range from £10,250 to £11,400.

Funding A variety of financial support is available, see: www.st-andrews.ac.uk/admissions/scholarships

Accommodation The university has a small stock of accommodation for couples, mainly in studio apartments and also some flats for students with families. For information contact: studacc@st-and.ac.uk

Facilities The university spends about £1.4m on books and journals each year; an extensive refurbishment of the library is underway. Sports facilities extend over 60 acres near the university halls.

There are dedicated postgraduate study areas and a postgraduate-only residence known as Deans Court.

Transport St Andrews is a walking town: you can get from one end to the other in under an hour. The nearest train station is Leuchars, which is on the main train line from London via Edinburgh. The nearest city is Dundee, approximately 30 minutes by bus or car. Edinburgh is 50 miles south and can be reached by bus, train or car. There is a small airport at Dundee and an international airport at Edinburgh.

Specialism The university has an excellent reputation in all the postgraduate subject areas delivered across four faculties: arts, science, divinity and medicine.

❝ STUDENT VIEW ❞

'St Andrews offers a lively, atmospheric and dynamic learning environment both academically and socially. This year has been challenging; I've been introduced to a more sophisticated level of study and am now attracted to a career in academia. As postgraduate senate officer, I've liaised with university working groups and the Academic Council to encourage postraduates to become more fully integrated into the community.' Ashley Cole, international security studies.

St George's, University of London

Cranmer Terrace,
London SW17 0RE

t 020 8725 2333
e enquiries@sgul.ac.uk
↗ www.sgul.ac.uk

» **www.sgul.ac.uk/postgraduate**

 3,784　**PG** 12%　(**UK**) 59%

St George's is one of the UK's best-known medical and health sciences universities. The campus, which shares a site and a history with St George's Hospital, is based in the lively and cosmopolitan area of Tooting, south-west London. St George's is home to a thriving, interdisciplinary postgraduate community, which is fully integrated into the hospital and associated Trusts. So students benefit from specialist clinical facilities and strong health sector links. It is widely known for pioneering the four-year postgraduate degree in medicine (MBBS4) and is now one of the first universities to offer the new postgraduate diploma in physician assistant studies.

London

Courses and qualifications Taught and research postgraduate qualifications in health, medical and biomedical sciences, leading to PgDip, MSc, MRes, MPhil, PhD and MD(Res) degrees.

Fees Fees vary for individual courses.
UK/EU students: £2,400 to £4,377 a year.
International students: £6,800 to £12,700.

Funding St George's, together with its partners Royal Holloway University and Kingston University, offers a number of fully-funded research scholarships each year.

Accommodation There are no specific spaces in halls of residence for postgraduates, but there are lots of reasonably-priced privately rented flats and houses around Tooting.
　Students have full use of the University of London Housing Services. This includes access to the housing database, where students can search for rooms to rent and like-minded roommates.

Facilities Specialist library resources and overnight computer access. There is a huge range of high-spec clinical facilities and specialist laboratories within both the university and the hospital.

Transport It's in London, near Tooting Broadway underground station. Earlsfield, Tooting and Wimbledon mainline stations are also close by and there are plenty of bus routes, so it's good for transport.

Specialism St George's specialises in research areas including cardiac and vascular sciences, cell signalling in medicine, infection and immunity, epidemiology and public health, genetics, medical and healthcare education, and mental health.
　Among the cutting-edge work being done at St George's is world-leading research into anti-HIV treatment, such as innovative microbicide gels.

❝ STUDENT VIEW ❞

'I love studying in a university which shares its site with a hospital. I see patients and visitors on site almost everyday and it brings a sense of reality, making me realise I am studying exactly what I love.' Nora Shrestha, postgraduate diploma in physician assistant studies.

St Mary's University College, Belfast

191 Falls Road,
Belfast BT12 6FE

t 02890 268320
www.stmarys-belfast.ac.uk

» www.stmarys-belfast.ac.uk/admissions/courseinfo.asp

 1,000 **PG** 12% (**UK**) 11%

St Mary's is a college of Queen's University Belfast, based in the Falls Road in the west of the city. The college has a long tradition of teacher education in undergraduate and postgraduate provision.

Belfast

Courses and qualifications There are four postgraduate courses leading to AdvCertEd, DASE, MEd or PGCE (Irish Medium Education).

Fees The fee for the one-year full-time PGCE (IME) is £3,225. For the master's degree, the fee will be £380 per 20-point module and £570 per 30-point module. The dissertation is equivalent to two 30-point master's level modules and attracts the equivalent fee of £1,140.

Funding UK/EU students enrolled on the PGCE (IME) course are eligible for a student loan. There are no scholarships or bursaries available for master's courses.

Accommodation The college does not have halls of residence or other accommodation but maintains a list of landlords in the local area who provide accommodation for full-time postgraduate students.

Facilities There are modern library and computing facilities; students are also entitled to use the library and computing resources at Queen's University Belfast.

Transport Frequent buses to Great Victoria Street bus and rail centre two miles away. Central station is 15 minutes by bus. Belfast's airports are easily accessible.

Specialism St Mary's University College has an excellent reputation in the field of teacher education.

St Mary's University College Twickenham

Waldegrave Road,
Strawberry Hill,
Twickenham TW1 4SX

t 020 8240 4000
e admit@smuc.ac.uk
↗ www.smuc.ac.uk

>> **www.smuc.ac.uk/study-here/postgraduate/index.htm**

 3,500   **PG** 9%

St Mary's University College was founded in 1850 as a Catholic
teacher training college, and about a third of its students
still take teaching courses, including PGCEs. The college is
popular with its undergraduates, who gave it good ratings in
recent National Student Surveys. St Mary's was granted its
own degree awarding powers in 2006 and is making plans to
slightly increase its size to gain university status.

Courses and qualifications MA, MSc, MPhil,
Pg Cert, PGCE, Pg Dip or PhD.

Fees Fees for taught programmes of study are
calculated by modules undertaken.
UK/EU students: £3,145 for the PGCE, £3,090
for MA/MSc.
International students: £7,200 for the MA, MSc,
MPhil or PhD.

Funding Non means tested loans of up to
£3,700 are available for PGCE students.

Accommodation There is postgraduate
accommodation in halls, though there is
no family accommodation available through
the university.

Facilities Good sports facilities — it is the
Institute of Sports' leading centre in London.
The college has also been identified as a training
base for the 2012 Olympics.

Transport Trains to Waterloo station from
Strawberry Hill take 35 minutes. Or take the bus
to Richmond underground station from where
you can travel in on the district line. The M3
and M4 are close by.

Specialism Education.

University of Salford

Salford,
Greater Manchester M5 4WT

t 0161 295 5000
e course-enquiries@salford.ac.uk
↗ www.salford.ac.uk

》 www.salford.ac.uk/study/postgraduate

 19,306   **PG** 17%

The university has an attractive waterside location in vastly regenerated Salford. It's about a mile and a half from Manchester city centre, with its great Victorian architecture, endless bars, clubs and shops and galleries and museums. £150m is currently being invested in new campus facilities with a palpable sense of ambition. A hefty proportion of students are from overseas and the university is renowned for its friendly atmosphere. Courses are created with future careers in mind, and there are some interesting options to choose from.

Courses and qualifications There are 87 programmes leading to MSc, MA, Pg Dip, Pg Cert, GCM, LLM.

Fees
UK/EU students: £3,300.
International students: range from £8,400 to £10,400.
For information see: www.isite.salford.ac.uk/money/fees/standard

Funding Funding is available for both home and international students.
For information see: www.pg.salford.ac.uk/funding/#internalfunding

Accommodation Accommodation is available for postgraduate students and undergraduates with children.
See: www.accommodation.salford.ac.uk

Facilities The leisure centre is open seven days a week and boasts a gym, swimming pool, sauna and spa, squash courts, climbing wall, snooker room and a multi-use sports hall. There are five libraries and good access to computers. Common rooms and other postgraduate facilities are specific to courses and subject areas.

Transport The campus is less than a mile and a half from Manchester city centre. It has excellent transport links with Salford Crescent railway station on campus and a regular bus service. It is only a couple of minutes' drive from the motorway network and less than 20 minutes' drive from Manchester International Airport.

Specialism In the RAE 2008, 83 per cent of Salford's research was internationally recognised. In the fields of architecture and the built environment and library and information management, 25 per cent of the work submitted was judged as world leading.

◀◀ STUDENT VIEW ▶▶

'I was looking for a postgraduate course in drug design and found the MSc analytical biosciences and drug design on Salford's website. It sounded like it met my requirements and the university was not too far to move to. Overall the course content was exactly what I expected and I graduated with distinction. I'm now studying for a PhD drug design at Salford and my project involves the discovery of new anti-cancer agents.'
Elizabeth Bennett, PhD student.

School of Oriental and African Studies (SOAS)

Thornhaugh Street,
Russell Square,
London WC1H 0XG

t 020 7637 2388
e study@soas.ac.uk
↗ www.soas.ac.uk

 www.soas.ac.uk/admissions/pg/postgraduate.html

 4,000 **PG** 40% (UK) or (EU) 50%

SOAS is part of the University of London and enjoys a central location in student-centric Bloomsbury, with a second campus a short distance away near King's Cross. It was initially founded in 1916 as a place to train British administrators for postings across the empire. These days, it's the UK's only higher education institution to focus on the languages, cultures and societies of Africa, Asia and the Middle East, with a worldwide reputation for its teaching and research. It has a close-knit, cosmopolitan and fascinating student population, with great student-to-teacher ratios.

London

Courses and qualifications More than 100 taught master's, plus research options. Study for an LLM, MA, MSc, MPhil, Pg Dip or PhD.

Fees
UK/EU students: £3,510 a year for research.
International students: £10,450 a year for research.

Funding SOAS offers nine Research Student Fellowships each year. Support is available through competition for scholarships and bursaries with SOAS and the University of London.

Accommodation There is limited accommodation available.

Facilities The library is recognised as a collection of national importance and IT provision is very good.

Transport It's very central to London, near Euston, St Pancras and King's Cross.

Specialism Africa, anthropology, East Asia, history, law, music, Near and Middle East, South Asia, South East Asia, and study of religions.

School of Pharmacy

29-39 Brunswick Square,
London WC1N 1AX

t 020 7753 5800
e registry@pharmacy.ac.uk
↗ www.pharmacy.ac.uk

»

 1,200   **PG** 33%

The School of Pharmacy is a specialist college of the
University of London. The college is based in the university
district of Bloomsbury, in the heart of London. It is dedicated
to teaching and research in pharmacy and pharmaceutical
sciences. There is a strong focus on four key areas of study;
drug discovery, formulation sciences, neuroscience, and
medicines use and health. New areas of significance, such as
behavioural medicine, paediatric pharmacy, gene therapy and
nanomedicine are being developed.

London

Courses and qualifications The School
of Pharmacy offers four different taught
postgraduate degrees leading to MSc. You can
also study for a Pg Dip or PhD.

Fees
UK/EU students: range from £4,400 to £13,370.
International students: £13,370.
There are exceptions, see the website for further
details.

Funding Funding is available for home and
international students. See the website for
details.

Accommodation This is very limited, for
information see: www.lon.ac.uk/halls

Facilities You can join two students' unions:
the school's own and the University of London
Union, a 10-minute walk away. ULU has great
sports and recreational facilities. Teaching
facilities are state of the art.

Transport Located in the heart of London.

Specialism Pharmacy and the pharmaceutical
sciences.

❝ STUDENT VIEW ❞

*'I came from Kuwait in 2005 to the School of Pharmacy to do an MSc in clinical pharmacy, but I think I have
gained a lot more that what I signed up for. I was privileged to receive a world-class education in one of the
most exciting cities of the whole world. I have enjoyed the experience so much that I have decided to stay on
to do a PhD. I am now halfway through my PhD, which is focusing on non-adherence to medications among
patients with diabetes. Despite all of the challenges I am enjoying every single minute and will really miss it
here when I go back home.'* Fatima Jeragh Alhaddad, PhD in clinical pharmacy.

Scottish Agricultural College

Edinburgh Campus, King's Buildings,
West Mains Road,
Edinburgh EH9 3JG

t 0800 269453
e recruitment@sac.ac.uk
↗ www.sac.ac.uk

» **www.sac.ac.uk/learning/prospective/postgrad**

 994   **PG** 19%

SAC (The Scottish Agricultural College) offers undergraduate and postgraduate courses designed to support the land-based industries and rural economy. Courses range from agriculture to business studies, environment, conservation, garden design and tourism. SAC has three campuses across Scotland – in Edinburgh, Ayr and Aberdeen, all of which are pleasant places to live and study.

Courses and qualifications There are five courses leading to Pg Dip, MSc, MPhil, PhD.

Fees
UK/EU students: £3,600.
International students: from £9,400 to £14,000.

Funding Postgraduate students may apply for SAC Centenary Bursaries.

Accommodation Family accommodation may be available at the Ayr and Aberdeen campus but is not guaranteed.

Facilities SAC has farms distributed around Scotland with a comprehensive range of farming activities represented including organic, livestock, arable and dairy. Science courses at SAC are supported by modern, well-equipped teaching laboratories and each campus has its own library.

Transport Good. Even the airport is pretty close.

Specialism Organic farming, food marketing and agri-business management, livestock sciences, poultry science, rural economics, crop science and environmental sustainability.

❝ STUDENT VIEW ❞
'Being a research students at SAC means I benefit from a wealth of theoretical and practical expertise. SAC has a huge network of staff and partners throughout the rural sector which ensures constant transfer and development of knowledge.' Edinburgh based PhD student.

University of Sheffield

Western Bank,
Sheffield S10 2TN

t 0114 222 1255
e pg.admissions@sheffield.ac.uk
↗ www.sheffield.ac.uk

» **www.sheffield.ac.uk/postgraduate**

 23,914   **PG** 24%

Sheffield is always a popular choice, and the university has almost 24,000 students enjoying life in the lively and friendly northern city. Lots of students get involved in the union, or in the wealth of societies and activities the university boasts. The student media are especially well thought of. University buildings are clustered close together about a mile to the west of the city centre, where you can find all the shops, bars and pubs you could desire. The clubbing here is particularly good. Sheffield has a strong academic reputation and provides good career prospects.

Courses and qualifications There are numerous programmes leading to MA, MSc, MPhil, PhD, MBA, PGCE, MArch, PhD with Integrated Studies, MSc(Eng), MMedSci, MClinDent, Pg Cert, Pg Dip, EdD, LLM, MSc(Res), MMid, DClinPsy, MMus, MD, DMedSci.

Fees
UK/EU students: range from £3,300 to £18,300.
International students: from £9,920 to £38,580.

Funding Funding is available for home and international students. See the website for details: www.sheffield.ac.uk/pgresearch/studentships and www.sheffield.ac.uk/nrphd

Accommodation There are several self-contained apartments and houses suitable for couples and families. For information contact: studentoffice@sheffield.ac.uk

Facilities The students' union is award-winning and has great facilities and events.

Transport The central position makes it good for getting about the rest of the country and there's a decent local public transport system too.

❝ STUDENT VIEW ❞

'I have good supervisors and the freedom to follow my own initiative. The university facilities are excellent. Having been in Sheffield for the past six years it is nice to see the needs of an ever-growing student body constantly updated and met.' Sam Clarke, PhD in civil and structural engineering.

Sheffield Hallam University

City Campus,
Howard Street,
Sheffield S1 1WB

t 0114 225 5555
e enquiries@shu.ac.uk
↗ www.shu.ac.uk

》 www.shu.ac.uk/study/pg/

 29,409　**PG** 25%

Sheffield Hallam is one of the largest universities in the country. It's based on two campuses, one in the bustling city centre and the other out in the leafy suburbs. Investment of £115m over the past 10 years has given the university modern, well-equipped teaching facilities. The university takes its links with business seriously, and has England's largest number of students on courses with work placements. Sheffield has great facilities and good transport links. It claims to be the greenest city in England, and is within easy reach of Leeds, Manchester and the Peak District.

Courses and qualifications There are 241 programmes leading to MBAs, MAs, MScs and doctorates as well as professional development degrees, diplomas and certificates.

Fees Fees differ in each category. See website for details.

Funding The student finance centre (SFC) deals with applications for bursaries and gives advice and information on loans. It also manages the access to learning funds and emergency loan schemes. Sheffield Hallam offers a postgraduate bursary for students who complete their undergraduate degree at Sheffield Hallam. To be eligible for the bursary, students must have received funding from the LEA for their undergraduate degree.

Accommodation It is possible to find good-quality rented, owned or part-owned housing in Sheffield to accommodate students with families. Detailed advice is given in the publication 'A Rough Guide to Househunting' which can be downloaded and is also available from accommodation services.

Facilities Good learning and teaching facilities, a lively students' union, plentiful sports provision and one of the UK's leading universities in e-learning. None specifically for postgraduates.

Transport Easy to hop on a train to London, Leeds or Manchester. Good public transport in town.

Specialism Art and design, history, metallurgy and materials, sports-related subjects, town and country planning, English language and literature, biomedical sciences.

❝ STUDENT VIEW ❞

'The main reason I returned to Sheffield was academic, my MSc supervisor has a very good reputation in the field of tourism and I wanted to benefit from his knowledge again. Also, on a practical level, Sheffield is still much cheaper than many other cities in the UK and because of its size, it is very convenient. The city also has some excellent nightlife and entertainment and is a great student city.'

University of Southampton

Highfield Campus,
University Road,
Southampton SO17 1BJ

t 023 8059 5000
e prospenq@soton.ac.uk
↗ www.soton.ac.uk

» www.soton.ac.uk/postgraduate/index.shtml

 24,500   **PG** 21%

Founded in 1952, Southampton is an innovative university with a diverse student population. Its main Highfield campus is located two miles from the centre of Southampton, with other sites spread across Southampton and Winchester. The active students' union recently launched a TV station to accompany its award-winning radio station.

Southampton

Courses and qualifications There are over 300 programmes leading to LLM, MA, MBA, MBV, MMus, MPhil, MRes, MSc, EdD, EngD, DClinP, DClinPsy, DM, PhD.

Fees
UK/EU students: range from £3,145 to £3,300.
International students: range from £9,380 to £23,280.

Funding Funding is available. For information visit: www.soton.ac.uk/postgraduate/feesandfunding/pgfundbyschool

Accommodation UK/EU postgraduates are offered a place in halls during their first year of study subject to certain criteria.
   International students are guaranteed a place in halls for the full normal duration of their degree programme subject to certain criteria. Families may be able to have university-owned accommodation.
   For information contact: accommodation@soton.ac.uk

Facilities A variety of multi-access computer servers are available to support postgraduate research. The university also hosts one of the UK's e-Science centres as part of the e-Grid.

All campuses and halls are equipped with state-of-the-art computer facilities that are available to all students. You can take advantage of self-service wired and wireless high-speed connections from many campus locations. When you're away from campus you will still have access to university central services. There are six libraries based around the university to satisfy all academic needs.
   Specialist equipment and assistive technology is available for people with disabilities, specific learning difficulties, or chronic medical conditions.

Transport There are good train and motorway links.

Specialism Engineering, computer science and medicine – also home to a number of world-leading research centres, including the National Oceanography Centre, Southampton, the Institute of Sound and Vibration Research, the Optoelectronics Research Centre, the Centre for the Developmental Origins of Health and Disease, the Mountbatten Centre for International Studies and the Southampton Statistical Sciences Research Institute.

❝ STUDENT VIEW ❞

'I chose to study at Southampton because it has such a good reputation and because nowadays employers seem to be looking for more and more from their applicants. I am hoping my postgraduate course will improve my employability and provide me with more opportunities.'

Southampton Solent University

East Park Terrace,
Southampton SO14 0YN

t 0845 6767000
e enquiries@solent.ac.uk
↗ www.solent.ac.uk

» www.solent.ac.uk/students/postgraduate/postgradstudy.aspx

 18,171 **PG** 4% (UK) 59%

Southampton Solent is one of the UK's newest universities, based in a lively city on the south coast. It is a modern university, close to the city centre and the waterfront. (Though it's not really a beach resort, more of an industrial port.) Unsurprisingly, maritime studies are a particular strength here, including courses in the design of yachts and small craft. Graduate employment rates are a particular source of pride for the university.

Southampton

Courses and qualifications There are 31 programmes leading to MA, MBA, MSc, LLM, PGCE, Pg Dip, MProf, PhD, MPhil.

Fees
UK/EU students: around £3,000.
International students: around £8,700.

Funding Usually offers a range of scholarships and bursaries ranging from £1,000 to £5,000.

Accommodation The university sets aside rooms within its halls of residence for postgraduate students, and provides guidance on securing accommodation within the private rented sector for families. For information contact: accommodation@solent.ac.uk

Facilities The sports centre comprises a multi-purpose sports hall, gym, changing facilities, saunas, wellness and massage rooms. The university also has its own newly-opened, purpose-built watersports centre at Warsash, at the mouth of the River Hamble. An innovative 'laptops for loan' service enables students to borrow laptops with the specific software packages they need for their course, from word processing packages to design software.

Transport The city has excellent transport links by road, rail and air, thanks to the nearby Southampton International Airport which links with a number of cities in the north of England, Scotland, Ireland and the Channel Islands.

◄◄ STUDENT VIEW ►►

'The MA media programme at Southampton gives you the chance to focus on both theoretical and vocational aspects. I also found it to be a perfect combination of professionalism and friendliness. Having gone on to undertake a PhD at Solent, I have had the chance to attend conferences, give papers, get my work published, and become a visiting scholar in Canada.' Eylem Atakav, MA in media.

Staffordshire University

College Road,
Stoke-on-Trent,
Staffordshire ST4 2DE

t 01782 294000
e admissions@staffs.ac.uk
↗ www.staffs.ac.uk

>> www.staffs.ac.uk/study_here/why_staffordshire/postgraduate_study/index.jsp

 15,719   **PG** 21%   (UK) 66%

Staffordshire University is located on two main campuses, in Stoke and Stafford, with a satellite campus in Lichfield. The Stoke campus lies close to the centre of Stoke-on-Trent, with easy access to the railway station and the amenities of the town. The Stafford campus is a mile and a half from Stafford town centre – a lively and picturesque market town. The business-orientated Lichfield campus lies some 15 miles from Stafford and is set near to the beautiful cathedral city. The university boasts a lively students' union and the cost of living in the area is relatively low, making it one of the most affordable universities.

Courses and qualifications Around 200 programmes leading to PhD, MPhil, Professional Doctorate, MA, MBA, MSc, LLM, Pg Dip, Pg Cert, PGCE.

Fees
UK/EU students: range from £2,880 to £4,680. MBA, £6,700.
International students: start at £9,395.

Funding Alumni are entitled to 15 per cent discount off subsequent courses. There is an early payment discount of 5 per cent where course fees are paid within first four weeks of teaching. Postgraduates in receipt of approved benefits may be entitled to a discount of up to 50 per cent.

Accommodation There's no university accommodation, but the university operates a landlord registration scheme whereby all properties have to be of a specific standard.

Facilities Facilities include a professionally-equipped media centre, music, film, TV and radio studios, a crime scene house, nature reserve, drama studio and mock courtroom. All facilities are shared with undergraduates.

Transport Stoke station is a minute away and has pretty good links in all directions.

Specialism Several including business/management/marketing, art, design and ceramics, cultural studies, media, journalism, engineering, computer science and informatics, design technology, health psychology, sports science, education, philosophy, environmental and sustainable development, forensic science, law.

❝ STUDENT VIEW ❞

'Staff are just so enthusiastic and helpful and I found studying this way really cost effective. I've enjoyed every minute of my time at Staffs and though it was hard work with a lot of tears, it has all been worth it'.
Jane Kennedy, PhD in local government performance.

University of Stirling

Stirling FK9 4LA

t 01786 473171
e admissions@stir.ac.uk
↗ www.stir.ac.uk

 www.external.stir.ac.uk/postgrad/index.php

 9,000   **PG** 22%   (UK) 61%

Stirling's campus is regularly described as one of the most beautiful in the world, set in 300 acres at the foot of the Ochil Hills. Stirling is the smallest city in Scotland, but still the local centre for shopping and nightlife. There are excellent facilities for sport and a recently refurbished arts centre on campus. A significant proportion of them are from the local area, but there's also a good representation of international students. Stirling was the first university in the UK to introduce the acclaimed semester system and is proud of the flexibility of its degrees.

Courses and qualifications Over 70 programmes leading to MSc, MPhil, PhD, MRes, MLitt, MEd, Pg Dip, Pg cert, EdD, LLB, LLM, MBA, TQFE.

Fees See website for full details: www.external. stir.ac.uk/postgrad/finance/index.php

Funding Some available, see: www.external. stir.ac.uk/postgrad/finance/scholarships/scholarships.php

Accommodation Limited family accommodation. See website for details.

Facilities There are 24-hour computer labs, an arts centre with theatre and cinema, extensive sports facilities and a publicly accessible art collection. Most departments offer postgraduate common rooms for informal meetings, social events and group study. Research students also benefit from the Stirling Graduate Research School (SGRS) which offers the following facilities: access to most computing and library facilities at the same level as a member of staff; email access to inter-library loans; space in which to work, in an office shared with other research students in your department; the use of some office facilities, including photocopying and telephones. Postgraduates also have access to the main campus facilities.

Transport Well connected to the UK road and rail networks and only 45 minutes from both Edinburgh and Glasgow.

Specialism Health and well-being, the environment, culture and society, enterprise and the economy, and sport.

Stranmillis University College

Stranmillis Road,
Belfast BT9 5DY

t 028 9038 1271
↗ www.stran.ac.uk

>> www.stran.ac.uk/informationfor/postgraduatestudents

 1,000   **PG** 10%   (UK) 100%

Founded in 1922 as a teacher training institute, Stranmillis
is now a college of Queen's University Belfast. Its campus is
based in a conservation area, part of 18 hectares of wooded
parkland, one mile south of the city centre. The college is
proud of being an inter-faith institution.

Courses and qualifications There are four
postgraduate qualifications available. Choose
from the PGCE, Mteach, MA or MEd.

Fees
UK/EU students: £3,145 (full time), £570 per
module for part-time study.
International students: £9,000.

Funding There are bursaries for PGCE students
only.

Accommodation There isn't any family
accommodation. See: www.stran.ac.uk/
informationfor/postgraduatestudents

Facilities A well-stocked library that will loan
laptops to students, students' union, halls of
residence, coffee bars and a sports centre.

Transport An hour by air from London. Good
links with Northern Ireland and the rest of
Ireland.

Specialism Education.

University of Strathclyde

John Anderson Campus,
16 Richmond Street,
Glasgow G1 1XQ

t 0141 552 4400
e scls@mis.strath.ac.uk
↗ www.strath.ac.uk

 » www.strath.ac.uk/postgrad

 26,001 **PG** 38%

Strathclyde emphasises 'useful learning' by tailoring degrees and teaching towards the requirements of future employers. It also takes a holistic approach to university life — acknowledging students come to university to do more than just learn, and encouraging them to get involved in student activities or check out what Glasgow has to offer. There are over 20,000 students, split between the central John Anderson campus (where many students also live) and another in the west of the city. The students' union building is one of the largest in the country, though Glasgow also has plenty to offer, from swanky bars to hushed art galleries and plenty of green spaces.

Courses and qualifications There are several courses leading to PGDE, MRes, DBA, EdD, MLitt, LLB, LLM, MArch, MEd, DEdPsy, EngD.

Fees Fees vary. Full details see: www.strath.ac.uk/registry/students/finance

Funding There is an on-line searchable database of scholarship and funding opportunities at: www.strath.ac.uk/studying/prospective/financingyoureducation/scholarships

Accommodation There is some. For information contact: student.accommodation@strath.ac.uk

Facilities Some of the best student libraries in Scotland, with specialist collections for the subjects taught here. There are a range of resources for students including an online forum. The university offers specialised skills training to enhance research skills, employability and IT literacy. See the postgraduate community website at: www.strath.ac.uk/postgrad

Transport Two railway stations and an airport, plus good public transport.

Specialism Business, engineering and science. The Strathclyde Business School is the only triple-accredited business school in Scotland and is in the top one per cent of business schools worldwide.

❝ STUDENT VIEW ❞

'It was the personal touch I received from Strathclyde that helped me make my decision to study here. Coming to Glasgow, and leaving my home in Delhi for the first time was the biggest decision I have ever made, but definitely the right one. Not only is the psychology department extremely friendly and accommodating, but Glasgow as a city is so welcoming.' Shilpi Gupta, PhD psychology.

University of Sunderland

City Campus, Edinburgh Building,
Chester Road,
Sunderland SR1 3SD

t 0191 515 2000
e student-helpline@sunderland.ac.uk
↗ www.sunderland.ac.uk

》 www.sunderland.ac.uk/study/postgraduate

 17,207 **PG** 12%

The university has a total student population of over 14,000, based at two main sites. The Sir Tom Cowie campus at St Peter's, next to the River Wear, has seen an investment of over £50m in recent years and at the City campus an ambitious redevelopment programme is under way. Sunderland is a modern city, close to Newcastle, and within easy reach of some stunning coastal scenery. The city has been the focus of regeneration and investment and is continuing to grow and develop. Courses focus on vocational development and there's a good careers service.

Courses and qualifications There are 130 courses on offer. Study for a LLM, MA, MBA, MPhil, MSc, PGCE, Pg Dip or PhD.

Fees
UK/EU students: £3,965 for full-time taught courses, £3,300 for research degrees.
International students: full-time non-laboratory degrees from £8,300, full-time laboratory-based degrees from £9,100.

Funding Scholarships of £1,575 are available to international students who are studying full-time on campus for a maximum of three years duration for PhD programmes and two years for MPhil programmes.

Accommodation Postgraduate accommodation is available. Scotia Quay is allocated to postgraduate and research students only. There are a small number of family flats and houses attached to halls. There are one bed flats suitable for couples, two bed flats and two bed houses suitable for families with one or two children but you are advised to apply early.

Facilities The Murray Library has recently undergone a major refurbishment, which has created a variety of areas to study in. There is also a Fairtrade cafe nearby. Libraries have got IT facilities, including a large number of PCs, scanners, networked printing facilities and wireless access to the internet. You can also borrow laptops from the university.

Transport There are good train links around the north-east. Road and rail transport to the rest of the UK is OK too.

❝ STUDENT VIEW ❞

'I came to Sunderland University as it is the A-rated university in the north east for my particular course. The facilities they offer are excellent and the organisation and structure of the course is well designed.'
Karen Maddock, PGCE (secondary education) mathematics.

University of Surrey

Guildford,
Surrey U2 7XH

t 01483 300800
e pg-enquiries@surrey.ac.uk
↗ www.surrey.ac.uk

 www2.surrey.ac.uk/postgraduate

 12,000   **PG** 34%   (UK) 39%

The main campus is on Stag Hill, in Guildford, adjacent to the cathedral. It's in charming parkland with its own lake. The new Manor Park campus, just under a mile away, has been undergoing recent development. Guildford is a rather smart town, with easy links to London. As befits a university that pioneered 'sandwich' degrees, 80 per cent of the students study on courses that include a work-based professional training year. The university is famous for its consistently outstanding employment record. The students' union has some of the best facilities in the country, and a packed calendar of events and activities.

Guildford

Courses and qualifications There are several courses leading to MA, MSc, MEng, MMath, MChem, MPhy, MPhil, PhD, PsychD, DClinP, EngD, MBA, DBA.

Fees
UK/EU students: from £3,000. MBA, £16,000.
International students: from £8,000. MBA, £16,000.

Funding There are bursaries. Contact the university for details.

Accommodation There is family and postgraduate accommodation. For details see: www.surrey.ac.uk/accommodation

Facilities Great resources for sport and physical activity, including a programme of 25 dance classes a week. There's a dedicated art gallery on campus and good library, graduate schools and study facilities.

Transport London is half an hour away by train.

Specialism All aspects of engineering as well as postgraduate medical studies, hospitality and MBAs.

University of Sussex

Sussex House,
Brighton BN1 9RH

t 01273 606755
e information@sussex.ac.uk
↗ www.sussex.ac.uk

 » www.sussex.ac.uk/pgstudy

  11,459   **PG** 25%   (UK) 61%

Sussex is the only university in England situated entirely within an area officially recognised as being one of outstanding natural beauty – the South Downs. Add to that the natural parkland environment of its friendly campus and the fact that it's only four miles from lovely Brighton, with its Pavilion, pier, beaches, bars and boutiques, and it's enough to make anyone jealous. As well as good amenities on campus, there is a large and active students' union. Sussex has a good academic reputation (the English department is particularly strong) and a history of innovative approaches to teaching and learning.

Brighton

Courses and qualifications There are 187 programmes leading to MA, MSc, LLM, Pg Dip, Pg Cert, PGCE, CPE, MPhil, DPhil, New Route DPhil, EdD.

Fees Fees vary. For details see: www.sussex.ac.uk/Units/publications/pgrad2009/fees_table

Funding Funding is available, see: www.sussex.ac.uk/Units/publications/pgrad2009/funding_table

Accommodation There are 60 small family flats in university-managed residences, mostly on campus. For information contact: housing@sussex.ac.uk

Facilities Profolio is a new professional researcher development programme for Sussex doctoral students – details can be found online at www.sussex.ac.uk/sp2/profolio

The launch of a new doctoral school in 2009 looks to enable postgraduate students and postdoctoral researchers to feel fully integrated as members of the university's wider research community. The role of the school will include the organisation of skills training for postgraduates and will look at the bursaries and financial support on offer for postgraduates.

There are also excellent library, IT and sports facilities, Wi-Fi, and an extensive sports programme.

Transport London is under an hour by train. Gatwick is half that.

Specialism The university is one of the world's leading institutions for development studies. It is ranked joint first in the world for technology and innovation management.

◄◄ STUDENT VIEW ►►

'Sussex offers a stimulating intellectual atmosphere and a supportive environment to study in. Studying here has helped me to hone my research and teaching skills and to question and analyse critically, as well as providing opportunities to network and socialise.' Sohela Nazneen, DPhil in development studies.

Swansea University

Singleton Park,
Swansea SA2 8PP

t 01792 205678
e admissions@swansea.ac.uk
↗ www.swansea.ac.uk

 » www.swansea.ac.uk/postgraduate

 13,835 **PG** 13% (**UK**) 63%

A contender for any 'best campus' award going, Swansea is virtually unparalled for its location. It sits in parkland overlooking the Swansea Bay, on the edge of the stunning Gower peninsula. Surfers, walkers and climbers adore it here. Swansea is a good place to shop, party or get some culture. The university is a consistently popular choice with applicants, and last year became independent from the University of Wales of which it had been a constituent member.

Courses and qualifications There are around 190 courses leading to MA, MSc, MPhil, MEng, MRes, PhD and MBA degrees.

Fees
UK/EU students: most courses £3,300.
International students: range from £9,300 to £11,900.
Fees for MBAs and professional courses can be found on the website.

Funding Swansea offers funding for taught and research degrees. It also participates in the International Research Students Awards Scheme and individual departmental and school funding is available.

Accommodation The university provides a range of family flats. Contact:
accommodation@swansea.ac.uk

Facilities Among the best rates of computing provision in the country; students can also borrow laptops from the university. The £20m sports village is adjacent to the campus and includes the UniGym — a fully equipped fitness centre with over 80 stations, a multi-purpose sports hall, climbing wall and physiotherapy/sports massage unit. The sports village is also home to the 50-metre Wales National Pool and a 25-metre 'warm-up' pool.

Transport The city centre is only a 10-minute journey from campus. Cardiff is an hour away by car and is well served by road and rail links.

Specialism Swansea University's Business School is the only one in Wales to offer accredited full-time and part-time MBAs. The school of medicine at Swansea also offers a unique 'fast-track' graduate entry medicine programme.

Swansea Metropolitan University

Mount Pleasant, Swansea SA1 6ED	**t** 01792 481000 **e** enquiry@smu.ac.uk ↗ www.smu.ac.uk

» **www.smu.ac.uk/sihe/pglist.asp**

 5,800   **PG** 23%

SMU was, until very recently, known as the Swansea Institute of Higher Education. It is based on several campuses in and around the city of Swansea, with easy access to Mumbles and the Gower peninsula. The institute was founded in 1992 and became a member of the University of Wales in 2004, but its roots go back more than 150 years. It offers courses under three main faculties – arts and design; applied design and engineering; and a third faculty broadly called 'humanities', but also encompassing accounting, business and tourism.

Swansea

Courses and qualifications There are approximately 50 courses leading to MA, MA (Ed), MBA, MPhil, MRes, MSc, PCET, PDET, PGCE or PhD. Professional qualifications include ACCA, CIMA, CIPD CPP, CIM and CILT.

Fees
UK/EU students: £2,950 for the MBA.
International students: £7,450 for the MBA.

Funding None available through the university.

Accommodation There is neither postgraduate-designated nor family accommodation on campus. For further information contact: accommodation@smu.ac.uk

Facilities There are three libraries, each with their own computing facilities attached.

Transport Swansea enjoys excellent road and rail links with all parts of Britain.

Specialism 3D computer animation; glass; transportation design; lean and agile manufacturing; non-destructive testing and evaluation.

University of Teesside

Middlesbrough,
Tee Valley TS1 3BA

t 01642 218121
e registry@tees.ac.uk
↗ www.tees.ac.uk

» **www.tees.ac.uk/sections/postgrad**

 22,387   **PG** 10%

Middlesbrough

Teesside's campus is close to the centre of Middlesbrough, a town undergoing a transformation — alongside a wide range of bars, cafes and clubs is a stunning new art gallery, Middlesbrough Institute of Modern Art. You're a short hop up to Newcastle if you really want to divest yourself of some of that excess cash in mammoth shopping centres. Or head into the lovely scenery, which is just as much fun, and cheaper. The campus has seen nearly a £100m investment over the past decade.

Courses and qualifications There are over 200 courses leading to MPhil, PhD, DProf, MProf, MBA, MA, MSc, MRes, LLM, PGCE, LLM, PGC, PGD, CMI, CIM, DBA, Pg Dip, Pg Cert, Doctorate, UCPCE, UCPPD.

Fees
UK/EU students: £3,950. MBA, £8,550.
International students: £8,250 to £11,000.

Funding UK and EU students on full-time taught postgraduate course are able to apply for a non means tested bursary of £2,400. Full fee paying international students are offered a bursary of £1,500 per year available as a fee reduction. International alumni are entitled to an additional bursary of £1,000 per year making a total bursary of £2,500. International students who pay their fees in full on or before enrolment will be entitled to a 5 per cent discount on fees (after the bursary has been deducted).

Accommodation Family accommodation is available. See: www.tees.ac.uk/sections/studentlife/accommodation_umh.cfm
Or contact: accommodation@tees.ac.uk

Facilities An award-winning students' union, and some brand new learning resources on campus, thanks to a programme of recent investment. Among unique facilities is the crime scene laboratory for all you budding CSI officers. No specific facilities for postgraduates.

Transport City centre campus, with direct rail links to York or Newcastle (both an hour away), Leeds and Manchester. The airport is 20 minutes away with direct flights to London.

Specialism History, cultural studies, design, nanotechnology and micro-systems, forensic science, engineering, computer and digital science, sociology and psychology, criminology, rehabilitation sciences and clinical practice.

❝ STUDENT VIEW ❞
'I would definitely recommend Teesside because the staff are great, very supportive. Not only do they encourage learning, but also self-development.' MSc criminology.

Thames Valley University

Ealing Campus St Mary's Road, Ealing W5 5RF
Slough Campus Wellington Street, Slough, Berkshire SL1 1YG
Brentford Campus Paragon House, Boston Manor Road, Brentford, Middlesex TW8 9GA
Reading Campus Kings Road, Reading, Berkshire RG1 4HJ

t 0800 036 8888   **e** learning.advice@tvu.ac.uk   ↗ www.tvu.ac.uk

» www.tvu.ac.uk/students/Postgraduate.jsp

 15,214   **PG** 11%   (UK) 70%

TVU is based on four campuses, which are all in the Thames Valley. Hence the name. It's not too far to go to get to the wild and crazy heart of London, but life around here is a bit more sedate and manageable. There a large, mixed student body, with lots of mature, part-time and ethnic minority students. Most are local and often commute from home. It's only recently that TVU could provide any accommodation for students; the fact that it now can suggests it's got an eye on a bigger and brighter future.

Courses and qualifications There are over 120 leading to Pg Cert, Pg Dip, MA, MSc, MBA, MPhil, PhD, DHSci, DMid, DMA, DNurs, LLM.

Fees Tuition fees vary according to the course, mode of study and a student's immigration status.
For full details, visit the university's website: www.tvu.ac.uk/fees

Funding There are several awards and scholarships available. Visit the university's website at: www.tvu.ac.uk
The International Office may also have information about scholarships. Contact: int.office@tvu.ac.uk

Accommodation TVU offers postgraduate students accommodation in its halls of residence, but there is no family accommodation available. For information contact: uas@tvu.ac.uk

Facilities The graduate school has a common room, which is used as a meeting and resource area for research students. The school also provides training workshops for research students and helps to facilitate research student seminars. Students have a chance to demonstrate their research to their peers at the university's annual MPhil/PhD conference.

The student services department offers TVU students a free, confidential, professional service in support of their academic studies. Information, advice and guidance is available on accommodation, funding, immigration issues, state benefits, tax credits, housing rights, disability, faith, counselling and health.

Learning resource centres at each site are well stocked and updated regularly. They have long opening hours; some with 24-hour access.

Transport There are shuttle buses between campuses, all of which (especially Ealing) are within easy striking distance of London.

Specialism Hospitality management, legal practice, international business management and computing interaction design.

Trinity College Carmarthen

Carmarthen SA31 3EP

t 01267 676767
e registry@trinity-cm.ac.uk
↗ www.trinity-cm.ac.uk

» **www.trinity-cm.ac.uk/english/prospectus/pg/index.asp**

 2,659   **PG** 12%   (UK) 90%

Trinity College Carmarthen (Coleg y Drindod Caerfyrddin) is a church college within the University of Wales. It offers arts and humanities degrees in a range of subjects from acting to film studies to Christianity and community studies. Students are based on a picturesque single campus in South Wales, with easy access to lovely countryside and the busy market town of Carmarthen.

Courses and qualifications There are 12 courses leading to MA, MSc, MPhil, PhD, MBA or PGCE, some are available through the medium of Welsh.

Fees
UK/EU students: standard fees are £3,150, the MBA is £3,780.
International students: £2,166 for the full-time Pg Cert, £4,334 for the Pg Dip and £2,166 for the dissertation.

Funding There's no funding for postgraduate study from the university.

Accommodation There is accommodation for postgraduates. A few flats are also available on campus, for information contact: d.doyle@trinity-cm.ac.uk

Facilities There's a sports hall (featuring a climbing wall) and fitness suite. The students' union is active and arts facilities in particular are very good, including a fully equipped theatre. There's a postgraduate lounge and a designated postgraduate area in the library.

Transport Close to the town centre and to the station for major rail links. Good access to the main road network.

Specialism Arts management, creative writing, education, tourism management.

 STUDENT VIEW »

'The MBA in tourism management has opened many doors for me; it has given me confidence in my ability and the enthusiasm to follow my dream. I would encourage anyone who wishes to study an MBA to apply for tourism management at Trinity College Carmarthen.' Elinos Walters, MBA.

Trinity Laban

King Charles Court,
Old Royal Naval College,
Greenwich, London SE10 9JF

t 020 8305 4300
e info@trinitylaban.ac.uk
↗ www.trinitylaban.ac.uk

 1,006   **PG** 23%   (UK) 56%

London

Trinity Laban is a conservatoire for music and dance, formed in 2005 from the merger of Trinity College of Music and the Laban School of Dance. It is based in Greenwich – a nice corner of south-east London. Trinity is housed at the glorious King Charles Court at the Old Royal Naval College while Laban is based to the west of Greenwich, nearer Deptford.

Courses and qualifications There are around 13 different courses leading to MMus, PGCE, Pg Dip, PGA, MA, MSc, MPhil, PhD.

Fees The cost varies according to course, see the relevant web pages for more info: www.laban.org/php/form.php?id=29 for Laban courses and www.tcm.ac.uk/fees for Trinity College of Music.

Funding A range of support is available. Again, all the details are provided on the funding web pages.

Accommodation For information contact: www.opalstudents.com

Facilities As you might expect, there are superb resources for practice and performance. Postgraduate students have access to all of the facilities across TCM and Laban which are available to the entire student body.

Transport It's in London, so easy access to the tube, national rail and bus services.

Specialism Specialist music and dance courses, including performance, composition, creative practice and choreography.

UHI Millennium Institute

Executive Office,
Ness Walk IV3 5SQ

t 0845 272 3600
e info@uhi.ac.uk
↗ www.uhi.ac.uk

» **www.uhi.ac.uk/home/courses/postgraduate-programmes**

 6,847   **PG** 5%

UHI Millennium Institute (UHI) is the only higher education institution in the Highlands and Islands of Scotland – covering 15 sites as far away from each other as Shetland, Lewis, Argyll and Perth. As well as more general vocational courses such as computing or business studies, the institute offers degrees in areas reflecting local industries and culture – such as aircraft engineering, electrical engineering with nuclear decommissioning studies, culture studies of the Highlands and Islands, Gaelic music or Gaelic language/ culture, marine science, sustainable forestry ... and, if all that tires you out, golf management. Many courses are offered on one site only, so check carefully.

Courses and qualifications There are 14 courses leading to MA, MSc, MPhil, PGCE or PhD.

Fees
UK/EU students: £3,235.
International students: range from £7,565 to £8,825.

Funding There is funding available. For further details, check: www.uhi.ac.uk/home/fees-and-funding

Accommodation The type of accommodation available depends on which site you are based. There's no family accommodation. For information see: www.uhi.ac.uk/accommodation

Facilities There's none specifically for postgraduates. Obviously facilities vary according to where you study. And UHI is good at off-campus delivery, through e-learning, video-conferencing and virtual learning environments.

Transport Depends on where you are, of course, but allow seven hours for the train to London. Less by air, of course. All campuses are easily accessible by bus.

Specialism Archaeology, theology, infection control, sustainable rural/mountain development.

University of Ulster

York Street,
Belfast,
Co. Antrim BT15 1ED

t 08700 400 700
e registryjn@ulster.ac.uk
↗ www.ulster.ac.uk

» **prospectus.ulster.ac.uk**

 23,578   **PG** 20%

Students are spread over four campuses in Belfast, Coleraine, Jordanstown and Magee (in Derry). A fifth, Campus One, is an online e-learning service offering mainly postgraduate and short courses. Many students are drawn from the local area. Add to that an innovative and dynamic approach and it's no wonder that Ulster sees itself as part of the economic and social regeneration of Northern Ireland.

Courses and qualifications Over 100 courses leading to MA, MD Pg Cert, Pg Dip or ProfDoc.

Fees Costs vary depending on the type of course chosen. Fees are established on a modular basis and range from set prices through to premium band courses. For further information visit: www.ulster.ac.uk/finance/fees/0809.html

Funding There are a variety of research studentships and some financial support for certain taught programmes. See the website for details.

Accommodation Family accommodation is available as part of the residential provision at the Jordanstown, Coleraine and Magee campuses. In addition, by August 2009, 22 new two-bedroom units will be available at the Jordanstown campus. These state-of-the-art facilities will include broadband and en-suite facilities as standard. For information see: www.ulster.ac.uk/accommodation

Facilities There is an impressive sports centre at Jordanstown, major arts venues at Coleraine and good learning resources. Research students have access to excellent facilities provided by each of the 17 research institutes. The university has completed a multi-million-pound programme of development on its learning resources centres, providing state-of-the-art facilities for all students. Ulster also boasts a high performance centre for sport, the University of Ulster Clinic, modern accommodation and wireless access.

Transport There are road and rail connections between the campuses and there are airports and ports to help you reach the rest of the UK and beyond.

Specialism Key research areas include bio-medical sciences, the built environment and art and design.

University College Birmingham

Summer Row,
Birmingham B3 1JB

t 0121 604 1000
e marketing@ucb.ac.uk
↗ www.ucb.ac.uk

» **www.ucb.ac.uk/asp/postgraduateDegrees.asp**

 7,862   **PG** 8%   (UK) 14%

UCB was formally known as the Birmingham School of Food, Tourism and Creative Studies. There are almost 8,000 students in total on a range of short courses and engaged in full and part time studies. The specialist nature of the college means that students have access to tailored facilities. There are also close links to employers. Birmingham is a fun place to study with all the attractions of a big city on your doorstep.

Courses and qualifications There are 10 courses leading to Pg Dip, Pg Cert, MA, MSc and PGCE.

Fees
UK/EU students: £2,200.
International students: £7,750.

Funding There are scholarships for international students. Contact the university for details.

Accommodation Postgraduate accommodation is available. For information contact: accommodation@ucb.ac.uk

Facilities There are restaurants and a spa that are used both as learning resources and as commercial centres: the public is actively encouraged to make use of them and, of course, so can students. New postgraduate teaching facilities, main campus research centre and well stocked, specialist library.

Transport Within easy reach of the city centre. Birmingham itself is well served by road, rail and air.

Specialism Hospitality, tourism and childcare.

❝ STUDENT VIEW ❞

'The managerial skills I studied at University College Birmingham such as leadership, empowerment and motivation are truly beneficial to my current role (as senior development manager at the Mandarin Oriental Hotel Group) and enable me to be a good team leader.' Billy Jin, MA in hospitality management.

University College Falmouth
incorporating Dartington College of Arts

Woodlane, Falmouth,
Cornwall TR11 4HR

t 01326 211077
e admissions@falmouth.ac.uk
↗ www.falmouth.ac.uk

» **www.falmouth.ac.uk/201/courses-7/postgraduate-courses-43.html**

 3,500 **PG** 14%

In 2005, University College Falmouth became the first institution in Cornwall to award its own degrees. Its courses focus on art and design, and they are taught in Falmouth and on the Tremough campus of the Combined Universities in Cornwall. In 2010 it is relocating to Falmouth. The university college is proud of its facilities and its focus on personal as well as academic development. Falmouth is famous for its harbour and as a centre of water-based fun. The rest of Cornwall is no less enticing, with everything from bracing cliff climbs to lounge-able beaches on offer.

Falmouth

Courses and qualifications There are 26 courses including various MA and PhD options.

Fees Fees are reviewed annually and can be viewed on the website: www.falmouth.ac.uk

Funding A variety of funding is available and is detailed in the postgraduate prospectus and on the website.

Accommodation There isn't any family accommodation, but plenty of suitable private accommodation is available locally. For information visit: www.tremoughservices/accommodation

Transport Falmouth can feel somewhat out on a limb. It does have easy access to the A39, which will take you all the way to Bath. Regular trains link the town to London and elsewhere, but it's a five-hour journey to the capital.

Facilities A range of specialist IT facilities are on offer to support its courses, including digital media applications and digital photography facilities. There are crèche facilities on the Dartington Hall Estate.

Specialism Art, design, media and performance.

❝ STUDENT VIEW ❞

'I chose Falmouth because of the 20th century focus of the MA course. I knew my interests lay in this particular period and the course offered the opportunity to really get to grips with the meanings of modernity.' Hilary Philips, MA 20th century art and design.

University College London

Gower Street,
London WC1E 6BT

t 020 7679 2000
↗ www.ucl.ac.uk

 www.ucl.ac.uk/prospective-students/graduate-study

 19,500   **PG** 38%   (**UK**) 62%

UCL is big, bustling and is consistently ranked among the best universities in the world, with an emphasis on innovative teaching and research excellence (it got its 20th Nobel prize in 2007). Its alumni include Gandhi, Alexander Graham Bell and, of course, Coldplay. The majority of its buildings are gathered around the impressive Octagon, topped by the famous dome, in Bloomsbury. It's an area famous for its literary and educational heritage and could hardly be more convenient for almost anything you care to think of. The diverse and friendly community means you can feel right at home in the centre of the city.

Courses and qualifications There are around 320 courses leading to MA, Pg Dip, MA, Pg Cert, MRes, MClinDent.

Fees For details visit: www.ucl.ac.uk/prospective-students/graduate-study/fees-costs

Funding A lot is available. See the scholarships and funding website at: www.ucl.ac.uk/scholarships

Accommodation For information visit: www.ucl.ac.uk/prospective-students/accommodation/residences/alternative-accommodation

Facilities Excellent library facilities (and Senate House, the huge University of London library, is virtually next door), its own on-campus theatre, a fitness centre and a great students' union.

Transport Perfectly placed for easy access to the London transport network, a couple of mainline stations and the Eurostar terminal. Much of central London is easily walkable from campus too.

Specialism There are many subjects that UCL is well regarded for at postgraduate level. Neuroscience is one of these.

 STUDENT VIEW ▶▶

'I chose UCL for its international reputation as a leading research institution and for its supportive learning environment. Not only does UCL offer world-class resources, it also offers a great network of staff and students who work together and generate innovative research.' Erica Yu, PhD in psychology.

University of Wales Institute, Cardiff

Western Avenue,
Cardiff CF5 2YB

t 029 2041 6070
e uwicinfo@uwic.ac.uk
↗ www.uwic.ac.uk

>> www3.uwic.ac.uk/English/StudyAtUWIC/Courses/Pages/PostgraduateAZ.aspx

 12,458   **PG** 34%   (UK) 40%

UWIC is one of the leading new universities in Wales, mainly due to its career-orientated courses that make graduates popular with employers. It's also a top sporting university with first-class facilities and a proud tradition of competition – and success. It's also recently announced a £46m fund for redeveloping and updating the campus facilities. The university is split between four campuses, with the Howard Gardens campus in the city centre itself. Cardiff is a lively, cosmopolitan and fun-loving capital city, but still manageable and easy to get around. There's some lovely countryside within easy reach and good transport links to the rest of the UK.

Courses and qualifications There are 75 courses including MA, MSc, PGCE, Pg Dip, Pg Cert, MBA, MPhil, PhD, EdD, MRes, DBMS, DBA.

Fees
UK/EU students: £3,300.
International students: £8,800.

Funding There are more than seven schemes on offer; these range from means tested bursaries, food industry bursaries, entry scholarship, sports scholarship, postgraduate scholarships, childcare bursaries and care leaver bursaries. Bursaries range up to £1,500 for a three-year course, whilst scholarships are paid as a one off £1,000 payment. Details of all the schemes can be found at: www.uwic.ac.uk/bursaries

Accommodation No family accommodation but the university will assist those with families to find private rented accommodation. For information contact: accomm@uwic.ac.uk

Facilities Learning materials are available on all campuses, as well as computing facilities. Resources for sport are especially good. No facilities specifically for postgraduates.

Transport There's a university shuttle bus between campuses, the city centre and popular student housing areas. Cardiff is good for road and rail: London is two hours by train.

Specialism Art and design, education, health sciences, management, sport.

<< STUDENT VIEW >>

'The MSc in advanced dietetic practice was a challenging but enjoyable experience for me. The individual modules I chose were all very relevant to my work and I was able to apply the knowledge and skills directly to my current working practice. Being able to undertake this on a part-time basis meant that I was able to fit it around my full-time work.' Nicola Lee, a senior dietician, completed the programme in 2007.

University of Warwick

Coventry CV4 7AL

t 02476 523523
e student.recruitment@warwick.ac.uk
↗ www.warwick.ac.uk

》 www2.warwick.ac.uk/study/postgraduate

 18,212   **PG** 40%

Warwick lies about three miles outside the centre of Coventry and on the border of Warwickshire. Warwick does have its own castle, though, so you might like to go there for a day trip. Coventry has all the other mod cons you require, though the modern (well, modern in the 1960s) main campus is charming and very well equipped. Consistently rated among the best universities in the country, Warwick is something of a leader in the academic field, with innovative approaches to community involvement and widening participation.

Courses and qualifications There are over 170 programmes. For a full list of taught courses see: www2.warwick.ac.uk/study/postgraduate/courses/coursea2z For research courses see: www2.warwick.ac.uk/study/postgraduate/courses/researcha2z

Fees Fees vary, see: www2.warwick.ac.uk/services/academicoffice/ourservices/finance

Funding Again see: www2.warwick.ac.uk/study/postgraduate/funding

Accommodation For information view: www2.warwick.ac.uk/study/postgraduate/living/accommodation
Or contact: accommodation@warwick.ac.uk

Facilities There's an impressive art collection on show at the arts centre, good sports facilities (including a climbing wall) and a large and welcoming library. Visit: www2.warwick.ac.uk/services/library/researchexchange

Transport Close to the M1/M6 intersection and half an hour to Birmingham by train; an hour and a quarter to London.

❝ STUDENT VIEW ❞

'I firmly believe that my experience at Warwick has helped me to develop both academically as well as personally. Warwick has played a significant role in enhancing my future career prospects and for me, being at Warwick has been the journey of a lifetime.' Sahil Juneja, MSC in management.

University of the West of England, Bristol (UWE Bristol)

Frenchay Campus,
Coldharbour Lane,
Bristol BS16 1QY

t 0117 32 83333
e admissions@uwe.ac.uk
↗ www.uwe.ac.uk

» www.uwe.ac.uk/study/pg

 27,676   **PG** 20%   (**UK**) 77%

Bristol UWE has grown considerably since it gained university status in 1992 and now has a student population of almost 30,000. Students are drawn from a wide range of backgrounds and the university is keen to take on students with a broad range of qualifications and experience. The graduate employment record is consistently impressive. Bristol UWE has four campuses across the city. Lovely Bristol is the largest city in the south-west, with an impressive music scene and cultural life and lovely historic buildings. It's very student-friendly and many first-time visitors fall instantly in love with it.

Courses and qualifications There are several leading to MA, MSc, MPhil, PhD, MBA, PGCE.

Fees
UK/EU students: full-time taught programmes are £3,600.
International students: £8,250 for classroom based taught programmes, £8,700 for non classroom based programmes.

Funding Some available, mainly for international students. See website for details.

Accommodation Family accommodation in private sector only. For information contact: accommodation@uwe.ac.uk

Facilities 24/7 access to computing facilities and a brand new sports centre for all your fitness needs. Graduate Schools provide specialist support and facilities.

Transport A university run bus service links the campuses to the city centre. On major rail routes, close to the M4 and M5 and not far from Bristol airport.

Specialism Teaching.

❝ STUDENT VIEW ❞

'I made the decision to enrol on the MSc health psychology so that I could eventually progress on to the professional doctorate. I chose UWE because the modules sounded really interesting and when I met the staff they seemed very friendly and enthusiastic. Once on the course I realised that it had also been planned very well and that the topics linked together brilliantly. The challenging and varied assignments have helped me to build my confidence and improved my time management skills. The support I received at UWE during my dissertation and when I required careers advice was fantastic.' Lauren, MSc in health psychology.

University of the West of Scotland

Paisley PA1 2BE

t 0141 848 3000
e info@uws.ac.uk
↗ www.uws.ac.uk

 » www.uws.ac.uk/courses/postgraduate.asp

 19,500 **PG** 9% (UK) 65%

UWS was, until recently, Paisley University. It is based on four campuses in the south and south west of Scotland, offering higher education to local people and giving students from outside the area a chance to live in a lovely part of the country. The main campus is in Paisley, six miles from Glasgow; a second is located in Ayr, a third outside Dumfries and the fourth in Lanarkshire. The university is one of Scotland's most vocational higher education institutions, boasting strong links with industrial and commercial partners. Courses are designed to meet the demands of industry and the professions, and recent developments include degrees in forensic science, computer animation, and exercise and health.

Courses and qualifications Over 40 programmes leading to MBA, MPhil, MSc, Pg Dip, Pg Cert, PGDE or PhD.

Fees
UK/EU students: £3,315.
International students: range from £7,500 to £8,300.

Funding There are various studentships available at the university. For more details please see: www.uws.ac.uk/research/research-studentships.asp

Accommodation Student accommodation is offered for students at both undergraduate and postgraduate level at the campuses in Ayr, Hamilton and Paisley. For information contact: accommodation@uws.ac.uk

Facilities The £6.8m library on the Paisley campus has room for 1,000 studious students. Extensive sports facilities will take care of the less studious. All students enjoy access to a wide range of facilities across all four of the campuses in Ayr, Dumfries, Hamilton and Paisley. Facilities include a students' association with a variety of affiliated clubs and societies; sporting facilities; library facilities and student services.

Transport By train, the main campus is 10 minutes from Glasgow. One hour from Edinburgh.

Specialism Business.

❝ STUDENT VIEW ❞

'I chose to undertake the MSc international marketing at the University of the West of Scotland for several reasons. British master's programmes are recognised and respected throughout the world and studying in English, as well as living in an English-speaking environment, gave me the opportunity to become truly fluent in the language. I had already studied at the University of the West of Scotland and had had a good experience — the standard of learning and teaching at the university is excellent.' Sylvain Baur, PgD/MSc international marketing.

University of Westminster

309 Regent Street,
London 1B 2UW

t 020 7911 5000
e course-enquiries@westminster.ac.uk
↗ www.westminster.ac.uk

» www.wmin.ac.uk/page-864

 22,000   **PG** 28%

If you want to be right at the heart of London, you could do worse than Westminster. Three of its campuses are in the middle of town; Harrow is slightly further flung, though still on the tube. In London, everything you could want is within easy reach. As the country's first polytechnic (in 1838), Westminster has a longstanding commitment to equal opportunities; lots of courses can be studied part-time and the student body is fantastically diverse. It puts careers at the centre of its mission and it's diligent about preparing students for their chosen profession.

Courses and qualifications There are around 160 different courses leading to MA, MSc, MBA, LLM, MEng, MMus, MPH, MPhil, PhD, Grad Dip, Pg Dip, Pg Cert.

Fees
UK/EU students: range from £3,800 to £6,500.
International students: range from £9,700 to £16,750.

Funding The university's scholarship programme is the largest of its kind in the UK, with £4.3m being awarded annually to over 500 UK/EU and international students. There are over 70 scholarships available to postgraduate students every year.

Accommodation The university does not offer family accommodation within its halls of residence, however it does offer a comprehensive housing advice service at both its central London and Harrow sites. For information contact: housing@westminster.ac.uk

Facilities Recently revamped gym facilities and there's a 45-acre sports ground by the river in Chiswick. Libraries on all sites, with 24-hour access in Harrow and Marylebone. The students' union boasts a £1m venue and an underground exhibition space; the student radio station is award-winning.

The facilities vary according to the type of course. There are dedicated computer labs and a common room for postgraduate students in the Westminster Business School.

Transport Three of the four campuses are in central London with excellent links. The fourth, in Harrow, is a 20-minute tube ride away, or there's a 24-hour bus service.

Specialism Business, journalism and mass communications, law, linguistics.

◀◀ STUDENT VIEW ▶▶

'I made the right decision when I chose to study at Westminster. Careers advice, in-depth lectures, interview workshops and visits from employers have all helped to shape my confidence. I feel more employable as a result. I'm ready to launch my new career.' Peter Alexandrou, graduate diploma in law.

University of Winchester

West Hill,
Winchester SO22 4NR

t 01962 841515
e course.enquiries@winchester.ac.uk
↗ www.winchester.ac.uk

» **www.winchester.ac.uk/?page=9037**

 5,200   **PG** 15%   (UK) 97%

Winchester is a fairly small university, which makes for a friendly, informal environment. Its long history as a teacher training college means that education is a still a focus, but there's a wide range of other degrees on offer, too. Winchester is a lovely cathedral city with a refined atmosphere, excellent shopping and great pubs and green spaces. There's another campus in Basingstoke.

Winchester

Courses and qualifications There are 56 programmes leading to MA, MSc, MPhil, PhD, PGCE, MBA, Pg Cert, Pg Dip.

Fees Fees vary depending on the course. As a guide:
UK/EU students: from £3,880.
International students: from £8,070.

Funding There is an alumni scholarship for students who have previously completed a degree at Winchester. There are bursaries and scholarships available for full-time PGCE students. The Winchester International Scholarship is for non-EU students studying a taught master's degree. See the website for details.

Accommodation Postgraduates are usually accommodated in the West Downs Centre and there are other quiet blocks set aside in the halls of residence. There is accommodation provided on campus for small families and couples. For information contact: housing@winchester.ac.uk

Facilities The £10m University Centre opened in 2007. It includes a 1,200 capacity venue space for concerts, club nights and other events complete with bars. Winchester also has an Olympic standard 400-metre eight-lane athletics track and an all-weather hockey and general sports pitch with floodlighting and an extended pavilion.

The Research and Knowledge Transfer Centre is a dedicated support service for postgraduate research students and administers all aspects of postgraduate research candidature. It offers advice and support throughout study and provides access to networked PCs, a meeting room and common room.

Transport A 10-minute walk to the city centre of Winchester and the train station. One hour away from London Waterloo and 20 minutes from Southampton.

Specialism Teaching, archaeology, theology and religious studies, creative writing and performing arts.

❝ STUDENT VIEW ❞

'One of the best experiences I've had at Winchester has been interacting with the lecturers, as virtually all of them have been in the industry and have great theoretical and practical knowledge. My eyes have been opened to the possibilities. Before the MSc, I thought I wanted to stay in the leisure industry. Since studying finance and corporate management, it's given me a taste for a whole new market.' Rich Gillespie, MSc in business management.

University of Wolverhampton

Wulfruna Street,
Wolverhampton WV1 1SB

t 01902 322222
e enquries@wlv.ac.uk
↗ www.wlv.ac.uk

» **www.wlv.ac.uk/Default.aspx?page=6941**

 23,166   **PG** 19%   (**UK**) 71%

Wolverhampton stresses innovation and enterprise, encouraging student 'start up' companies and leading initiatives in this area. It has a successful focus on employability, with excellent business links, collaborative working and opportunities for students to gain experience. Wolverhampton is a bustling city in its own right and its four campuses are easily accessible, but the attractions of Birmingham are only a short distance away. Plus there is some lovely scenery nearby for a bit of rest and relaxation.

Courses and qualifications There are over 100 leading to MA, MSc, MPhil, PhD, Pg Cert, GD, PGCE, MPH, Pg Dip, LPC, CPE, LLDip, LLM, CIM, CIMA, MBA, MMus, DBMS.

Fees The fees vary depending on the subject and students are encouraged to contact the academic school offering their course for further details.

Funding Studentships/bursaries are available each year for research students. Further details are available on the website: www.wlv.ac.uk There is a loyalty discount for international students who progress from an undergraduate to a postgraduate programme.

Accommodation There is dedicated postgraduate accommodation. For information contact: residences@wlv.ac.uk
No family accommodation but there is a website containing private sector accommodation: www.mlas-online.co.uk

Facilities Each campus has a Learning Centre. There is a strong focus on IT and audio-visual facilities, as the university secures its reputation as a national leader in e-learning. Walsall campus' sports centre hosts many large regional, national and international sports events and is one of few national judo centres of excellence, being used as the training facility for 2012 Olympic contenders. The Arena Theatre, based at the city campus, is one of the busiest and most successful theatres in the Midlands.

Transport All campuses linked by a free shuttle bus. Wolverhampton has excellent transport links and Birmingham is just a short train or tram ride away.

Specialism Excellence in computational linguistics, statistical cybermetrics, healthcare science, leadership and management and construction management.

❝ STUDENT VIEW ❞

'I have been pleased at the University of Wolverhampton to find an atmosphere of encouragement for my PhD research. With the assistance of my director of studies I have been able to develop my areas of interest in a supportive academic environment. There is no other university in the world that offers a PhD in dance medicine and science, so I'm proud to be associated with an institution that has a pioneering spirit.'
Jeffrey A. Russell, PhD student.

University of Worcester

Henwick Grove,
Worcester WR2 6AJ

t 01905 855000
e study@worc.ac.uk
↗ www.worcester.ac.uk

 www.worc.ac.uk/courses/112.html

8,000   **PG** 20%

Hayfever sufferers might be interested to learn that all of the UK's national pollen forecasts are now supplied by the university's pollen and aerobiology research unit. Worcester is investing £120m in the development of a new city-centre campus and a further £60m on a unique library and history centre, which will be the first joint university and public library in the UK. There are currently 8,000 students at Worcester and the majority come from the local area, but applications from further afield are increasing. Worcester itself is a charming little city with lovely countryside nearby.

Courses and qualifications There are 51 programmes. See the website for details.

Fees
UK/EU students: £3,600 for a MA or MSc.
International students: £6,000 for a MA or MSc.

Funding There is no financial support for postgraduates from the university.

Accommodation For information contact: accommodation@worc.ac.uk

Facilities The library has over 150,000 books and 600 journal print titles, 150 computers available and is open seven days a week during term time. Computers are also available in 24-hour open access rooms across the campus. Excellent sports facilities too.

Transport The campus is a 15-minute walk from the city centre. A frequent bus service also links the two. Worcester has good rail and motorway links (M5), which put Birmingham within 45 minutes and London just over two hours from the city centre.

Specialism The university carries out research into archaeology and heritage, business and information technology, education, English literary studies, environmental and biological sciences, geography, health, history, psychology, sociology, sport and exercise sciences, theatre studies and drama.

Writtle College

Chelmsford, Essex CM1 3RR	t 01245 424200
	e info@writtle.ac.uk
	↗ www.writtle.ac.uk

» **www.writtle.ac.uk/pge_MainDisplay.cfm?ID=10**

 1,222   **PG** 14%

Writtle College is an agricultural college based two miles from Chelmsford in Essex. Established in 1893 it is now a partner college of the University of Essex and offers courses in a full range of land-based subjects. The main campus is surrounded by its own estate, farm and gardens — the college says this serves as a 'green laboratory' for students.

Courses and qualifications There are 55 courses leading to PG Cert, PG Dip, MA, MSc, MBA, MSc, MPhil, PhD.

Fees
UK/EU students: £3,645.
International students: £8,000.

Funding Eligible students can apply for Marshall Papworth Scholarship, International student scholarship (internally funded), bursaries via the Alice Noakes Charitable trust, GTA for research students.

Accommodation No accommodation for families. For information contact: student. services@writtle.ac.uk

Facilities The active students' union keeps things lively on campus and a range of sporting facilities are available to all students. The estate provides plenty of hands-on learning experience. There is a postgraduate common room.

Transport Situated two miles from Chelmsford town centre and just a short walk from the main bus route through Writtle village. There are buses from Chelmsford station to the campus.

Specialism All courses are specialist areas with a land-based focus including; horticulture, animal biology, equine science, garden design and landscape architecture.

University of York

Heslington,
York YO10 5DD

t 01904 430000
e admissions@york.ac.uk
↗ www.york.ac.uk

>> **www.york.ac.uk/graduatestudy**

 11,500 **PG** 20%

York enjoys a collegiate system similar to Oxbridge, though the divisions don't seem to be as rigid as at those universities. Most students are based on the landscaped campus on the outskirts of the city. The campus is undergoing a process of expansion and improvement. York is an interesting city, with a history stretching back to Roman times and the evidence of it all around you.

Courses and qualifications There are around 200 courses leading to MA, MSc, MRes, MPhil, Pg Dip, PGCE, Pg Cert and PhD.

Fees
UK/EU students: the standard full-time postgraduate tuition fees are £3,300 per annum. *International students:* £9,510 per annum for classroom based study, £12,555 for laboratory.

Funding There are between 30 and 40 studentships and scholarships available for graduate students under the university's postgraduate awards scheme. Many departments offer their own studentships and scholarships.

Accommodation There is limited accommodation for families. The university offers advice and guidance to help students find suitable privately rented accommodation which is readily available in the city and of good value. Contact: accommodation@york.ac.uk

Facilities Libraries, computer rooms, restaurants, bars, shops, a fully-equipped sports centre, tennis and squash courts, health centre, theatres and concert halls are all within easy walking distance on campus.

Wentworth College is specifically designed for postgraduates and provides accommodation and common rooms. There is a graduate student association that organises events specifically for postgraduates.

Transport The campus itself is compact and generally traffic-free. York city centre is 20 minutes' stroll away, or less than 10 minutes by bus — a fast, direct service runs every 10 minutes. Much of the city is pedestrianised and there are plenty of cycle routes. A fast all-night train puts Leeds and Manchester within easy reach.

Specialism York is regarded as a leading university for research and teaching, both nationally and internationally.

<< STUDENT VIEW >>

'I came to York as an undergraduate and have chosen to continue my postgraduate studies here. The teaching is of an excellent standard, and the variety of the research interests ensures a diversity of topics available at both undergraduate and postgraduate level. The MA was useful in clarifying my research interests and my PhD supervision has been exemplary.' Owen Hulatt, philosophy.

York St John University

Lord Mayor's Walk,
York YO31 7EX

t 01904 624624
e admissions@yorksj.ac.uk
➚ www.yorksj.ac.uk

》 www2.yorksj.ac.uk/default.asp?Page_ID=3268&Parent_ID=255

 5,300   **PG** 12%   (**UK**) 15%

St John's descends from two Victorian Anglican teacher training colleges. Over the years, it has gone through various incarnations and won full university status in 2006. Its course programme has diversified a bit, too, though you can, of course, still train to teach here. Almost half of the students are over 21. There's also a male-female ratio of 30:70. The campus is located almost literally a stone's throw from York Minster, the stunning medieval cathedral. All the other amenities of the charming and compact city centre are on your doorstep.

Courses and qualifications 27 taught courses leading to MA, MSc, MPhil, PhD, MBA, PGCE, Pg Cert, GradDip, Pg Dip, MA, MSc, PGCE from York St John University. MPhil and PhDs from University of Leeds.

Fees There is a range of fees across subjects, and qualifications and final costs are usually dependent on module combinations. See the website for details.

Funding There is funding available, see the website for details.

Accommodation There is some studio accommodation which is suitable for postgraduates and couples. For information contact: accommodation@yorksj.ac.uk

Facilities Recent investment has seen new facilities for study and teaching being built on campus. There is good sports provision, including a climbing wall, an internet cafe and impressive lecture theatres. A postgraduate centre based in a new £15m building opened in 2008.

Transport St John's is just a few minutes' walk or cycle ride from the city centre. The city is on the main east coast rail line — handy for London and Edinburgh. Leeds and Manchester are easy to get to, too.

Specialism Teaching, creative writing and literature, leadership and management, and health and life sciences.

Glossary of abbreviations

ACCA	Association of Chartered Certified Accountants
AdvCert	Advanced Certificate
AdvCertEd	Advanced Certificate in Education
AdvDip	Advanced Diploma
AMusD	Doctor of Musical Arts
AMusM	Master of Musical Arts
AppEd	Applied Educational ... plus specialism
ArtsD	Doctor of Arts
BArch	Bachelor of Architecture
BCL	Bachelor of Civil Law
BLandArch	Bachelor of Landscape Architecture
BVC	Bar Vocational Course
BVetMed	Bachelor of Veterinary Medicine
BPhil	Bachelor of Philosophy
Cert Ed	Certificate in Education
ChildPsyD	Doctor of Child Psychology
ChM	Master of Surgery
ClinPsyD	Doctor of Child Psychology
CIM	Chartered Institute of Marketing
CIMA	Chartered Institute of Management Accountants
CIPD	Chartered Institute of Personnel and Development
CIPFA	Chartered Institute of Public Finance and Accountancy
CIPS	Chartered Institute of Purchasing and Supply
CMI Diploma	Chartered Management Institute Diploma in Management
CMI Executive Diploma	Chartered Management Institute Executive Diploma in Management
CMS	Certificate in Management Studies
CPE	Common Professional Examination
DAppEdPsy	Doctor of Applied Educational Psychology
DArt	Doctor of Arts
DASE	Diploma in Advanced Study of Education
DBA	Doctor of Business Administration
DBMS	Doctor of Biomedical Science
DClin	Doctorate in Clinical Psychology
DClinP	Doctorate in Clinical Psychology
DClinPsy	Doctorate in Clinical Psychology
DDS	Doctor of Dental Surgery
DDes	Doctor of Design

DEdPsy+	Doctorate in Educational Psychology
DHC	Doctorate in Healthcare
DHSci	Doctorate in Health Science
DipHE	Diploma in Higher Education
DipSW	Diploma in Social Work
DJourn	Diploma in Journalism
DLang	Diploma in Language
DLP	Distance Learning Programme
DM	Doctor of Medicine
DMan	Doctor of Management
DMid	Doctor of Midwifery
DMin	Doctor of Ministry
DMS	Doctorate in Management Studies
DNurs	Doctorate in Nursing
DPharm	Doctorate in Pharmacy
DPhil	Doctorate in Philosophy
DProf	Doctorate in Professional Studies
DPS	Doctorate in Professional Studies
DPsych	Doctorate in Psychology
DPT	Doctor of Practical Theology
DrPH	Doctorate in Public Health
DrPS	Doctorate in Professional Studies
DSocSci	Doctorate in Social Sciences
EdD	Doctor of Education
EdM	Master of Education
EdPsychD+	Doctorate in Educational Psychology
EMBA	Executive Masters in Business Administration
EngD	Doctor of Engineering
EURMsc	European Master of Science
EYPS	Early Years Professional Status
FMM	Fellowship in Manufacturing Management
ForenPsyD	Forensic Psychology Practice Doctorate
GCM	Graduate Certificate in Management
GDip	Graduate Diploma
GDL	Graduate Diploma in Law
Grad Cert	Graduate Certificate
Grad Dip	Graduate Diploma
GTP	Graduate Teacher Programme
IMP	International Marketing and Pathways
IMS	Institute of Management Studies

IntMasters	International Masters in Business Administration	MPhys	Master of Physics
LicDD	Licence in Divinity (Doctorate)	MRes	Master of Research
LLD	Doctor of Laws	MProf	Master of Professional Practice
LLDip	Legal Practice Course	MSc	Master of Science
LLM	Master of Laws	MScD	Master of Science in Dentistry
LPC	Legal Practice Course	MScEcon	Master of Science (Economics)
MA	Master of Arts	MSCR	Master of Science in Clinical Research
Macc	Masters in Accounting	MSt	Master of Studies
March	Master of Architecture	MSW	Master of Social Work
MARes	Master of Research	MTeach	Master of Teaching
MBA	Masters in Business Administration	MTech	Master of Technology
MBiol	Master of Biology	MTh	Master of Theology
MBS	Master of Business Studies	NRPhD	New Route Doctor of Philosophy
Mchem	Master of Chemistry	OTT	Overseas Trained Teacher Programme
MClin	Master of Clinical ... plus specialism	PAQ	Professional Accounting Qualification
MClinDent	Master of Clinical Dentistry	PCert	Postgraduate Certificate
MClinSci	Master of Clinical Science	PCET	Post-Compulsory Education and Training
Mcomp	Master of Computers	PDET	Professional Development Education and Training
MChem	Master of Chemistry	PDP	Personal Development Planning (for Postgraduates)
MD	Doctor of Medicine		
MDes	Master of Design	PGC	Postgraduate Certificate
Meng	Master of Engineering	Pg Dip	Postgraduate Diploma
MEnt	Master of Enterprise Technology	PgC	Postgraduate Certificate
MEnv	Masters in Environment, Science and Society	Pg Cert	Postgraduate Certificate
MEd	Masters in Education	Pg Cert PAE	Postgraduate Certificate in Performing Arts Education
MFA	Masters of Finance and Accounting	PGCE	Postgraduate Certificate in Education
Mfin	Master of International Finance and Financial Institutions	PGCHE	Postgraduate Certificate in Higher Education
MGPrac	Master of Museum and Gallery Practice	PGDE	Postgraduate Diploma in Education
MHPrac	Master of Heritage Practice	PgD	Postgraduate Diploma
MInnov	Master in Innovation	PhD	Doctor of Philosophy
MJur	Master of Jurisprudence and Political Theory	PhDFA	Doctor of Philosophy (Fine Art)
MLitt	Master of Literature	ProfDoc	Professional Doctorate
MM	Master of Music	ProfGCE	Professional Graduate Certificate in Education
MMath	Master of Mathematics	PsychD	Doctor of Psychology
Mmin	Master of Ministry	SocScD	Doctor of Social Sciences
MMPrac	Masters in Museum Practice	TESOL	Teaching English to Speakers of Other Languages
Mmus	Master of Music	ThD	Doctor of Theology
MnursSci	Master of Nursing Science	TQFE	Teaching Qualification in Further English
MOpera	Master of Opera	UCPCE	University Certificate in Postgraduate Continuing Education
MPA	Masters in Public Administration		
MPA	Masters in Public Health	UCPPD	University Certificate in Postgraduate Professional Development
MPharm	Master of Pharmacy		
MPhil	Master of Philosophy	Univ Dip	University Diploma
MPhilStud	Master of Philosophy		